# White-Collar and
# Economic Crime

# White-Collar and Economic Crime

**Multidisciplinary and
Cross-National Perspectives**

*Edited by*
**Peter Wickman**
State University of New York,
College at Potsdam

**Timothy Dailey**
Clarkson College of Technology

**LexingtonBooks**
D.C. Heath and Company
Lexington, Massachusetts
Toronto

**Library of Congress Cataloging in Publication Data**
Main entry under title:

White-collar and economic crime.

Papers presented at a symposium held Feb. 7–9, 1980, at the State
University of New York College at Potsdam and sponsored by the Re-
search Committee on Deviance and Social Control of the International
Sociological Association.
Includes index.
1. White collar crimes–United States–Congresses. 2. Corporations–
United States–Corrupt practices–Congresses. I. Wickman, Peter M.
II. Dailey, Timothy. III. International Sociological Association. Research
Committee on Deviance and Social Control.
HV6635.W44            364.1'68            81-47561
ISBN 0-669-04665-5                        AACR2

*Copyright © 1982 by D.C. Heath and Company*

Published simultaneously in Canada

Printed in the United States of America

International Standard Book Number: 0-669-04665-5

Library of Congress Catalog Card Number: 81-47561

# Contents

                    Corporate Capitalism   *Harold C. Barnett*                  157

*Part III*          *Social Control: Sanctions and Deterrent Effects*          171

Chapter 11          Legal Control of Safety on British Offshore Oil
                    Installations   *W.G. Carson*                               173

Chapter 12          Social Control and the Legal Profession
                    *Jerry Parker*                                              197

Chapter 13          Traditional and Corporate Theft: A Comparison of
                    Sanctions   *Laureen Snider*                                235

Chapter 14          The Social Organization of White-Collar Sanctions:
                    A Study of Prosecution and Punishment in the
                    Federal Courts   *John Hagan, Ilene Nagel,* and
                    *Celesta Albonetti*                                         259

                    Index                                                       276

                    About the Contributors                                      283

                    About the Editors                                           286

# Preface

*John P. Clark*

Casual observations about the nature and effects of white-collar crime now abound in social-science, public-policy, and mass-media presentations. Systematic attention to its structure and processes is more rare. The chapters in this volume are examples of the latter. Even so, the rather helter-skelter substantive character of even this scholarly treatment probably reflects, among other things, one of white-collar crime's unique aspects. Traditionally, criminological topics have been identified, at least partially, by their specific prohibition in the criminal law. White-collar crime is known for its elusiveness in that arena. Some have cried out in despair about thorny definitional problems. Others have contributed to its further specification, usually into some variant of two subcategories: organizational and occupational crime.

The chapters in this volume tend toward an organizational perspective, that is, organization as offending party and organization as controller. In fact, in the current burst of scholarly interest in white-collar crime (or "white-collar law-breaking," Reiss and Bidermann 1980), substantial strain toward organizational-level analysis is evident. A focus of analysis on the occupational bases of crime is not common. Further, relatively less emphasis is being placed on individual offenders. Increasingly, however, organizational structures and processes are being compared for understandings of corporate actions, particularly those that include the violation of law.

Perhaps more encouraging is the companion trend toward analyses that are more than single-case studies. Historic apologies for having to limit one's social-scientific investigation to a single, and usually atypical instance of law violation apparently is no longer valid. Indeed, a problem at the opposite extreme has suddenly arisen, that is, how to digest in scholarly ways the great volume and complexity of cases on which data are now available. For example, three recent National Institute of Justice reports grapple with this issue: *Data Sources on White-Collar Law-Breaking* by Al Reiss and Al Biderman *(1980);* *Illegal Corporate Behavior* by Marshall Clinard (1979); and *The Internal Revenue Service: Measuring Tax Offenses and Enforcement Response* by Susan Long (1980). It is interesting to speculate whether such studies could have been pursued in some fashion before this time.

A variant of that problem reveals the interaction among training of social-service researchers, the quality of data analyzed, and the scholarship produced. It is evident that the traditional training of criminologists or other social scientists who seriously wish to study much of what is subsumed under white-collar crime is probably inadequate to utilize fully the available data sources, both primary and secondary, and to grasp conceptually the social-organizational forces involved. The key now to the generation of higher-order interactions among researcher training, data resources, and analytical conceptualizations appears to be the exposure of interested scientific investigators to training appropriate to the research tasks to be performed. As such, training in complex organizations, economics, certain management practices, administrative law, and so forth would seem desirable.

Several long unresolved issues cry out for greater attention from the literature of white-collar crime. Methods for the study of the internal and external operations of organization are still heavily socio-psychological in their origin and therefore sometimes inadequate to handle simultaneously the many sets of variables drawn from large corporate bodies. As anyone knows who has worked extensively with modern corporate bodies, definitions of organization are sometimes difficult, scientific sampling of organizational acts rare, determination of the locus of decision-making power elusive, and so forth. In such circumstances, innovative research methods will be required before great contributions can be expected.

Another significant issue must receive some attention before great strides can be made from an organizational perspective on white-collar crime. In such literature, acts attributed to the organization are often assumed to be explainable by certain circumstances being experienced inside the corporation. That inside conditions are in some fashion converted into actions constituting lawbreaking outside the organization is often left unexplicated. Is it that an internal criminological climate fosters types of acts that are externally defined as lawbreaking? In other words, what social organization within the organizations in question brings about the actions that by external definition are seen as instances of organizational lawbreaking? Although these sound like elementary issues, they are of major consequence to a full understanding of individual-level offending.

The list of extremely stimulating and important issues raised by the contributions in this volume is long. We have apparently entered an era of more objective study of white-collar crime. Less evident is the ideological commitment of the investigator and more explicit are the methods, data sources, theoretical formulations, and analytical paths of the scientific researcher. Disciplines have finally awakened to the potential knowledge to be gleaned from systematic treatment of rules and laws concerning corporate bodies, how corporate bodies operate in the presence of these rules and laws, and how societies inherit the consequences.

# Acknowledgments

*Peter Wickman* and
*Timothy Dailey*

This is to acknowledge and underscore the idea that this book is the result of the collaborative efforts of many individuals and organizations who made the work of the editors and contributors possible. We greatly appreciate the efforts and support of those who made the White Collar and Economic Crime Conference possible and contributed to the success of this volume. This includes the Conversations in the Disciplines Program of the State University of New York (SUNY); the Associated Colleges of the St. Lawrence Valley; the Research Committee for the Sociology of Deviance and Social Control of the International Sociological Association; and Paul Friday, the president of that organization. We extend our appreciation to the members of the conference planning committee: Edward Albert, SUNY, Potsdam; Ram Chugh, SUNY, Potsdam; Stuart Hills, St. Lawrence University, Canton; and Jon Bergstrom, college relations, SUNY, Potsdam. We would, of course, like to thank each of the authors for his or her contribution to this volume. We must also thank the numerous participants in the conference, who made it a success. And we extend a special note of appreciation to Gilbert Geis for his keynote address; to Mark Richard of the U.S. Department of Justice; to Joe Conason of *The Village Voice;* to the honorable Ralph Guy, U.S. district judge, Detroit; to Charles Walsh, assistant U.S. attorney, District of New Jersey; to William Chambliss, Lawrence Sherman, Hal Barnett, Michael Block, Susan Long, F. Peter Poerting, *Bundeskriminalamt* (Federal Republic of Germany), and John Clark; and to those who served as moderators, chairpersons, and participants for the various sessions. Finally, we acknowledge the editorial assistance and encouragement provided by Margaret N. Zusky and the staff of Lexington Books. The secretarial assistance of Kathleen Howe and Betty Wells is also greatly appreciated.

# Introduction

## Peter Wickman and
## Timothy Dailey

The research studies reported in this book are indicative of the renewed attention being given to the illegal behavior of "respectable" individuals and organizations. They suggest something of the changing emphases in criminology as well as the growing public concern with white-collar crime. Since Edwin H. Sutherland first coined the term *white-collar crime* over forty years ago to describe crimes committed by persons of "respectability and high social status," it has been a domain of criminology that has received little attention compared with that given to other forms of crime.

Although the public tends to be indifferent, public policy ambivalent, and scholars inattentive, there is a growing awareness of the seriousness of white-collar crime in modern industrialized societies.[1] The increased attention focused on white-collar offenses by the publicized events that surrounded and followed the Watergate exposés (for example, illegal corporate political contributions, bribery of foreign officials by U.S.-based global corporations, domestic spying by the Central Intelligence Agency (CIA), illegal surveillance and break-ins by the Federal Bureau of Investigation (FBI), political scandals such as "Koreagate" and "Abscam," and further abuses of power) seems to suggest that the incidence of such illegal behavior is increasing. Yet the chapters in this book, by scholars from both sides of the Atlantic, demonstrate that there is a ubiquitous and continuing pattern of such behavior, motivated by economic gain, which pervades corporate, professional, and political organizations both on the national and the international scene. This pattern is observable in countries that operate both under capitalist and socialist economies.

It is difficult to obtain accurate estimates of the extent of white-collar crime, however, since there is no centralized official reporting system to provide data comparable to those on "street crime" provided by the FBI's *Uniform Crime Reports* (UCR). Of course, it is generally accepted that much of the official data on street crime lack both validity and reliability. The UCR data, however, do give some indication of trends in crimes reported to police and of police response in terms of arrests, number of persons charged, and so forth. Although the UCR also include arrest data on white-collar offenses by individuals (such as embezzlement, fraud, and forgery), it does not report corporate offenses such as antitrust violations, corporate bribery, product safety and health hazards, and consumer or securities fraud. Such data are located in relatively inaccessible reports of various regulatory agencies, such as the Federal Trade Commission, the Securities and Exchange Commission, the Environmental Protection Agency, the Internal Revenue Service, and many other federal agencies and commissions. A recent report by the Committee on Economic Offenses of the American Bar Association concludes that there have been few official data collected in this area and that the data available are of "questionable validity" because of the lack of uniform standards for the collection of economic-crime statistics among the relevant agencies. As Gilbert Geis stated in a recent article, "the nonexistence of an official accounting system for white-collar crime suggests something about the state of our priorities," although he notes that the "complexities inherent in this task have doubtless contributed to the absence of such a system."[2]

The paucity of valid data may have been the stimulus for a number of recent efforts to plot the magnitude of the problem by estimating the exorbitant costs of such crimes. The Joint Economic Committee (JEC) of the U.S. Congress estimated the cost of white-collar crime for 1976 at $44 billion, compared with $5.11 billion for other crimes against property (including $1.11 billion for arson). This estimate is comparable to the $40 billion figure set by the U.S. Chamber of Commerce in 1974. Half of this latter figure was due to consumer fraud, illegal competition, and deceptive business practices. The Chamber of Commerce data excluded long-range costs of antitrust violations and other corporate crimes such as violations of health and safety standards. (In 1968 the Justice Department's Antitrust Division had estimated that violations of the Sherman Antitrust Act cost $35 to $40 billion each year).[3]

Emphasizing the economic effects of white-collar crime, which may be spread over a great number of victims, obscures the fact that there are serious physical—albeit apparently accidental—effects. In a recent article, Laura Schrager and James Short catalogue some of these harmful effects of organizational crime on employees, consumers, and the general public. They note that conservative estimates placed the number of deaths resulting from occupational accidents at 14,200 in 1971. About 20,000,000 serious injuries are associated with consumer products, 110,000 of which result in permanent disability and 30,000 in death each year. The harmful effects of using the environment for dumping wastes that contain substances such as polychlorinated biphenyls (PCBs) are still being uncovered.[4]

More difficult to estimate are the broader social consequences of illegal behavior by organizations. Although its major focus was traditional crime, the Crime Commission stated that organizational crimes "are the most threatening of all ... because of their corrosive effect on the moral standards by which American business is conducted."[5] For instance, some research tentatively suggests that corporations that have been charged with violations are confronted with an increased incidence of employee fraud and theft. And although research is scarce in this area, it may be argued that such crimes lead to an erosion of confidence in the legal system, as well as to a breakdown in crime-control efforts. As Professor Geis noted in his recent testimony before the Subcommittee on Crime: "I believe the failure of the criminal justice system to mount an effective campaign against street offenders is largely a function of the fact that prosecutors, judges, and the rest of us know too well that a vast amount of criminal activity by middle and upper class persons is largely ignored."[6]

It is little wonder, then, that ten years after the Crime Commission noted in its brief review of the topic, "the public tends to be indifferent to business crime and even to sympathize with those apprehended,"[7] public opinion began to reflect more concern with this issue. In 1977 Marvin Wolfgang reported that in a random survey of over 8,000 households, many respondents ranked white-collar crime (such as factory pollution, corporate bribery of a government official, political corruption, and fraud against a government program) as being as serious as robbery, aggravated assault, and kidnapping, and even more serious than the theft of amounts in excess of $1,000. In 1978, 89 percent of those responding to a Harris poll agreed that "more than anything else they wanted Congress to do something about corruption in government."[8] It may be that public concern seldom moves beyond "a few fleeting outbursts of indig-nation," as Professor Geis has noted, for "the harm from white collar offenses tends to be diffuse and scattered among the population with individual citizens feeling only a small part of the effects."[9]

The federal government's efforts to develop an effective policy for the control of white-collar crime have been uneven, but some beginnings have been made. Currently, Congress has under consideration a provision in the proposed Federal Criminal Code that would regard officials of organizations as having behaved "recklessly" if they did not control activities of groups for which they were administratively responsible. Yet one cannot but agree with Geis that "populist political rhetoric" sometimes replaces policy. Professor Geis's comment was in reference to a speech by former President Carter an-nouncing that the Justice Department was to undertake "a major new effort in white collar crime."[10] Subsequently, officials of the Law Enforcement Assistance Administration (LEAA) announced that funding for research and action projects on white-collar crime would be reduced for fiscal 1979 as part of that agency's budget cut.[11]

The American Bar Association's Committee on Economic Offenses, in its 1979 report analyzing the federal enforcement policy against economic and white-collar crime, concluded that: "This program is under-funded, undirected, uncoordinated, and is in need of the development of priorities."[12] The com-mittee noted two problems that were directly related to ineffective efforts: the lack of uniform data on the incidence of white-collar crime, and the absence of centralized congressional oversight of the federal effort to control white-collar crime. The committee's report stated further "that if the public were aware of the extent of the economic crime violations in the (government) pro-gram agencies . . . it would reflect badly on . . . agencies and . . . officials charged with the responsibility . . . to prevent or detect violations of law."[13]

However, several projects funded by LEAA have increased federal enforcemert efforts and prosecution of white-collar offenses. One such project, which provided funds to the National District Attorneys' Association's Economic Crime Project, was designed to coordinate the prosecution of white-collar crimes at the state level. By August 1976, the efforts of the sixty-two participating district attorneys had obtained 2,149 convictions for economic crimes, 1,177 of them felony convictions.

The LEAA has also funded research projects such as the grant of over $1 million to a group of scholars at Yale University. The monies have funded studies of such topics as how white-collar crimes are prosecuted, and problems of transnational bribery. This funding also enabled Albert Reiss and Albert D. Biderman to assess the current and potential availability of statistical data in federal agencies on white-collar crime. This originally involved the scrutiny of the records of thirty federal agencies to ascertain how they classify and deal with events that come to be defined as white-collar crime.[14]

This summary of official policy, or lack of it, with respect to crimes of the powerful, as contrasted with the criminal-justice system's focus on protecting society from street offenders, would seem to have presaged a renewed effort for systematic research on this issue. Yet this domain of criminology has been left relatively unattended until the late 1970s, except for a brief flurry of research following Edwin H. Sutherland's presidential address to the American Sociological Society in 1939. For instance, a two-volume review of theoretical and empirical research in criminology from 1945 to 1972, the *Criminology Index* (1975), lists nearly 3,700 articles or books; yet only 92 of these, about 2.5 percent, dealt with economic crime—that is, white-collar, corporate, or organized crimes.[15]

Interest in the study of white-collar crime by social scientists was rekindled in 1968 with the publication of a collection of readings on the subject edited by Gilbert Geis.[16] It is noteworthy that the increased momentum of research on the subject was not yet apparent when the revised edition was published in 1977. Fewer than one-third of the works included had been published since the appearance of the first edition. In the introductory essay to the revised edition the editors noted the developments that they contended would stimulate increased scholarly concern on this issue: the militant consumer-advocacy movement of Ralph Nader and others, the renewed interest in laws regulating business malpractice and governmental malfeasance, and more-vigorous enforcement efforts by federal agencies. The need for studies of white-collar crime to become a part of the mainstream of social-science research, to draw from diverse disciplines, to accumulate data from previous case studies, to develop and test hypotheses, and to focus on the type of research that represents a cumulative process, was also stressed by the editors as a prerequisite for promoting the revival of social inquiry in the area.[17]

The quality of the work on white-collar and economic crime included in this book attests, we believe, to such a renaissance of concern with this complex subject. These chapters illustrate the ability of social scientists to apply refined concepts and perspectives from related disciplines, such as economic and political theory and organizational behavior, to the substantive areas of white-collar crime. Several of the scholars represented here have formerly concentrated on studies of traditional forms of lawbreaking activity. Now, however, they have contributed, we believe, to the momentum of increased interest and activity in this domain of criminology, which is one of "preeminent intellectual and policy significance," initiated by Edwin H. Sutherland.[18]

This book will augment the growing list of publications on the subject that have appeared since 1975. At least seven collections of readings on white-collar and economic crime have been edited by economists and sociologists over the past six years. Monographs by academics include works that vary in scope and orientation and include, among others: August Bequai's *White Collar Crime: A 20th Century Crisis* (1978); John Conklin's *Illegal but Not Criminal* (1977); Colin Goff and Charles Reason's *Corporate Crime in Canada: A Critical Analysis of Anti-Combine Legislation* (1978); and Susan Rose-Ackerman's *Corruption: A Study in Political Economy* (1978).

The chapters in this book represent the end product of a majority of the papers presented at a symposium on white-collar crime. The occasion, a conference convened on the campus of the State University of New York, College at Potsdam, 7-9 February 1980, was part of the ripple of recent national conferences that attest still further to the mounting attentiveness to this topic. This meeting was also international in its intent and focus, for, although funded by grants from the State University of New York and the Associated Colleges of the St. Lawrence Valley, it was also sponsored by the Research Committee on Deviance and Social Control of the International Sociological Association. Five of the essays included here—those by Professors Sheleff, Łoś, Reasons, Carson, and Snider—typify the cross-national ambience of this conference.

The papers presented at the conference covered a wide spectrum of scholarly concerns and perspectives relevant to white-collar and economic crime. The sessions were planned and organized to promote scholarly interchange on such critical issues as the following:

1. *The changing social definitions of white-collar crime.* What have we learned from recent events, such as Watergate, relative to the morally ambiguous evaluations of the various publics?

2. *The need to extend traditional sociological inquiry to include eocnmic analysis and perspectives on organizational behavior.* What is the function of economic gain in these types of crime, and are there certain organizational structures that are criminogenic?

3. *How might organized crime intersect or overlap with upperworld crime both on the national and the international scene?* Would more research on organized crime provide insights into the organizational nature of upperworld economic crime on both micro and macro levels?

4. *The extent, nature, and socioeconomic significance of white-collar crime*

*compared with traditional street crime.* What biases, empathies, and limitations do middle-class social scientists bring to such inquiry?

5. *The extent to which corporate crime and political corruption exist as apparently unavoidable facts of national and international economic structures.* Do the political economies of modern industrialized nations—either capitalist or socialist—create concentrations of power that make the abuse of such power inevitable? Do the dimensions of the global political economy create conflicts of cultural and legal definitions, so that what is viewed as illegal in one nation is an acceptable, or even necessary, practice in another?

6. *The relative effects of various sanctions.* What are the relative deterrent effects of formal versus informal sanctions? of economic sanctions such as fines versus imprisonment?

7. *The importance of the regulatory process and control efforts.* Do the interplay and complexity of relations between offenders and the system and between law violators and agencies of social control require a different understanding from that of traditional crime? How do variables such as the power and influence of those subject to regulation and control affect the laws and the control of information required to substantiate charges of illegal behavior?[19]

To a remarkable degree—some termed it "serendipity"—the papers and symposia focused on these interrelated issues. Consequently, these are themes that cut across and pervade the three parts of this book. The three parts then organize the various chapters into rather broad parameters representing various dimensions for scholarly research on white-collar and economic crime. Each part is introduced by an overview essay.

The four chapters in part I make a significant contribution by providing a reexamination and expansion of perspectives and focuses for further research. The first chapter provides a historical context and a study in the sociology of knowledge through a biographical analysis. The other chapters extend the parameters of inquiry into political-economic dimensions and macro emphases.

The chapters in part II focus on organizational patterns and structural concomitants and consequences of white-collar and economic crime. Organizational factors as well as political-economic considerations also have implications for social-control efforts, as the four chapters in part III demonstrate. These chapters provide a descriptive and quantitative analysis of research studies relevant to social control, sanctions, and presumed deterrent effects.

In summary, the chapters of this book, admittedly, do not constitute a comprehensive coverage of the domain of white-collar and economic crime. They do represent, in addition to augmenting a renewed interest in the topic, some of the solid and systematic scholarly research that is ongoing in the area.

Thus they also typify efforts to broaden the boundaries of the focus of inquiry and to demonstrate the interworking between developing theory and sound research. It is hoped that this volume will contribute to the continuation of research emphasis in this area.

## Notes

1. American Bar Association, Section of Criminal Justice, *Economic Offenses* (Washington, D.C.: American Bar Association, 1977), p. 5.

2. Gilbert Geis and Ezra Stotland, "Introduction," in Geis and Stotland, eds., *White Collar Crime: Theory and Research* (Beverly Hills: Sage Publications, 1980), p. 10.

3. Cited in Peter Wickman and Phillip Whitten, *Criminology: Perspectives on Crime and Criminality* (Lexington, Mass.: D.C. Heath and Company, 1980), p. 88. See also Miriam Saxon, *White Collar Crime: The Problem and the Federal Response* (Washington, D.C.: U.S. Government Printing Office, 1978), pp. 8-10.

4. Laura Shill Schrager and James F. Short, "Toward a Sociology of Organizational Crime," *Social Problems* 25, No. 4(April 1978):413-416.

5. The President's Commission on Law Enforcement and the Administration of Justice, *The Challenge of Crime in a Free Society* (Washington, D.C.: U.S. Government Printing Office, 1967), p. 5; hereafter referred to as Crime Commission.

6. Statement of Gilbert Geis, *Hearings before the Subcommittee on Crime* (Washington, D.C.: U.S. Government Printing Office, 1978), p. 22.

7. Crime Commission, p. 104.

8. Saxon, *White Collar Crime*, p. 16.

9. Saxon, *White Collar Crime*, p. 16; see also Prepared Statement of Edelhertz, *Hearings Before the Subcommittee*, p. 5; see also Prepared Statement of Geis, *Hearings Before the Subcommittee*, p. 23.

10. Statement of Gilbert Geis, *Hearings Before the Subcommittee*, p. 21.

11. Saxon, *White Collar Crime*, p. 21.

12. American Bar Association, *Economic Offenses*, pp. 5-7.

13. American Bar Association, *Economic Offenses*, p. 20.

14. Saxon, *White Collar Crime*, pp. 22-23.

15. Marvin Wolfgang, Robert M. Figlio, and Terrence Thornberry, *Criminology Index, 1945-1972* (New York: Elsevier, 1945), cited in Stanton Wheeler, "Trends and Problems in the Sociological Study of Crime," in Peter Wickman and Phillip Whitten, eds., *Readings in Criminology* (Lexington, Mass.: D.C. Heath and Company, 1978), p. 5.

16. Gilbert Geis, ed., *White Collar Criminal: The Offender in Business and the Professions* (New York: Atherton, 1968).

17. Gilbert Geis and Robert Meier, eds., *White Collar Crime: Offenses in Business, Politics and the Professions* (New York: Free Press, 1977), pp. 1–4.

18. See chapter 1 by Gilbert Geis and Colin Goff.

19. Adapted from Stanton Wheeler's Presidential Address to the Society for the Study of Social Problems, 1975; "Trends and Problems in the Sociological Study of Crime," in Wickman and Whitten, eds., *Readings in Criminology,* p. 8–9.

# Part I
# White-Collar Crime
# Reexamined: Expansion of
# Conceptual Perspectives
# and Emphases

Geis and Goff begin this section with the analytical biography of Edwin Sutherland in chapter 1. They ask why Sutherland "erupted" in his work on white-collar crime, given his earlier "meticulous" focus on traditional concepts of crime. Sutherland's innovative concept of crime is traced to influences of his midwestern, rural, and religious background. According to Geis and Goff, Sutherland's groundbreaking has not been vigorously pursued because of his reliance on differential association, definitional ambiguity, and historical factors. The remaining chapters in this section (chapters 2, 3, and 4) seek to expand Sutherland's ideas, especially his theoretical ideas, by recognizing economic and political forces.

In chapter 2 Smith advocates joining the concepts of white-collar and organized crime under the concept of enterprise—a spectrum along which entrepreneurial activity is more or less legal, depending on the political constraints placed on economic activity. Departing from Sutherland's moral emphases, Smith tells us to look at what the actors do and at the political circumstances under which their activity is evaluated, rather than at their character and appearance.

Sheleff, in chapter 3, expands Sutherland's concerns in an international direction, but follows in Sutherland's moral path as he insists that the problems of international crime are often truly or naturally criminal in the harm they do, whether or not they are so labeled legally. The lack of clear definition and procedure in much international law leads Sheleff to call not only for more research but also for more action to understand and curb such problems as pollution, destruction and theft of nations' historical artifacts, waste of natural resources, and infringement of human rights.

In chapter 4 Charles Reasons also takes us beyond Sutherland's focus in that his essay distinguishes between *white-collar crime*—acts by individuals against business—and *organizational crime*—acts by business against others. Reasons surveys available information about the extent and nature of organizational crime in Canada, including governmental offenses. He includes analyses of economic offenses (unfair marketing, price fixing); human-rights violations (eavesdropping, blacklisting); and violent personal injuries (auto deaths, asbestosis, pollution). Reasons advocates broader application of criminal law to the liability of organizational violations.

1

# 1

# Edwin H. Sutherland: A Biographical and Analytical Commentary

*Gilbert Geis* and *Colin Goff*

The thirty-fourth annual meeting of the American Sociological Society (ASS)—convened in Philadelphia in 1939 during the academic recess between Christmas and the New Year—was held jointly with the fifty-second gathering of the American Economic Association (AEA). On 27 December, Jacob Viner of the University of Chicago delivered his presidential address to the AEA. According to the program, his topic was to have been "Does Gold Have a Future?" But Viner's thoughts on this matter must remain uncertain. By the time of the session, he had abandoned his announced subject. The presidential address now bore the imposing title "The Short View and the Long in Economic Policy," and had nothing to say about the prospects for gold (Viner 1940).

The joint meeting of the AEA and the ASS was held at the Benjamin Franklin Hotel, which still stands at Ninth and Chestnut Streets in downtown Philadelphia. Room rates ranged from $3.50 to $6.00. Newspapers of the day were reporting that the Archbishop of Canterbury had suggested prayers in support of Finland's resistance to a Russian invasion; that the British were instituting sugar and meat rationing; and that Mussolini had paid a visit to the Pope. At home, it was noted mournfully that Roosevelt's fiscal proposals included the seventh unbalanced federal budget in a row. Elsewhere, Al Capone had been admitted to a Baltimore hospital with an undisclosed ailment, and probes by Martin Dies's House Committee on un-American Activities were said to have bared a "Red drive" on the West Coast.

Viner's presidential address was at eight o'clock on the evening of 27 December. He was followed to the podium in the hotel's Crystal Room by Edwin H. Sutherland of Indiana University, president of the sociological society, whose title was "The White Collar Criminal." Sutherland's address altered the field of criminology in fundamental ways throughout the world, although it would take all of the more than forty years since that night for the impact of the address to be appreciated fully and reflected in the mainstream of criminological work.

Paper delivered at the Conference on White Collar and Economic Crime, State University of New York College, Potsdam, New York, 7 February 1980. The following persons have contributed information and insights to our work: Russ Dynes; Robley Geis; Peter Wickman; Lamar Empey; John Braithwaite; Henry Pontell; Paul Jesilow; Marvin Wolfgang; Ron Huff; Robert Meier; Robert Lowry, librarian, Grand Island, Nebraska; Verle D. Dority, secretary, Grand Island College Former Student Association; Rachel R. Shorthill, Special Corrections librarian, William Jewell College; Mark R. Patterson, director of alumni affairs, Sioux Falls College.

## Sutherland's Heritage

Sutherland was 56 years old at the time of his presidential address. Little in his earlier work would have prepared the audience for his fiery indictment of persons who ever after would be known by the label that Sutherland put on them that night: *white-collar criminals.* In addition to its scholarly component, Sutherland's material clearly represented a strong personal and political testament. His work on white-collar crime abounds with expressions of indignation, anger, and vituperation. Note as but one example (though one of the most inflammatory) the following from *White Collar Crime,* the monograph Sutherland wrote in 1949:

> . . . the utility corporations for two generations or more have engaged in organized propaganda to develop favorable sentiments. They devoted much attention to the public schools in an effort to mold the opinion of children. Perhaps no groups except the Nazis have paid so much attention to indotrinating the youth of the land with ideas favorable to a special interest, and it is doubtful whether even the Nazis were less bound by considerations of honesty in their propaganda. [p. 210]

This seems a surprising outburst from a person who uniformly is described by those who knew him well as "imbued with sincerity and objectivity," "soft-spoken," a man of "paternal wisdom" who "never taught in terms of sarcasm, ridicule, or abuse" (Odum 1951, p. 802). As his colleague at Indiana University, Jerome Hall, observed, Sutherland was "distinguished by an attitude of extraordinary objectivity and thorough inquiry maintained on a high level" and was an individual who "knew how to keep his feelings and personality from intruding into the discussion" (1951, p. 394). What clues might we find in Sutherland's heritage that would help account for his eruption on white-collar crime, which contrasts so markedly with his much more meticulous, even rather pedantic, earlier work in criminology?

Fortunately, details of Sutherland's family background are readily recaptured. In 1935 his father, a Baptist educator and minister, then 87 years old, wrote three book-length manuscripts, one of them an account of his own life. The typescripts, which were deposited by their author in the library of the Baptist Historical Society in Rochester, New York, provide considerable insight into the milieu and the ideological atmosphere that constituted Sutherland's early environment.

These manuscripts set forth some of the principles held by Edwin Sutherland's father that undoubtedly served to fashion the son's character. Both father and son were critical, tough on others (Sutherland 1937), and unstintingly self-critical (Sutherland 1944). They shared also a traditional dedication to service, to doing good, to making the world a better place, and to taking the side of the underprivileged and downtrodden. Most notably, there is a religious commitment that, at its best, demands that the ethics of Christianity be attained in the marketplace. At times, the tone of Sutherland's work on white-collar crime is reminiscent of the preaching of outraged biblical prophets. There is a theological insistence that something other than strict legal denotation demark the realm of acceptable behavior, a matter that would involve Sutherland in considerable debate with those who adhered more firmly to law-book codes as the only criteria by which criminological judgments should be made (Tappan 1947). Snodgrass (1972, p. 223) has pointed out that "Edwin grew up to love bridge, golf, cigarettes, magazines, movies and jigsaw puzzles," and that he was not particularly religious as an adult. But he remained a man of "compulsive virtue and integrity. . . . While he may have given up the orthodoxy of his Baptist upbringing, he never lost its scruples" (Snodgrass 1972, p. 227).

Sutherland certainly was tougher on entrenched interests than was his father. In one segment of the elder Sutherland's *History of Nebraska Baptists* (G. Sutherland 1935a, p. 25), he praises the railroads for providing free passes to itinerant religious preachers. This policy, George Sutherland suggests, arose from the railroads' awareness that ministers brought stability and prosperity to an area, thus ultimately benefiting the railroads. This puts the self-interest of both preachers and the railroads in a benevolent light. The son was less benign; indeed, railroads take some of the heavier blows in his work on white-collar crime (Sutherland 1949, pp. 89–94).

The independence of the frontiersman constituted an essential aspect of Sutherland's patrimony. In his study of homeless men in Chicago (Sutherland and Locke 1936), Sutherland points out how migration from the protective rural countryside into the jungle of the city had been disconcerting for so many shelter residents. So it must have been for Sutherland as well. The ruses and rudeness, the predation and pitilessness—all must have been unnerving for the Baptist minister's son from Nebraska when he first came to Chicago.

Sutherland's mixture of rural integrity and self-reliance, his combined fear and scorn of city-bred sophistication, and his religious zeal for social reform also marked the characters of a large number of the early leaders of American sociology (Geis 1964). In time, Sutherland was indoctrinated by the prevailing imperatives of his sociological trade into the ethos of "scientific" objectivity. Especially in his textbook, he was unsparing in his exposure of the false syllogism, the sloppy logic, the unsupported inference, and the generalization rooted in fancy rather than fact. But behind all this lay his Nebraska Baptist heritage, a heritage that would break through—for better and for worse—when Sutherland in his later years came to study and write about white-collar crime.

## Sutherland's Forebears

Edwin Sutherland's great-grandparents migrated to Canada from Scotland and ultimately settled in the fishing and lumbering village of St. George, New Brunswick, where George Sutherland, Edwin's father, was born in 1848. In the 1850s depressed economic conditions drove the Sutherlands to Wisconsin. The family settled in Eau Claire, where George was graduated from high school. The

Sutherlands supported themselves by farming; almost eighty years later, George Sutherland would recall that an unfair share of the chores fell to him. "My father," he wrote critically, "was not interested in farming. He would rather visit his neighbors than plow a furrow or hoe a row of potatoes."[a] From his mother George acquired a strong religious sense, from his father a fervid antagonism toward liquor, "the great corrupter of mankind" (1935b, p. 155). George's earliest experiences with organized religion are recounted in the independent, self-deprecatory tone that so permeates his description of his life:

> Soon after my uniting with the church I was made a clerk. . . . I do not think that I made a particularly brilliant clerk, but I attended the church meetings and took down what was done. I was criticized because I did not speak loud enough and did not read loud enough. It was said that my reports could not be heard. They could have remedied that, since my resignation was always before the Church. [1935b, p. 21]

After finishing high school, George Sutherland taught locally. In 1872, when he was first old enough to vote, he marked his ballot for the candidate of the Prohibition party. He reveals a great deal about himself and about attitudes that must have been transmitted to his children when he recounts the nature of his affiliation with the Prohibition party:

> I was not very active. . . . I met with them a few times. I was on one occasion president of the state nominating convention in Nebraska, but the people who composed the party seemed to me to be angular, stiff, non-conciliatory, refusing to go out of their way a tittle of a hair's breadth to win an adherent. [1935b, p. 35][1]

In 1876 Sutherland was ordained a Baptist minister, an event that led him to observe, more than fifty years later, "I was a good deal more orthodox on that day than I am at the present time" (1935b, p. 94). He received a divinity degree from the Baptist Union Theological Seminary of the University of Chicago the following year. In 1881 he was appointed to teach Greek and bookkeeping at the Nebraska Baptist Seminary in Gibbon, which was then in its second year of operation. Gibbon, named after a Civil War general, lies almost adjacent to the Platte River in the southeastern part of the state. It was a frontier town, founded ten years earlier by the Soldier's Free Homestead Colony, a group of sixty families brought together in the East by a speculator desiring to settle lands ceded to the Union Pacific Railroad to encourage roadbed construction (Vohland 1971).

Edwin H. Sutherland was born in Gibbon on 13 August 1883. Less than a year later, the family relocated in Kansas, where for the next nine years George

---

[a]George Sutherland, "Autobiography," unpublished manuscript (Rochester, N.Y.: American Baptist Historical Society, 1935b). Reprinted with permission.

Sutherland served as head of the history department. "It is my judgment," he would later write, "that for the man who likes books and young people, teaching in a college is the height of human bliss" (1935b, p. 144). The father's point was not lost on the Sutherland children. Edwin's brother became an educational psychologist, teaching for a while at the University of Illinois, at Yale, and later at Louisiana College, a Baptist school in Pineville;[2] the youngest child, George, became a pediatrician on the faculty of Rush Medical College in Philadelphia.

When the Nebraska Baptist Seminary, in dire financial straits, moved thirty miles east to become Grand Island College, George Sutherland was recruited for the presidency. He remained in that office for eighteen years, from 1893 to 1911. During this period the college was in incessant financial difficulty, a predicament that it managed to overcome, according to the school's historian (Hinton 1970), only because of the extraordinary energy and personality of its president.

After leaving the presidency of Grand Island College in 1911, Sutherland accepted a position in St. Louis with the Society for the Friendless, a group dedicated to aiding former prison inmates. Sutherland reports going to the public library to read up on criminology, since "I knew little about the business in which I was engaged" (1935b, p. 162). While he was at work, his overcoat was stolen. He was neither amused nor sympathetic:

> While I had been industriously gathering information on behalf of those in prison or who ought to be there, some of these people were showing their customary gratitude to one who was trying to do them good. I had the discomfort of going home through rain and storm, cold and shivering. That criminal was not unlike others for whom good men had labored and made sacrifices. [pp. 1935b, pp. 162-163]

Sutherland soon found that despite his considerable labors he was raising hardly more than enough money to pay his own salary, with little left to help former inmates. His employers seemed satisfied, but Sutherland, believing that under the circumstances his solicitations were unethical, quit. He dabbled for a while in real estate,[3] and he did some teaching at Grand Island College. ("I was asked to withdraw from the teaching force of the college," he writes, "for the reason that my personality was so striking and impressive that no president could stand up against me" (1935b, p. 177). After that, he preached and did pastoral work at neighboring churches on a contract basis. In 1929, when he was 81, Sutherland again was named president of Grand Island College. He held that position for the next two years, until during the Depression Grand Island College was absorbed by Sioux Falls College in South Dakota.

Sutherland barely mentions his family in his 181 pages of autobiographical memoir. He states that he married Lizzie T. Pickett in 1877 and that she was from Connecticut (they had met in Chicago), "active in Christian service," "a good Sunday school teacher," and "one who led the singing and prayer meetings" (1935b, p. 100). That is all that we will learn from her husband about Lizzie Pickett. The Sutherland children, too, are discussed in only a single paragraph, but affectionately:

> I had three children when I went to Ottawa. Arthur, born in Minock [Illinois]; Nellie, born in Chicago, and Edwin, born in Gibbon. During our nine years sojourn in Ottawa there came to us four more, Bertha, Lillian, Stanley, and Fred. Seven is a large number to those who have none. Some seemed to think that it was too large a number for respectable people to have. On the meager salary I received, we found it hard to feed and clothe them. But when they had grown up, when they were occupying important places in the world of service, when at times they gathered together in the old homestead, it looked then as though there were none too many, that without them, the world would be much poorer. [1935b, p. 149]

The final line of Sutherland's reminiscences reads, "Perhaps my executors will complete this autobiography by writing here an account of my decease" (1935b, p. 181). No one did. George Sutherland died at the age of 95, on 11 December 1943, four years after his son's presidential adress to the American Sociological Society.


## Sutherland's Career

Almost all of Edwin Sutherland's earlier years, up to the age of 21, were spent in Grand Island, Nebraska. This city, which had a population of about 6,000 in Sutherland's time, owed its early growth to a favorable position as a railroad distribution point. It is located almost in the center of the United States, and was founded there in 1866 (less than two decades before the Sutherlands arrived) partly in the quixotic belief that its location would persuade the federal government to place the national capital in Grand Island (Works Progress Administration 1939).

Sutherland received the A.B. degree from Grand Island College, where his father was president, in 1904.[4] He was one of seventy students to complete a baccalaureate degree during his father's eighteen year tenure at the college. Most of those enrolled at Grand Island did academic work that today would be equivalent to the level of the later years of high school. Sutherland immediately went to teach Greek and Latin at Sioux Falls College in South Dakota, Grand Island's sister Baptist institution. While he was in Sioux Falls, from 1904 to 1906, Sutherland enrolled in a correspondence course in sociology offered by the University of Chicago. The course, a prerequisite for graduate study in history (the field that Sutherland intended to pursue) used a textbook by Charles R. Henderson, a Baptist minister turned sociologist. Henderson, a man much in the spirit of Sutherland's father, was once described by a journalist who watched him preside over an international penology conference as "giving fire, dignity, and spiritual earnestness to the gathering" (Geis 1971, p. iv). It is particularly noteworthy that the edition of Henderson's textbook that Sutherland used contains a number of statements that Sutherland himself would echo more than thirty years later in setting forth his ideas about white-collar crime.[5] Note, for instance, this pronouncement by Henderson:

> The social classes of the highest culture furnish few convicts, yet there are educated criminals. Advanced culture modifies the form of crime; tends to make it less coarse and violent, but more cunning; restricts it to quasi-legal forms. But education also opens up the way to new and colossal kinds of crime, as debauching of conventions, councils, legislatures, and bribery of the press and public officials. The egoistic impulses are masked and disguised in this way, the devil wearing the livery of heavenly charity for a cloak of wrong. Many of the "Napoleons" of trade are well named, for they are cold-blooded robbers and murderers, utterly indifferent to the inevitable misery which they must know will follow their contrivances and deals. Occasionally eminent legal ability is employed to plan raids upon the public in ways which will evade the penalties of the criminal code, and many a representative of financial power grazes the prison walls on his way to "success."
> [1901, p. 250]

The correspondence course led Sutherland to change his graduate concentration to sociology when he attended the University of Chicago from 1906 to 1908. He also worked during part of this period with the Juvenile Protective Association in the city. A significant portion of his academic work was with W.I. Thomas, an iconoclast who may well have been influential in moderating the hold of religious orthodoxy on Sutherland's mind. From 1909 to 1911, Sutherland returned to Grand Island as a faculty member. In 1911 he went back to the university, where two years later he received the Ph.D. degree. His dissertation, done in conjunction with the work of the Chicago Commission on Unemployment, was titled, "Unemployment and Public Employment Agencies."

Sutherland then took a teaching position in the sociology department at William Jewell College in Liberty, Missouri, another Baptist institution, where he spent the six years between 1913 and 1919. At William Jewell, where he occupied the John E. Franklin chair of sociology, his teaching assignments included classes in Trade Unionism, Social Problems in Rural Life, Socialism, Charities and Corrections, and Social Politics. In 1918 Sutherland married Myrtle Crews, his landlady's daughter. They would have one child, a daughter.

After leaving William Jewell, Sutherland engaged in something of a Cook's tour of the Big Ten universities. He taught at the University of Illinois for seven years (1919-1926); went to the University of Minnesota for three (1926-1929); and then to the University of Chicago for five years (1930-1935). Failing to secure a tenure guarantee at Chicago, he departed for Indiana University and remained there for the next fifteen years, until his death in 1950. He made brief excursions throughout his career for visiting appointments at the University of Kansas (1918); Northwestern University (1922); the University of Washington in St. Louis (1942); and San Diego State College during the summer before he died. There was also a year, 1929, with the Bureau of Social Hygiene in New York City, a period that included a brief trip to England to examine the prison system.

What can be said about Sutherland's career pattern? Certainly, there is some indication of a parochial tendency in that Sutherland never ventured very far for very long from the social milieus that he understood and with which he was probably particularly comfortable. In other words, he was exposed to little that might directly challenge his midwestern upbringing, although his years in Chicago must have broadened considerably his understanding of crime and criminals. By the time he came to write on the subject of white-collar crime, Sutherland had spent virtually all of his life very far indeed from the center of political and economic power in the Unites States. In this country, cities such as Washington and New York are where things happen, where wealth and power (and white-collar crime) are concentrated, where meaningful field work can be undertaken at the source rather than with second-hand reports in the library. Sutherland could not draw on friendship networks, personal discussions, or similar sources for information and viewpoints about white-collar crime. The national and international corporate and political world was for him an almost entirely alien environment. This may explain why, in trying to document white-collar crime by means of case histories, Sutherland (1949, pp. 226–228) resorts to a pedestrian recital of the small-time shenanigans of a college student who worked on weekends as a shoe salesman—a story, according to Donald Cressey, based on Sutherland's personal experiences.

White-collar-crime studies, in fact, have suffered continuously from the age-old tradition of locating major centers of learning in geographically remote and bucolic settings, presumably so that contemplation is not disturbed by mundane affairs. It is noteworthy that scholars based in New York, including Paul Tappan, Richard Quinney, and Erwin Smigel at New York University, make up a sizable percentage of the limited cadre of persons who have contributed significant material on white-collar crime. Washington, D.C., unfortunately, has no preeminent university within the city, although several institutions are now striving for such distinction. Clinard (1952) did his work on the black market as a form of white-collar crime following a wartime assignment with the Office of Price Administration in Washington; and much of the recent white-collar-crime scholarship of a team at Yale University, under the direction of Stanton Wheeler, has been based on the assignment of researchers to federal regulatory agencies in Washington. Sutherland's own work on white-collar crime clearly reflects his upbringing and the pattern of his academic career, and can be much better understood and interpreted when it is examined in this light.

## The Presidential Address

At least two dozen persons who participated in the American Sociological Society meetings of 1934 are alive today. Not surprisingly, given the time interval and the generally untheatrical nature of such academic events, none of the handful to whom we have talked recalls Sutherland's address. Thorsten Sellin of the University of Pennsylvania, a member of the program committee in 1939 and now living in retirement in New Hampshire, says that he no longer "can remember a thing" from that night. Sellin had known Sutherland for some time, however. In 1927, on a visit to his parents' home in Minneapolis, Sellin paid a special call at the University of Minnesota, where Sutherland was teaching, in order to become acquainted. The two maintained close ties through the years. Sutherland, Sellin observes, was "a very, very retiring person. Modest. Chary of hullabaloo. Very quiet."[a]

As noted, Sutherland's earlier work gave virtually no indication that he suddenly would turn his attention to white-collar crime. His criminology textbook, in its tenth edition in 1978—the revisions having been undertaken by Donald Cressey after Sutherland's death—and perhaps the longest survivor in the realm of social science texts, had paid hardly any attention to the kinds of criminal activity that formed the focus of the Philadelphia talk.

Later, in a speech before the Toynbee Club of DePauw University in Indiana, Sutherland (1956a) would say that he had been collecting material on white-collar crime since 1928, more than a decade before his groundbreaking presidential address. We have found only one published clue to this work: a passing observation in a 1932 article that advocates the use of the concept of "culture" in understanding the crime patterns of immigrants to America. Sutherland (1932, pp. 59-60) notes of his idea: "It is not suggested as a total explanation of delinquency even in the delinquency area, and it certainly does not explain the financial crimes of the white-collar classes." Further, in a 1936 book, written with Harvey J. Locke (one of Sutherland's very few collaborators), the authors employ the term *white collar worker* as a classificatory category to distinguish the 7 percent of the people living during the Depression in Chicago's shelters for unemployed men who had been "professional men, business men, clerks, salesmen, accountants, and men who previously held minor political positions" (p. 62). Obviously, the terms *crime* and *white collar* were prominent in Sutherland's professional vocabularly; given his subject matter, their denotive linkage was almost inevitable.

Sutherland's presidential address, some 5,000 words in length, merits close analysis. The *Philadelphia Inquirer,* in a prominently placed news story the following day, took note of Sutherland's address in terms which suggested that it

[a]Thorsten Sellin, Telephone conversation with Gilbert Geis, 12 January 1980.

had pointed to a radical departure from accepted approaches to criminal-behavior theories. The report was headlined "Poverty Belittled as Crime Factor," with the subhead "Sociologist Cites Fraud in Business." Sutherland's audience of economists and sociologists was said to have been "astonished" by the presentation. Certainly the reporter was taken with Professor Sutherland's speech, which he suggested in a figurative sense "threw scores of sociological textbooks into a wastebasket." The *Inquirer* writer thus inadvertently offered an observation that time has proved to have been more hopeful than prescient.

The *New York Times* also gave Sutherland favorable, albeit more restrained, coverage. Its news report suggested that Sutherland launched a pointed attack against white-collar criminality. This is the first, though hardly the last, commentary that refused to take seriously Sutherland's patently disingenuous disclaimer at the end of the first paragraph of his paper. Sutherland made a comparison between crime in the upper class and crime in the lower class which he contended was "for the purpose of developing theories of criminal behavior, not for the purpose of muckraking or the reform of anything except criminology" (p. 1). The *New York Times* story implied that the reporter knew better: he could recognize a muckrake when he saw one.

Perhaps fearing to seem defensive both the *Inquirer* and the *Times* in their stories gave prominent mention to Sutherland's implied criticism of the press. "In many periods," Sutherland said, "more important crime news can be found on the financial pages than on the front pages" of the nation's dailies. The papers also noted Sutherland's scarcely profound observation that white-collar crime of his day was more suave and deceptive than such crime had been in the time of the robber barons. They also found newsworthy the observation that much of white-collar crime was like "stealing candy from a baby"; that is, that the matchup between offender and victim was highly uneven. It has been remarked (Snodgrass 1973) that Sutherland appears in awe of the skills of professional criminals such as Chic Conwell, the con artist whose autobiographical observations Sutherland published under the title, *The Professional Thief* (1937). But his awe turns to scorn when the thief is a businessman, when it is power and not finesse that allows the haves to prey upon the have-nots.

## "White-Collar Criminality"

Given the joint nature of the professional meeting at which he was speaking, Sutherland at the outset tried to draw the scholarly community of economists into a concern with white-collar crime, a mission that had little success either then or since. For economists, white-collar criminal acts are usually viewed as no more than one among many calculated business risks; apprehension by the authorities means only that a cost is added to the loss side of the ledger. There is in economics virtually no material examining the efficacy of variant penalty

structures on business behavior, or relating organizational structure and function
to law violation. The farthest economists (as well as political scientists) are apt
to venture into the study of white-collar crime is to address questions about
whether corruption in developing countries is functional or dysfunctional (for
general reviews, see Caiden 1979; Heidenheimer 1970). That economists lately
have come to regard traditional forms of crime and penalties such as capital
punishment as matters worthy of attention may indicate that with time they will
begin to focus on white-collar crime, on offenses that one might have thought,
given their expertise, would have captured their disciplinary fancy earlier.

Sutherland's presidential address gropes ponderously toward a definition for
white-collar crime, an issue that has preoccupied many scholars since his time.
Sutherland's definition is placed in a footnote, presumably indicating that he
found the matter of little inportance. Elsewhere, Geis has suggested that the
footnoted statement seems like "a parody of pedantic obscurantism" (1974,
p. 284), and many readings thereafter have offered no reason to alter this
judgment. The footnote states:

> . . . "[W]hite-collar" (upper) and "lower" classes merely designate per-
> sons of high and low socioeconomic status. Income and the amount of
> money involved in the crime are not the sole criteria. Many persons of
> "low" socioeconomic status are "white-collar" criminals in the sense
> that they are well-dressed, well-educated, and have high incomes, but
> "white-collar" as used in this paper means "respected," "socially ac-
> cepted and approved," "looked up to." Some people in this class may
> not be well-dressed or well-educated, nor have high incomes, although
> the "upper" usually exceed the "lower" classes in these respects as well
> as in social status. [p. 9]

In his 1949 monograph Sutherland would note, also in a footnote, that he
meant to employ the term *white collar* in the sense that Alfred A. Sloan, Jr. did
(1941), that is, "principally" to refer to business managers and executives
(Sutherland 1949, p. 9). It is an eccentric reference. Sloan, who had become the
president of General Motors, made a fortune during the halcyon days of the
automobile industry. Certainly Sutherland did not mean to restrict his inquiries
to men of Sloan's enormous wealth and power. Sloan and Sparkes (1941) contains neither any references nor anything of particular relevance to social or
business stratification, the matters of importance to Sutherland. A biographical
sketch of Sloan notes that he characteristically wore collars "of an arresting
height and as stiff as a Buick mudguard" (Sloan 1940, p. 472). Perhaps, if he
knew of this, Sutherland was impressed enough with its symbolism to have
Sloan represent the class whose crimes form Sutherland's research topic. Oddly,
Sutherland, who was a meticulous person in such respects, incorrectly cites the
title of Sloan's book, which was actually *Adventures of a White Collar Man*, not
*An Autiobiography of a White Collar Worker*. It is not unlikely that Sutherland,

who by the time his monograph appeared was suffering noticeably from stomach pains (Sellin 1980) and was near the end of his life, wrote the introductory chapter of *White Collar Crime* last, and in haste.

There are a number of themes set forth in Sutherland's presidential address that should have (but as yet have not) been addressed by later scholars. Many of the ideas are repeated; few are investigated. Sutherland maintains, for instance, that white-collar crime is more deleterious to a community's morale than is street crime:

> White-collar crimes violate trust and therefore create distrust, which lowers social morale and produces social disorganization on a large scale. . . . Other crimes have relatively little effect on social institutions or social organizations. [p. 5]

Many of us may agree, but the issues require restatement in a testable form—and testing. Sutherland insists that white-collar criminals tend to be relatively protected from the harsher consequences of lawbreaking, in part because of a class congruence between them and those responsible for writing and enforcing laws and exacting penalties. Again, the thesis needs to be broken down into operationally defined variables and empirically verifiable hypotheses.

Taking only Sutherland's presidential address, the following items are among those propositions advanced that ought to be examined more closely:

1. "White-collar criminality is found in every occupation, as can be discovered readily in casual conversation with a representative of an occupation by asking him what crooked practices are . . . in his occupation" (p. 1).
2. The practice of politics is more honest than the conduct of business (p. 3).
3. "Political graft almost always involves collusion between politicians and businessmen, but prosecutions are generally limited to the politicians" (p. 4).
4. White-collar criminals are not regarded as really criminals by themselves, the general public (see Schrager and Short 1980), or by criminologists (p. 7.)
5. Differences in the implementation of the criminal law are due chiefly to the disparity in the social positions of white-collar and lower-class offenders (p. 7), and not, for instance, to the complexity of proof for one as against the other type of behavior.
6. Because of their social status, upper-class persons, potential white-collar offenders themselves, have a "loud voice" in determining what goes into the statutes and how the criminal law affecting them is implemented and administered (p. 6; see Shover 1980).
7. "Even if poverty is extended to include the economic stresses which afflict business in the period of depression, it is not closely correlated with white-collar criminality" (p. 9).

A major problem with Sutherland's work on white-collar crime and, arguably, a significant reason for the relative dearth of work on the topic during the past four decades, seems to us to lie in his ineffectual and almost pretentious effort to force the review of white-collar crime into a grand theory of criminal behavior. Sutherland may have sensed the difficulty himself; in many instances (see Sutherland 1956b) he was his own sharpest critic. "I believe the concept of white-collar crime is questionable in certain respects and I hope to elaborate on these in a later publication," Sutherland wrote to Paul Tappan on the last day of 1946 (Schuessler 1973, p. xxi). That further statement was never forthcoming; perhaps, had it been, white-collar crime would have grown more successfully as a subject of research and theory. Absent clarification by Sutherland, however, his dicta became dogma.

Sutherland implacably insisted that a single theory be made to explain the entire range of criminal behavior, and he placed that burden on a rather simple collection of statements about human learning that he called *differential association* (Sutherland 1947, pp. 5-9). "Favorable" or "unfavorable" learning with respect to the imperatives of the criminal law was seen by Sutherland as the process distinguishing noncriminal from criminal behavior. Differential association was derived in part from Lindesmith's (1951) analytical induction, which, like differential association, seems beyond scientific demonstration, though—as Cressey (1961) has observed—the theory has considerable pedagogical utility, if one's aim is to stimulate critical thinking about the importance of values and culture in shaping the form and the extent of criminal behavior.

The difficulty is that white-collar offenses, however they come to be defined, are extremely heterogenous acts and are not susceptible of decent understanding by means of a rudimentary learning theory. Antitrust violations may resemble, say, Medicare fraud in that the perpetrators have more education than do persons who commit muggings. But the fraud and the restraint of trade cannot satisfactorily be explained by differential association. Emphasis on differential association, in fact, deflects attention from significant ideological matters such as power relationships and other social-structural issues.

Sutherland saw no need to make clear-cut distinctions among white-collar crimes. For him, the same theoretical approach would do for any kind of business, professional, or political violation as for any other type of criminal-law violation. Sutherland believed that what he saw as sociologically unified groups (such as professional thieves) and as logically unified acts (such as white-collar crime) should for social-scientific purposes be considered analytical units (Schuessler 1973, p. xxvii), and then all together be regarded as susceptible to understanding by means of differential association. It is significant that the theory itself, with only slight modifications, could be employed to analyze all human behavior, but that it has never been taken as seriously in other branches of sociological or psychological research as it has in criminology.

"White-collar crime" is a political designation, rendered, like "crime" itself, by those who want to label, study, or call particular attention to certain kinds of social and political harm, real or imagined. The harms and their perpetrators designated by criminal law tend to have a very loose connective character: To provide some of them with a common name, such as white-collar crime or white-collar criminals, allows attention to be focused in a shorthand manner. Wrangling, both sophisticated and sophistical, over the "proper" definition of white-collar crime will never be satisfactorily resolved unless the overt and covert purposes, both political and scientific, underlying the search for definition, are clearly indicated. But fruitful approaches to the examination of behaviors that common sense indicates to be white-collar crime can be launched without resolution of the term's definition (see Bernstein and Hagan 1980).

At the time that he delivered his presidential address, Sutherland was caught in a sociological ethos that demanded from him a focus on scientific, value-free, and causal analysis. These professional norms would dominate the discipline for another decade (Bramson 1961, pp. 93–94). Sutherland's broadside attack on prominent crime-causation theories of his day (and of today), such as the focus on poverty, was in reality an assault on a creation of his own making. By demonstrating that poverty does not cause white-collar crime, Sutherland presumed that he had demonstrated that poverty does not cause any crime. This proposition succeeds only if it is granted that the essential task is to locate theories that can describe the cause of all crime. Poverty may be significant in the genesis of innumerable kinds of criminal and noncriminal behavior; to neglect its importance because it lacks direct relevance to white-collar offenses may be to divert attention from important aspects of social inequity.

In his presentation, Sutherland might have focused on the issue that Cressey (1961) later raised: why white-collar crime had for so long been neglected as an object of study, an issue that could yield fruitful theoretical insights. Perhaps, had Sutherland taken this or other alternative paths toward his professional goal of making his material "scientific," the result would have been both more evocative and more provocative of subsequent, cumulative, paradigmatic work on white-collar crime. As it was, the spate of studies that immediately followed Sutherland's efforts (see Geis and Meier [1977] for a collection of these materials) all felt compelled to look at their data in relation to the applicability of differential-association theory. For none did the theory quite fit (see Clinard 1952; Cressey 1953); but, once the task had been set, the job became to refine differential-association analysis rather than to look too far afield for other kinds of explanatory mechanisms and models.

The scholarly career of the concept of white-collar crime is captured effectively by a recent review of criminological literature. A survey of 100 leading (that is, most cited) scholars in the field found that they regarded Sutherland's work on white-collar crime as the fourth-most-important contribution ever made on the subject. But Sutherland was virtually neglected in terms of a concomitant count of citations. Becker's *The Outsiders* and the Glueck and Glueck's *Unraveling Juvenile Delinquency* were found to have been cited 648 times each. Cloward and Ohlin's *Delinquency and Opportunity* had 535 citations. Sutherland's work on white-collar crime had a mere 44 citations (Wolfgang, Figlio, and Thornberry 1978). The discrepancy between the scholars' ratings on importance, on the one hand, and the actual number of citations in the work on white-collar crime, on the other, attests to a condition of benign neglect. Undoubtedly, the "importance" rating would have risen had more later work on white-collar crime been conducted; as it is, until very recently white-collar crime as a subject of criminological effort has represented something of a historical sport.

In addition, Wolfgang and his colleagues found that out of nearly 3,700 books and articles they reviewed, only 92, or approximately 2.5 percent, dealt with white-collar or corporate criminality, even when studies on organized crime were included in the tabulations. If the organized-crime studies were removed from the category, no more than 1.2 percent of all writings in criminology dealt with subjects such as corporate crime, fraud, embezzlement, corruption, and bribery.

A study conducted with respect to material included in *Sociological Abstracts* from 1945 to 1972 yielded the same result. In most of the years, there was no more than one article devoted to white-collar crime. The most in any single twelve-month period was nine, in 1964, and most of these were on the subject of organized crime (Wheeler 1976, p. 528).

This situation is puzzling in light of the common belief that many persons are drawn to criminal-justice research and teaching careers out of reformist zeal. Schuessler (1973) has suggested that the affluence of U.S. society during recent decades undermined concern with white-collar crime, a hypothesis that deserves scrutiny. The political atmosphere during the McCarthy era of the 1950s probably muted criticism by academics and others of establishment persons and organizations. Perhaps, having lain dormant, the subject of white-collar crime needed especially favorable conditions for the kind of renaissance that it is now experiencing. The increased personnel in criminology also may be related to renewed interest in white-collar crime, as scholars seek to cultivate intellectual fields that have not yet been adequately harvested. The prod of Marxist criminology assuredly has also given credence and impetus to a critical posture toward persons in powerful positions in the society and toward the arrangements that got and keep them there. The work of Ralph Nader also has demonstrated the feasibility of gathering meaningful information about white-collar crimes.

For Sutherland, these developments would have been a matter of some personal pride (Schuessler 1973). Our review of Sutherland's background and career, as well as the panegyrics of his colleagues and many of his former students, stress his dedication to a search for truth and describe a personality marked by decency, integrity, and compassion. Sutherland fundamentally was a populist, agrarian liberal. He had no interest in the overthrow of capitalism, although he certainly leaned toward socialism as the preferable economic system. On the podium in Philadelphia in 1939, what Sutherland really said—once the camouflage is removed—is that white-collar crime is wrong—indeed, that often it is despicable—and that sociologists and economists ought to pay close attention to such matters and join with him in a crusade to do something about them.

Sutherland's work on white-collar crime has been subject, perhaps, to overly vigorous strictures in this paper. It will receive much harder blows as the pace and depth of study of white-collar crime increases. It must be recognized, however tough the critiques, that they are the kinds of backhanded accolades that mark significant scholarly work. That he must be attended to is the glory of Sutherland's contributions. He himself seemed, at least in print, amiable about this process of scientific maturation.

Sutherland's work on white-collar crime—his very invention of the term—is deeply and strongly rooted in our intellectual and public soil. We could cover page after page with illustrations of the manner in which Sutherland's pioneering contributions have influenced public policy and common understanding. That at this conference, almost a hundred years after Sutherland's birth in a frontier village on the Nebraska plains, we attend to his singlehanded creation of a realm of preeminent intellectual and policy importance is the most-significant tribute that he could have desired.

### Notes

1. Sutherland was a member of the Anti-Saloon League's executive council in Nebraska, but he does not appear to have played a prominent part in the group's work. The league's Nebraska branch, founded in 1897 (Shelden 1931), is discussed in detail by Wenger (1971), who finds that it does not fit Gusfield's (1966) classical sociological analysis of the prohibition movement as a "symbolic crusade."

2. We have not yet resolved a contradiction in our sources on this matter. Snodgrass (1972, p. 219) places Arthur at Louisiana College; but the director of the Norton Memorial Library at the college reports that a survey of the catalogues for the 1930's and 1940's had not turned up a Sutherland on the Louisiana College faculty. An inquiry was also made of certain persons on the campus who might have some personal knowledge, and this effort was also fruitless.

3. An inferential bit of evidence with respect to the influence of father on son comes in an article by Edwin Sutherland in which, among other things, he discusses "professions in which the problem is to control human behavior" and free associates in his representation of such professions to the four occupations that his father had followed: "salesmanship, teaching, preaching, and social work" (p. 109).

4. The Grand Island Alumni Directory summarizes Sutherland's scholarly contributions in only a few words. It reads: "Dr. Edwin H. Sutherland. Class of 1904. Prof. of Sociology, Indiana U. Author of Book on Criminology. Deceased 1950."

5. Henderson was also an avid advocate of indeterminate sentences, a position enthusiastically and rather uncritically adopted by Sutherland (1924; see Geis 1976).

## References

Bernstein, Ilene Nagel, and Hagen, John L. "The Social Organization of Criminal Justice Processing in Ten American Cities." *American Sociological Review* 1980.

Bramson, Leon. *The Political Content of Sociology*. Cambridge, Mass: Harvard University Press, 1961.

Caiden, Naomi. "Shortchanging the Public." *Public Administration Review* 39(May–June 1979):294–298.

Clinard, Marshall B. *The Black Market: A Study of White-Collar Crime*. New York: Holt, 1952.

Cressey, Donald R. *Other People's Money: The Social Psychology of Embezzlement*. New York: Free Press, 1953.

——. "Preface." In Edwin H. Sutherland and Donald R. Cressey, *Principles of Criminology*, 6th ed., pp. v–vi. Philadelphia: Lippincott, 1960.

——. "Foreword." In Edwin H. Sutherland, *White Collar Crime*, pp. iii–xiii. New York: Holt, 1961.

Geis, Gilbert. "Sociology and Sociological Jurisprudence." *Kentucky Law Journal* 52(Winter 1964):267–293.

——. "Introduction." In Eugene Smith, *Criminal Law in the United States*, pp. i–xii. Dubuque, Iowa: Brown Reprints, 1971.

——. "Avocational Crime." In Daniel Glaser, ed., *Handbook of Criminology*, pp. 273–298. Chicago: Rand-McNally, 1974.

——. "Revisiting Sutherland's Criminology (1924)," *Criminology* 14(November 1976):303–306.

Geis, Gilbert, and Meier, Robert F., eds. *White-Collar Crime: Offenses in Business, Politics, and the Professions*, rev. ed. New York: Free Press, 1977.

Gusfield, Joseph R. *Symbolic Crusade*. Urbana: University of Illinois Press, 1966.

Hall, Jerome. "Edwin H. Sutherland, 1883–1950." *Journal of Criminal Law and Criminology* 41(November–December 1950):393–396.

Heidenheimer, Arnold J. *Political Corruption: Readings in Comparative Analysis*. New York: Holt, Rinehart and Winston, 1970.

Henderson, Charles R. *Introduction to the Study of the Dependent, Defective, and Delinquent Classes*, 2nd ed. Boston: D.C. Heath, 1901.

Hinton, Herbert E. *A Brief History of Grand Island College.* Rochester, N.Y.:
    American Baptist Historical Society, 1970.
"Hits Criminality in White Collars." *The New York Times,* 28 December 1939,
    p. 12.
Lindesmith, Alfred R. "Edwin H. Sutherland's Contributions to Criminology."
    *Sociology and Social Research* 35(March–April 1951): 243–249.
Odum, Howard W. "Edwin H. Sutherland, 1883–1950." *Social Forces* 29(March
    1951):348–349.
"Poverty Belittled as Crime Factor." *Philadelphia Inquirer,* 28 December 1939,
    p. 17.
Schrager, Laura Shill, and Short, James F., Jr. "How Serious a Crime? Percep-
    tions of Organizational and Common Crimes." In Geis and Stotland, *White-
    Collar Crime,* pp. 14–31.
Schuessler, Karl, ed. *Edwin H. Sutherland on Analyzing Crime.* Chicago: Univer-
    sity of Chicago Press, 1973.
Sellin, Thorsten. Telephone conversation, 12 January 1980.
Shelden, A. *Nebraska: The Land and the People.* Chicago: Lewis Publishing
    Company, 1931.
Shover, Neal. "The Criminalization of Corporate Behavior: Federal Surface Coal
    Mining." In Gilbert Geis and Ezra Stotland, eds., *White-Collar Crime:
    Theory and Research,* pp. 98–125. Beverly Hills, Calif.: Sage, 1980.
Sloan, Alfred Pritchard Jr. *Current Biography 1940,* pp. 741–743.
Sloan, Alfred Pritchard, Jr., and Sparkes, Boyden. *Adventures of a White-Collar
    Man.* New York: Doubleday, Doran, 1941.
Snodgrass, Jon. "The Gentle and Devout Iconoclast." Pp. 217–308 In Snodgrass,
    "The American Criminological Tradition: Portraits of the Men and Ideology
    in a Discipline," pp. 217–308. Ph.D. diss., University of Pennsylvania, 1972.
——. "The Criminologist and His Criminal: The Case of Edwin H. Sutherland
    and Broadway Jones." *Issues in Criminology,* 8(Spring 1973):1–17.
Sutherland, Edwin H. *Criminology.* Philadelphia: Lippincott, 1924.
——. "Crime and the Conflict Process." *Journal of Juvenile Research* 13(Jan-
    uary 1929):38–48.
——. "Social Process in Behavior Problems." *Publications of the American
    Sociological Society* 26(August 1932):55–61.
——. *The Professional Thief.* Chicago: University of Chicago Press, 1937.
——. "White-Collar Criminality." *American Sociological Review* 5(Feburary
    1940):1–12.
——. *Principles of Criminology,* 4th ed. Philadelphia: Lippincott, 1947.
——. "Crime of Corporations." In Albert Cohen, Alfred Lindesmith, and Karl
    Schuessler, ed., *The Sutherland Papers,* pp. 78–96. Bloomington: Indiana
    University Press, 1956a.
——. "Critique of the Theory." In Cohen, Lindesmith, and Schuessler, *The
    Sutherland Papers,* pp. 30–41, 1956b.

——. *White Collar Crime.* New York: Dryden, 1949.

——. "Critique of Sheldon's *Varieties of Delinquent Youth.*" *American Sociological Review* 16(February 1951):10–13.

Sutherland, Edwin H., and Locke, Harvey J. *Twenty Thousand Homeless Men: A Study of Unemployed Men in Chicago Shelters.* Philadelphia: Lippincott, 1936.

Sutherland, George. "History of Nebraska Baptists," unpublished manuscript. Rochester, N.Y.: American Baptist Historical Society, 1935a.

——. "Autobiography," unpublished manuscript. Rochester, N.Y.: American Baptist Historical Society, 1935b.

Tappan, Paul W. "Who is the Criminal?" *American Sociological Review* 12(February 1947):96–102.

Viner, Jacob. "The Short View and the Long in Economic Policy." *American Economic Review* 30(March 1940): 1–15.

Vohland, Mabel. *Trail Dust to Star Dust.* Kearney, Neb.: Zimmerman Printing and Lithographers, 1971.

Wenger, Robert E. "The Anti-Saloon League in Nebraska Politics." *Nebraska History* 52(Fall 1971):267–292.

Wheeler, Stanton. "Trends and Problem in the Sociological Study of Crime." *Social Problems* 83(June 1976):526–534.

Wolfgang, Marvin E.; Figlio, Robert M.; and Thornberry, Terence P. *Evaluating Criminology.* New York: Elsevier, 1978.

Works Progress Administration. *Nebraska: A Guide to the Cornhusker State.* Lincoln: Nebraska State Historical Society, 1939.

# 2 White-Collar Crime, Organized Crime, and the Business Establishment: Resolving a Crisis in Criminological Theory

*Dwight C. Smith, Jr.*

## Introduction: The Paradigm Crisis

The purpose of this chapter is to explore some consequences of taking seriously the notion that there is a crisis in criminological theory concerning both white-collar and organized crime, and of assuming that the best response lies in a unified approach to both. The crisis is evident in a continuing and growing body of anomalies that current literature acknowledges but cannot resolve within existing theories, and in the inability of researchers to modify or improve those theories satisfactorily.

The anomalies of organized crime are the easier ones to detect. The most obvious concern the ethnic stipulations of conventional theory and emerge in attempts to apply a Sicilian-based paradigm to blacks, Hispanics, Orientals, and other groups. The white-collar-crime paradigm has appeared to be more resilient, perhaps in part because of the absence of ethnic specification. Close examination of the literature, however, reveals that the anomalies themselves have not been the only problem for researchers. In each area, the theory itself has been a matter of continuing contention. The debate over white-collar-crime theory began almost as soon as Sutherland (1940) introduced the concept. As late as 1977, Geis and Meier reported that there still remains "a pressing need for accumulation of case studies, for hypothesis development and testing, and for the kind of research that moves forward by careful additive processes" (Geis and Meier 1977, p. 4). Likewise, the prevailing theory of organized crime has been under continuing attack since its formulation in the 1950s.

The remarkable fact about these debates, from a scientific standpoint, is that there has been so little focused effort placed on reformulation of either theory. One could hardly imagine such a relaxed acceptance of obvious anomalies and theoretical controversy in the physical sciences. The contrast may be a useful illustration of Kuhn's view of the social sciences as "protoscience" (1970, pp. 244-245). But times do change. In the last few years there have been noteworthy signs of renewed and more-substantial interest in upgrading the quality of theory and research in both areas. The recent Clinard report on corporate crime (Clinard et al. 1979) and the recent National Institute of Justice (U.S. Department of Justice 1980) solicitation for new research on organized crime are illustrative rays of hope. Signals and solutions are not the same, however. The primary issue remains: What theoretical base will provide the best approach to either white-collar or organized crime, or to both?

The answer to be examined here is the concept that enterprise, not crime, is the governing characteristic of both phenomena, and that their criminal aspects are best understood when we, recognize that enterprise takes place across a spectrum of legitimacy. A spectrum-based theory of enterprise promises a framework for a better understanding of the interrelationships, and the distinctions, among legitimate business, white-collar crime, and organized crime. Clues to such an enterprise paradigm have long been evident in the literatures of crime and business, but their implications have not been taken seriously enough in the past. Let us look, then, at what such a theory entails; at what it replaces; and at some of the immediate consequences that a new theory may have on our understanding of the intersection between business and crime.

## A Spectrum-Based Theory of Enterprise:
## The Paradigm of the Future

Behind every theory lies a set of prior assumptions concerning the way in which that theory's portion of the universe is supposed to act. In this case, three prior assumptions are of particular importance: (1) that enterprise occurs across a behavioral spectrum that includes both business and certain kinds of crime; (2) that behavioral theory regarding organizations in general and businesses in particular can be applied to that entire spectrum; and (3) that whereas theories about secrecy (or conspiracy) and ethnicity may be pertinent to an understanding of business behavior—legal or criminal—they are necessarily subordinate in that understanding to a theory of enterprise. These three assumptions will be discussed in greater detail.

### A Spectrum of Enterprise

There is a range of economic activity that is continuous "from the very saintly to the most sinful" (Wilkins 1965, pp. 46–47). Any business can be conducted across this range of behavior; legality—the litmus test that traditionally has separated business from crime—is an arbitrary point on that range. The point of legality varies according to industry and can be relocated if new laws are passed. It is a factor in the business environment, not an intrinsic characteristic of the processes by which legal goods and services are produced as opposed to the production of illegal ones.

It is not enough to say that there is a spectrum in any industry. One must also be able to classify activity across that spectrum. This is a two-step process. The first step obviously is to group businesses that reflect similar problems of manufacture or that share common products or services. The natural starting point would probably be the government's *Standard Industrial Classification Manual (SIC Manual)*, a typology "intended to cover the entire field of economic activity" (U.S. Office of Management and Budget 1972, p. 9). It has some deficiencies, notably its deference to ownership as a higher distinction than common product or service, and its limitations with respect to classification of conglomerates. For present purposes, however, its deficiencies need not be resolved. The system it embodies is sufficiently indicative for us to assume that an operable classification can be developed. The second step of this assumption can then be pursued: the design of a system by which business activity could be ranked according to criteria defining legal business practices.

An example illustrating both of these steps would be a marketplace for security and enforcement services. This market does not exist within the SIC typology, because publicly financed police protection is considered part of public administration, whereas detective and protective services are establishments within the general umbrella of private services. The inappropriateness of the ownership distinction is increasingly obvious in this case, as private police forces grow in importance in today's economy. If we ignore ownership, and recognize public police and private security forces as complementary "businesses," then the spectrum concept becomes viable. We can then go further, to recognize that the posse, vigilantes, the lynch mob, and the "enforcer" are also part of that marketplace. Obviously, criteria are at work by which some of these mechanisms are defined as illegal and others as legal, even if only under limited circumstances—and by which some are "more legal" than others. Whatever these criteria may be (and they must obviously vary by marketplace and technology), they give operational significance to the concept of a spectrum of enterprise.

*A Focus on Organizational Behavior*

However formal or informal they may be, organizations enable entrepreneurs to deal with the dynamics of the marketplace. They develop and function in response to the challenges posed by their environments. It is essential to understand that relationship because modifications in the environment can affect and limit illegal behavior. Thompson (1967, p. 13) sets the stage:

> Most of our beliefs about . . . organizations follow from one or the other of two distinct strategies. The closed-system strategy seeks certainty by incorporating only those variables positively associated with goal achievement and subjecting them to a monolithic control network.

The open-system strategy shifts attention from goal achievement to survival, and incorporates uncertainty by recognizing organizational interdependence with environment. A newer tradition enables us to conceive of the organization as an open system, indeterminate and faced with uncertainty, but subject to criteria of rationality and hence needing certainty.

## The Primacy of Enterprise Theory

A problem that has plagued organized-crime theory is the relative significance of conspiracy and ethnicity. (The fact that a similar debate has not arisen within white-collar-crime theory is a point to which we shall return in the following section.) Organized crime has been a recognized phenomenon in the United States for fifty years. During this time, particularly since 1951, there has been a continuing debate over its significance and origins. The two main points of view in this debate have been expressed by the adherents of *enterprise* as a key to its understanding, and by the adherents of *conspiracy*. A third position in the debate, one of somewhat lesser influence, has been expressed by the adherents of *ethnicity*. This three-way debate flowered during the 1970s and tended, mistakenly, to be based on the assumption that *either* conspiracy, ethnicity, or enterprise was the explanation for organized crime—to the exclusion of the other two. On further reflection, it is clear that each contains some truth and that a complete explanation for organized crime must integrate all three theories. The problem then becomes one of establishing a useful relationship among them.

Enterprise is the principal but not exclusive explanation for the events commonly identified as organized crime. Market dynamics operating past the point of legitimacy establish the primary context for the illicit entrepreneur, regardless of his organizational style or his ethnic roots. His task environment is markedly different, primarily because of the absence of regulation to ensure order and to protect property rights. An operating strategy is required, which is explained in part by conspiracy theory, since conspiracy may be the best device by which to further outlawed economic activity. A mechanism through which order and stability can be maintained is also necessary, and is best explained by ethnicity, since ethnic ties are most likely to ensure trust among persons who cannot rely on the law to protect their rights and obligations within a cooperative but outlawed economic activity (Smith and Alba 1979, pp. 36–38).

With these assumptions as a base, a spectrum-based theory of enterprise takes shape. It begins with some preliminary statements about organizations in general, because the heart of any enterprise is its core technology. It comprises the technical functions by which it is able to create and dispose of its end product or service. It exists within a task environment, a set of external conditions that enable it to function but that simultaneously offer hazards to its survival. In very general terms, the task environment for a business consists of four primary forces: suppliers, customers, competitors, and regulators.

The *core technology* of an enterprise is the area of activity that responds to closed-system strategies. These aim at maximum goal achievement within bounded rationality. The *task environment* is the area of entrepreneurial activity that responds to open-system strategies, which aim at survival in an arena characterized by uncertainty. The function of enterprise is, through risk taking, to direct an activity in such a way that both open- and closed-system requirements are met in a balanced fashion.

The result of efforts to protect an enterprise's core technology is the creation of a territory, or *domain*. This consists of a set of claims staked out in terms of a range of products, a population served, or services rendered. Domain produces stability, efficiency, and increased profits. Consequently, the focus of the entrepreneur is on protecting and expanding that domain, which is, however, not an arbitrary or unilateral task. The entrepreneur interacts with his environment, a large share of which will be other entrepreneurs equally intent on establishing their own domains as either suppliers, customers, or competitors—and, in some instances, as regulators. Thompson (1967, p. 28) notes again:

> Only if the organization's claims to domain are recognized by those who can provide the necessary support, by the task environment, can a domain be operational. The relationship between an organization and its task environment is essentially one of exchange, and unless the organization is judged by those in contact with it as offering something desirable, it will not receive the inputs necessary for survival. . . . The specific categories of exchange vary from one type of organization to another, but in each case, . . . exchange agreements rest on *prior consensus regarding domain.* [Emphasis in original.]

These conditions govern any establishment, without respect to its technological processes, the nature of its product, or the legality of either product or process. There are other differences, however, that reflect the entrepreneur's place on a spectrum of legitimacy. These differences are most notable at the point of legality, but that point is not always precise. A variety of behaviors may emerge in a gray area that surrounds the point of legality. An area of ambiguity and controversy may well develop, to which a large body of litigation adheres.

As one approaches that point of legality, the task environment changes. Different competitors and customers may be more prominent, and the entrepreneur's response will differ accordingly. There is a spectrum of entrepreneurial willingness to operate under different degrees of legitimacy; there is a similar spectrum of customers (Smith 1978). As they interact, market stratification occurs (Smith 1980). Certain kinds of customers will deal regularly with certain kinds of businessmen. As the process of exchange takes place, the balance between power and dependency that defines the entrepreneur's domain (Thompson 1967) may be maintained (if the market is stable) or may shift; the legitimacy of the enterprise may or may not bear on that balance.

The terminology and metaphors of normal business theory are obvious and essential characteristics of a spectrum-based theory of enterprise. It is equally obvious that this theory covers ground that has been mined previously by sociologists and criminologists. Little proof is needed that entrepreneurs and customers occasionally behave legally and occasionally illegally. That motivation and opportunity are critical factors in their choice of behaviors is also unarguable. The significance of a spectrum-based theory of enterprise is that it provides a framework within which to consider and evaluate "legitimate and illegitimate opportunity structures" (Cloward and Ohlin 1961, p. 150). The new elements arguing for a reexamination of older constructs rest on two expectations: (1) that "opportunity" relates to a spectrum of behavioral possibilities, and (2) that the decisive factors in determining "opportunity" relate to the dynamics of the marketplace as it changes character across that spectrum.

## Are Conventional Theories Obsolete?

The fact that the terminology and metaphors of white-collar-crime theory are essentially those of business analysis eases its incorporation within a spectrum-based theory of enterprise. Organized-crime theory is a different matter. The conventional description of organized crime uses a distinctive set of metaphors and an entirely different vocabulary. According to the adherents of this theory, organized crime is the product of a group of alien (or alien-minded) conspirators, who owe their allegiance to an Italian-dominated underworld that will stop at nothing (1) to protect itself by corrupting and nullifying legitimate government, and (2) to expand its empire by infiltrating legitimate businesses. In this fashion, they carry their immoral values and illegal practices into the upperworld. The alien-conspiracy view emphasizes secret arrangements, undertaken for criminal purposes and characterized by the reputations of the unsavory persons who have directed or encouraged those arrangements. In describing them, this view emphasizes its own set of code words: Mafia, families, underbosses, *omerta,* infiltration. The enterprise perspective follows an entirely different style of analysis and discourse. It emphasizes an interplay between environment and entrepreneur that is characterized by the kinds of business obligations demanded by a competitive but illegal marketplace. It also uses the language of business analysis: task environment, domain, crucial contingencies, dominant coalitions.

The advantage of a unique set of metaphors and a separate language is that it enables the alien-conspiracy advocate to maintain that the events identified with organized crime are somehow "different." One immediate consequence is that two persons discussing the same set of activities may sound as though they are talking about entirely separate circumstances. The crucial question at that point is: Can claims of difference really be justified? Is it reasonable still to assume that loansharking bears no relationship to banking, or that fencing bears no relationship to retailing, or that narcotics importation and the wholesale trade have nothing in common until an "infiltrator" starts to undermine? When a businessman restrains trade, is his behavior really different from that of the mobster who cooperates with others to establish territorial lines for numbers banks? If a businessman and a mobster sign a sweetheart labor contract, is one a "white-collar criminal" and the other a "member of organized crime infiltrating legitimate business," or are they symbiotic consumer and supplier, respectively, of an otherwise legal business being conducted, in this instance, in an illegal way? When such questions can be raised, an "enterprise" perspective begins to make sense.

A switch from the alien-conspiracy perspective to an enterprise perspective entails more than the adoption of new metaphors and a new language. Organized-crime theory has its own set of prior assumptions, which must be recognized as obsolete, and discarded, so that the assumptions preceding an enterprise theory can replace them. Five prior assumptions hold special significance behind organized-crime theory. They have been described at length elsewhere (Smith 1980, pp. 361-370); they can be summarized as follows.

1. *Business and crime are distinct categories.* Business theorists and criminologists have traditionally worked and studied independently. In business literature, for example, there is no recognized category of "the theory of the criminal firm." When business schools offer courses in business ethics, they are most likely to cover bribery, corporate spying, and price fixing as dysfunctional aberrations from the model of business as a legal activity. Likewise, when criminologists have looked at criminal activity in the business sphere, it has been as a distinctive category—the "businessman who went wrong"—not to be confused either with crime in general or with general business practices. Although there are exceptions—and increasingly so in the last decade—the prevailing sense among both criminal-justice practitioners and the public at large remains an expectation closer to the beliefs of the 1960s. Cynicism and the sardonic epigram aside, "business" and "crime" come from separate and incommensurable roots.

2. *Business is best described by the labels of legal undertakings.* The *Standard Industrial Classification Manual's* taxonomy of business is supposed to cover the entire field of economic activity, but it does not. The designers of the manual had only legitimate businesses in mind. *Establishment,* as the entity through which economic activity takes place, may be the critical linguistic turning point, as it conveys strong overtones of institutional authority and sanction. It is defined as "an economic unit, generally at a single physical location, where business is conducted or where services or industrial operations are performed" (U.S. Office of Management and Budget 1972, p. 10). They need not be large or commercially significant units. For example, "Singing Societies" is an establishment

within the industry (Code 8641) known as "Civic, Social, and Fraternal Organizations." The only reason for excluding the fence and the loanshark, among other illegal businesses, is that they are not sanctioned or licensed—"established."

3. *Within an industrial classification, the principal distinctions are by size and ownership, not legality.* Once the product or service of an industry has been specified, and the ownership and size of its establishments has been described, the *SIC Manual* makes no further distinction with respect to the manner in which a business is organized and managed. That some firms may be more willing, say, to engage in marginally deceptive advertising, or that some establishments or industries may be more vulnerable to cutting corners and to legal hair splitting, is of no concern to systems that classify businesses.

4. *Business = the Professionally Managed Corporation.* In the midtwentieth century, the dominant force within the "capitalist engine" was held to be the large corporation. The entrepreneur, the mainspring of classic capitalism, would be swallowed by the large corporation. The entrepreneurial function would inevitably be taken over by the salaried staffs of research-and-development units; innovation would become routine. Schumpeter (1942) forecast this state of affairs. His Darwinian analysis of natural selection and survival of the fittest in the marketplace had a major effect on the way business was perceived prior to the mid-1960s. The established, large firm is still a dominant object on the economic landscape, but one of the surprises of the postwar years was the survival of entrepreneurship in the face of Schumpeter's prediction (Harwood 1979). It took a while for observers to realize they were watching a natural phenomenon, but by the mid-1960s the postwar entrepreneurial renaissance had been augmented by an emerging sense of the continuing profession of entrepreneurship.

The significance of this development is that there are now two coexistent models of business activity, and two accompanying business personalities, the entrepreneur and the corporate hierarch. In the early 1960s, when conventional organized-crime theory was being developed, the hierarch was the only recognized style. It was recognized by the ability to manage the tasks of business—planning and forecasting, goal and priority setting, financial allocation and control—in a setting dominated by established structure, channels, rational design and decision making, and a calculation of long-range corporate profits and losses.

5. *The corporate model can be projected onto organized crime.* Structural models of organized crime began with the Kefauver committee, but its descriptions were minimal. If there was a hierarchical system of status and power within criminal syndicates, no one bothered to describe it. Seven years later, the McClellan committee was diverted into a study of criminal organization. Three new operating characteristics emerged then: conspiracy; a tie-in, in some fashion, to business activities; and ethnicity. The "Apalachin conclave" of 1957 was a more-tangible sign of organization than previous notions of gangs; since

common ethnic ties seemed a major clue to what was going on there, investigators began charting family and marriage relationships as the basis of "organization." When Joseph Valachi's stories of Cosa Nostra surfaced in 1963, organization came into its own. He described hierarchy, conscious efforts to manage and control, survival through changes of leadership, and an apparently more rational process of decision making and supervision. Crime and business might still be separate entities, but the old gang-derived criminal metaphor was now insufficient. New mental pictures were needed. To some, it was the military: "in the Cosa Nostra's paramilitary organization, [Valachi] was on the order of a master sergeant working out of headquarters" (Maas 1969, p. 59). The business analogy became the rallying point, however; and when Meyer Lansky was credited apocryphally with boasting that "we're bigger than U.S. Steel" (Cressey 1969, p. 243; Salerno and Tompkins 1969, p. 225), the business–organized-crime parallel was complete.

Even though the structural imagery of large business was adopted, its accompanying understandings of business operations were ignored. Crime and business were still separate entities. The business model was simply a visual overlay, to which the organized-crime school could attach Valachi's terminology of boss, underboss, lieutenant, and soldier. The idea that a criminal business might most closely resemble the less-structured and more-independent entrepreneur was not yet available as a viable alternative.

Perhaps more importantly, the assumptions of the alien-conspiracy school were not compatible with modern understanding of organizational behavior. Working apart from conventional assumptions about the legitimate firm, organized-crime analysts adopted the closed-system strategy as their operating model. The open-systems strategy was inappropriate; a monolithic organization could hardly be described as simply surviving, much less as being governed by uncertainty. Thompson's third alternative of combining open- and closed-system models came to flower after organized-crime theory had been established. As a result, conventional theory ignored (or missed) the crucial concept of interdependence and its operating principle: the necessity of exchange agreements between organization and environment as a precondition to survival and growth.

Until recently, the alien-conspiracy theory has been impervious to the demands of enterprise theory. Two interrelated conditions contributed to this circumstance: the control of both theory and its evidence by government agencies. Thus, they generally have been beyond the province of scholars outside government circles. The theory itself was enunciated in the essentially political forums of a Senate investigations committee (U.S. Senate Permanent Subcommittee on Investigations 1965) and a presidential commission (U.S. President's Commission on Law Enforcement and Administration of Justice 1967). These committees gave the theory formal status, which has compounded the tasks of amendment or replacement. They also endowed it with problems of credibility since, as Hawkins (1969, pp. 26–28) points out, such a forum is hardly conducive to the production of counterevidence or to realistic testing of a proposition. The data in which the theory was grounded have, with few exceptions, remained closed to researchers despite Cressey's plea (1967, p. 60) for open files, new questions, and new evidence. As a result, researchers have been unable to engage in the sort of theoretical testing of the original evidence that would be routine in any other field.

The immediate consequence is that public policy has remained mired in the concept of "Mafia." It is governed by statutory provisions that were adopted in 1968 and 1970, and by an enforcement commitment to a theory that no one (except literary entrepreneurs and diehard ideologues) believes any more, but that no one has been able to supplant in a sufficiently formal way. Revisionists have laid siege to it since 1969, but with discouragingly little sign of success until the signals of change noted earlier began to appear.

Whereas existing white-collar-crime theory may be more compatible with an enterprise approach, it has also suffered from the limits of data and theory. Prior to the Clinard report, facts about white-collar crime were gathered in near-random fashion and within "the pragmatic view that everybody pretty much knows what is meant by white-collar crime" (Geis and Meier 1977, p. 254). But pragmatism has had its cost. The absence of rigorous definition has hampered cumulative, integrated research. The limits of a protoscience are thereby revealed; its tolerance for diversity has been an effective stumbling block to scientific advances. Any testable proposition has been fair game, and researchers have been encouraged to work relatively independently. White-collar-crime theory has been as diffuse as organized-crime theory has been monolithic.

Still, one universal problem within white-collar-crime theory stands out, the cause of which similarly and more directly affects the organized-crime school. That cause is an exaggerated concern for certain characteristics of the perpetrator. In the case of organized crime, the result is an ethnic preoccupation. This leads to easy acceptance of an "enemy" model of an alien, parasitic conspiracy rather than to a symbiotic model (as is characteristic of the enterprise school) that reflects the interdependence between illicit entrepreneurial behavior and its environment.

The problem for white-collar-crime theory is an exaggerated concern for an occupational uniform—the white collar. This forces an artificial mixture of two criminal circumstances that appear to share an opportunity structure but that are, in reality, entirely different events. There are, on the one hand, offenses *of* business, activities that occur in the course of an exchange relationship involving the sale of a product or service. There are also offenses *against* business (embezzlement, theft, pilferage, and so forth) that do not reflect such an exchange. Although the distinction is by no means new, it has not been resolved on a theoretical level because of the tolerance occasioned by a flexible approach to white-collar-crime theory.

A spectrum-based theory of enterprise can emerge once it is recognized that offenses *against* business belong elsewhere in a comprehensive typology of crime. Such a shift would accomplish two useful objectives. First, it would facilitate studies of relational as opposed to nonrelational theft, and of certain kinds of part-time crime, along the lines that Ditton (1977) and others have been pursuing. Second, it would facilitate a recognition that crimes *of* business and organized crime, being fundamentally entrepreneurial, are best understood together as alternative ways in which business can be conducted illegally.

## Some Consequences of Enterprise Theory

The most immediate and important consequence of a spectrum-based theory of enterprise is that it will lead us to think about crime and business in a different way. Thus, white-collar crime is not simply a dysfunctional aberration. Organized crime is not something ominously alien to the American economic system. Both are made criminal by laws declaring that certain ways of doing business, or certain products of business, are illegal. In other words, criminality is not an inherent characteristic either of certain persons or of certain business activities but rather, an externally imposed evaluation of alternative modes of behavior and action.

The U.S. experiment with Prohibition illustrates this truth. The Volstead Act did not alter the chemical processes of distillation and fermentation; and it did not change the ways in which alcoholic beverages could be packaged, transported, sold, or consumed. It simply stipulated that certain activities in that sequence were henceforth illegal. A new point of legitimacy was imposed on the spectrum of enterprise. That changed the regulatory aspect of the liquor industry's task environment, but not the essential character of its core technology. In response, entrepreneurs willing to engage in risk taking had a different set of crucial contingencies with which to contend. Repeal of the Volstead Act represented a second shift in the point of legitimacy, one that produced its own set of business responses.

A spectrum-based theory of enterprise enables us to see that *organized crime and the crimes of business are the results of the process by which political (that is, value-based) constraints are placed on economic activity.*

A second consequence of what has been said so far about a spectrum-based theory of enterprise is that it requires considerably more thought. Its description in this chapter is not intended as a final formulation. Rather, it is an attempt to illuminate a way of looking at entrepreneurial behavior that will enable analysts to explain or predict the ways in which legal, illegal, and illicit businesses emerge from a common marketplace. Those explanations or predictions could then provide a framework within which existing concepts of enterprise can be modified and applied to emerging problems of fraud, abuse, and crime. At this point in its development, however, its claims are more modest: It remains an invitation to further questions. For example, not all criminal activity should fall within a concept of enterprise; but where should the line be drawn? Further, there appears to be a distinction between operating an illegal business and conducting a legal business in an illegal way. If the distinction is real, how should it be specified, and what implications will it have for further exposition of entrepreneurial theory? Also, some illegal and legal enterprises parallel or supplement government functions, as illustrated by earlier comments about a marketplace for security and enforcement services. To what extent should some government activities be recognized as entrepreneurial? Or, alternatively, what distinction between government and business should be maintained? Finally, not all white-collar crime is entrepreneurial; and the distinction between crimes *of* business and crimes *against* business may not be the same as the distinction between entrepreneurial and nonentrepreneurial activity. How should that boundary be defined, and what theoretical construct will be required for nonentrepreneurial white-collar crime?

The incompleteness and imperfection of a preliminary statement produce challenges to be met rather than objections or barriers to further discussion. The foregoing questions may result from an attempt to construct too wide a theoretical base, and may resolve themselves through further debate. They suggest, however, that the perception and definition of roles may have great importance. It is a definition that becomes increasingly difficult to prepare, as persons are recognized as behaving in accordance with multiple roles. However the foregoing boundary questions are ultimately resolved—whether by economic determinists who conclude that all property-related crime is entrepreneurial in nature, or by the adherents of other philosophical positions—one central point remains. In order for the nature of illegality in the entrepreneurial sphere to be perceived and understood more clearly, a concept of enterprise is needed that is not limited by the line of demarcation between entrepreneurial behaviors that are legal and those that are not.

We need not wait for a final theoretical formulation to emerge before we look at some of the implications of what has been said so far. Indeed, a look at some of these implications may provide helpful clues for further investigation. Let me suggest some that come most easily to mind.

1. A spectrum-based theory of enterprise is a tool for analysis, not evaluation. It is value free. It will not tell the researcher that a particular activity is good or bad; it will simply show how that activity relates to alternative forms of activity. Such a caution is not ordinarily required, but the researcher must work within the historic context of other research. In the case of organized-crime studies, that context bears a heavy value content. The purpose of organized-crime theory in the past has been to convey moral judgments, not to facilitate objective study. Resistance to unorthodox findings has been clear, continuous,

and consistent, from Kefauver's dismissal of his skeptics as "a strangely assorted company of criminals, self-serving politicians and plain blind fools" (1951, p. 12) to Kwitny's latest diatribe against "irresponsible self-deception" in organized-crime research (1979, p. 50). The future researcher will risk similar criticism until enterprise theory is more widely accepted.

2. To say that business crimes are a function of constraints on economic behavior may sound simplistic—nothing more than the truism that laws produce crime. The intent of stating the problem in this fashion runs deeper, however. Its aim is to free the analysis of business crime from the confines of a particular economic theory or system. The constraints that define illegal activity are necessary in any society in which demands exceed resources. Otherwise, society risks the extremes of economic and political anarchy or a totalitarian alternative in which "might makes right." Consequently, business crimes—whether the reference is to what U.S. residents have conventionally termed organized crime or to the crimes of privately or publicly controlled business—are inevitable in any economy.

3. Some of the political constraints imposed on an economy are intended to improve or open up market performance—antitrust laws, small-business assistance, and so forth. Most of them are not related to market performance but are imposed on the marketplace because of noneconomic (often humanitarian) considerations. Examples include child-labor laws, affirmative action, environmental protection, and the still-emerging regulation of hazardous-waste disposal. Some of these constraints are so long standing that they have become accepted as economically desirable, even though they were once highly political and considered to be unwarranted intrusions into the marketplace. We should recognize, however, the meaning of "intrusion." Accepted operating expenses are not intrusions, and a constraint will by definition cease to be an external intrusion when it has been internalized as a factor of production.

4. As long as political pluralism is valued, the debate over appropriate constraints will continue. It will continue to generate a degree of ambiguity that will affect efforts to define precisely the criminality of entrepreneurial behavior. For example, the U.S. economic system has been based historically on an exploitative approach to energy and waste disposal. A political debate over the desirability of charging for energy replenishment or for more-stringent waste-disposal requirements carries the threat of unbalancing complex accounting structures by which varieties of energy-consumption and waste-disposal processes heretofore have been balanced. When certain forms of exploitation are no longer considered desirable, the effects will vary by industry or even by establishment within an industry. A close division of public opinion is more likely to produce a greater tendency toward illegal behavior than a clear consensus.

5. Even in the absence of accepted pluralism, constraints on the marketplace will continue and will create opportunities for illegal behavior. When there is no competitive market, accommodations may be made to create gray-market

options—for example, for the produce of the farmer's private plot. Still, some form of economic crime—whether parallel in its intent or structure to "organized" or to "white-collar" crime—is inevitable in socialist as well as capitalist economies. As long as demands are perceived to exceed resources, there will be constraints. Economic crime cannot then be eliminated, short of a total, puritanical, fanatical form of social control. Even then, the problem of watching the watchers will remain.

6. The principal distinction between organized crime and the crimes of businesses, as they have been perceived up to now, seems to be that the former are primarily product oriented, whereas the latter are process oriented. That distinction appears to hold in all areas of economic behavior. If true, perhaps it helps explain why the two areas of inquiry have not been combined in the past.

7. Although conventional wisdom distinguishes between government and business, some government activities are simply the result of its having nationalized, or socialized, portions of the market spectrum, and having substituted taxes (in some instances) for fee-for-service payment. The core technology of an activity may be altered slightly in the process, but the nationalized enterprise still "competes"—whether its supporters recognize it or not—with the private remnants of the marketplace. The gambling industry is an apt illustration of the manner in which ownership can add confusion to a marketplace already divided between legal and illegal behavior. Is state-run off-track betting supposed to compete with bookies, or not? The inability to transcend ownership and to see the continuation of such natural marketplaces is a major handicap to the understanding and control of some economic behavior.

8. Ethnicity is one of the best ways of generating trust in the nonregulated arena of illegal business activity. Consequently, it may be a critical factor in ensuring the success of a particular venture. Under some circumstances, including both opportunities for organized crimes and opportunities for crimes of business, conspiracy may be a necessary tool for the successful implementation of an illegal business activity. The effects of ethnicity and conspiracy are not confined to illegal activity, however. The old-boy networks of business, education, and government reflect a combination of ethnicity and conspiracy that thrived prior to the mid-1960s. Once the artificial barrier of legality is lifted, it may be possible to see a universality of both characteristics throughout all business activity.

9. A spectrum of legitimacy is not simply a quantitatively oriented measure of the legality of process and product. It contains qualitative elements as well, summarized best by the notions of *standing* and *reputation*. Many of the crimes of businesses succeed because their perpetrators enjoy high standing and reputation that masks the ways in which they have responded illegally to the contingencies and constraints of their task environments. The ways in which standing and reputation are defined and applied may be high-priority research targets in the field of economic crime.

10. Most organized crimes remain segregated in conventional analyses because the "normal" criteria of standing and reputation are compounded by a

politically inspired debate over the propriety of a product. The consequence is a heavy shadow of moral opprobrium from which some entrepreneurs emerge as pariahs. The process by which a marketplace is legitimated (or blacklisted), and the interplay of pariah status may also be an important area of research.

11. There is a tendency for marketplaces to become stratified, and for inter-market exchanges (that is, the businessman who becomes the customer of a bank or other resource supplier) to reflect such a stratification. Firms with standing become customers of their qualitative equals; pariahs are more likely to deal with each other. When stratification occurs close to the point of legality, it produces continued business associations that can be interpreted, in conventional wisdom, as signs of an organizational relationship. That interpretation may be incorrect. Still, it will reinforce any kernel of truth that does exist regarding continuing illegal networks, thereby adding unwarranted support to some notions associated with organized crime.

## References

Clinard, Marshall B., Jeager, Peter C.; Brissette, Jeanne; Petrashek, David; and Harries, Elizabeth. *Illegal Corporate Behavior.* Washington, D.C.: U.S. Department of Justice (Law Enforcement Assistance Administration), 1979.

Cloward, Richard A., and Ohlin, Lloyd E. *Delinquency and Opportunity.* New York: Free Press, 1961.

Cressey, Donald R. "The Function and Structure of Criminal Syndicates." In U.S. President's Commission on Law Enforcement and Administration of Justice, *Task Force Report: Organized Crime*, pp. 25-60. Washington, D.C.: U.S. Government Printing Office, 1967.

——. *Theft of the Nation: The Structure and Operations of Organized Crime in America.* New York: Harper and Row, 1969.

Ditton, Jason. *Part-Time Crime.* London: MacMillan, 1977.

Geis, Gilbert, *and* Meier, Robert F., eds. *White-Collar Crime: Offenses in Business, Politics, and the Professions.* New York: Free Press, 1977.

Harwood, Edwin. "The Entrepreneurial Renaissance and Its Promoters." *Society* 16(1979):25-31.

Hawkins, Gordon. "God and the Mafia." *The Public Interest* 14(1969):24-51.

Kefauver, Estes. *Crime in America.* New York: Doubleday, 1951.

Kuhn, Thomas S. "Reflections on My Critics." In Imre Lakatos and Alan Musgrave, eds., *Criticism and the Growth of Knowledge*, pp. 231-278. Cambridge; Cambridge University Press, 1970.

Kwitny, Jonathan. *Vicious Circles: The Mafia in the Marketplace.* New York: Norton, 1979.

Maas, Peter. *The Valachi Papers.* New York: G.P. Putnam's Sons, 1969.

Salerno, Ralph, and Tompkins, John S. *The Crime Confederation: Cosa Nostra and Allied Operations in Organized Crime.* Garden City, N.Y.: Doubleday, 1969.

Schumpeter, Joseph. *Capitalism, Socialism, and Democracy*. New York: Harper, 1942.

Smith, Dwight C., Jr. "Organized Crime and Entrepreneurship." *International Journal of Criminology and Penology* 6(1978):161–177.

——. "Paragons, Pariahs, and Pirates: A Spectrum-Based Theory of Enterprise." *Crime and Delinquency* 26(1980):358–386.

Smith, Dwight C., Jr., and Alba, Richard S. "Organized Crime and American Life." *Society* 16(1979):32–38.

Sutherland, Edwin H. "White-Collar Criminality." *American Sociological Review* 5(1940):1–12.

Thompson, James D. *Organizations in Action*. New York: McGraw-Hill, 1967.

United States Department of Justice. National Institute of Justice. "A Program of Research in Organized Crime." Mimeographed, 1980.

United States Office of Management and Budget. *Standard Industrial Classification Manual*. Washington, D.C.: U.S. Government Printing Office, 1972.

United States President's Commission on Law Enforcement and Administration of Justice. *Task Force Report: Organized Crime* (including report, annotations, and consultants' papers). Washington, D.C.: U.S. Government Printing Office, 1967.

United States Senate Permanent Subcommittee on Investigations. *Report on Organized Crime and Illicit Traffic in Narcotics*. Washington, D.C.: U.S. Government Printing Office, 1965.

Wilkins, Leslie T. *Social Deviance*. Englewood Cliffs, N.J.: Prentice-Hall, 1965.

# 3 International White-Collar Crime

*Leon Sheleff*

## Introduction

Any attempt to delineate the nature of white-collar crime in the realm of international law suffers from the two major drawbacks inherent in the two constituent areas—that of white-collar crime and that of international law—with their mutual lack both of clear and acceptable definition and of a recognized effective means of control.

Yet these obstacles are by no means insurmountable. In both areas, creative and compelling actions have been taken in recent years to raise public awareness, to map out campaigns, and to seek meaningful changes in the law.

Sutherland would indeed be surprised to see the tremendous developments that have emerged from his first tentative probings into the netherworld of corporate activities (Sutherland 1940, 1949); Oppenheim might be no less surprised to see the extent to which efforts in the field of international law are being devoted to topics (such as the protection of the environment) that formed no more than passing comments in his treatise on international law (Oppenheim 1955). Grotius, considered the father of international law, would no doubt be bewildered—and perhaps even distressed—to know of the inroads that have been made into his pioneering concept, which later became almost sacrosanct, of the free and open seas (de Pauw 1965).

Indeed, in some respects, much of the lack of understanding of both white-collar crime and international law may be due to an optical illusion—an incorrect perception of their roles in modern legal systems. This misperception, partly a relic of what once was, is partly perhaps the result of a deliberate effort to keep these areas marginal in public awareness and official response—an effort fostered by those who have the most to gain from the notions of the past and the most to lose by any new developments in international law.

The problem may also be compounded by the fact that criminologists working in the area of white-collar crime are insufficiently attuned to the international and transnational implications of their work, and insufficiently aware of ongoing changes in the field of international law; international lawyers, likewise, have a corresponding lack of appreciation of legal, policing, and criminological work in white-collar crime.

This chapter represents an attempt to bridge this gap. It will suggest that some of the real issues of white-collar crime may well be outside the range of national purview and, further, that the full extent of white-collar crime (particularly

39

in its newer manifestations) can be grasped only in an international framework. Thus, to give one example, there has been almost no criminological work on the looting of national treasures. Although this is a serious problem—in economic, human, and national terms—it has received little attention. Should criminologists evince an interest in this area, they will soon discover that the cause of the problem lies not in the avarice of local thieves in countries that, though rich in treasures, are often economically backward, but in the cultural aspirations of enlightened administrators of respected institutions (such as museums, art galleries, and universities) of the wealthy and developed countries of the world, who have the finances and the desire to acquire forbidden treasures.

It was Sutherland who first warned us that a full appreciation of crime in general and a validation of theories of crime both depended on a willingness to see crime in its widest dimensions, embracing not only the traditional forms and concepts of crime, but also those marginal areas in which criminality had not been specifically spelled out, or for which special definitions had been advanced and special procedures established. A perusal of newspaper reports convinced Sutherland that the widespread evasive activities among leading public corporations, for which there were special administrative procedures, were, in reality, of a criminal nature.

The debate that grew out of Sutherland's original assertions is not yet over (Gilbert, Geis, and Meier 1977). In siding with those of sociological bent who have insisted on looking at the social reality, rather than with those of legal inclinations who stress the legal form, I shall attempt to suggest that a similar extension of the idea of criminality may be applicable in the field of international law.

Among international lawyers themselves, discussions of the emerging field of international criminal law concentrate on such topics as drug trafficking, smuggling, slavery, terrorism, genocide, crimes against humanity, and crimes of war (Bassiouni and Vanda 1973; De Schutter 1972), but ignore such areas as environmental pollution on the high seas; the looting of art and architectural treasures; the depletion of natural resources; international finance manipulations; illicit arms deals; violations of trade agreements; unfair exploitation of labor (migrant, children, women); and fraudulent transnational economic deals.

In some of these areas there are indeed pronouncements of international law—either in the quasi-legislative actions of international bodies (such as the International Labor Organization), or in the judge-made law of the International Court of Justice or of international arbitration tribunals, or in the impact of customary law as detailed by recognized scholars in their authoritative textbooks.

However, a key point must be stressed at the outset: although several strict measures have been taken, these are generally only in the realm of civil and administrative law. But if we adopt the approach set out by Sutherland, we may see that a civil or administrative approach is useful only for convenience or as an acknowledgment of power relationships.

## The Social Reality of International "Delinquency"

The nature of the problem may be gauged by examining a leading international law case from the 1930s, the importance of which has increased over the years as the problem that was addressed, then of only marginal and localized concern, has become one of major international dimensions.

The case, known as the Trail Smelter Case, dealt with pollution across international boundaries. An arbitration tribunal came to the conclusion that "no state has the right to use or permit the use of its territory in such a manner as to cause injury by fumes in or to the territory of another . . . when the case is of serious consequence and the injury is established by clear and convincing evidence" (Trail Smelter Arbitration Tribunal 1941, p. 684).

Two points must be stressed: (1) This was a case in tort, the action being for damages and an injunction. (2) The case was the first of its kind to discuss transnational air pollution. In fact, unable to find any precedents in international law, the tribunal relied on rules that had been laid down in connection with water pollution (for example, by upstream users) and within national boundaries of federal countries (for example, the various riparian states within the United States).

Once liability is conceded in tort law, the possibility arises of attributing criminal liability as well. As a number of criminal-law jurists have pointed out, the differences between tort and criminal law are often mainly fortuitous, the result of historical accident. However, one clear difference does exist—the rule of *nulla poena sine lege,* that is, there can be no punishment without a prior legal definition of a crime. If the Trail Smelter case was the first of its kind, then prior to that time there must have been little awareness of a problem; thus it was only natural and fair that the initial attribution of responsibility should be through civil proceedings. But once awareness has been aroused, and once the nature and dimension of a problem have been clearly perceived, the question inevitably becomes: What sanction and what form of procedure are the most desirable and the most efficacious?

Further, as long as the damage is to a particular state, (that is, there is a recognized victim), the civil procedures certainly retain their relevance and importance, since the direct victims are likely to be the most zealous in safeguarding their rights and in pursuing their interests. However, when the damage is diffuse and there is no one direct victim, then there is the greatest need for criminal sanctions and for powerful enforcing agencies.

Since the days of the Trail Smelter case, pollution outside national boundaries—on the open seas and in the atmosphere—has become of major concern. Often there is no direct victim who will be sufficiently affected to institute proceedings, which may themselves be costly and complicated. The nature of the problem is compounded by the fact that the damage caused by any one aberrant party is likely to be minimal, and that it is only the *cumulative* effect— of oil being dumped, of emissions from supersonic transports entering the upper strata of the atmosphere and remaining there—that is the real threat. To combat such insidious dangers, a concerted effort is needed, involving clearly defined regulations, predetermined sanctions, and a recognized enforcing agency.

Until now, the growing concern in these areas has found only partial expression in international law, mainly in conventions that empower states to act only insofar as their own coastal areas, or their own ships on the open seas, are concerned. This latter rule becomes almost meaningless given the fact that the maritime navy of some states is state owned and state run, and given the fact that much marine shipping uses flags of convenience whereby the state itself has little or no control over shipping companies working largely out of wealthy developed countries.

The 1972 Stockholm Convention on the Environment (Barros and Johnston 1974, p. 299) came out with strong declarations for concerted action but refrained from declaring pollution to be an international crime like piracy or trafficking in drugs; the ongoing Convention on the Law of the Seas has also, up to now, refrained from any such action. Of course, there are traditional arguments that have been used against international crimes and that may well apply here, including in particular the argument that the means of enforcement are lacking at present in that there is no international police force and no international criminal court of law. Where international crimes are recognized, it is still the individual states that apply them or, rarely—as with war crimes—ad hoc courts of the victorious states. And there seems little chance of change in the near future. See Besharov (1973) for discussion of an international court of criminal law.

Yet it is precisely this glib reiteration of the conventional wisdom that requires reexamination. In earlier times, the idea of holding the state liable was unthinkable; similarly, the idea of a corporation being considered a legal entity caused many problems until the exigencies of burgeoning commerce and trade forced such a fiction to become a reality in the legal world.

Legal concepts and legal powers must be adapted to changing social and political realities. It is indisputable today, for instance, that the formerly firm concept of the freedom of navigation on the high seas is in dispute. It was of value—and of great value—for as long as the human perception of the sea was of unlimited bounty bestowed by nature. But as we come to realize that this bounty is not boundless, we are obliged to take steps to prevent its despoliation through pollution or its depletion for the sake of economic enrichment (Teclaff 1974, p. 104).

If the sea is no longer open, then who is to bear responsibility for its protection? Can we trust this function to the maritime nations, some of whom—the smaller ones—lack the resources to patrol the vast spaces of the open seas, whereas others—the larger countries, which have at least some of the resources—lack the will and, in any case, often are themselves direct or collusive parties to some of the major delinquencies, including deliberate breaches of world conventions (for example, the hunting of certain protected species of whales by the Soviet Union and Japan).

It may be naive to believe that sovereign nations will voluntarily surrender their rights over their citizens and their property while on the high seas. But if we take a longer historical view, we see that the state with its exclusive powers emerged only as the result of a long struggle, in which the central ruling authority only gradually succeeded in extending its direct legal control over its territory and its subjects. When this control was lacking, there was often resort to vigilante actions, ranging from legitimate protective measures to exploitative practices that included extortion and lynching (see Rosenbaum and Sederburg 1976).

This struggle that occurred within sovereign nations may now be replicating itself in the world community as a whole. We see even the practice of vigilante actions to fill a legal void. Thus, at the individual level, one may note the actions of groups of keenly concerned individuals determined to prevent destruction of the natural resources; for instance, a ship has been set up as a raider to search out ships involved in illicit hunting of whales, and to incapacitate them by ramming them; similarly, on a number of occasions, small boats have sailed into areas in which nuclear-bomb trial explosions were scheduled. In one instance these actions were a direct result of the impotence of the world community, after France ignored appeals from the governments of Australia and New Zealand and then successfully warded off legal actions brought by these two countries in the International Court of Justice (Nuclear Test Case 1974).

Such actions may be expected to increase in the future as people become more aware and concerned, as the damage becomes more widespread, and as the inability of the community of nations to act becomes more apparent. Further, at the national level, individual states may be confronted with similar problems when they realize that the present rules of international law and/or the means of enforcement are inadequate to cope with many of the new problems of international life. Canada's legislation pertaining to the Arctic seas is perhaps the best-known example of a state arrogating to itself power to take strong action against ships of any nation on the high seas—specifically within a certain distance (100 miles) of Canada's shore, even though Canada has recognized the 12-mile limit for territorial waters.

According to the Arctic Waters Pollution Prevention Act (International Legal Materials 1970; Utton 1974), agents of the Canadian government are empowered to board ships on the open sea in the Arctic up to 100 miles from shore and to examine whether they conform to the safety provisions of Canadian legislation. Where the Canadian regulations are violated, a number of options are available, including criminal and civil sanctions for contravening the law, or the seizure of the ship when safety and ecological considerations justify such drastic action. One justification for Canada's law is the fragile nature of the Arctic environment, where oil spills could have long-range, devastating effects. Another is the fact that the discovery of oil in the Arctic regions has raised the possibility of greatly increased shipping in the area, including the use of ships armed with ice breakers for the winter months when the sea becomes tundra. This raises the question of whether or not tundra itself constitutes some third form of planetary surface, in addition to land and water. Be that it may, international lawyers

have had a field day debating whether Canada is making new law or breaking the
old law. If the latter, then in any case its action may be seen as akin to vigilante
actions taken by groups of citizens who realize that the central authorities are
unwilling or unable to maintain the requisite standards of order and safety. In
the course of time the very fact of vigilante actions necessitates orderly responses
by the central authorities, and this is precisely what may happen as a result of
Canada's innovative legislative and enforcement activities.

The Arctic is, of course, unique; but it exemplifies, in extreme and concentrated form, the nature of the problem. Canada's concern relates to its shore-
line and the sea in the immediate vicinity. But what about remote areas of the
sea? What interest are individual countries entitled to show in the open sea in
general? Are landlocked countries to be given any say? What rights do countries
in one hemisphere have over occurrences in another hemisphere? What of the
seabed and the continental shelf? How are all of these to be protected? Can they
be protected without the use of stern criminal sanctions, and what would be the
means of enforcing such sanctions?

The problem may be handled at two levels—in terms of philosophical
beliefs, and in terms of underlying legal concepts.

Lynton Caldwell suggests that there are five socioecological concepts
that must underlie all our thinking on legal solutions to problems of pollution
at the international level:

1.  Unity of the biosphere. Its logical implication is universal participation of all
    responsible political jurisdictions in any effort or attempt to cope globally
    with human–environment relationships.
2.  Unique nature of the earth. Life outside the earth is unknown at this stage,
    and if it exists elsewhere it is liable to be rare. There is, therefore, a need
    to preserve what we have.
3.  Universality of the natural and cultural human heritage. Whatever our
    differences, we are all citizens of the Earth, a biological reality reinforced
    by the mobility of the human species and the intermingling of racial and
    cultural groups.
4.  Limitations of national sovereignty. Once considered the cornerstone of
    the law, national sovereignty is slowly being diminished, partly because it
    it becoming manifest that nations on their own cannot protect even them-
    selves and their citizens from environmental damage.
5.  Humankind has obligations as the custodian of the earth (Caldwell 1974,
    pp. 12-24).

Caldwell ends by suggesting that these five concepts need to be "woven into
a comprehensive and coherent interpretation of man and his place in nature that
is fully socially and politically operational." Meanwhile, however, "we do not,
as yet, have a body of ecological concepts that are simultaneously political
concepts" (1974, p. 23).

As long as a philosophy of this type remains only inchoate, there will be difficulties in gaining acceptance of more-stringent environmental controls, particularly with criminal sanctions. Yet even now demands have been made for a recognition of the international criminal-law aspects of environmental damage.

Barend van Niekerk has pinipointed the key factors in such a development. Arguing for the establishment of an international definition of the crime of pollution, he claims that the essential predetermining factors are already present (van Niekerk 1976, p. 68; Lee 1971, p. 203). First, there is a strong environmental norm already existing in international law, as can be seen from the host of conventions dealing with the environment, except that the sanctions are generally nonpenal. Second, almost every country in the world today has legislation, including criminal sanctions, against pollution. Finally, environmental pollution across national boundaries and outside national boundaries affects the quality of life for all humankind, and may be considered no less deleterious for human welfare and the future of humanity than the accepted international crimes.

Van Niekerk concedes that there is a serious problem in enforcing environmental regulations. Although he acknowledges the present weakness of supranational bodies, he reminds us that in earlier times, in the battle against piracy, the limited prospects of full enforcement did not deter the community of nations from taking the necessary steps, once they became aware of the dangers of inaction. Indeed, as van Niekerk argues, the mere fact of declaring an act to be a crime will have significance even if effective enforcement is not immediately forthcoming.

Finally, van Niekerk points out that the problem of pollution is not national, but international; that actions must be allowed against both states and individuals; that the measures adopted should involve strict preventive measures, with penalties for violation; and that the penalties should be oriented not so much toward the traditional punishments but more toward compensations.

Van Niekerk's article ends on a positive note with the suggestion that it may be easier to institute criminal sanctions in this area than in other, more-accepted areas of international criminal law, because environmental action has fewer political connotations than do, for example, acts of terrorism, whose perpetrators may be regarded by some countries as freedom fighters.

This optimism may be premature and only partly justified. It may well be that in the long run a supranational body with police, judicial, and enforcement powers will be more likely to come about for preserving the environment than for controlling other international crimes. In the meantime, though, there should be no illusions: The ecology has political connotations that will affect the capacity of such a body to act along the lines laid down by van Niekerk. Ecology provides a counterpoint to economics; it is economic factors, specifically, that are largely the cause of pollution and the reason for the weak societal response. Action now being taken at the national level began only after the ecological crisis had reached enormous proportions, and even now too little is being done.

The truth is that the temptation to freeload and the short-term rewards of free-riding (reaping benefits at the expense of others) are too large (see Wertheimer 1977, p. 302). Indeed, there is even a potential paradox here. As more-stringent measures are taken against pollution at the national level, there is a likelihood that the open seas will be increasingly exploited—as a dumping ground for bilge; for radioactive wastes; and even for ordinary household garbage, with ships being hired to transport such garbage out into the far reaches of the sea.

The idea of free-riding, of reaping the short-term benefits with impunity at the exepnse of others, may be seen most clearly in the difficulties involved in enforcing strict standards for the hunting of endangered species of whales. For important whale-hunting countries, the immediate direct economic benefits to themselves far outweigh the long-term diffuse damage to the world.

The ecology is directly affected by economics and so is bound up with politics as well. It is these factors that may well determine the prosepcts of a recognized international crime. In fact, we are really dealing with the kind of problem that Sutherland raised at the national level four decades ago—namely, that of impressing on the public the true criminal nature of acts that have traditionally been defined more moderately as "mere" civil wrongs.

Similar considerations apply to the prospects of conserving humanity's cultural treasures of the past. It is true that most countries that possess archeological (or even geological) treasures have taken steps to legislate for the protection of these treasures. They do so out of both national pride and national economic considerations. Thus, inasmuch as the laws on searching for and exporting artifacts are broken, the criminal sanction of the state is available. However, these measures at the national level are not always meaningful, and sometimes in their zealousness may be counterproductive.

Inasmuch as there is enforcement, it is the local "small fish" who get caught; the prestigious institutes and their directors and curators in other countries remain, for the most part, immune not only to penal sanctions but also to sanctions of almost any kind. What is the nature of the problem? In a fascinating account, Meyer—a political scientist by education, a journalist by profession, and an archeologist by avocation—has dealt directly with the issue (Meyer 1977). To whom, he asks, does the past belong?

Many would answer: to the nation in whose territory the finds are. However, there is another aspect to this question: Just as with ecology, the lofty realms of academic archeology are sustained by the earthy—and sometimes murky—foundations of economics and politics. Archeological finds can become of immense importance for present-day national philosophies. Meyer notes that in some countries archeology is an important factor in the search for a national identity and national pride. Unfortunately, in some cases concentration on these national aspects has led to a desire not just to conserve, but to hoard: to limit the number of foreign archeologists allowed to dig, and to restrict severely or ban totally the export of artifacts. Under such conditions, an illegal trade becomes almost inevitable. Calls have gone out in the past to commit all countries to allow legitimate, if controlled, activity of archeologists. Meyer notes that "while it is true that some countries rich in antiquities—notably Iran, Israel, and Egypt— have made some provision for a legal trade, the prevailing dogma is that the past is indivisible national property. The impulse springs in part from the memory of past exploitation. But it also indicates the myopic limitation of the nationhood outlook" (Meyer 1977, pp. 186–187).

The very existence of too severe restrictions on digging and on trading may cause museums to use illicit means of attaining the treasures they want. This existence of illicit trade also attracts into the international trade disreputable people who are drawn by the excitement of illicit activity and the promise of big financial returns.

Meyer writes of one such dealer who told him that it was precisely the illicit nature of the work that attracted him: "You must not forget one thing; I am a pirate. I enjoy piracy. I like the moment at the airport when they look at my passport and glance at my bag, for I take the very best pieces with me, on the airplane" (Meyer 1977, p. 16).

It can be argued that for the most part, laws do exist, and that some national governments are indeed conscientious in prosecuting. The reality is different, however. Although laws may be extensive—in some cases too extensive— implementation is often lax. It is impossible to guard all the sites, and the police and the courts have other responsibilities that are generally regarded as far more important. When cases are brought before the courts, the typical considerations of white-collar crime apply, with judges often showing tolerance that is not always compatible with the nature of the offense.

But the real problem lies much deeper. Looting at sites by low-level workers, or even the intricate and delicate manipulations of international dealers, take place only because there is an international market of museums, hungry for scoops in a tightly competitive and secretive market. The directors and curators of these institutions do not sully themselves with the looting of archeological sites, but they reap the benefits, which are so attractive that they cause an escalating round of further demands for illicit activity.

The problem of archeological looting is an international one. For although it is the objects of a specific country that are now being stolen and removed across the border, it is basically the treasures of all humankind that are being affected; in some specific cases, elements of essential knowledge are lost for all time the moment one upsets the provenance—the total picture of the artifacts.

Adopting an approach similar to that of Caldwell and van Niekerk with respect to the environment, Meyer suggests that we should

see our collective cultural remains as a resource whose title is invested in all humanity. It is a non-renewable resource; once exhausted, it cannot be replaced. And in our lifetime we may see it dwindle meaninglessly away, not so much because anyone has willed it, but because not enough people are aware that the problem exists. [Meyer 1977, pp. 203-204]

He argues that in a sense the archeological finds belong not only to the nation concerned, but to humanity as a whole. How is the world community acting as guardian in this respect? What more could be done?

What are the prospects of recognition for the necessary controls? Awareness of potential disaster and destruction has led to some second thoughts as to how the human heritage is to be preserved, researched, recorded, and suitably presented. If, on the one hand, museums with lavish funding cannot be allowed to cart away the treasures of another country, then on the other hand, countries with treasures cannot hoard them exclusively because of excessive national pride.

International controls may be the only answer, and Meyer has called for a comprehensive conference similar to the 1972 Conference on the Environment, held in Stockholm. Even so, the basis for an international-law approach exists— minus the criminal-law aspect.

In 1970 a Convention on the Means of Prohibiting and Preventing the Illicit Import, Export and Transfer of Ownership of Cultural Property was held. (For the full text of the convention see Meyer [1977], pp. 291-301.) The articles of this convention refer to the need for international cooperation as a means of protecting each country's cultural property, the need to stop illicit trade in such properties, and the need to establish adequate and appropriate rules and bodies to ensure proper control of such property. The convention stresses the need for national legislation to prevent museums and similar institutions from acquiring cultural property originating in another state that has been illegally exported. Article 9 of the convention allows parties that are the victims of pillage to call on other states to participate in a concerted international effort to stop the pillage.

The convention itself makes no direct reference to penal measures or sanctions, but the spirit of its declaration relates to actions of a criminal nature— there is harm to a specific victim, the world community of nations is affected, there is a need for control. All that is lacking is the actual formal sanction. But, of course, this begs the question and touches on the very issue raised by Sutherland. Are we to be bound by formal legal definitions, or are we to look at the real nature of the act described? In this case, however, the lack of a formal sanction is not just a function of special consideration being given to this aberrant act but is a consequence of a far larger problem, the lack of an international machinery. Nevertheless, this has not prevented the international community from declaring a series of acts to be considered as international crimes, even though they leave the actual sanctioning power to the signatory states. Why, then, are these white-collar acts not similarly considered to be international crimes? There are a number of reasons that this is so.

First, there is a lack of a sufficient awareness of the nature of the problem, again the very issue addressed by Sutherland. Second, again in line with Sutherland's thinking, there is a reluctance to recognize these acts as being of a criminal nature because of the kinds of people involved—respectable people who possess all the rationalizing and neutralizing capacity to explain that what they are doing is for the good of others and not for personal aggrandizement.

However, there are indications that a significant transformation is gradually taking place. Whereas in the past there was a casual willingness to evade local regulations, including occasionally the exploitation of the diplomatic pouch for such purposes, today a new set of ethics is slowly being forged, in which explicit rules are laid down for the conduct of the search for acquisitions. A number of museums have made their own statements about the rules that they will follow, and some have even declared their intention to return cultural property in the event that turns out to have been removed illegally from the country of origin. In a number of instances, as a gesture of goodwill, property has been returned many years after its removal—a rough equivalent to the *nolo contendere* plea used in the United States to allow a company or person to make expiation for the wrongful act without conceding criminality (see Meyer 1977, p. 105).

Let us sum up the position in this area. If we look beyond the formal definition and examine the actual nature of the act, we see that:

1.  The act is considered a crime in the country of origin.
2.  There is an international norm expressed in official declarations.
3.  The problem can be resolved only by concerted international action.
4.  Those responsible for the problem have in recent years evinced a change of heart in recognizing the error of their past ways, in essence acknowledging their wrongdoing.

It is not obvious that all we lack is the official definition? In essence, we are dealing with an international delinquency.

The vulnerability of developing countries to possible exploitation by wealthy nations is seen in many other areas as well. It is impossible to make a detailed description, but there are a number of ideas that might be probed in greater depth. For instance, the increasingly stringent consumer measures being adopted in the more-advanced industrial countries—in terms of safety and health regulations—may very well lead (if they have not already done so) to a situation in which products that are unable to meet the new higher demands of the producing country will find their way into developing countries, only too eager to reap some of the presumed benefits of modern affluent living without checking too carefully the quality of the product, or without even having the necessary information or instruments to avoid the infiltration of such products into their market.

Beyond this, some products of debatable value may, through a sophisticated advertising campaign that artificially and needlessly raises consumer expectations, be introduced into areas that have no need for them. An interesting inverse pattern may even develop. As a product becomes exposed to attack in the developed country in which it is produced, it may seek newer markets in areas where there is no knowledge of the debate over the product's dubious qualities. Thus, in the last decade, there has been a move in several Western countries to encourage women to return to the traditional method of breastfeeding their babies, since most recent medical evidence indicates that this natural means of feeding babies is far superior to the use of artificial milk substitutes.[1] Paradoxically but not entirely coincidentally, even as this new awareness spreads among women in developed areas, there is a new demand being made in developing countries for such products, by women who often lack the wherewithal to invest in the purchase of such products. Recently, there has been a campaign directed against some of the exporters of these baby foods, some of whom have been forced to restrict their trading activities in other parts of the world. What manner of activity are we dealing with? Is there a need for transnational regulations? Is there a need for an international convention? Would this be an unjustifiable interference against free trade? Can international standards be set up akin to those laid down by national food and drug administrations? Who would enforce such regulations—the developing country that lacks the resources and the personnel, or the developed industrial country that lacks the willingness and that may be exposed to pressures from the companies involved?

At a recent international conference on infant and young-child feeding, recommendations were made to put a halt to advertising and sales promotion of artificial substitutes for breast milk, and to establish an international code for the marketing of such products. The recommendations involved concerted activities by exporting and importing countries; by international agencies; and by advertising, consumer, and professional groups. The recommendations, however, fail to indicate firm measures for enforcement.[2]

A further way in which commercial relations allow for exploitation of the developing world by powerful commercial companies is through price manipulation, whereby the company may keep prices low, even selling at a loss, in their home country, and make its profits by raising prices in other parts of the world. This is an issue that requires sophisticated economic and accounting measures. Indications of this practice may be noted in the public storm that has arisen in the last year or two as several oil companies have declared large profits at a time of supposed energy crisis. Their explanation for their good financial position is that, although their economic position is weak in their home base, their overseas dealings have been successful. To what extent have these dealings been exploitative? Further, given the phenomenon of multinational companies, it may be asked whether national bodies remain capable of maintaining control over the trade practices of these companies, which have extensive opportunities to manipulate their accounting practices—for instance, for taxation purposes (see Wallace 1976, especially pp. 25-38, 80-89, 107-120). Similar questions may be raised as to the possibility of ensuring adequate safety and health controls in shipping without international enforcement.

The vulnerability of weaker consuming nations to the blandishments of the developed world is only one aspect of international trade. Sometimes the consuming country constitutes the source of the problem. In many countries, international commercial transactions are dependent on willingness to make under-the-counter payments, generally to highly placed government officials in the purchasing country. A number of international scandals in the past few years (for example, the Lockheed case and the involvement of the crown prince of the Netherlands) have focused some attention on the economic dimensions and political implications of the problem. Here, as in the case of the museums, there has been a certain amount of soul searching and an attempt at clarification of the human and ethical aspects of the problem. But can this be done at the national level only? For instance, a company or a nation determined to avoid any bribes may find itself unable to compete with rival companies or nations. Little is known of the full details of corruption, but several writers have pointed out that there is often a tendency in new countries for those recently elevated to positions of authority to exploit their power for their personal aggrandizement while simultaneously justifying their activities through typical neutralization techniques—pointing out, for instance, the contribution that they have made in the past to the very independence of the country, or emphasizing that it is only the foreigner who is being exploited; that the country will derive numerous advantages from the consummation of the deal; that everyone else is doing it; that the country is too poor to provide a proper official recompense for the important work being done; or that the payments themselves are not really bribes, but more akin to commission for the efforts expended.

Wraith and Simpkins (1953) have drawn a parallel between the scope for corrupt behavior in new countries in Africa and similar problems in England at an early stage in its industrial development. More recently, Clinard and Abbott, in their survey of crime in the developing countries, have summed up the situation: "It is generally agreed that corruption of government officials is an acute problem in most developing countries in Asia, Latin America, and Africa and that many persons have amassed large fortunes in political office (1973, pp. 51-52). They provide a list of countries that have enacted special laws against corruption or have appointed commissions of enquiry.

The acute nature of the problem may be seen from the ambivalence that it causes. As Clinard and Abbott claim:

> In developing countries corruption is seldom really regarded as a "crime," even though it is specified as a crime. Many developing countries, for example, have long had traditions of making "gifts" to persons in authority or to gain some personal advantage. Sometimes giving a gift fits accepted custom, but asking for it does not. [1973, p. 53]

Similarly, Lloyd, in *Africa in Social Change,* draws attention to the deeper cultural background of the problem. Corruption in many cases

> is difficult to define. Office-holders in traditional societies received much of their remuneration in gifts for services rendered, and the ambitious regularly advanced their interests through the patronage of the more influential members of the community. In general, the lavishness of gift exchange greatly exceeded that in contemporary Western society (which is not without its system of bribes). And in contrast, the impersonality of bureaucratic relationship is alien to the African [Lloyd 1969, pp. 249–250]

Given this kind of situation, given the discrepancies between the bureaucratic modern state and the traditional forms of authority, how is the problem of corruption to be resolved, particularly at the international level against the background of differing cultural and ethical frameworks. Although the issue was raised in many discussions of the economic, political, and human aspects of life in developing countries, the world community as such seems reluctant to confront the problem head on because of its explosive nature. Clinard and Abbott draw attention to the fact that despite the broad ramifications of the problem, the 1970 U.N. Congress on the Prevention of Crime and the Treatment of Delinquency, in which the discussion centered on developing countries, carefully avoided the problem of white-collar crime.

Thus, in regarding the mutual corrupting affects of kickbacks and bribes, it seems clear that we again confront a problem that plagues so much discussion of white-collar crime—namely, a reluctance to deal with the question honestly and openly. In any event, I would suggest that here too we are facing an international delinquency.

It should not be thought that the problem of international trade is limited to trade between the developed and the developing world. One of the countries most affected by the Canadian Arctic Waters Act was the United States, and developed countries have had similar problem in trying to control the dumping of steel across the border. Legislation has been passed to deal with the tensions that have arisen. The form of the legislation is civil, but the intent seems to be to define a criminal act (see, for example, "Steel Dumping" 1972, especially Slayton 1972).

Tribunals have been set up to discuss complaints of companies victimized by what is termed "predatory dumping" in order to destroy competitors in other countries. The tribunal is of an administrative nature—but is not its work in the field of international trade similar to that of the tribunals that Sutherland exampled?

There are other problems that have clear overtones of international white-collar criminality. The issue of boycotts has raised many delicate questions because they are normally set up for political reasons. Yet some writers have argued that they should be outlawed, whereas others have argued that they are legitimate as long as no coercive or violent methods are used to enforce them (see Friedman 1959, pp. 445–447). But again, what is coercion? Is a threat not to deal with a company unless it ceases trading with another country to be considered coercive?

There have also been a number of instances in which countries have expropriated the property of foreign nationals without making due compensation. Is this the equivalent of stealing their property? Acknowledging that there are complicated ideological issues involved (such as nationalization in a socialist economy), Wolfgang/Friedman nevertheless argues for a recognized norm that the expropriating nation make compensation, particularly in those cases in which the company was originally invited to trade. He concludes that where a state has undertaken to protect foreign companies or individuals against expropriation then "a breach of such undertaking will be clearly an international delinquency" (Friedman 1959, pp. 455–456).

The list of such problems is lengthy and includes instances ranging from countries that "steal" works of art by systematically refusing to abide by international copyright regulations providing for royalties to the writer or artist (see Nowell-Smith 1968; Kaplan 1967), to countries that are guilty of "tax evasion" in their persistent refusal to pay their regular dues to international organizations, while claiming all the rights and privileges of membership. The question is whether the time is not ripe to enforce a basic principle of "no representation without taxation."

Manifestly, there is ample room for much creative criminological work in these and related areas, some of which may necessitate some basic rethinking of fundamental concepts. Is this work doomed to remain purely academic, an exercise in intellectual futility, or are there prospects of its having an impact on the world community of nations? Is there any hope of international white-collar crime being considered part of the emerging international criminal law? Further, is there any hope that this emerging criminal law will ever have the requisite power to enforce rules and to impose sanctions?

Although superficially the prospects may look dim and distant, in reality we may well be at the beginning of an upsurge in the efficacy of international criminal law. This is emerging at present, particularly at the regional level and in the realm of human rights, and especially among the European community of nations, where several of the constituent member states have been challenged and indicted on charges of violating human rights (see, for example, Robertson 1977).

Although this issue may seem far removed from those that seem to form the core of international white-collar crime, there is actually the potential for much overlap. This is borne out in an interesting book by Paul Gormley, who discusses the environment at the international level as being basically a human-rights issue (Gomley 1976). At the center of his thesis is the fact that "in looking toward the development of an environmental philosophy and, likewise, the susequent emergence of international environment law, encouragement can be obtained from the success already achieved in the protection of human rights" (Gormley 1976, p. 47). In fact, in many instances human-rights issues interact with those of white-collar crime. The work of the International Labor Organization is of prime importance in this respect. Over the past fifty years it has been laying down a series of rules by which member nations may judge the adequacy and equity of their labor relations. The underlying philosophy has been that of applying criteria of social justice, in particular in ensuring minimum standards for the protection of workers—hours of work, holidays, work condition, and so forth.

There is a particularly strong overlap among the three areas—human rights, the environment, and white-collar crime—in the efforts of some countries to advance industrialization and in the economic exploitation of areas inhabited by simple tribes living in regions of unique environmental qualities. As Gorinsky writes:

> The newly-independent nations of South America, Africa and the Far East are imitating not only the industrial structure and increased urbanization of the West but also, unhappily, its treatment of harmless and simple people. They are copying today the ruthlessness and savagery that the Europeans showed to the indigenous populations of North America and Australia when they first met them. [Gorinsky 1971; Arens 1976]

Gorinsky's article is a plea for a concerted effort to protect these people from destruction of their habitat and way of life—and sometimes even from genocide—justified by the dictates of industrial progress and financial profitability.

Historically, there is ample evidence indicating how a lack of concern for commercial aberrations may have serious human-rights and political implications. Joseph Borkin's description of the history of the I.G. Farben is a classic case study of the impact of commercial activities on political developments (Borkin 1978). Of particular interest is the fact that some of the leading officials of the company were actually sentenced to imprisonment in 1923 for evading regulations laid down in the occupied area of Germany. They avoided serving the sentences by crossing into the unoccupied area of Germany, where they were able to evade the penalty for their crimes. Later, this company made key contributions to the Nazis' preparation of their war machine in the 1930s, as well as using forced labor in their plants during World War II.

A further serious attack on basic human rights is the continuing exploitation of children in work situations, in flagrant violation of international regulations. The pious declarations that accompanied the recently concluded International Year of the Child have failed to deal in a meaningful way with this continuing denial of the fullness of the childhood years that results from the calculated exploitation of young people in the interest of profit. Where countries countenance such exploitation, there is every need for the world community to respond and to spell out categorically that such exploitation constitutes an international delinquency. The young, an especially vulnerable group, surely are entitled to the special concern of the family of nations.


## Conclusion

It should be stressed that in arguing for the incorporation of white-collar crime into the rubric of international criminal law, I am not arguing for the imposition of a whole host of penalties that penological experience has shown to be ineffective. As we develop a new international criminal law, an openness must also be shown to the newer forms of enforcement and of sanctions—of compensation, injunctions, mediation, and arbitration. This would not undermine the thrust of international criminal law because in many respects national criminal law also is moving in this direction. In any event, it is not the punitive and stignatizing features that are the most attractive or significant aspect of criminal law but, rather, that the *enforcement becomes the concern of the society as a whole, in this case of the world community of nations.* And practically, it means that there should be a major investment in the personnel, the machinery, and the organizational infrastructure required for enforcement.

Further, despite the attempts by many jurists, philosophers, and sociologists of the law to deny that there is a connection between law and morality, I hold to the view that such a connection does exist—that law, particularly criminal law, is in many respects the expression of the deepest values of a society (see Sheleff 1976, p. 140). It is a statement of morality, of purpose, of intent, of awareness of a problematic situation. This, above all, is why harmful acts—such as pollution of the environment, depletion of natural resources, economic exploitation of the weak, illicit trade of art and archeological treasures, and other similar acts— should be incorporated within the rubric of international criminal law.

In a larger sense, then, the call for a recognition of the reality of international white-collar crime is a call not for punitive vengeance but for the recognition of the unity of the human race and the commonality of its concerns, fortified by an expression of the desire to cooperate across national borders in order to cope with problems that confront us all.


## Notes

1. For recent research on this question, see *Proceedings of the International Symposium on Breast Feeding,* held in Tel Aviv in February 1980 (Amsterdam: Excerpta Medica, 1981).

2. See Joint WHO/UNICEF & *Infant and Young Child Feeding,* Geneva, October 1979 (Geneva: World Health Organization, 1979). See also World Health Organization Vote of May 1981 in which the United States was the only nation to vote against a resolution calling for action by importing nations to regulate artificial (powdered) baby food.

References

Arens, Richard. *Genocide in Paraguay*. Philadelphia: Temple University Press, 1976.

Barros, J., and Johnston, D.M. *The International Law of Pollution*. New York: Free Press, 1974.

Bassiouni, M.C., and Vanda, V.P., eds. *A Treatise on International Criminal Law*. Springfield, Ill.: Charles C. Thomas, 1973.

Borkin, Joseph. *The Crime and Punishment of I.G. Farben*. New York: Free Press, 1978.

Caldwell, Lynton. "Concepts in Development of International Environmental Policies." In L.A. Teclaff and A.E. Utton, eds., *International Environmental Law*, pp. 12–24. New York: Praeger, 1974.

Clinard, Marshall B., and Abbott, Daniel J. *Crime in Developing Countries: A Comparative Perspective*. New York: Wiley, 1973.

de Pauw, Frans. *Grotius and the Law of the Sea*. Institut de Sociologie, Brussels: 1965.

De Schutter, Bart. *Bibliography of International Criminal Law*. Leiden: Sijthoff, 1972.

Friedman, Wolfgang. *Law in a Changing Society*. London: Steven and Sons, 1959.

Geis, Gilbert, and Meier, Robert, eds. *White Collar Criminal*, 2nd ed. New York: Free Press, 1977.

Gorinsky, "Cultures in Conflict: Amerindians in New Societies." *Yearbook of World Affairs* 88(1971).

Gormley, W. Paul. *Human Rights and Environment: The Need for International Co-operation*. Leyden: Sijthoff, 1976.

*International Legal Materials* 9(1970):598.

Kaplan, Benjamin. *An Unhurried View of Copyright*. New York: Columbia University Press, 1967.

Lee, F.G. "International Legal Aspects of Pollution of the Atmosphere." *University of Toronto Law Journal* 21(1971):203.

Lloyd, P.C. *Africa in Social Change*. Baltimore, Md.: Penguin, 1969.

Meyer, Karl E. *The Plundered Past: The Story of the Illegal International Traffic in Works of Art*. New York: Atheneum, 1977.

Mueller, Gerhard O., and Besharov, D. "The Scope and Significance of International Criminal Law." In Bassiouni and Vanda, *International Criminal Law*, pp. 129–143.

Nowell-Smith, S. *International Copyright Law and the Publisher in the Reign of Queen Victoria*. Oxford: Clarendon Press, 1968.

Nuclear Test Case (Judgment). Australia v. France. 1974. ICJ 253; *id*. New Zealand v. France. 457.

Oppenheim, L.F.L. *International Law: A Treatise*. London: Longmans, Green, 1955.

Robertson, A.H. *Human Rights in Europe,* 2nd ed. Manchester: Manchester University Press, 1977.

Rosenbaum, Jon H., and Sederberg, Peter C., eds. *Vigilante Politics.* Philadelphia: University of Pennsylvania Press, 1976.

Sheleff, Leon. "Morality, Criminal Law and Politics." *Tel Aviv University Studies in Law* 2(1976):140.

Slayton, Philip. "The Canadian Legal Response to Steel Dumping." In "Steel Dumping into Canada and the United States, pp. 81-94. *Canada–United States Law Journal* 2(1972):17-115.

Sutherland, Edwin H. "White Collar Criminality." *American Sociological Review* 5(1940):1.

_____ . *White Collar Crime.* New York: Holt, Rinehart and Winston, 1949.

Teclaff, Ludwik A. "International Law and the Protection of the Oceans from Pollution." In Teclaff and Utton, *International Environmental Law,* ch. 5.

Trail Smelter Arbitration Tribunal. *American Journal of International Law* 35(1941):684.

Utton, Albert E. "The Arctic Waters Pollution Prevention Act, and the Right of Self-Protection." In Teclaff and Utton, *International Environmental Law,* pp. 140-153.

van Niekerk, Barend. "Environmental Pollution–The New International Crime." *South African Law Journal* 93(1976):68.

Wallace, Don. *International Regulation of Multinational Corporations.* New York: Praeger, 1976.

Wertheimer, A. "Victimless Crimes." *Ethics* 87(1977):302.

Wraith, Ronald, and Simpkins, Edgar. *Corruption in Developing Countries: A Comparative Perspective.* New York: Wiley, 1973.

# 4

# Crime and the Abuse of Power: Offenses and Offenders beyond the Reach of the Law

*Charles E. Reasons*

Traditionally, students of crime have viewed upperworld crime or "crime at the top" as white-collar crime: that is, crime committed by a person in a position of trust for his or her personal gain. Therefore, emphasis has been placed on individuals and their needs, goals, attitudes, and behavior. However, such emphasis has caused us to neglect the ever increasing significance of organizations in our daily lives. It fails either to consider adequately the physical harms that are a consequence of organizational offenses or to deal with the special characteristics of illegal behavior in organizational settings.

> Organizational crimes are illegal acts of omission or commission of an individual or a group of individuals in a legitimate formal organization in accordance with the operative goals of the organization, which have serious physical or economic impact on employees, consumers or the general public. [Schrager and Short 1978]

In distinguishing between white-collar and organizational crimes, we are recognizing the daily impact that private and public organizations have on our lives as workers, consumers, and members of the general public. Therefore, the behavior of individuals is placed within the context of the organization. For example, whereas an employee who embezzles from the employer is guilty of a white-collar offense, the same employee may also be involved in price fixing or misleading advertising as part of the policies, practices, and/or procedures of the organization. In the latter offenses, the white-collar offender is carrying out organizational goals. Such a distinction forces us to look at organizational changes and control as a means of redressing harms, rather than solely at individual sanction. For example, sanctioning a police officer for illegal entry or illegal mail opening may not in itself remedy the practice if the organizational goals and practices of the police force reinforce such behavior.

Adapted from a preparatory paper for the Sixty United Nations Congress on the Prevention of Crime, prepared for the solicitor general of Canada, 1 March 1979. Not to be quoted or reproduced without permission of the author. Particular thanks is due to research assistants Trudie Smith and Ken Tighe. This paper reflects the opinions of the author and not necessarily those of the Office of the Solicitor General. Slightly revised version of a paper presented to the International Conference on Economic and White Collar Crime, New York, February 1980.

Finally, I would argue that we must transcend a merely formal legal definition of crime in order to address victims *without* crimes. That is, there may be harms being committed against workers, consumers, or the general public that need to be criminalized. For example, the presence of unsafe or unhealthful conditions in the workplace may not be criminal, although the consequences may include thousands of deaths and injuries. Thus, there is a need to determine the magnitude and scope of harms that should be criminalized.

Although the distinction between white-collar and organizational crime may be difficult to make in certain instances, it provides a general framework for analyzing and prescribing change in specific substantive areas. Therefore, the following section will describe the nature and scope of specific crimes of the powerful in Canadian society within the context of this distinction.

**White-Collar Crime**

Much of the concern with white-collar and business crime has been directed toward employee theft. One authority suggests that supervisory personnel have accounted for more than 60 percent of business dishonesty over the past decade (Davies 1978a). Furthermore, it has been estimated that such business crime in Canada in 1977 cost companies and consumers more than $4 million—$11 million a day—with some security agents saying that this means a 15-percent increase in price paid for goods and services to cover employer-employee dishonesty (Davies 1978a). Furthermore, insurance companies estimate of 30 percent of company liquidations in North America are the result of fraud. However, only an estimated 5 percent of the criminals are apprehended and brought before the courts (Davies 1978b). Computer theft is another form of white-collar crime that has received increased attention within the last few years. Computer thefts often involve sizable amounts, with the Stanford Research Institute identifying eighty-five incidents, thirty-three of which totaled $13 million in losses (Parry 1976).

The Royal Canadian Mounted Police (RCMP) instituted a Commercial Crime Branch in the late 1960s to address such employee crimes, as well as other white-collar offenses (Magee 1973). Their activity has been directed toward such offenses as fraudulent bankruptcies; securities scandals; municipal, provincial, or federal kickbacks and briberies; frauds on and by every level of government; tax evasions; and a variety of other business-related crimes (Harlwood 1977). In 1976 the dollar value of the branch's caseload was $359,714,201. Bankruptcies accounted for more than $70 million, frauds for $241 million, tax matters for $7.5 million, security for $5 million, and assistance to foreign authorities for $3.76 million. More than $1 million in fines were imposed, with $22 million in monies recovered from only 2,500 charges laid (Harlwood 1977, p. 62). The superintendent of the RCMP Commercial Crime Branch estimates that Canadians are defrauded of $1 billion a year (Weissman 1975). Stolen securities appear to be increasingly evident, with their counterfeiting on the rise (Weissman 1975). Only about 5 percent of bankruptcies in Canada are investigated by the RCMP, with 75 percent of these found to be fraudulent (Magee 1973, p. 27). Tax evasion in a number of forms is also being investigated by the Department of National Revenue, although there are only about 200 convictions each year out of more than 12.5 million filings. It is estimated that about $20 million in Canadian income was deposited in foreign banks in 1974 to avoid taxation (Mathias 1974).

Bribery and political kickbacks are another type of white-collar crime, often involving politicians. A number of cases have been revealed in New Brunswick, raising the question of how widespread such practices are throughout Canada (Mathias 1977). The charges in New Brunswick include intimidation, bribery, kickbacks, and blackmail (Plaskin 1978). The allegations include payoffs to the conservative government in order to obtain government contracts. Evidence of such practices leads us into the study of organizational crime carried out by government agencies and political parties.

The Sky Shops (Urquhart 1976), Hamilton Harbour ("Dredging Up" 1975), and 1978 Olympics ("Contracts" 1979) cases all indicate that the use of political power for private gain is present in Canadian society, although we have only just begun to assess its nature and magnitude. This brings us to the topic of corporate bribes, which will be specifically addressed in the section on organizational crimes.

All of the aforementioned types of white-collar offenses, as well as others, are pursued largely through the RCMP Commercial Crime Branch and other agencies. Nonetheless, we know much less about such crimes than about traditional crimes.

## Organizational Crime

I have divided organizational offenses into economic crimes, human-rights crimes, and violent personal-injury crimes.[1] Within each of these categories, I will review materials regarding their nature and scope.

### Economic Crimes

What often comes to mind when corporate crime is mentioned are such things as misleading advertising, price fixing, bribery, and other types of economic offenses. A large number of corporate economic offenses are policed by the Department of Consumer and and Corporate Affairs, which has sole jurisdiction over twenty-four acts, and coenforcing power with the Department of Health and Welfare or of Agriculture over another six. The major pieces of legislation are the Food and Drugs Act, the Hazardous Products Act, the Weights and Measures Act, the Textile Labeling Act, and the Combines Investigation Act. In one of the few studies in this area, the six-month period from October 1974 to March 1975 was analyzed to determine the number of convictions and penalties under all but the Combines Investigation Act (Snider 1978). Forty-one individuals or firms were convicted of fifty-nine charges, with an average fine of $442.50 per person or firm under the Food and Drug Act, and with no one imprisoned. Under the Weights and Measures Act, eight firms or individuals were convicted on a total of eighteen charges, and $1,050 in fines assessed, with no imprisonment. Finally, no prosecutions were completed during this period under the Hazardous Products or Textile Labeling Acts.

The Combines Investigation Act, passed in 1889, is the key piece of legislation directed at corporations. Its purpose is largely to prohibit unfair marketing practices in the Canadian economy, including illegal monopolies, mergers, advertising, and other unfair practices. Between 1889 and 1972, 145 reports were completed and 125 published by combines enforcers. Although there are provisions for up to two years incarceration, no one was jailed during this period (Goff and Reasons 1976). In 1979 five prominent Canadian businessmen were sentenced to jail terms for rigging bids on dredging contracts, and eight companies were fined $6.5 million ("Five Jailed" 1979). They are, of course, appealing the decision. Most of the prosecutions have been against smaller, less-powerful corporations, with penalties being fines or orders of prohibition.

In recent years misleading advertising has largely occupied the enforcement staff, while price fixing, mergers, and monopolies have largely been neglected. However, these latter actions are potentially the most economically harmful. For example, it has been estimated that lost output attributable to the presence of monopolies and shared monopolies in Canada costs $4.5 to $6 billion a year (Gonick 1975, p. 22). Concentration and monopolization are often the consequence of mergers. Aggregate concentration (the percentage of economic activity accounted for by the largest firms in Canada) decreased from 1923 to 1975, but industrial concentration (the fraction of total activity in a given industry attributable to a fixed number of the largest corporations in that industry) increased in Canadian manufacturing industries from 1948 to 1972. Both aggregate and industrial concentration are higher in Canada than in the United States (*Report of the Royal Commission* 1978). Prior to 1960, no mergers were successfully prosecuted by the government, whereas of the 3,572 mergers occurring between 1960 and 1972, nine were prosecuted and three convicted; the penalties assessed were two Orders of Prohibition and one fine of $40,000. Thus, since 1923 when mergers came under the auspices of the Combines Investigation Act, only 0.003 percent of the total number of mergers have been charged, resulting in 0.0005 percent of the mergers being convicted (Goff and Reasons 1978), pp. 91–110). A recent price-fixing case resulted in a fine of $150,000 being levied against Levi Strauss for eight counts of price fixing.

Although this was the largest fine assessed in such a case, the company made a net profit of $3.25 million in 1974 and $1.8 million in 1975, two of the years during which it fixed prices ("Levi Strauss" 1979). A recent Supreme Court of Canada decision made the Canadian competition law essentially useless because of the difficulty of defining *unduly*. Thus, the conviction of three huge sugar companies by a lower court was thrown out; and attempts to prosecute for conspiring to "prevent, or lessen, unduly, competition" were made even more difficult ("Sugar Trio" 1980).

In conclusion, the limited data on Consumer and Corporate Affairs enforcement suggest that prosecutions are infrequent and are directed at smaller, non-dominant companies, with fines and orders of prohibition used as sanctions.

As noted in the section on white-collar crime, bribery may be an organizational crime when it is done to further the interests of the organization. The bribery cases in Newfoundland, which suggest that a political organization may use this technique to fatten its coffers, brings us to the practice of party financing and contributions. Although corporate contributions are legal in Canada, it may be a practice in need of criminalizing (Urquhart 1978). Also, the use of bribes by corporations has increasingly come under scrutiny with the revelation that many U.S. multinational corporations are involved in bribing foreign customers and government officials (Ungea 1976; Jacoby, Nehenkis, and Ells 1977). Control of such crimes would be greatly aided by the establishment and strict enforcement of public-disclosure laws, conflict-of-interest laws, and freedom-of-information legislation.

Other economic harms that may be profitably made crimes include excessive profits, land speculation, and employer ripoffs. Whereas Canadian prices increased 11 percent in 1978 and salaries approximately 7 percent, profits rose 21 percent, to $9.3 billion. Also, an independent study recently released by the Economic Council of Canada concluded that customers contributed between $200 and $500 million in excess profits to bank coffers between 1968 and 1973 ("9.3 Billion" 1979; Oake 1979). This, coupled with the great increase in housing costs (Lorimer 1978), have led to calls for antiprofiteering legislation. Another example of harm done by organizations is the failure of employers to remit payroll deductions for employees. Whereas bank robbers, extortionists, and kidnappers made off with $5.17 million in 1975, employers received $7.9 million through such theft from workers (Goff and Reasons 1978, p. 11). These and other harms should be addressed to determine their nature and scope and the possibility of criminalization.

## Human-Rights Crimes

In a democratic society a fundamental right of the citizenry should be the right to know. Access to information on which the government is basing decisions and policies is essential to any government for the people. In Canada the public has very little access to information that may be vital to the Canadian people either individually or collectively.[2] In 1971 former federal Solicitor General Jean-Pierre Goyer circulated among five of his fellow cabinet members a list of some twenty-five Canadians who were believed to be "subversives." The list contained mainly civil servants and university professors thought to be organizing for the overthrow of the government. Subsequent blacklists were revealed, although they were denied by the Executive. Secret files on politicians, social activists, and others have been kept by the government. The Solicitor General's Department, the RCMP Security Branch, and the Canadian Armed Forces keep files on political groups, business organizations, and individuals that they regard as a threat to national security. To what extent is such information used by the prime minister's office and the privy council's office, or by other government agencies? Are these persons or organizations a threat to the state or merely to the party in power? These and other questions arise when we attempt to open up the government to the citizenry.

We should be concerned about the nature, extent, and use of government information about its citizens. There are approximately 15,000 files or other types of records held by government institutions at the federal level, distributed among 87 government departments and institutions, with at least 22 types of records that are beyond the public realm. There are 72 federal statutes prohibiting the release of certain records. Although the Canadian Human Rights Act of 1977 provides access to government records, there are 22 exemptions, such as national defense or security, information given by confidential sources, and matters that might reveal information on individuals other than those making an inquiry. Also, the minister of justice has wide discretion in determining the "public benefit" in weighing whether or not to release information. The most-controversial and potentially most-damaging information will likely remain withheld because the burden of proof is on the citizen to show what is specifically desired and why, although in a democracy the opposite should be the case. Furthermore, the lack of any independent judicial review of both the criteria and the process of government categorizing and dissemination of information makes the legislation largely ineffective. It provides the opportunity for the abuse of power by the government in using such categories and secrecy for its own political ends. The need for more public access to "public" institutions is apparent in the revelations concerning the RCMP. Canada needs separate freedom-of-information legislation, like that in Sweden and the United States, that places the burden of proof for denying access on the government and allows for independent judicial review. This will go a long way toward reducing possible violations of human rights and making the government a public institution.

The police in a democratic society should be subject to the rule of law and to control by the citizenry and their representatives. Within the last few years there have been increasing revelations concerning illegal and questionable activities of the RCMP, including illegal wiretaps; kidnapping; the use of agents provocateurs; illegal opening of mail; burglary; theft; destruction of property; and surveillance of suspected political activists in universities, unions, and native organizations, among others (Dewar 1978a, b; Lewis 1977; "R.C.M.P." 1978; Benedict 1979). Throughout its history the RCMP has conducted surveillance of political and social activists, particularly among labor unions (Brown and Brown 1973; Mann and Lee 1979). A federal commission established to inquire into the wrongdoing of the RCMP (the McDonald commission) has nearly completed its study, and it is becoming increasingly clear that illegal activity is part of the organizational policies and practices of the force and that the RCMP is in need of external social control in a democratic society. For example, a former RCMP security-service personnel testified that as a Mountie dealing with susepcted subversive groups, he often broke into their headquarters to get information ("RCMP Break-Ins" 1980).

The policing of the police is also necessary at the local level. When civil rights and liberties are violated, there is a need for adequate redress. A victim of police action may suffer property damage or destruction, loss of liberty, personal injury, or even death (Craig 1977). Although a citizen may make a criminal prosecution, file a civil suit, and/or file a formal complaint to the department, such remedies are largely inadequate. For example, most disciplining is done internally, with no independent external review or adjudication. Since illegally obtained evidence can be admissible in court, interrogation before access to counsel is routine (Borovoy 1977; Stewart 1970; Henshel 1977; Barton 1970). More attention needs to be paid to detailing the nature and extent of such organizational crimes against human rights and possible effective remedies.

The potential for abuse of civil rights and personal freedom is also evident in the increasing use of electronic eavesdropping. It appears that the Protection of Privacy Act introduced in 1974 is actually an erosion of the right of privacy (Title 1978; Manning and Bronson 1977; Smith 1970; Burns 1975-1976). Unlike some other countries, Canada permits evidence gained from illegal wiretaps to be used as evidence; and there is inadequate external review of the granting of legal wiretaps. Furthermore, the justification for legal wiretaps has largely been expressed in terms of combating organized crime, although the evidence does not confirm its worth in this area. Thus, government surveillance of its citizens through social-control agencies is not adequately controlled.

Finally, the entire area of human rights needs more societal attention and more-effective means of redress. Individual and institutional discrimination on the basis of sex, age, race, ethnicity, sexual orientation, or other irrelevant personal characteristics need to be more vigorously combatted through criminalization of such discriminatory practices (MacKay 1978; McDermott 1976-1977; Fisher 1977). A final "crime" of the greatest magnitude is the way we treat our native population. These "crimes against humanity" include inadequate housing, poor health services, short lifespan, high unemployment rates, high infant-mortality and maternal-mortality rates, and inferior education and social services, among other conditions. The current plight of the Canadian native population is due not to circumstance but to a history of government policies and practices, neglect, and lack of concern. When we look at human-rights violations in other countries, we should not forget the massive violation of human dignity and social justice evident in Canada (Goldenberg 1971; Frideres 1975; Manzer 1974; Reasons and Perdue 1981).

*Violent Personal-Injury Crimes*

Although there is more-obvious physical dnager and harm from some "street crimes" such as murder and assault, the belief that organizational crimes are not violent is false. For example, Ford Motor Company has lost several civil suits and is currently under indictment in Indiana for reckless homocide and criminal recklessness concerning the Pinto's fuel tanks. More specifically, it has been re-vealed in court that the representatives of this organization calculated that the costs of changing an unsafe gas tank were nearly three times the expected costs of suits arising because of deaths and injuries (Jacobson and Barnes 1978; "Ford Is Indicted" 1978). Thus the policies and practices of the organization patently put profit over the saving of lives of consumers. Another example is the 1976 fire in the Wentworth Arms Hotel in Hamilton, which killed six people. Sub-sequent investigations found thirty safety violations, including the hotel pro-cedure of turning off fire-alarm bells at night to prevent false alarms ("30 Safety Violations" 1978). Whether it be in manufactured products or in accommoda-tions, volence against the consumer may be the result of an organization's policies and practices.

Violence in the workplace is also related to organizational wrongdoing. For example, in the United States illegal working conditions are the cause of 30 percent of on-the-job injuries; and another 24 percent are due to legal but unsafe conditions. Both accidents and diseases are related to safety and the workplace in Canada. Elliot Leyton's *Dying Hard* vividly portrays the violent deaths from industrial diseases that workers in St. Lawrence's fluorspar mines suffer (Leyton 1975). More recently, Lloyd Tataryn extensively documents the diseases perpetrated by companies dealing with asbestos, uranium, and arsenic in Canada (Tataryn 1979; McQuaig 1980; pp. 45–50). Much of this suffering resulted from the lack of proper safety and health standards and/or from the lack of their enforcement. The Saint Johns Calgary Report of 15 January 1979 points out that 50 percent of the workers exposed to asbestos die of cancer, compared with 25 percent of the general population. In Alberta, annual construction accidents rose from 15,076 in 1970 to 27,920 in 1977, with more than 280,568 working days lost in 1977 because of accidents and over $29 million paid in compensation. There are forty-eight occupational-health inspection officers in the province, and, at any given time, an estimated 10,000 construction sites. In order to visit each site biweekly, each officer would have to make twenty visits a day. In 1977, of 16,761 sites inspected there were 9,883 violations, none of which were prosecuted. Of forty-eight charges made against all industries for 1977 violations of the Occupational Health and Safety Regulations of Alberta, eight led to convictions. Only fines were levied, ranging from $300 to $3,500, but with five being less than $800 (Ross 1979). Undoubtedly, many of the deaths and injuries were due to improper safety standards. Stringent standards and vigorous enforcement, coupled with stiff penalties, can deter such crimes and their subsequent violent effects. The same type of deterrence can be used to combat occupational disease (Pearson 1978; see also George 1976; Glasbeek and Rowland 1979). This real health hazard has been the result of a combination of poor (or no) standards and laxity of enforcement. The likelihood of asbestos workers dying at the hands of a street assailant is minuscule compared with the real violence to which they may be exposed daily. In a 1975 case, the owner of a Hamilton building site was fined $100 for excavating without proper bracing after three workers died when a pit wall collapsed. Thus violation of the safety codes that killed three workers only resulted in a fine of $100. The assault on the worker will be continued until collective efforts are made to reduce it (Reasons, Peterson, and Ross 1981).

The general public is exposed to organizational crimes when the environment is polluted or potential hazards are posed. For example, the environmental section of *Maclean's*, 2 October 1978, notes that in St. Pierre Jolys, Manitoba, there are 300 tons of lethal rat poisoning stored in the city, contrary to government law. Where are polychlorinated biphenyls (PCBs) and other toxic wastes stored? Are they stored according to regulations, and are the regulations adequate? What pollutants are being emitted in the air, on the ground, and in the water—and what is being done about it? Penalties for pollution appear to be minuscule and not a deterrent (Good 1971).

When alleged defects in manufactured products or violation of safety standards are investigated and substantiated, they are usually interpreted as quirks or accidents with possible civil, but not criminal, liability. In Quebec, about 45 construction workers die on the job each year while approximately 13,500 are injured. According to Real Mireault, head of the Quebec Construction office, "Employers should stop blaming accidents on workers and instead enforce safety regulations and give their employees safety training" ("Workers Accident Rate" 1976).

Although persons might use the threat of violence in robbery, they seldom employ it. Likewise, the probability of injuries and deaths from organizational crime may be low in relation to the number of offenses. Nonetheless, although both types of offenses periodically result in injury and death, only street crimes bear the brunt of full prosecution. For example, mercury poisoning from the Dryden Chemical Plant in Northwestern Ontario is evident among native people in the area; but this is unlikely to lead to criminal charges (Singer and Rodgers 1975). Such a decision is based largely on legal conceptions of causation, intent, and culpability, all of which mitigate corporate responsibility. Nonetheless, physical harm, injury, and often death result from this disease. Whether death or injury occurs at the hands of an assailant in a face-to-face encounter, or is due to poisoning and disease caused by an impersonal corporation, the end result is similar.

We know very little about such organizational harms. It is imperative that we direct more attention to this area because we are all consumers, workers, and members of the general public. It is increasingly evident that our bodily safety will be more secure if we attack these types of harms, which are much more likely to harm us than the acts of rapists, muggers, or other assailants. Such organizational harms necessitate a new approach toward culpability. Although manufacturers or construction companies do not necessarily intend to harm persons by producing substandard products or maintaining unsafe and un-healthy workplaces, they provide the basis for such physical harm to occur. Therefore, any harm that does occur as the consequence of such violations should be dealt with severely. Strict liability laws and/or the use of criminal negligence would provide the impetus to deter such crimes, coupled with better policing and prosecution. Establishment of national safety and health standards with criminal penalties and provision for large fines would also be helpful. The crisis in the workplace that is increasingly being recognized in the United States needs greater attention in Canada (Ashford 1977). Workers should have access to medical research done by employers and should participate in establishing and policing regulations. Furthermore, they should have the right to refuse work that is unsafe and/or unhealthy, with no threat of recrimination. Increasing attention must be paid to consumer safety, product standards, and pollution standards, and to their enforcement. Although the physical harms mentioned here may not be dramatic, they are nonetheless taking their yearly toll in human life and suffering.

## Conclusion

The major issues to be resolved include determining the extent and nature of white-collar and organizational crimes and how best to combat them; initiation of action to attack these crimes of the powerful; and development of a appropriate approach to using the criminal law for organizational liability, for example, a concept of strict liability. Canada must commit itself to addressing crimes of the powerful more adequately through more research, better laws, vigorous enforce-ment of current laws, and recognition of harms done by organizations to our economy, human rights, and physical safety. By fostering comprehensive and demanding standards in the area of organizational harms, Canada will join the international community in recognizing the ever increasing power and effect large organizations have over our lives and the need to control this power adequately.

## Notes

1. As will become evident in the subsequent discussion, some of these are harms that in my opinion warrant criminalization.

2. This discussion is based on Barry N. Crump, "Freedom of Information Legislation in Canada: Discretionary Secrecy, Political Deviance and Surreptitious Labeling" (Paper presented to the session on the Sociology of Legal Control, Annual Meeting of the Canadian Sociology and Anthropology Association, London, Ontario, 29 May–1 June 1978.

## References

Ashford, Nicholas Askounes. *Crisis in the Workplace; Occupational Disease and Injury.* Cambridge, Mass.: MIT Press, 1977.

Barton, Peter G. "Civilian Review Boards and the Handling of Complaints Against the Police." *University of Toronto Law Journal* 20(1970):448–469.

Benedict, Michael. "Past Imperfect, Future Tense." *The Canadian,* 3 February 1979, pp. 4–6.

Borovoy, A. Allan. "Denial of Civil Liberties by Police in Canada." *Canadian Labour,* 16 September 1977, pp. 10–12.

Brown, Lorne, and Brown, Caroline. *An Unauthorized History of the RCMP.* Toronto: James Lorimer, 1973.

Burns, Peter. "Electronic Eavesdropping and the Federal Response: Cloning a Hybrid." *University of British Columbia Law Review* 10(1975–1976):36–63.

"Contracts May Have Been Tied to Donations Chairman." *Calgary Herald,* 18 January 1979, p. A22.

Craig, Ellis. "The Innocent Victims of a Police Action." *University of New Brunswick Law Journal* 26(1977):34–36.

Davies, Graham. "Ripping Off the Company." *Financial Times of Canada,* 10 July 1978a, pp. 1, 6.

——. "Corporate Theft." *Financial Times of Canada,* 17 July 1978b, pp. 2–3.

Dewar, Elaine. "Free?" *The Canadian,* 16 September 1978a, pp. 3–7.

——. "Free?" part 2. *The Canadian,* 23 September 1978b, pp. 11–14.

"Dredging Up a Harbour Scandal." *Time Canada,* 10 March 1975, pp. 6–7.

Ferguson, T.M. "Tax Talk." *Canadian Business Magazine* 50(October 1977):117.

Fisher, Hugo. "The Human Rights Covenants and Canadian Law." *Canadian Yearbook on International Law* 15(1977):42–83.

"Five Jailed for Bid-Rigging." *Calgary Herald,* 11 June 1979, p. 1.

"Ford Is Indicted on Criminal Counts over Pinto Deaths." *Globe and Mail,* 14 September 1978, p. 1.

Frideres, James F. *Canada's Indians: Contemporary Conflicts.* Scarborough: Prentice-Hall of Canada, 1975.

George, Anne. *Occupational Health Hazards to Women: A Synoptic View.* Ottawa: Advisory Council on the Status of Women, October 1976.

Glasbeek, Harry J., and Rowland, Susan. "Are Inquiry and Killing at Work Crimes?" *Osgoods Hall Law Journal* 17(December 1979):507–594.

Goff, C., and Reasons, C. "Corporations in Canada: A Study of Crime and Punishment." *Criminal Law Quarterly* 18(August 1976):468–498.

_____ . *Corporate Crime in Canada: Critical Analysis of Anti-Combines Legislation.* Scarborough: Prentice-Hall of Canada, 1978.

Goldenberg, Sydney L. "Crimes Against Humanity, 1945–1970." *Western Ontario Law Review* 10(1971):1–55.

Gonick, C. *Inflation or Depression.* Toronto: James Lorimer, 1975.

Good, P. "Anti-Pollution Legislation and Its Enforcement." *University of British Columbia Law Review* 6(1971):215–236.

Harlwood, Ed. "Cops and Corporate Robbers." *Canadian Business Magazine* 50 (May 1977):62–64, 66 ff.

Henshel, Richard L. "Controlling the Police Power." *Canadian Forum* 57(November 1977):11–13.

Jacobson, Philip, and Barnes, John. "£66 in Damages: The Car That Carried Death in the Book." *Sunday Times,* 12 February 1978, pp. 4 ff.

Jacoby, N.; Nehenkis, P.; and Ells, R. Bribery and Extortion in World Business." New York: Macmillan, 1977.

"Levi Strauss Fined $150,000 for Price Fixing." *Calgary Herald,* 31 January 1979, p. H7.

Lewis, Robert. "The Parliament Hill Mob." *Maclean's Magazine,* 11 July 1977, pp. 14–16.

Leyton, Elliott. *Dying Hard: The Ravages of Industrial Carnage.* Toronto: McClelland and Stewart, 1975.

Lorimer, James. "Land Grab." *The Canadian,* 2 December 1978, pp. 6–9.

Magee, David. "White Collar Crime—A High Risk Venture." *Canadian Commerce* 137(October 1973):26–28.

Mann, Edward, and Lee, John Alan. *The RCMP vs. the People.* Don Mills, Ont.: General Publishing Company, 1979.

Manning, Morris, and Bronson, Cecil. "Wiretapping: The Morality of Snooping." *Canadian Lawyer,* October 1977, pp. 24–29.

Manzer, Ronald. *Canada: A Socio-Political Report.* Toronto: McGraw-Hill Ryerson, 1974.

Mathias, Philip. "Hiding Cash Abroad to Escape Tax, Becoming a Popular Game?" *Financial Post* 68 (October 1974), p. 15.

_____ . "How Widespread Are (New Brunswick) Political Kickbacks?" *Financial Post* 28 71 May 1977, pp. 1, 4.

McDermott, Niale. "The Credibility Gap in Human Rights." *Dalhousie Law Journal* 3(1976–1977):262–274.

MacKay, A. Wayne. "Human Rights in Canadian Society: Mechanisms for Raising the Issues and Providing Redress." *Dalhousie Law Journal* 4(1978):739–779.

McQuaig, Linda. "Occupational Death." *Macleans Magazine,* 19 May 1980, pp. 45–50.

"9.3 Billion in Company Profits Helps NDP's Federal Inquiry Call." *Calgary Herald,* 7 February 1979, p. A3.

Oake, George. "Large Corporate Profits Enrage Labor." *Calgary Herald,* 8 February 1979, p. 1.

Parry, James. "Computer Theft: You May Be the Last to Know." *Canadian Business* 49(May 1976):63–70.

Pearson, Jessica S. "Organizational Response to Occupational Injury and Disease: The Case of the Uranium Industry." *Social Forces* 57(September 1978):23–41.

Plaskin, Robert. "Newfoundland B'ys Will Be B'ys." *Macleans Magazine,* May 1978, p. 28.

"R.C.M.P." *C.A.U.T. Bulletin* 35(October 1978):18 ff.

"RCMP Break-Ins Routine, Inquiry Told." *Calgary Herald,* 26 June 1980, p. 1.

Reasons, Charles E.; Paterson, Craig; and Ross, Lois L. *Assault on the Worker: Occupational Safety and Health in Canada.* Toronto: Butterworth, 1981.

Reasons, C.E., and Perdue, W.D. *The Ideology of Social Problems.* Sherman Oaks, Calif.: Alfred Publishing Company, 1981.

*Report of the Royal Commission on Corporate Concentration.* Ottawa: Minister of Supply and Services Canada, March 1978.

Ross, Lois L. "Those Daring Young Men on the Skyscraper Beams." *Saint Johns Calgary Report,* 16 February 1979, pp. 14–15.

Schrager, Laura Shill, and Short, James F. "Toward A Sociology of Organizational Crime." *Social Problems* 26(1978):411–412.

Singer, Gail, and Rodgers, Bob. "Mercury: The Hidden Poison in the Northern Rivers." *Saturday Night,* October 1975, pp. 15–22.

Smith, J.A. Clarence. "The Invasion of Privacy by Electronic Listening Devices." *Colloque International De Droit Compare* 8(1970):205–210.

Snider, D. Laureen. "Corporate Crime in Canada: A Preliminary Report." *Canadian Journal of Criminology* 20(April 1978):142–168.

Stewart, Walter. "Entrapment: Should a Policeman Encourage Thievery to Catch a Thief?" *Macleans Magazine,* October 1970, p. 8.

"Sugar Trio Wins Supreme Court Battle." *Calgary Albertan,* 20 July 1980, p. 17.

Tataryn, Lloyd. *Dying for a Living: The Politics of Industrial Death.* Montreal: Deneau and Greenberg Publishers, 1979.

"30 Safety Violations Found after Hotel Fire." *Calgary Herald,* 5 October 1978, p. 1.

Title, Morris M. "Canadian Wiretap Legislation: Protection or Erosion of Privacy." *Chitty's Law Journal* 26(1978):47–49.

Ungea, Harlow. "American Report: Bribes: Just a Fact of Life for Corporations."
    *Canadian Business* 49(August 1976):22.
Urquhart, Ian. "The Skyshops Five." *Macleans Magazine,* 3 May 1976, pp. 19–21.
──── . "The Bucks Start Here—Behind Every Great Leader Is an Equally Great
    Bagman." *Macleans Magazine,* 15 May 1978, p. 44.
Weissman, Tom. "Float of Stolen Stocks and Bonds $27 Million or More."
    *Financial Post,* 29 March 1975, p. 23.
"Workers Accident Rate Excessive." *Calgary Herald,* 10 June 1976, p. 13.

# Part II
# Organizational and Structural Concomitants and Consequences

## Introduction

The chapters in part II analyze corporate crime as a function of organizational and structural factors. As Kramer points out in chapter 5, corporate crime is organizational behavior. He provides a theoretical framework of the organizational characteristics for consideration, using the Ford Motor Company and its Pinto safety problems as illustration. His contention is that the goals, type of structure, and environment are organizational characteristics relevant to the probability of corporate crime.

In chapter 6, Susan Long uses quantitative analysis to test the impressionistic assumption that the developing underground economy—fueled by a heavy tax burden and inflation—has contributed to income-tax noncompliance. Her statistical comparison of data from Internal Revenue Service (IRS) returns and national income figures from Department of Commerce surveys shows an uncertain relationship between the growth in the subterranean economy and noncompliance. Apparently, we will have to look beyond such simplistic models if we are to tap the effects of the reported taxpayers' revolt.

The remaining chapters in part II focus more explicitly on the relevance of political economy to white-collar and economic offenses. In chapter 7, Łoś analyzes the contradictions between communist economic theory and practice to show how economic crime is inevitable at many levels of the economy. The political constraints on economic activity create both the behavior and the social-legal definition of it as criminal, making crime necessary to cope with the artificial and unrealistic aspects of the political ideology. Łoś thus takes us beyond Sutherland's focus on the values of the actors to see, for example, how political decisions can make it necessary for economic organizations to become corrupt merely to conduct ordinary transactions with some success.

Block, in chapter 8, provides cross-national analyses of economic crime as a function of types of societal organizations, especially capitalist ones. Using theft as the crime for analysis, he finds, contrary to "radical" theory, no reason to believe that more "collective control over resources or a greater degree of equality in income distribution" would lead to less crime. Snider's critique of Block (chapter 9), stresses the inadequacies of his data and the erroneous assumptions of his quantitative analyses, and also contends that his version of Marxist theory of crime verges on the simplistic. She briefly sets forth alternative explanations, including cultural change, and a more-complex Marxist perspective to argue that the two factors on which Block relies—public ownership and in-equality—may not be theoretically adequate for the problem of explaining theft-rate variations between capitalist and socialist nations.

In chapter 10 Barnett discusses the reproduction, historically, of corporate crime under capitalism, and focuses on the conflict between material output and enforcement benefits. The three areas of product safety, environmental protec-tion, and antitrust and labor violations are analyzed from the point of view of the relative costs, and the different bearers of these costs, under various enforce-ment policies. Given structural limits on the severity of legal constraints, Barnett asks whether capitalism and crime are inevitably linked. He proposes that a more "participatory economic democracy" would lead to a positive change in this link.

# 5 Corporate Crime: An Organizational Perspective

*Ronald C. Kramer*

*[T]he nation's leading corporations are committing destructive acts against man and nature. Specifically, all of this is being done systematically and repeatedly, rather than randomly and occasionally. The crimes are being committed as a standard operating procedure. In order to insure profits at a minimum of expense, these corporations are willfully engaging in crime. The corporations themselves as legal entities, as well as some of the corporate officials who make specific decisions, are criminal. And what is most frightening is that once these systematic crimes become normal operating procedure, they are not the responsibility of any one individual in the corporation. Rather they are corporate crimes, in the sense that the corporation itself is criminal.*
—Marshall B. Clinard and Richard Quinney, *Criminal Behavior Systems*
(New York: Holt, Rinehart and Winston, 1973), p. 212.

In recent years there has been an upsurge of interest in the topic of corporate crime. Although we still lack a precise definition of the concept, it generally refers to the illegal and/or socially harmful acts (of omission or commission) engaged in by corporations themselves as legal entities. This definition is not restricted to violations of the criminal law only, but includes any corporate action that could be punished by the state, regardless of whether it is punished under administrative, civil, or criminal law.[1] Such a definition, it should be noted, excludes consideration of the occupational and economic crimes committed by high-status individuals for their own personal gain: acts that are normally included in the concept of white-collar crime (see Sutherland 1949, p. 9; Edelhertz 1970, pp. 3–4; Clinard and Quinney 1973). As Clinard points out, "corporate crime is, of course, white collar crime, but it is white collar crime of a particular type" (1979, p. xiii).

By *corporate crime*, therefore, I refer to illegal and/or socially harmful behaviors that result from deliberate decision making by corporate executives in accordance with the operative goals of their organizations. These corporate crimes, I argue, constitute one of the most-crucial problems facing our society

This is a revised version of a paper presented at the Conference on White Collar and Economic Crime: Trends and Problems in Research and Policy: Multidisciplinary and Cross-National Perspectives, held at SUNY College of Arts and Science, Potsdam, New York, 7–9 February 1980. This work was supported by a fellowship from the Faculty Research Fund, Western Michigan University.

today. Criminal acts by the nation's corporations cause greater social harm than any other type of crime. The economic costs alone of such corporate offenses as price fixing, consumer fraud, and monopolistic practices (to mention only a few) are immense. The late Senator Philip Hart once estimated that the annual cost of corporate crime was between $174 and $231 billion (Clinard 1979, p. 16). Ralph Nader (1978) has made similar estimates. These costs simply dwarf the economic costs of "street crimes" such as robbery and burglary, which are estimated to be between $3 and $4 billion a year (Conklin 1977).

The impact of corporate crime, however, is not limited to its economic costs. There are also serious "physical costs" associated with the criminal acts of corporations. Each year corporate crime is responsible for thousands of deaths and injuries (Clinard 1979; pp. 15-16; Reiman 1979, pp. 44-94). As with the economic costs of corporate offenses, these physical costs far exceed those caused by the more-traditional violent street crimes reported on the Federal Bureau of Investigation's (FBI's) Uniform Crime Reports. For example, over 100,000 deaths a year are attributed to occupationally related diseases, the majority of which are caused by the willful violation of health and safety laws by corporations (see Ashford 1976; Berman 1978; Page and O'Brien 1972; Swartz 1975, pp. 15-20; U.S. Department of Labor 1972). This compares with an average of 18,000 murders and nonnegligent manslaughters per year reported on by the FBI during the 1970s.

Employees are not the only victims of corporate crimes. The general public is often victimized simply by being in an environment made unsafe by corporate acts. As Schrager and Short (1978) have noted, the "potential impact ranges from acute environmental catastrophes such as the collapse of a dam to the chronic effects of diseases resulting from industrial pollution (p. 415). Consumers are a segment of the general public who are victimized by corporate violence. It has been estimated that approximately 20 million serious injuries annually are associated with consumer products, with 110,000 resulting in permanent disability and 30,000 resulting in death (Schrager and Short 1978). As Clinard (1979) has concluded: "Far more persons are killed through corporate criminal activities than by individual criminal homicides; even if death is an indirect result, the person still died" (p. 16).

The case of the Ford Pinto illustrates dramatically that the physical costs of corporate wrongdoing can be enormous. Hundreds of people have died or suffered severe burn injuries because Pinto automobiles have a design defect that causes the gasoline tank to explode and burn on rear-end impact (Dowie 1977; CBS News 1978). Internal Ford documents show that the company knew of the design defect, but that it went ahead and manufactured the car anyway, and then kept it on the road for eight years without making the changes needed to make it safe (Dowie 1977).

The Ford Motor Company has lost numerous civil suits concerning deaths and injuries that have resulted from Pinto crashes. One California jury awarded a young Pinto burn victim $125 million in *punitive damages* (Dowie 1978, p. 52; Harris 1978, p. 1; Jacobson and Barnes 1978, p. 1; Gamlin 1978). In May 1978 the U.S. Department of Transportation (1978) made a finding of a safety defect in Pinto fuel tanks. In June of that year, the National Highway Traffic Safety Administration forced Ford to recall some 2 million Pinto automobiles because of the defect (Kelderman 1978; Karr and Apcar 1978). Then, in September 1978, an Elkhart County, Indiana, grand jury returned a criminal indictment charging the Ford Motor Company with three counts of reckless homicide (Sharp 1978). These charges stemmed from the deaths of three teenage women in a 1973 Pinto that exploded and burned when it was struck from behind by a van near Elkhart on 10 August 1978.

Although the Ford Motor Company was acquitted in this particular case (primarily because the judge severely restricted the amount of evidence that could be presented to the jury [Lenhoff 1980]), the fact that this indictment was even issued is highly significant. The indictment and the trial, along with the other official actions taken against the Ford Motor Company in connection with the Pinto, demonstrate that many people in our society are coming to recognize the serious physical costs associated with corporate crime, and that they feel something needs to be done to control the behavior of corporations. This growing public concern about the seriousness of corporate crime was underscored in a recent column by Jack Anderson. He referred to the increased awareness by the people of the United States, as well as by lawmakers, that the consequences of illegal actions by big-business executives can be more deadly than even those of well-publicized mass murders. He also noted the growing public demand for corporate executives—whose decisions, although motivated by profit, nevertheless result in death and injury to thousands—to face sanctions at least as severe as those meted out to the "street kid" who holds up the neighborhood merchant (Anderson 1980).

Given the great social harm caused by corporate violence, there is an obvious need for our society to devise more-adequate controls over corporate behavior. Corporate offenses have traditionally been dealt with by administrative and civil laws and penalties. Many legal scholars, however, have begun to reevaluate the methods used to control corporations, and a number of them recommend the use of criminal sanctions (Elkins 1976; Kriesberg 1976; McVisk 1978; "Developments in the Law" 1979; Stone 1975; Yoder 1978). As Elkins (1976) puts it, "The social good now demands the use of all available means to control corporate power, including the use of criminal sanctions (p. 73).

I argue, however, that society will not be able to devise more-adequate social controls of any kind over illegal corporate behavior until we develop some empirically based theoretical explanations of this complex social phenomenon. As Kriesberg (1976) has argued, "effective legal policy concerning corporate crime must be found on an understanding of the decision-making process underlying corporate action" (p. 1092). At present, neither criminologists nor legal policymakers understand that decision-making process very well. Kriesberg contends further that there is a basic problem that stems from the law not having been founded on a clear perception of the process of decision making that it must mold if it is to deter corporate illegality. Although lawmakers and judicial officials have their own conceptions of how such illegality occurs, when it comes to formulating a regulatory statute or reviewing admissible evidence, they work within certain assumptions with respect to the occurrence of corporate crime and the most effective deterrence of such illegality. Nevertheless, legal policy fails to be based empirically on an analysis of the corporate decision-making process that details the actual patterns and strategies of deterrence implicit in such assumptions . Consequently, since the assumptions of legal policymakers may often be untested, or not clearly articulated, and decisions grounded upon these assumptions may often be misdirected (Kriesberg 1976, p. 1099).

The challenge to criminologists, therefore, is clear: to develop empirically based explanations of corporate decision making and illegal organizational behavior. The purpose of this chapter is to make a contribution to that effort by developing a preliminary theoretical framework for the study of corporate crime.

### Previous Theory and Research on Corporate Crime

The first empirical study of corporate crime was carried out by Edwin Sutherland (1949). He reviewed the records of seventy large corporations and found that each corporation had one or more "decisions" (administrative, civil, or criminal) made against it. Sutherland attempted to explain these violations through his theory of differential association:

> The data which are at hand suggest that white collar crime has its genesis in the same general process as other criminal behavior, namely, differential association. The hypothesis of differential association is that criminal behavior is learned in association with those who define such behavior favorably and in isolation from those who define it unfavorably, and that a person in an appropriate situation engages in such criminal behavior if, and only if, the weight of the favorable definitions exceeds the weight of the unfavorable definitions [1949, p. 234]

Other research on corporate crime has found support for the theory of differential associations. Clinard (1946) in his study of violations of wartime regulations, noted that many of these violations could be explained satisfactorily by a theory of differential association, although he did identify several "limitations" in the perspective. In a study of regulatory violations in the New England shoe industry, Lane (1953) observed that his results seemed to confirm the differential-association hypothesis. Finally, Geis (1967), in his analysis of the heavy-electrical-equipment price-fixing case concluded that "many of Sutherland's ideas concerning the behavior of corporate offenders . . . receive substantiation (p. 150).

Recently, behavioral scientists have attempted to move beyond Sutherland by identifying other significant social-psychological factors that may be related to corporate crime. Monahan and Novaco (1979), for example, have attempted to derive testable hypotheses concerning corporate violence by drawing on the existing research on individual violence and aggression. They have also examined research on moral reasoning, moral development, and moral behavior as a source of hypotheses that could be applied to corporate criminality (Monahan and Novaco 1979).

The major problem with Sutherland's differential-association theory, as with the psychological analysis of Monahan and Novaco, is that individuals remain the unit of analysis. Corporate crime is *organizational* crime, and its explanation calls for an *organizational* level of analysis.[2] Theories that focus on social-psychological learning processes involving corporate executives cannot adequately explain why corporations as social and legal entities violate the law. As Schrager and Short (1978) point out:

> Preoccupation with individuals can lead us to underestimate the pressures within society and organizational structure, which impel those individuals to commit illegal acts. . . . Recognizing structural forces . . . does not negate the importance of interaction between individuals. . . . It serves to emphasize organizational . . . etiological factors, and calls for a macrosociological . . . level of explanation. [p. 410]

There have been repeated calls for the development of an organizational perspective on corporate crime (Ermann and Lundman 1978a, b; Gross 1978, 1980; Reiss 1966; Schrager and Short 1978; Wheeler 1976). In fact, prior research has touched on some of the structural and organizational factors related to corporate crime. Sutherland (1949), for example, did note that the corporation's position in the economic structure has great significance in the variations among the corporations as to the number of violations of law (p. 259). Lane (1953), in his study of the New England industrial shoe firms, focused on the structure of the corporation and its industry-wide position as these related to lawbreaking activity (pp. 152–154). Geis (1967) pointed out that extrinsic conditions such as the condition of the market and the level of enforcement activity influenced the price-fixing agreements in the heavy-electrical-equipment industry (p. 150). Finally, Leonard and Weber (1970), in their study of criminogenic market forces in the auto industry, highlighted the importance of market structure to corporate criminal behavior. No one, however, has developed a systematic organizational perspective on corporate crime.

Future work in the area of corporate crime in general, and corporate violence in particular, will have to develop, more systematically, an organizational framework for analyzing corporate lawbreaking, and provide an empirical evaluation of the utility of that framework for explaining these behaviors. This paper represents a preliminary attempt to develop and apply such a framework. It will be developed from materials drawn from the extensive literature on the sociology of organizations and illustrated with data taken from a preliminary analysis of the Ford Pinto case.

## Organizational Factors Related to Corporate Crime

An organizational perspective on corporate crime assumes that behavior in corporations is organizationally based. That is, organizational factors are viewed as playing an important part in determining how individuals within a corporation will act. Hall (1977) has made this argument with regard to organizational decision making:

> Many decisions in organizations . . . are organizational decisions. That is, the organization has set the parameters for decision-making and the individual simply follows the procedures that have been prescribed for him. These rather programmed types of decisions are usually at a low level. But more important decisions about future organizational directions and policies are also strongly influenced by organizational factors. The whole area of tradition and precedent, power position within the organization, and the organization's relationship with its environment have an impact on how individuals within the organizational hierarchy make decisions on behalf of the organization. Organizational considerations thus pervade the decision-making process. [p. 26]

The task for criminologists is to identify and examine the organizational factors that account for the illegal and/or socially harmful acts of individuals within corporations on behalf of the corporations themselves. In order to identify these organizational factors, we must develop a more-specific definition of organizations. This paper adopts the definition formulated by Hall (1977):

> An organization is a collectivity with a relatively identifiable boundary, a normative order, ranks of authority, communications systems, and membership-coordinating systems; this collectivity exists on a relatively continuous basis in an environment and engages in activities that are usually related to a goal or a set of goals. [pp. 22–23]

This definition recognizes the complexity of organizations and identifies some of the diverse elements and factors that make them up. Three of these factors are hypothesized to have a significant relationship to corporate criminal behavior: (1) the goals of the organization; (2) the structure of the organization; (3) the environment of the organization. The nature of each of these organizational factors and its influence on the illegal actions of corporations will be examined in this section.

*Organizational Goals*

Since all organizations are justified and evaluated in terms of their success or failure in goal attainment, an analysis of organizational behavior (of any kind) must focus on the concept of organizational goals. The focus on goals is seen by most sociologists as the central characteristic of organizations (Blau and Scott 1962; Etzioni 1964; Hau 1977; Parsons 1963; Perrow 1961). Even though there are a number of problems with the concept of organizational goals, the analysis of corporate crime must begin with an examination of the nature of organizational goals and their consequences for organizational behavior.

Organizational goals are essentially abstractions that are distilled from the desires of members and from environmental and internal pressures. Perrow argues that these abstract values must be translated into more-specific directives in order for the organization to act. He distinguishes between "official" and "operative" organizational goals. According to Perrow (1961), official goals are "the general purposes of the organization as put forth in the charter, annual reports, public statements and other authoritative pronouncements." (p. 855). On the other hand, operative goals "designate the ends sought through the actual operating policies of the organization; they tell us what the organization actually is trying to do, regardless of what the official goals say are the aims" (p. 855). Assuming that we can determine the operative goals of corporations, how do these organizational goals influence the commission of criminal acts by corporations?

One answer to this question has been advanced recently by Edward Gross (1978). He argues that all organizations are *inherently criminogenic*. By this he means "that there is built into the very structure of organizations an inherent inducement for the organization itself to engage in crime" (p. 56). This inherent inducement is the organization's commitment to goal attainment. As Gross (1978) points out:

> as arrangements which are committed to goal attainment or perform-
> ance, organizations will often find themselves in difficulties. They live
> in competitive environments, even in socialist society, in which there
> are always insecurities, and uncertainties in supplies, money, sales, and
> security support. . . . Given a situation of uncertainty in attaining goals,
> and one in which the organization is judged (directly, or indirectly by
> sales or other indicators) by its success in goal attainment or perform-
> ance, one can predict that the organization will, if it must, engage in
> criminal behavior to attain these goals. [p. 57]

Following this perspective, one can argue that corporate criminality is related to the primary goal of business corporations in a capitalistic economy: profit maximization.[3] Numerous studies have suggested that "pressure for profits" is the single most compelling factor behind business crime (Conklin 1977). As Balkan, Berger, and Schmidt (1980) note: "Corporations exist to make profits. A corporation must accumulate and grow, or be surpassed by competitors and destroyed. Any means to this goal is considered acceptable"

(p. 175). Clinard (1979), too, argues that the "desire to increase profits provides one explanation for a wide range of corporate deviance, from refusal to install pollution control equipment to well planned decisions to produce a shoddy product that will wear out and then need to be replaced" (p. 57). He also points out:

> certain industries, as for example the drug and chemical industries, are characterized by severe competition and strong profit drives that are linked to demands for continuous innovation of new products. Under these conditions, the pressures to falsify test data, market new products before their full effects are known, or engage in unethical sales techniques can have disastrous results on human beings as well as on the environment [p. 7]

The Ford Motor Company's decision to manufacture and keep on the market an automobile (the Pinto) that it knew to be unsafe was clearly influenced by the profit goals of the corporation. First of all, during the late 1960s Ford became concerned with the rising number of imports sold in the United States. Fearing that its foreign competitors were going to capture the entire U.S. subcompact market, Ford rushed its new subcompact (the Pinto) into production. To have the Pinto ready for the 1971 model year, Ford shortened the product-development process from 43 months to 25 months (Dowie 1977, pp. 20–21). The shortening of this process meant that Ford was already tooled up for production when the design defect was discovered (Dowie 1977, pp. 20–21). Since tooling up the assembly-line machinery is very expensive, Ford would have suffered severe financial problems by changing the design of the Pinto at that late date. Ford officials, therefore, decided to go ahead and manufacture a car they knew to be defective, rather than suffer a loss in profits by changing it.

Furthermore, Ford officials made an explicit decision to continue to manufacture the Pinto without making changes in it, based on a "cost-benefit analysis" that said it would not be profitable to make the safety changes (see table 5-1). In this internal cost-benefit analysis, Ford actually placed a dollar value on human life (Grush and Saunby 1973). This document clearly demonstrates that "pressure for profits" directly influenced Ford's decisions with respect to the Pinto.

Profit maximization is not, of course, the only organizational goal that influences corporate behavior. Product-characteristic goals also appear to be important. According to Perrow (1970), goals regarding the characteristics of products—quality, quantity, type, cost, styling, and so on—do have an important effect on organizational behavior. In many cases, these product goals are the "subgoals" into which the more-abstract profit goal has been translated. These product goals exert a great deal of pressure on people in lower level of the organization. Furthermore, as Perrow has noted, many organizational actors

**Table 5-1**
**Benefits and Costs Relating to Fuel Leakage Associated with the Static Rollover Test Portion of FMVSS.208**

| Benefits | Costs |
|---|---|
| Savings: 180 burn deaths, 180 serious burn injuries, 2,100 burned vehicles. | Sales: 11 million cars, 1.5 million light trucks. |
| Unit cost: $200,000 per death, $67,000 per injury, $700 per vehicle. | Unit cost: $11 per car, $11 per truck. |
| Total benefit: 180 × ($200,000) + 180 × ($67,000) + 2,100 × ($700) = $49.5 million. | Total cost: 11,000,000 × ($11) + 1,500,000 × ($11) = $137 million. |

Source: E.S. Grush and C.S. Saunby, "Fatalities Associated with Crash Induced Fuel Leakage and Fires," Interoffice memorandum, Ford Motor Company, 1973, p. 6.

become committed to the product goals; they then can take on the character of vested interests:

> When an organization adopts a certain strategy with regard to product characteristics, or finds that it has such a strategy, a great number of interests become invested in this way of doing its job, and the strategy takes on the character of an independent, autonomous goal [1970, p. 159]

The Ford Motor Company's commitment to certain product goals concerning the Pinto automobile seems to have played a major role in its decisions about the manufacture of that car. The product objectives for the Pinto were clearly stated in the Pinto "green book," a thick, top-secret manual that contains a step-by-step production plan for the model (Dowie 1977, pp. 21–22). These product goals were also contained in a paper by Ford executive F.G. Olsen (1971), published by the Society of Automotive Engineers. Two of the most-important product goals for the Pinto were: (1) it was to weigh less than 2,000 pounds and 2) it was to cost less than $2,000. Because of the pressures exerted to attain these goals, several important safety modifications were rejected because they added weight and cost to the car (Dowie 1977, p. 22). Safety was not a product goal for the Ford Pinto automobile.

In summary, then, I have argued that the analysis of corporate crime must begin with an examination of the nature of organizational goals and their consequences for organizational behavior. Following Gross, I have hypothesized that organizations, as arrangements committed to goal attainment, will engage in criminal behavior if they encounter serious difficulties in attaining their goals (especially profit goals). I have also suggested that product-characteristic goals may also help to shape the decision-making process that leads to corporate criminal acts. Organizational goals, however, never stand alone as factors related to corporate crime. They must always be linked to both the internal structure of the corporation and its environment, as we will see in the next two sections.

## Organizational Structure

A second organizational factor that needs to be taken into account in the analysis of corporate crime is the internal structure of the corporation. The relationship between organizational structure and illegal corporate behavior must be examined if we are to understand and control corporate criminality. By organizational structure, sociologists usually mean "the distributions, along various lines, of people among social positions that influence the role relations among these people" (Blau 1974). The structure of an organization, therefore, refers to such things as the division of labor, the hierarchy of authority, and the normative system, among others. Organizational structure, according to Hall (1977) serves two basic functions:

> First, structures are designed to minimize or at least regulate the influence of individual variations on the organization. Structure is imposed to ensure that individuals conform to the requirements of the organization and not vice versa. Second, structure is the setting in which power is exercised (structure also sets or determines which positions have power in the first place), in which decisions are made (the flow of information which goes into a decision is largely determined by structure), and in which the organization's activities are carried out. [p. 102]

Organizational structure is related to corporate crime in a number of ways. First of all, the internal structure of the organization may have a significant impact on the organization's goals. For example, Stone (1975) has suggested that the organizational structure may translate the profit goal into more-specific subgoals within the corporation, the attainment of which requires or leads to criminal behavior.

> As corporations become more complex, they tend to subdivide into various departments according to geographical divisions (manufacturing areas and distribution territories), functionally defined groups (finance, sales, advertising, legal), and so on. The central organization cannot leave each of these groups at large to realize "profit" as it sees best. Rather, the farther and farther down the operational ladder one moves, the more the "profit goal" has to be translated into subgoals—targets and objectives for the shop, the department, the plant, the division, the subsidiary. It is these subgoals that define the task environment of the people actually engaged in production at such a plant, not some abstract "corporate profit" [p. 43]

It appears that the organizational structure of the Ford Motor Company translated an abstract profit goal into more-specific subgoals within the corporation: the product-characteristic goals discussed in the previous section. These subgoals (the Pinto was to weigh less than 2,000 pounds and cost less than $2,000) defined the task environment of the people engaged in the production of the Pinto; and attainment of these subgoals required the rejection of safety modifications to the car.

The relationship of organizational structure to corporate crime, however, goes far beyond the influencing of corporate goals. As Cressey (1976) notes:

> Perhaps the persistence in outlawed behavior is related to the corporate form itself, as well as to the attitudes and behavior patterns of corporation directors. Thus, it is possible that corporation crime, like Cosa Nostra crime, persists because it is "organized," meaning that it is perpetuated by an apparatus rather than by individuals occupying positions in the division of labor constituting the apparatus.

This suggests that criminality may be rooted in the corporate structure itself. For example, a number of criminologists have argued that there is a relationship between the internal normative system of a corporation and corporate violations of the law. Ermann and Lundman (1978b) assert that an important element of all organizational crime is that it "must find support in the norms of a given level or division of the organization" (p. 57). Furthermore, they argue that "the action must be known to and supported by the dominant administrative coalition of the organization" (p. 57). Clinard and Quinney (1967) also argue that "lawbreaking can become a normative pattern within certain corporations, and violation norms may be shared between corporations and their executives (p. 213).

The Ford Motor Company's decision to manufacture and keep on the market a car that it knew to be unsafe can be analyzed in terms of the internal normative system at Ford: the way in which certain norms were built into the structure that supported those norms. For example, it appears that safety was not a strongly held norm at Ford, that it was not a part of the role prescription of Ford engineers or executives, and that a concern for safety was negatively sanctioned. Dowie illustrated this in an interview with a Ford engineer:

> When it was discovered the gas tank was unsafe, did anyone go to Iacocca (the President of Ford) and tell him? "Hell no," replied an engineer who worked on the Pinto, a high company official for many years, who, unlike several others at Ford, maintains a necessarily clandestine concern for safety. "That person would have been fired. Safety wasn't a popular subject around Ford in those days. With Lee (Iacocca) it was taboo" . . . "So you see," continued the anonymous Ford engineer ironically, "there are a few of us here at Ford who are concerned about fire safety." He adds: "They are mostly engineers who have to study a

lot of accident reports and look at pictures of burned people. But we don't talk about it much. It isn't a popular subject. I've never seen safety on the agenda of a product meeting and, except for a brief period in 1956, I can't remember seeing the word safety in an advertisement. I really don't think the company wants American consumers to start thinking too much about safety—for fear they might demand it, I suppose."[a]

Normative expectations built into organizational roles shape the premises of decision making within corporations and, therefore, shape behavior (Simon 1957). It is not that Ford officials wanted to build an unsafe car, but that they made decisions about the Pinto based on certain premises (safety doesn't sell, production deadlines must be met, product objectives must be followed, and so forth) that are organizationally determined. As Perrow (1979) notes, such "premises are to be found in the 'vocabulary' of the organization, the structure of communication, rules and regulations and standard programs, selection criteria for personnel, and so on—in short, in the structural aspects (p. 149).

In addition to the influence of organizational norms, roles, and rewards, another structural feature of corporations that appears to be related to criminal behavior is that of *organizational level.* Given the elaborate hierarchy of authority within most corporations, important decisions may be made at different levels within the organization. As Clinard (1979) points out, the decentralizatin of decision making in the corporate structure may diffuse personal responsibility for deadly decisions:

> Their mammoth size, combined with the growth trends of diversification and merger, require that corporations decentralize their decision making structures and operating procedures in order to produce efficiently. Decentralization is, almost by definition, accompanied by the establishment of elaborate hierarchies, based on authority position and functional duties. This allows the abdication of personal responsibility for almost every type of decision, from the most inconsequential to those that may have a great impact on the lives of thousands. [p. 7]

As Clinard goes on to note:

> Under these conditions almost any type of corporate criminality, from production of faulty or dangerous products to bribery, bid-rigging and even theft is possible. Executives at the higher levels can absolve themselves of responsibility by rationalizing that the operationalization of their broadly stated goals has been carried out, without their knowledge. A sharp split can develop between what the upper levels believe is going on below and the actual procedures being carried out below. There may even be genuine ignorance about the production level. It is also not

---

[a]Mark Dowie, "Pinto Madness," *Mother Jones* (September–October 1977):21. Reprinted with permission.

simply that the lower levels, for whatever reasons, do not wish to inform the higher ups; often the upper levels do not want to be told. Decentralization is also often accompanied by other potentially harmful processes. No single individual at the highest levels may make a decision to market a faulty product or take short cuts on product testing; instead, such decisions are made in small steps at each level. [p. 7]

Although it is difficult to document with currently available data, it does appear that such a diffusion of responsibility occurred with respect to the production of the Ford Pinto. The decision to manufacture and keep on the road a defective automobile was made in small steps at different levels within the corporate hierarchy at Ford. The structure, therefore, separated the men who were making these decisions from the consequences of their actions. The Ford executives who created the Pinto never had to confront the victims produced by their occupational decisions. As Jackall (1980) points out, "such depersonalization reinforces the avoidance of responsibility endemic to hierarchical, segmented structure" (p. 356).

In summary, then, I argued that the analysis of corporate crime must include an examination of the nature of the internal structure of the organization and the influence of this structure on organizational behavior. I suggested that the organizational structure may translate the abstract goals of the corporation into more-specific subgoals, the attainment of which requires or leads to criminal behavior. Following Ermann and Lundman, I hypothesized that illegal corporate behavior is supported by the normative system of a given level or division of the corporation, and that it is known to, or at least tacitly sanctioned by, the dominant administrative coalition of the corporation. In addition, I hypothesized that the decentralization of decision making within the corporation diffused responsibility for corporate decisions and makes illegal actions more likely to occur.

*Organizational Environment*

Formal organizations, such as business corporations, operate within a complex sociocultural environment. Corporate decisions and actions are shaped significantly by the environment in which the organization exists. As Aldrich (1979) has noted: "Many questions of interest to organizational sociologists today require a perspective on organizations that takes account not only of the internal structure of organizations but also the forces in their environments that set limits to organizational discretion" (p. 1). The environment of the corporation, therefore, is the third organizational factor that needs to be considered in the analysis of corporate crime.

The environment of an organization consists of any and all elements external to the organization, be they economic, political, cultural, technological, or interorganizational. Environmental elements influence corporate behavior not only directly but also indirectly through their impact on the internal structure and goals of the organization (Crozier 1964). The environment of the corporation, therefore, is significantly related to the commission of corporate crimes. As Clinard (1979) notes:

> It can be argued that the socio-cultural environment within which the modern American corporation operates may actually encourage criminal or deviant behavior. Corporate norms of doing business may conflict with one or several societal norms. A corporation that emphasized profits about business ethics and ignores corporate social responsibility to the community, the consumer, or to society is likely to have difficulties in complying with legal norms [p. 8]

Concerning the general environment of the corporation, two sets of conditions are of special significance. The first are economic conditions: The state of the economy in which the corporation is operating is crucial. The second set of conditions are legal conditions: Laws of all kinds are important external constraints on organizations. As Geis (1967) has pointed out in his analysis of the heavy-electrical-equipment price-fixing case, criminologists need to examine the influence of both of these general-environmental conditions on corporate criminal behavior:

> The ebb and flow of the price-fixing conspiracy also clearly indicates the relationship, often overlooked in explanations of criminal behavior, between extrinsic conditions and illegal acts. When the market behaved in a manner the executives thought satisfactory, or when enforcement agencies seemed particularly threatening, the conspiracy desisted. When market conditions deteriorated, while corporate pressures for achieving attractive profit and loss statements remained constant, and enforcement activity abated, the price-fixing agreements flourished. [p. 150]

As Geis indicates, market conditions are significantly related to corporate criminal acts. The market often imposes constraints on the attainment of corporate goals. Corporate crime results when management chooses to circumvent these market constraints in an illegal manner (Barnett 1980). In the Ford Pinto case, market conditions (the strong competition from Volkswagen and the Japanese automakers) pressured Ford to rush into the production of subcompact automobiles. As previously noted, this led to the shortening of the product-development process for the Pinto. When the design defect was discovered, it was too late (from Ford's point of view) to redesign the car without Ford suffering a huge financial loss due to retooling. Thus, market conditions did, indirectly, play a role in Ford's decision to manufacture a car that it knew to be unsafe.

In addition to market conditions, there are legal conditions that influence corporate crime. Laws are important external constraints on organizations. Hall (1977) notes that

> organizations must live with federal, state, and local laws as constraints in their environments. At the very least, they set many of the operating conditions of many organizations, ranging from specific prohibitions of certain kinds of behavior to regulations requiring reporting of income and staffing at periodic times of the year. [p. 306]

As Geis noted, the level and direction of law-enforcement and regulatory activity may discourage certain kinds of corporate lawbreaking while encouraging others. Lauderdale, Grasmick, and Clark (1979) have recently argued that "the fluctuation in corporate crime rates is a reflection of changes in constraints (threats) endogenous to corporate environments rather than changes in corporate action, per se" (p. 152). Federal regulation of the auto industry has, traditionally, been very lax. Constraints on corporate criminality, therefore, have been weak or nonexistent. At the time that Ford decided to produce the Pinto, there were no federal safety standards that applied to the Pinto's design problems. Furthermore, the National Highway Traffic Safety Administration was unable to exert much countervailing pressure on any of the auto makers with respect to the issue of safety. The absence of such pressure made it easier for Ford to disregard safety features in planning the production of the Pinto, and made it easier for Ford to keep the car on the market without changing its design defect.

Concerning the relationship between legal conditions and corporate behavior, it is important to note, as Hall (1977) does, that: "Among the strategies that organizations develop for dealing with their environments, a critical one is to attempt to share the environment itself" (p. 314). Corporations, of course, with their great social power, have the ability to shape their legal environments significantly. As Lauderdale, Grasmick, and Clark (1979) point out, when one examines the relationship between corporations and regulatory agencies "one becomes inescapably aware of the active role corporate bodies play in helping to shape the effect external threats have upon their action" (p. 154). In the Pinto case, Ford was able to control its legal environment very effectively and to neutralize various political forces that posed an external threat to the company's actions. For years Ford lobbied against the adoption of federal standards that would have required them to make design changes in the Pinto (Dowie 1977, pp. 23–32). Ford was able to use its great organizational power to neutralize the National Highway Traffic Safety Administration and to delay the passage of Federal Motor Vehicle Safety Standard (FMVSS) 301 for eight years while the company reaped enormous profits from a dangerously defective automobile.

In conclusion, this section has argued that the analysis of corporate crime must also include an examination of the environment of the corporation. Not only do environmental conditions influence illegal corporate behavior directly, but they do so indirectly as well through their impact on the goals and internal structure of the corporation. It was hypothesized that market conditions may operate as constraints on the attainment of corporate profit goals, pressuring corporations into illegal acts in the attempt to circumvent these constraints. It was also hypothesized that the absence of effective legal constraints may allow corporate violations to occur. Finally, it was argued that the analysis of corporate crime must also take into account the great power that corporations have to shape their legal environment significantly.

## Summary and Conclusion

This chapter represents a preliminary attempt to develop a theoretical framework for the study of corporate crime. Previous theory and research on this topic, with its focus on social-psychological learning processes involving corporate executives, has suffered from an individualistic bias. This chapter has argued that corporate crime is organizational crime and that its explanation therefore calls for an organizational level of analysis. Such a perspective argues that strictly organizational factors can account for much of the behavior of individuals without corporations. The task for criminologists is to identify and examine the organizational factors that account for illegal corporate behavior.

I have hypothesized that there are three major organizational factors that are related to the commission of corporate crimes: (1) organizational goals, (2) organizational structure, and (3) organizational environment. First, it was hypothesized that organizations, as arrangements committed to goal attainment, will engage in criminal behavior when they encounter serious difficulties in attaining goals. Second, it was hypothesized that illegal corporate behavior is: (1) supported by norms at a given level or division of the corporation and sanctioned (directly or indirectly) by the dominant administrative coalition of the corporation; and (2) made more probable when the decentralization of decision making within the organization diffuses responsibility for corporate decisions. Finally, it was hypothesized that general environmental conditions, such as economic market structures and law-enforcement activities, may pressure corporations into law violations (in the case of the former) or may fail to constrain or deter such violations adequately (in the case of the latter).

Some initial empirical support for these hypotheses was found in a preliminary analysis of the Ford Pinto case. Further research, of course, is needed to test and refine these hypotheses and to generate new hypotheses concerning the relationship between organizational factors and corporate crime. Given the great social harm (economic and physical) caused by illegal corporate acts, and the need to devise more-adequate social and legal controls over corporate behavior, such criminological research and theory development is urgently needed.

## Notes

1. This is the position taken by Sutherland (1949):

The essential characteristic of crime is that it is behavior which is prohibited by the State as an injury to the State against which the State
may react, at least as a last resort, by punishment. The two abstract
criteria generally regarded by legal scholars as necessary elements in a
definition of crime are legal description of an act as socially harmful
and legal provision of a penalty for the act. [p. 31]

Clinard (1979) has taken a similar position in his recent study, *Illegal
Corporate Behavior,* arguing that, "From a research point of view . . . corporate
crime includes any act punished by the state regardless of whether it is punished
under administrative, civil, or criminal law" (p. xvi).

2. It should be noted that one section of the Monahan and Novaco paper
does address an organizational level of analysis.

3. Concerning the primary goal of a business corporation, Conklin (1977)
quotes a corporate executive:

The goal of a business corporation is to make a profit . . . the only goal
of a business corporation is to make a profit . . . more fully, the only goal
of a business corporation is to make the maximum possible profit . . . .
Completely, the only goal of a business corporation is to make the
maximum possible profit over a long period of time. [p. 41]

## References

Aldrich, Howard E. *Organizations and Environments.* Englewood Cliffs, N.J.:
    Prentice-Hall, 1979.
Anderson, Jack. "Deadly Decisions by Profit-Seekers." *Detroit Free Press,* 10
    October 1980, p. 14.
Ashford, Nicholas A. *Crisis in the Workplace: Occupational Disease and Injury.*
    Cambridge, Mass.: MIT Press, 1976.
Balkan, Sheila; Berger, Ronald J.; and Schmidt, Janet. *Crime and Deviance in
    America: A Critical Approach.* Belmont, Calif.: Wadsworth, 1980.
Barnett, Harold C. "Corporate Capitalism, Corporate Crime." Paper presented
    at the Conference on White Collar and Economic Crime: Trends and Prob-
    lems in Research and Policy, Potsdam College of Arts and Science, Potsdam,
    N.Y., 7–9 February 1980.
Berman, Daniel M. *Death on the Job: Occupational Health and Safety Struggles
    in the U.S.* New York: Monthly Review Press, 1978.
Blau, Peter M. *On the Nature of Organizations.* New York: Wiley, 1974.
Blau, Peter M., and Scott, Richard W. *Formal Organizations.* San Francisco:
    Chandler, 1962.
CBS News. "Is Your Car Safe?" *60 Minutes,* vol. 10, no. 40. Broadcast over
    the CBS television network, Sunday, 11 June 1978.

Clinard, Marshall. "Criminological Theories of Violations of Wartime Regulations." *American Sociological Review* 2(June 1946):258-270.

_____. *Illegal Corporate Behavior.* Washington, D.C.: National Institute of Law Enforcement and Criminal Justice, 1979.

Clinard, Marshall, and Quinney, Richard. *Criminal Behavior Systems,* 2nd ed. New York: Holt, Rinehart and Winston, 1973.

Conklin, John E. *Illegal but Not Criminal: Business Crime in America.* Englewood Cliffs, N.J.: Prentice-Hall. "

Cressey, Donald R. "Restraints of Trade, Recidivism, and Delinquent Neighborhoods." In James F. Short, ed., *Delinquency, Crime, and Society.* Chicago: University of Chicago Press, 1976.

"Developments in the Law—Corporate Crime: Regulating Corporate Behavior Through Criminal Sanctions." *Harvard Law Review* 92(1979):1227-1375.

Dowie, Mark. "Pinto Madness." *Mother Jones,* September–October 1977, pp. 18-32.

_____. "Ford's Unpluggable Leak: The Sins of Harley Copp." Mother Jones, May 1978, p. 52.

Edelhertz, Herbert. *The Nature, Impact and Prosecution of White-Collar Crime.* Washington, D.C.: U.S. Government Printing Office, 1970.

Elkins, James R. "Corporations and the Criminal Law: An Uneasy Alliance." *Kentucky Law Journal* 65(1976):73-129.

Ermann, David M., and Lundman, Richard J. *Corporate and Governmental Deviance.* New York: Oxford University Press, 1978a.

_____. "Deviant Acts by Complex Organizations: Deviance and Social Control at the Organizational Level of Analysis." *Sociological Quarterly* 19(Winter 1978b):55-67.

Etzioni, Amitai. *Modern Organizations.* Englewood Cliffs, N.J.: Prentice-Hall, 1964.

Gamlin, Joanne. "Jury Slaps Massive Fine on Ford in '72 Pinto Crash." *Business Insurance,* 20 February 1978, p. 19.

Geis, Gilbert. "The Heavy Electrical Equipment Antitrust Cases of 1961." In M. Clinard and R. Quinney, eds., *Criminal Behavior Systems,* 1st ed., pp. 131-150. New York: Holt, Rinehart and Winston, 1967.

Geis, Gilbert, and Stotland, Ezra, eds. *White-Collar Crime: Theory and Research.* Beverly Hills, Calif.: Sage, 1980.

Gross, Edward. "Organizational Crime: A Theoretical Perspective." In N.H. Denzin, ed., *Studies in Symbolic Interaction,* pp. 55-85. Greenwich, Conn.: JAI Press, 1978.

Grush, E.S., and Saunby, C.S. "Fatalities Associated with Crash Induced Fuel Leakage and Fires." Interoffice memorandum, Ford Motor Company, 1973.

Hall, Richard H. *Organizations: Structure and Process,* 2nd ed. Englewood Cliffs, N.J.: Prentice-Hall, 1977.

Harris, Roy J., Jr. "Why the Pinto Jury Felt Ford Deserved $125 Million Penalty." *Wall Street Journal,* 14 February 1978, p. 1.

Jackall, Robert. "Crime in the Suites." *Contemporary Sociology* 9 (May 1980): 356.

Jacobson, Philip, and Barnes, John. "£66m Damages: The Car That Carried Death in the Boot." *London Times,* 12 February 1978, p. 1.

Karr, Albert R., and Apcar, and Leonard M. "Car Trouble: Government Pressure Propels Auto Recalls Toward a New High." *Wall Street Journal,* 16 August 1978, p. 1.

Kelderman, Jake. "Pinto Recall to be a Costly Project." *Automotive News,* 19 June 1978, p. 2.

Kriesberg, Simon. "Decisionmaking Models and the Control of Corporate Crime." *Yale Law Journal* 85(July 1976):1091-1129.

Lauderdale, Pat; Grasmick, Harold; and Clark, John P. "Corporate Environments, Corporate Crime and Deterrence." In M.D. Krohn and Ronald Akers, eds., *Crime, Law, and Sanctions.* Beverly Hills, Calif.: Sage, 1979.

Lenhoff, Alan S. "Rulings Threaten Pinto Case." *Detroit Free Press,* 23 January 1980, p. 1.

Leonard, William N., and Weber, Marvin Glenn. "Automakers and Dealers: A Study of Criminogenic Market Forces." *Law and Society Review* 4(February 1970):407-424.

McVisk, William. "Toward a Rational Theory of Criminal Liability for the Corporate Executive." *Journal of Criminal Law and Criminology* 69(Spring 1978):75-91.

Monahan, John, and Novaco, Raymond. "Corporate Violence: A Psychological Analysis." In A. Lipsitt and B. Sales, eds., *New Directions in Psychological Research.* New York: Van Nostrand, 1979.

Nader, Ralph. "Testimony before the Subcommittee on Criminal Laws and Procedures, Committee on the Judiciary, U.S. Senate." In *Reform of the Federal Criminal Laws,* part XI. Washington, D.C.: U.S. Government Printing Office, 19 ___, pp. 7863-7941.

Olson, F.G. "Engineering the Pinto." *Society of Automotive Engineers.* Detroit, 1971.

Page, Joseph A., and O'Brien, Mary-Win. *Bitter Wages.* New York: Grossman, 1972.

Parsons, Talcott. "A Sociological Approach to the Theory of Organizations." In T. Parsons, *Structure and Process in Modern Societies.* New York: Free Press, 1963.

Perrow, Charles. "The Analysis of Goals in Complex Organizations." *American Sociological Review* 26(December 1961):854-865.

_____ . *Organizational Analysis: A Sociological View.* Belmont, Calif.: Brooks/ Cole, 1970.

_____ . *Complex Organizations: A Critical Essay,* 2nd ed. Glenview, Ill.: Scott, Foresman, 1979.

Reiman, Jeffery. *The Rich Get Richer and the Poor Get Prison.* New York: Wiley, 1979.

Reiss, Albert J. "The Study of Deviant Behavior: Where the Action Is." *Ohio Valley Sociologist* 32(1966)1-12.

Schrager, Laura Shill, and Short, James F., Jr. "Toward a Sociology of Organizational Crime." *Social Problems* 25(June 1978):415.

Sharp, Eric. "Ford Motor Indicted in Indiana for Homicide in Pinto Fire." *Detroit Free Press,* 14, September 1978, p. 1.

Simon, Herbert A. *Administrative Behavior,* 2nd ed. New York: Macmillan, 1957.

Stone, Christopher. *Where the Law Ends: The Social Control of Corporate Behavior.* New York: Harper and Row, 1975.

Sutherland, Edwin H. *White Collar Crime.* New York: Dryden, 1949; reissued by Holt, Rinehart and Winston, 1961.

Swartz, Joel. "Silent Killers at Work." *Crime and Social Justice* 3(Spring–Summer 1975):15-20.

U.S. Department of Labor. *The President's Report on Occupational Safety and Health.* Washington, D.C.: U.S. Government Printing Office, 1972.

U.S. Department of Transportation. "DOT Finds Defect in Pinto Fuel Tanks." *DOT News Release,* 8 May 1978.

Wheeler, Stanton. "Trends and Problems in the Sociological Study of Crime." *Social Problems* 23(June 1976):525-534.

Yoder, Stephen. "Criminal Sanctions for Corporate Illegality." *Journal of Criminal Law and Criminology* 69(Spring 1978):40-58.

# Growth in the Underground Economy? An Empirical Issue

*Susan B. Long*

The notion that increasing tax loads and inflationary pressures, particularly in the 1960s and 1970s, have led to a burgeoning of the so-called underground economy has gained credence recently. Coverage in the news media, from articles in the popular and business press (see, for example, Ross 1978; Klein 1979; Lenhart 1978), to television network shows such as "60 Minutes," have treated the issue less as a hypothesis than as a proven fact. However, data in support of this contention are often impressionistic or reliant on untested assumptions that changes in currency ratios or in the circulation of large-denomination money are reliable indicators of changes in the level of cash transactions unreported on income-tax returns.[1]

Using two data sources on U.S. personal income—one based on national income and product accounts, the other based on amounts reported on federal income-tax returns by individuals—estimates of the amount of income improperly omitted from returns and the rate of underreporting were derived for the thirty-year period since World War II. Results show that rather than increasing, the estimated rate of income underreporting has steadily declined over the post–World War II period. A sensitivity analysis of the robustness of these estimates leads to some qualifications in the reliability of these estimated trends.

## Monetary-Based Indexes of Unreported Income

Evidence of inexplicably large and growing amounts of currency are well documented. There is a large amount of currency in circulation—$100 billion in notes and coin in 1979. Estimates of how much of this currency is held by individuals (rather than by businesses, other organizations, or persons from foreign

Paper presented at the Conference on White Collar and Economic Crime: Trends and Problems in Research and Policy; Multidisciplinary and Cross-National Perspectives, at State University of New York College, Potsdam, New York, 7–9 February 1980. Support for this research was received under grants from the U.S. Department of Justice, Law Enforcement Assistance Administration (Grant Nos. 78-NI-AX-0007 and NI-AX-0132) and the National Science Foundation (Grant No. SOC-7825039). This research is part of a larger study conducted by the author on federal income-tax enforcement. Any opinions, findings, and conclusions expressed are those of the author and do not necessarily reflect those of the supporting agencies.

countries) vary, but are on the order of $600 to $1,000 per household, or $500 to $600 per adult. Second, the amount of currency in circulation has been growing—up from roughly $30 billion two decades ago (Klein 1979). Despite the increasing use of checks and charge accounts in economic transactions, the rate of growth of currency in circulation has exceeded growth in demand deposits (checking accounts), but not that in personal outlays (compare figures 6–1 and 6–2). Most rapid has been the increase in large-denomination currency ($100 bills) which has been more rapid than the increase in volume of final sales (see figure 6–3).[2]

*Alternative Estimation Procedures*

A number of economists have attempted to use monetary data to develop an estimate of tax noncompliance. All are based on the assumption that "excess" demand for cash occurs because persons desire to hide income-generating transactions (both legal and illegal) on which no payment of taxes is made. Estimates vary both in how "excess" currency is determined and in how this excess estimate is translated into income-tax underreporting.

Gutmann (1977), for example, rests his estimate on the ratio of cash to checking deposits (see figure 6–1.) Using 1937–1941 as his base or normal period, he calculates the amount of currency that would be held today if no change in this cash-to-checking-account-deposits ratio had occurred. The "excess" amount of currency held over this estimate is translated into $176 billion in unreported income in 1976, on the assumption that each dollar of this excess currency generates $Q$ times as much unreported income annually from the "underground economy," where $Q$ is the ratio between GNP and the money supply (cash plus demand deposits). More recently, Feige (1979) derived an estimate of unreported income of between $226 and $369 billion for 1976. In contrast to Gutmann's method, Feige uses the ratio between total transactions per year (money supply × velocity of money) and income. Assuming the ratio in 1939 to be "normal," Feige attributes the increase in this ratio to unreported income from the irregular economy not reflected in reported GNP.[3] Henry (1976) uses the amount of large denomination currency not attributable to normal economic transaction needs to derive an estimate of $80 billion in unreported income attributable this single source alone.

*Shortcomings of Currency-Based Approaches*

Monetary-based indexes of tax noncompliance (unreported income) share a number of serious shortcomings. First and foremost, there is no independent means to verify the assumed connection between changes in monetary relationships and income underreporting. People have many reasons other than tax evasion for holding currency or for making cash transactions.

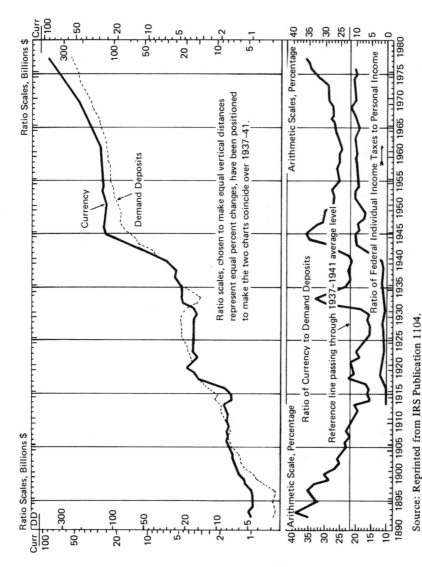

Source: Reprinted from IRS Publication 1104.

**Figure 6–1.** Relationships of Currency Outside Banks to Demand Deposits; and Tax Ratio

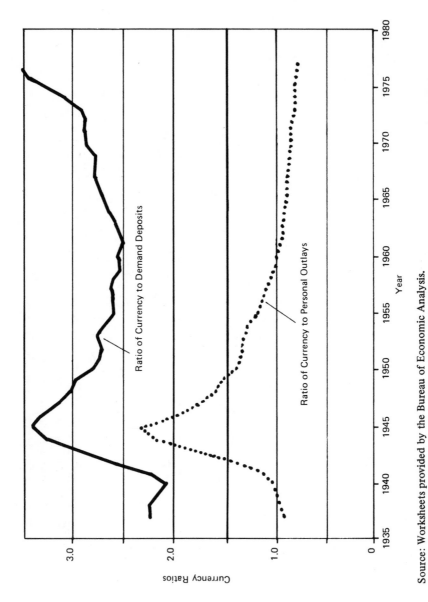

Source: Worksheets provided by the Bureau of Economic Analysis.

**Figure 6-2.** Ratio of Currency to Demand Deposits versus Personal Outlays, 1937–1977

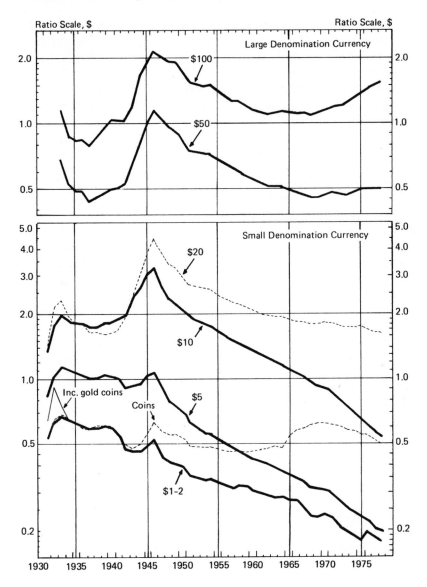

Source: Reprinted from IRS Publication 1104.
**Figure 6–3.** Currency in Circulation, by Denomination, per $100 of Final Sales

Second, there are a large number of other plausible factors that could explain changes in any of the monetary relationships that have been used. Changes in the turnover rates or transaction velocity of cash and demand deposits; changes in foreign holdings of currency or in currency "hoarding"; changes in cash management and monetary practices (such as the introduction of repurchase agreements [RPs], the use of credit cards and NOW accounts, and so forth) are a few of the alternative explanations that have been cited in the economic literature. Examining the ratio of currency to demand deposits, for example, others have shown that the ratio has increased apparently not because of a rise in currency over historic trends, but because of a corresponding fall in demand deposits (see figure 6–4). For a number of other laternative influences, there exist little if any reliable data on either their magnitude or their change over time, thus complicating attempts to incorporate these factors directly into the estimation procedure.[4]

Third, monetary-based indexes of noncompliance are also highly unstable. Small changes in the base period, measurement error, or other assumptions produce very large changes—often on the order of a $100 billion or more—in the estimates. For example, if Gutmann had used a base period of 1935–1939 or 1925–1929 (instead of 1937–1941), his procedure would result in an estimate of $165 billion or $262 billion, rather than $176 billion (U.S. Department of the Treasury, 1979, p. 48); Feige notes that changes of $100 billion or more in his estimates result from slight changes in his assumptions. Such sensitivity is probably inherent in monetary-based indexes of tax underreporting because effects of relatively small changes in estimated "excess" cash holdings are magnified by the multipiler (transaction velocity, ratio between money and income, and so forth) used to translate cash into income generated over the course of a year.[5]

## Other Measures of Income-Tax Noncompliance

In contrast to monetary-based measures of income underreporting, there are at least two other empirical measures of income underreporting on tax returns for time-series trends (Long 1979). The first, which will not be considered at length here, is derived from the IRS Taxpayer Compliance Measurement Program (TCMP), a program of continuing scientific surveys established in 1962. Here a stratified random sample of returns (or nonfilers in a geographic area) are given an intensive audit. Appropriately weighted, survey results are then used to estimate tax violations that would be detected if all returns were audited. National data on income-tax returns filed by individuals are available for tax years 1963, 1965, 1969, and 1973; additional information is available on surveys of nonfilers (based on geographic sampling and area canvasses). I have examined these elsewhere for indications of time trends in noncompliance (Long 1979; see

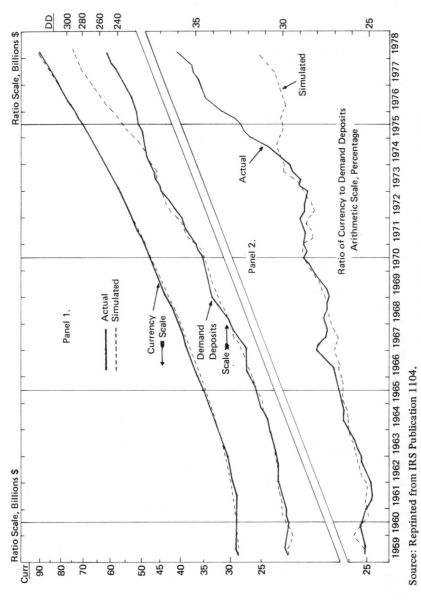

Source: Reprinted from IRS Publication 1104.

**Figure 6-4.** Relationships between Actual and Model-Simulated Currency and Demand Deposits

see also U.S. Department of the Treasury 1979, p. 151). Results are mixed. No clear evidence emerges for declining tax compliance, at least in the 1963–1973 period for which TCMP data are now available.

The focus of this chapter is on a second type of measure of tax violations based on the difference or residual left when two sets of income data are compared: the first based on income reported on tax returns from IRS statistics of income series, the second based on national income figures from the *Survey of Current Business* of the Department of Commerce. After translating the data into a common definition of *income* and adjusting for income received by individuals falling below federal income-tax filing requirements, the difference between these two aggregate totals should—to the extent the original two series are accurate—measure the amount of income improperly omitted from tax returns because of underreporting or the failure to file.[6]

*Residual Estimates of Income Underreporting*

Results for selected years previously calculated by economists Kahn (1960) and Goode (1976) are shown in table 6-1. U.S. personal income (Commerce) and income reported on nontaxable and taxable returns (IRS) are shown in columns 1, 4, and 8, along with the adjustments made by Kahn and Goode (columns 2 and 5) in deriving the residual they reported (column 9). I have translated these residuals into annual underreporting rates (column 9/column 7, shown in column 10).

Because we are dealing with figures on gross income before exemptions, deductions, and credits are taken, neither the absolute level nor the rate of underreporting is directly translatable into unpaid taxes. In 1970, for example, the average tax paid on reported adjusted gross income was 13.3 percent, and on net income, 20.9 percent, or between one-sixth and one-fifth of reported incomes (U.S. Department of the Treasury; *Statistics of Income,* 1970). The tax on estimated underreporting could be higher or lower than these average rates, depending on how this underreporting was distributed across tax brackets and income sources, and between filers and nonfilers.[7] Simply applying average tax yields would imply an estimated tax underpayment of $6 to $9.5 billion in 1970.[8]

Tax noncompliance, as indexed by this residual estimator, also shows a very consistent downward trend. Since only two time points are available after 1955, and these two by Goode may have been calculated by somewhat different assumptions than those by Kahn for the earlier period, I recalculated the entire series using Department of Commerce data on personal Income for the period 1947–1977, already adjusted to income defined for federal tax purposed by the Bureau of Economic Analysis (BEA) (internal BEA tabulations). From this

**Table 6-1**
**Derivation of Estimate of Personal Income Improperly Omitted from Federal Income-Tax Returns**
*(in billions of dollars)*

| Year | U.S. Personal Income (Per Inc) (1) | Net Adjustment Required for Comparability With Income for Tax Purposes (Adj) (2) | Adjusted Personal Income (3) | Adjusted Gross Income (AGI) Received by Individuals below Tax: Filing Payment Requirements | | | Adjusted U.S. Personal Income Required to Be Reported on Tax Returns (7) | Adjusted Gross Income (AGI Tax) Reported on Taxable Returns (8) | Residual (R) Income Not Accounted for on Returns (9) | Under-reporting Rate (10) |
|---|---|---|---|---|---|---|---|---|---|---|
| | | | | AGI Reported on Nontaxable Returns (4) [a] | Estimated AGI Received by Others Not Required to File or Pay (5) | Total (6) | | | | |
| 1945 | 171.1 | 30.9 | 140.2 | 2.4 | 1.8 | 4.3 | 135.9 | 118.1 | 17.8 | 13.1 |
| 1946 | 178.7 | 22.6 | 156.1 | 16.0 | 2.2 | 18.2 | 137.8 | 118.7 | 19.1 | 13.9 |
| 1947 | 191.2 | 19.6 | 171.6 | 14.4 | 2.3 | 16.7 | 154.8 | 135.9 | 19.0 | 12.2 |
| 1948 | 210.2 | 25.4 | 184.8 | 21.5 | 2.4 | 23.8 | 161.0 | 142.7 | 18.3 | 11.4 |
| 1949 | 207.2 | 22.9 | 184.3 | 22.0 | 2.2 | 24.2 | 160.1 | 139.0 | 21.1 | 13.2 |
| 1950 | 227.5 | 26.1 | 201.4 | 20.6 | 1.7 | 22.3 | 179.1 | 159.3 | 19.9 | 11.1 |
| 1951 | 255.6 | 29.0 | 226.6 | 19.1 | 2.4 | 21.5 | 205.1 | 183.9 | 21.2 | 10.3 |
| 1952 | 272.5 | 31.9 | 240.6 | 18.7 | 2.5 | 21.2 | 220.8 | 197.3 | 22.1 | 10.1 |
| 1953 | 288.2 | 33.7 | 254.5 | 18.2 | 2.5 | 20.8 | 233.7 | 210.5 | 23.2 | 10.0 |
| 1954 | 290.1 | 37.1 | 253.0 | 19.6 | 2.3 | 21.9 | 231.1 | 209.7 | 21.4 | 9.3 |
| 1955 | 310.9 | 38.2 | 272.7 | 18.9 | 2.1 | 21.1 | 251.6 | 229.6 | 22.0 | 8.9 |
| 1960 | 401.3[b] | 52.3 | 349.0 | 18.3 | 6.9 | 25.2 | 323.8 | 297.2 | 26.6 | 8.9 |
| 1970 | 808.3 | 125.5 | 682.8 | 21.4 | 6.8 | 28.2 | 654.6 | 610.3 | 44.3 | 6.8 |

Source: 1945–1955: columns (3)–(6), (8)–(9) from C. Harry Kahn, *Personal Deductions in the Federal Income Tax* (Princeton University Press, National Builder of Economic Research, 1960), pp. 194–195. 1960: columns (1)–(4), (8) from Richard Goode, *The Individual Income Tax* (Washington, D.C.: Brookings Institution, 1976), pp. 33, 305–306. [Goode does not give exact dollar figure for column (5) but states he estimates it to be 1 percent of total AGI (p. 33, fn. 34) which would be approximately $6.8 billion.] I calculated the remaining columns for each year, based on these authors' figures, except for 1945–1955, column (1) from U.S. Department of Commerce, National Income and Product Accounts, reprinted in U.S. Bureau of Census, *Historical Statistics of United States, Colonial Times to 1970*, 1975, p. 224.

aColumn (4) + column (5) may differ slightly from column (6) because of rounding.

bFigure now given for U.S. personal income in 1960 is 401.0, from *Historical Statistics of United States, Colonial Times to 1970* (Washington, D.C.: U.S. Bureau of the Census, 1975), p. 224. This would result in estimated underreporting of $26.3 billion out of $296.9 billion, or 8.85 percent.

series, I subtracted income reported on returns from IRS *Statistics of Income* annual volumes, along with an estimate of income received by persons falling below federal tax requirements (utilizing the method reported by Goode (1964, p. 223).[9] Results are shown in table 6-2, and the resultant estimated under-reporting rate for this time series is graphed in figure 6-5.

Variations on this residual method have previously been utilized by Gold-smith (1951), Stocker and Ellickson (1959), Holland and Kahn (1955), and Kahn (1968) to estimate residuals by type of income—interest, dividends, rent, wages and salaries, business and professional income, farm and nonfarm income, (sometimes using other survey sources on income). Estimated underreporting rates vary by income source. Somewhat higher rates of underreporting of busi-ness income, and particularly of farm income, result from residuals reported by Stocker and Ellickson (1959, p. 122; a rate of 11.9 percent on 1955 farm receipts, for example), and a much lower underreporting rate of wages and salaries of only 2 percent from residuals estimated for 1961 by Kahn (1968). Pechman and Okner (1974), deriving estimates of the distribution of tax burdens by income level, utilize a statistical match for individuals covered by the 1967 Survey of Economic Opportunity and those filing tax returns in 1966 (IRS *Statistics of Income* 1977), and compare the aggregate totals by type of income resulting from the blown-up sample to adjusted Department of Commerce national income totals allocating the residuals by income type. The Office of the Secretary of the Treasury, Office of Tax Analysis, using a similar approach, has developed estimates of underreporting of dividend and interest income.

Most recently, the IRS study group on the subterranean economy used the residual method in estimating underreporting of interest and dividend income for 1976. They also examined trends between Department of Commerce income and IRS tax data on wages and salaries as well as total personal income. IRS estimated that more than 16 percent of interest and dividend income, but only 1 percent of wages and salary, was not reported for 1976 using the residual method (U.S. Department of the Treasury 1979).[10]

*Limitations of the Residual Method:*
*Validity and Reliability of Estimates*

The accuracy of the estimates derived from the residual-indicator approach are a direct function of the reliability of the basic Department of Commerce and IRS income statistics, the validity of the adjustments made to ensure comparability between the two income series, and the robustness of the estimates to departures from these standards.

Data on income reported on return are derived from IRS *Statistics of In-come* (SoI) series, which have been published annually since 1916.[11] Since 1926, SoI data on dividuals have been based on sample information. Current samples for individual returns now average around 200,000 (out of over 60 million filed).

**Table 6–2**
**Estimated Rate of Income Underreporting on Federal Income-Tax Returns, 1947–1977**
**(Based on NIPA and SOI Tax Data on Individuals)**

| Year | Adjusted Personal Income (1) | Adjusted Gross Income (AGI) Received by Individuals below Tax-Filing Payment Requirements | | | Adjusted U.S. Personal Income Required to Be Reported on Tax Returns (5) [(1) − (4)] | Adjusted Gross Income (AGI Tax) Reported on Taxable Returns (6) | Residual Income Not Accounted for on Returns (7) [(5) − (6)] | Estimated Under-reporting Rate (8) [(7)/(5)] |
|---|---|---|---|---|---|---|---|---|
| | | AGI Reported on Nontaxable Returns (2) | Estimated AGI Received by Others Not Required to File or Pay (3) | Total (4) [(2) + (3)] | | | | |
| 1947 | 172.6 | 14.4 | 6.0 | 20.5 | 152.2 | 135.9 | 16.3 | 10.7 |
| 1948 | 186.4 | 21.5 | 8.1 | 29.6 | 156.7 | 142.7 | 14.0 | 9.0 |
| 1949 | 183.7 | 22.3 | 9.3 | 31.5 | 152.1 | 139.1 | 13.0 | 8.5 |
| 1950 | 202.1 | 20.6 | 8.4 | 29.0 | 173.1 | 159.3 | 13.8 | 8.0 |
| 1951 | 228.5 | 19.2 | 7.0 | 26.2 | 202.3 | 183.9 | 18.3 | 9.1 |
| 1952 | 240.9 | 18.8 | 6.2 | 24.9 | 216.0 | 197.3 | 18.7 | 8.6 |
| 1953 | 255.5 | 19.4 | 5.4 | 24.8 | 230.7 | 210.5 | 20.3 | 8.8 |
| 1954 | 253.8 | 20.6 | 6.4 | 27.0 | 226.8 | 209.7 | 17.1 | 7.5 |
| 1955 | 273.9 | 19.8 | 5.4 | 25.2 | 248.7 | 229.6 | 19.1 | 7.7 |
| 1956 | 294.2 | 19.0 | 5.2 | 24.2 | 269.9 | 249.6 | 20.4 | 7.5 |
| 1957 | 306.7 | 19.1 | 5.1 | 24.2 | 282.4 | 262.2 | 20.3 | 7.2 |
| 1958 | 311.2 | 20.0 | 6.5 | 26.5 | 284.7 | 262.2 | 22.5 | 7.9 |
| 1959 | 333.9 | 18.8 | 6.6 | 25.4 | 308.4 | 287.8 | 20.7 | 6.7 |
| 1960 | 346.1 | 19.4 | 6.4 | 25.9 | 320.3 | 297.2 | 23.1 | 7.2 |

**Table 6-2** Continued

| Year | Adjusted Personal Income (1) | Adjusted Gross Income (AGI) Received by Individuals below Tax-Filing Payment Requirements | | | Adjusted U.S. Personal Income Required to Be Reported on Tax Returns (5) [(1) − (4)] | Adjusted Gross Income (AGI Tax) Reported on Taxable Returns (6) | Residual Income Not Accounted for on Returns (7) [(5) − (6)] | Estimated Under-reporting Rate (8) [(7)/(5)] |
| | | AGI Reported on Nontaxable Returns (2) | Estimated AGI Received by Others Not Required to File or Pay (3) | Total (4) [(2) + (3)] | | | | |
|---|---|---|---|---|---|---|---|---|
| 1961 | 359.1 | 19.7 | 7.0 | 26.7 | 332.4 | 311.3 | 21.2 | 6.4 |
| 1962 | 378.5 | 19.2 | 7.8 | 27.0 | 351.4 | 330.6 | 20.8 | 5.9 |
| 1963 | 398.3 | 19.8 | 7.6 | 27.4 | 370.9 | 350.4 | 20.4 | 5.5 |
| 1964 | 340.8 | 22.2 | 7.6 | 29.8 | 401.0 | 376.0 | 25.0 | 6.2 |
| 1965 | 466.4 | 21.3 | 7.4 | 28.7 | 437.7 | 409.3 | 28.4 | 6.5 |
| 1966 | 508.9 | 20.1 | 6.6 | 26.7 | 482.2 | 450.2 | 32.0 | 6.6 |
| 1967 | 541.6 | 19.2 | 6.0 | 25.2 | 516.4 | 487.4 | 28.9 | 5.6 |
| 1968 | 595.6 | 18.0 | 5.7 | 23.7 | 571.9 | 538.3 | 33.6 | 5.9 |
| 1969 | 644.7 | 17.4 | 4.0 | 21.4 | 623.3 | 588.2 | 35.0 | 5.6 |
| 1970 | 677.3 | 21.4 | 7.1 | 28.5 | 648.8 | 610.3 | 38.5 | 5.9 |
| 1971 | 719.9 | 22.3 | 9.1 | 31.4 | 688.5 | 651.3 | 37.2 | 5.4 |
| 1972 | 793.2 | 28.6 | 10.0 | 38.6 | 754.6 | 717.4 | 37.2 | 4.9 |
| 1973 | 887.5 | 27.4 | 9.2 | 36.7 | 850.8 | 799.7 | 51.1 | 6.0 |
| 1974 | 966.1 | 25.1 | 5.7 | 30.8 | 935.2 | 880.4 | 54.9 | 5.9 |
| 1975 | 1,009.0 | 49.5 | 13.2 | 62.7 | 946.3 | 898.3 | 48.0 | 5.1 |
| 1976 | 1,118.3 | 49.4 | 12.1 | 61.6 | 1,056.7 | 1,004.4 | 52.3 | 4.9 |
| 1977 | 1,238.0 | 61.3 | 19.6 | 80.9 | 1,157.1 | 1,094.4 | 62.7 | 5.4 |

Source: U.S. Department of the Treasury, Internal Revenue Service, *Statistics of Income*, 1947-1976, 1977 (preliminary); internal tabulations, Bureau of Economic Analysis; U.S. census annual population estimates. Data as reported in columns (1), (2), (6); remaining estimates by author on the basis of figures reported by these sources.

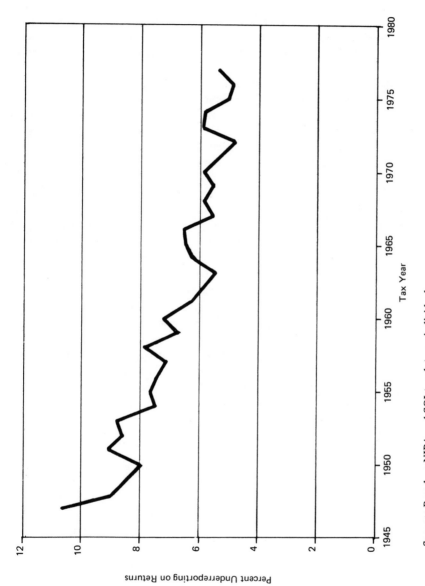

Source: Based on NIPA and SOI tax data on individuals.

**Figure 6-5.** Estimated Rate of Income Underreporting, 1947–1977

The population of returns or sampling frame for any one year consists of all returns received and processed by the IRS. Although most returns are for the current time period, "delinquent returns for prior years, revenues processed during the same period, (are) included in the sample to compensate for current-year returns filed after the cutoff data for receipt of sample returns for (any one) report" (*Statistics of Income,* Individual Returns 1975, p. 215). Information recorded is based on reported amounts, before any adjustments from enforcement activities.

Sampling and nonsampling limitations of the data, as well as changes in the tax law that affect comparability over time, are discussed in each SoI volume. Because of the size of the sample and the efficiency in sampling design, sampling variability for national total estimates is low. On adjusted-gross-income figures used for the residual indicator, the coefficient of variation at the national level is estimated at 0.11 percent. Although changes in the tax laws pose problems for year-to-year comparisons, "fortunately the definition of adjusted gross income . . . remained largely unchanged" in the post–World War II period (Duncan 1978, p. 191)

The National Income and Product Accounts (NIPA) of the Department of Commerce provide the second measure of aggregate personal income for the residual-estimator approach. Unlike SoI, NIPA estimates are not based on a single sample, but represent the compilation of numerous surveys, other informational sources, estimates, and adjustments.[12]

As a basis for estimating tax underreporting, NIPA data have at least two major limitations. First, income earned from informal activities outside the context of regular business establishments is probably underrepresented. (And, of course, income earned from illegal activities normally will not be included.) Second, NIPA estimates are not independent of tax data, since return information is used in the estimation process.[13] Indeed, Duncan and Shelton in their review of government statistics over the past fifty years report that impetus for improvement and expansion in SoI tabulations during the post–World War II period came from "the fact that national income and product accounts (NIPA) . . . could be improved by use of these data.[14]

Kahn (1964, p. 138) notes that "in its estimates of unincorporated business income, the [Commerce Department] relies heavily on tax return information." It is true that the wage and salary component of national income is derived primarily from reports to state unemployment-insurance authorities, not from income-tax information. Despite the fact that wages and salaries make up around two-thirds of total personal income, underreporting in this area is very low. Thus, most of the difference between NIPA and SoI data arises in areas other than wages and salaries—areas in which NIPA's reliance on tax data is greater.

In addition to lack of independence between the SoI and NIPA income series, additional sources of error are introduced by the sizable adjustments required to transform NIPA income figures into "income" as defined for federal income-tax purposes (see note 6). Net adjustments have been on the order of 20 percent; and because both positive and negative adjustments occur, the absolute amount of these adjustments is even higher. Economists both inside and outside government differ on what the appropriate adjustments should be. Compare, for example, Kahn (1960) and Goode (1976); Bureau of Economic Analysis and IRS adjustments (U.S. Department of the Treasury 1979, appendix E). Because of the magnitude of these adjustments, small changes can significantly affect the residual estimate and thus introduce a major source of potential error. (In these estimates, for example, no adjustment has been made for the first $100 of dividends received, although these are not taxable.)

Because most people file returns and those who do not typically have low incomes, the adjustment made for income received by persons under the level required for federal income-tax payments is of less consequence. In 1974, for example, only an estimated 3 percent of the total population of the country was unaccounted for on federal income-tax returns (both taxable and nontaxable returns filed). Although this figure is undoubtedly too low (because of underenumeration of the census and the double counting that occurs in tax data because some persons, particularly students, are allowed to file *and* be counted as dependents on their parents' returns, the relative amount involved in this adjustment is quite small (representing since the mid-1960s only 1 percent of total personnel income).

*Robustness of the Residual Estimator*

A sensitivity analysis shows that the estimated magnitude and rate of underreporting using the residual method are greatly affected by small changes in the measures used, particularly in the estimate of U.S. personal income (see table 6-3). If the estimate for personal income is even 1 percent too low, the estimate for underreporting would be 20 percent larger; a 10-percent underestimate of adjusted gross income would triple the level of predicted unreported income on returns. Since differences of 1 or more percentage points could easily arise from underenumeration, failure to pick up income generated in the so-called underground economy outside regular market channels, or inaccuracy in the adjustments, the residual estimator is far from robust.

Table 6-3 also compares the effects of a 10-percent error (both in under- and overenumeration) of other factors that enter into the estimation process. Although effects are not as large as those observed for income, the effects of underenumeration of the U.S. population (or those of claiming too many dependents on returns) work in the opposite direction. However, changes in the estimate used for the average income of persons whose income falls below reported requirements has only an insignificant effect on our estimator.) Thus

**Table 6-3**
**Sensitivity of Estimates of Income Underreporting on Federal Tax Returns, 1947–1977**
**(Based on NIPA and SOI Tax Data on Individuals)**

| | | | Estimated Income Underreported (Billions of Dollars) | | | | | | | |
| | Actual Estimate | | If Values Actually 10 Percent Larger for: | | | | If Values Actually 10 Percent Smaller for: | | | |
| | | | Personal Income (NIPA adj.) | | U.S. Population (Census) | | Income or Population below Filing Requirements | | Income Reported as Nontaxable on Returns | |
| Year | Dollars | Rate (%) | Dollars | Rate (%) | Dollars | Rate (%) | Dollars | Rate (%) | Dollars | Rate (%) |
|---|---|---|---|---|---|---|---|---|---|---|
| 1947 | 16.3 | 10.7 | 33.6 | 19.8 | 11.0 | 7.5 | 16.9 | 11.1 | 16.9 | 11.0 |
| 1948 | 14.0 | 9.0 | 32.7 | 18.6 | 7.2 | 4.8 | 14.9 | 9.4 | 14.9 | 9.3 |
| 1949 | 13.0 | 8.5 | 31.4 | 18.4 | 6.1 | 4.2 | 13.9 | 9.1 | 13.9 | 9.0 |
| 1950 | 13.8 | 8.0 | 34.0 | 17.6 | 6.7 | 4.0 | 14.6 | 8.4 | 14.6 | 8.3 |
| 1951 | 18.3 | 9.1 | 41.2 | 18.3 | 10.9 | 5.6 | 19.0 | 9.4 | 19.0 | 9.3 |
| 1952 | 18.7 | 8.6 | 42.7 | 17.8 | 11.2 | 5.4 | 19.3 | 8.9 | 19.3 | 8.8 |
| 1953 | 20.3 | 8.8 | 45.8 | 17.9 | 12.3 | 5.5 | 20.8 | 9.0 | 20.8 | 8.9 |
| 1954 | 17.1 | 7.5 | 42.5 | 16.8 | 8.9 | 4.1 | 17.7 | 7.8 | 17.7 | 7.7 |
| 1955 | 19.1 | 7.7 | 46.5 | 16.8 | 10.7 | 4.5 | 19.6 | 7.9 | 19.6 | 7.8 |
| 1956 | 20.4 | 7.5 | 49.8 | 16.6 | 11.7 | 4.5 | 20.9 | 7.7 | 20.9 | 7.7 |
| 1957 | 20.3 | 7.2 | 50.9 | 16.3 | 11.4 | 4.2 | 20.8 | 7.3 | 20.8 | 7.3 |
| 1958 | 22.5 | 7.9 | 53.7 | 17.0 | 13.5 | 4.9 | 23.2 | 8.1 | 23.2 | 8.1 |
| 1959 | 20.7 | 6.7 | 54.1 | 15.8 | 11.3 | 3.8 | 21.3 | 6.9 | 21.3 | 6.9 |
| 1960 | 23.1 | 7.2 | 57.7 | 16.3 | 13.5 | 4.4 | 23.8 | 7.4 | 23.8 | 7.4 |
| 1961 | 21.2 | 6.4 | 57.1 | 15.5 | 11.3 | 3.5 | 21.9 | 6.6 | 21.9 | 6.5 |
| 1962 | 20.8 | 5.9 | 58.6 | 15.1 | 10.4 | 3.0 | 21.6 | 6.1 | 21.6 | 6.1 |
| 1963 | 20.4 | 5.5 | 60.3 | 14.7 | 9.5 | 2.6 | 21.2 | 5.7 | 21.2 | 5.7 |

| Year | | | | | | | | | | |
| --- | --- | --- | --- | --- | --- | --- | --- | --- | --- | --- |
| 1964 | 25.0 | 6.2 | 68.0 | 15.3 | 13.2 | 3.4 | 25.7 | 6.4 | 25.7 | 6.4 |
| 1965 | 28.4 | 6.5 | 75.0 | 15.5 | 16.0 | 3.8 | 29.1 | 6.6 | 29.1 | 6.6 |
| 1966 | 32.0 | 6.6 | 82.9 | 15.6 | 19.1 | 4.1 | 32.7 | 6.8 | 32.7 | 6.7 |
| 1967 | 28.9 | 5.6 | 83.1 | 14.6 | 16.0 | 3.2 | 29.5 | 5.7 | 29.5 | 5.7 |
| 1968 | 33.6 | 5.9 | 93.2 | 14.8 | 20.0 | 3.6 | 34.2 | 6.0 | 34.2 | 6.0 |
| 1969 | 35.0 | 5.6 | 99.5 | 14.5 | 21.2 | 3.5 | 35.4 | 5.7 | 35.4 | 5.7 |
| 1970 | 38.5 | 5.9 | 106.3 | 14.8 | 23.7 | 3.7 | 39.2 | 6.0 | 39.2 | 6.0 |
| 1971 | 37.2 | 5.4 | 109.1 | 14.4 | 21.3 | 3.2 | 38.1 | 5.5 | 38.1 | 5.5 |
| 1972 | 37.2 | 4.9 | 116.5 | 14.0 | 18.6 | 2.5 | 38.2 | 5.1 | 38.2 | 5.0 |
| 1973 | 51.1 | 6.0 | 139.8 | 14.9 | 31.7 | 3.8 | 52.0 | 6.1 | 52.0 | 6.1 |
| 1974 | 54.9 | 5.9 | 151.5 | 14.7 | 36.6 | 4.0 | 55.4 | 5.9 | 55.4 | 5.9 |
| 1975 | 48.0 | 5.1 | 148.9 | 14.2 | 23.5 | 2.5 | 49.4 | 5.2 | 49.4 | 5.2 |
| 1976 | 52.3 | 4.9 | 164.1 | 14.0 | 26.1 | 2.5 | 53.5 | 5.1 | 53.5 | 5.0 |
| 1977 | 62.7 | 5.4 | 186.5 | 14.6 | 30.1 | 2.7 | 64.6 | 5.6 | 64.6 | 5.5 |

Source: Sensitivity analysis by author using data and estimates reported in table 3.18.

actual direction of bias is difficult to predict without more information. Errors in our data or in the adjustments made could either inflate or deflate our estimator. What is clear, however, is that the absolute level or rate of underreporting derived from this approach is highly unstable.

In contrast, the slope (reduction over time) in the estimated underreporting rate is quite robust. The effects of a change in any one of the factors, as shown in table 6-3 and figure 6-6 is to shift the entire plot of underreporting over time up or down, without greatly affecting its slope. Thus only differential changes in the magnitude error over time in population or income estimates could account for this observed decline. Although population underenumeration may have declined over time, the effect of plausible shifts in completeness of population counts is much too small to produce estimation errors large enough to account for the observed trend in underreporting. (Something on the order of a 30-percent underenumeration of population, at a minimum, would be required in the immediate post–World War II period.) Although population counts would need to improve to explain these differences, national income to produce estimates of personal income would have to grow consistently *less* complete to account for the movement in our estimates of underreporting. More and better data should have increased the completeness of information on income from regular business establishments (other things equal). Standing alone, this would produce an apparent rise—not a decline—in estimated income underreporting on returns. Current speculation about the so-called informal or underground economy argues that other things are not equal—that there has been a very sizable growth in the unreported "cash" economy. Estimates on the order of Gutmann's (discussed earlier) of 10 percent of GNP, are in fact comparable to estimates for income underreporting for the immediate post–World War II period based on the residual method. However, to explain the estimated trend shown in table 6-2, one would need to accept both the assumption that proportionately the informal economy today is much larger than immediately after World War II, and that the trend toward this increase in the informal or cash economy has been progressive and gradual. In contrast, most of the speculation about the growth in the unreported cash informal economy has portrayed this change as a new or comparatively recent trend (paralleling recent increases in taxes and inflation)—not one of progressive increase over the entire postwar period. The Gutmann method, for example, would require the rise to have started at least by 1963 when the currency-to-checking-account ratio began its upward climb back to the levels present immediately after World War II (see figures 6-1 and 6-2).

Composition shifts in sources of income provide one plausible explanation that involves gradual change. Over time, the proportion of income derived from wages and salaries (where income underreporting is estimated to be low) has increased, whereas that from self-employment sources (where underreporting is believed to be much greater) has declined.[15] (see figure 6-7). Nonetheless,

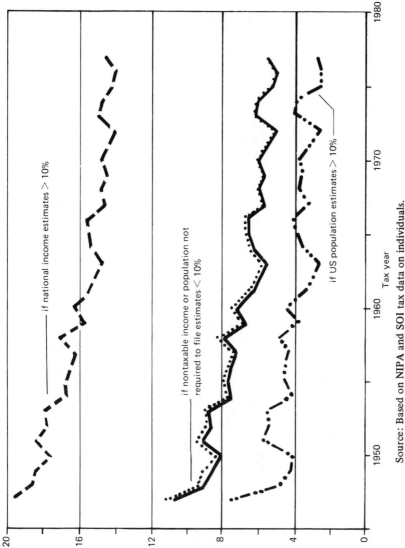

if national income estimates > 10%

if nontaxable income or population not required to file estimates < 10%

if US population estimates > 10%

Tax year

Source: Based on NIPA and SOI tax data on individuals.

**Figure 6-6. Stability of Estimated Income Underreporting, 1947-1977**

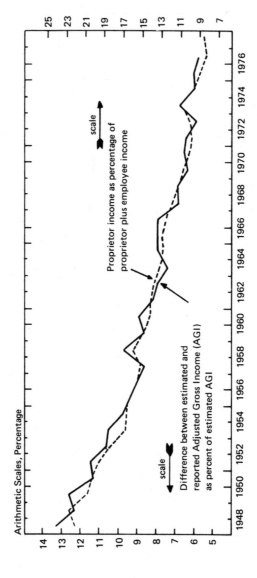

Source: Reprinted from background files of IRS Study Group on the Subterranean Economy (declining percentage of adjusted gross income of individuals from self-employment or "proprietor" income).

**Figure 6-7.** "Unreported Income" Related to Importance of Proprietor Income

even when only the wage and salary component of personal income is examined over time, estimates for income-underreporting rates still decline (see U.S. Department of the Treasury 1979, appendix I, and related background files on the subterranean economy.)

Thus ultimately the question of increasing or decreasing tax compliance remains open. Whereas the residual method results in estimates of decreasing levels of tax noncompliance, the sensitivity of the residual method to errors in estimating personal income mitigate against drawing any firm conclusions. Clearly, however, more than the simplistic monetary-based models are required.

## Notes

1. Measures of informal economic activities, sometimes referred to as the "irregular economy" (Ferman, Berndt, and Selo, 1978), have also been suggested as an alternative index of tax noncompliance. The assumption is that such activity is engaged in to avoid payment of income taxes or, at least, that income so obtained is not reported. (Activities outside regularly established business or market transactions—such as barter, self-employed moonlighting, self-employed casual labor—existed long before the enactment of income-tax statutes (see lazo 1933). Information on the extent of the irregular economy or its relationship to tax noncompliance are largely absent and have limited efforts to develop indexes in this area. (See, however, some preliminary efforts of IRS to develop estimates [Pub. 1104, appendix G].)

2. Final sales (equivalent to gross national product (GNP)–changes in inventory) as used in figure 6-3 is a more-inclusive base than personal outlays minus imputations) as used in figure 6-2, because final sales include outlays (purchases) by other than those in the personal sector (for example, business, government, and so forth).

3. The estimate is based on the assumed constancy of the ratio: (total transactions)/(income), where income = (reported GNP + unreported income). For his estimate of $226-$369 billion, Feige assumes unreported income to be zero in 1939. Because total transactions are not measured directly, several assumptions are required in the derivation of velocity of currency. Changes in one of these assumptions (that is, the average transaction life of paper money) produces the variation in his estimate of $226 to $369 billion dollars. Based on the same method, his estimate for 1978 is $542-704 billion, or up to one-quarter of the reported GNP. Feige notes that slight changes in other assumptions could alter his estimate by several hundred billion dollars.

4. See Anderson (1966, 1977); Laurent (1970, 1979); Goldfeld (1976); Paulus and Axilrod (1976); Porter and Thurman (1979); Porter and Mauskopf (1978); Garcia (1978); Gutmann (1977, 1978, 1979), Cagan (1958, 1965); Porter (1979); Molefsky (1979); U.S. Department of the Treasury 1979, appendix B, and IRS background files on underground economy; McDonald (1956); Kaufman (1965).

5. Monetary-based indexes of noncompliance focus on tax violations from income underreporting. Understatement of tax liability can also occur because of overstatement of deductions, expenses, and so forth (see note 8). Some monetary-based indexes, such as Gutmann's, estimate only one subtype of income underreporting—that related to unreported *cash* transactions.

6. *Income* as that term is used in national income and product accounts must be reduced for types of income not treated as taxable under the statute, and increased to include transfer and other payments that are "income" for tax purposes, but not for economic uses.

7. Income from some sources is more likely to be partially offset by business expenses or other adjustments; for nonfilers, income will be offset by allowable deductions.

8. Tax underreporting—as distinguished from income underreporting—also results from *over*claiming of deductions, exemptions, expenses, credits, and other adjustments to income. These are not examined here. However, estimates for these are available from the IRS Taxpayer Compliance Measurement Program.

9. Goode assumed that the average income of the population not covered by tax returns was equal to that of persons represented on nontaxable returns.

10. For wages and salaries, IRS made no adjustment for income received by persons falling below income-tax-return filing requirements.

11. In response to a statutory requirement first enacted in the Revenue Act of 1916, annual volumes have been published "with respect to the operation of the income tax laws, including classifications of taxpayers and of income, the amounts allowed as deductions, exemptions, and credits, and any other facts deemed pertinent and valuable" (IRS Sec. 6108(a)).

12. NIPA estimates for personal income are in fact themselves a residual measure, left after subtracting receipts by entities other than persons (that is, corporations, foreign entities, governments, and so forth).

13. They report:

As the number of items tabulated and the industry and other breakdowns for which each item was shown became larger and larger in the 1950's and 1960's, the use of income tax statistics spread to most phases of NIPA. Indeed, by the 1960s, the only major parts of NIPA which made very little use of these data were (1) wages and salaries, which depended chiefly on the unemployment insurance statistics, (2) most of the final product estimates, and (3) the current estimates, because of the lag in producing income tax data and the fact that they are only annual. [p. 190]

14. In addition to data reported on returns, the Department of Commerce has utilized "blow-up" ratios to adjust for underreporting on returns derived from IRS Taxpayer Compliance Measurement Program surveys, as well as its early predecessor, the 1948–1949 Audit Control Program.

15. Some of this reported decline in self-employment income may have arisen from a trend towards increasing incorporation of businesses. In that case, income underreporting would only be moved from the individual to the corporate sector.

## References

Anderson, Paul S. "The Rise of Currency in Circulation During World War II." *National Banking Review* (March 1966):359-367.

———. "Currency in Use and in Hoards." *New England Economic Review* (March-April 1977):21-30.

Cagan, Phillip. "The Demand For Currency Relative to the Total Money Supply." *Journal of Political Economy* (August 1958):303-328.

———. *Determinants and Effects of Change in the Stock of Money, 1875-1960.* New York: National Bureau of Economics, 1965. Distributed by Columbia University Press.

Duncan, Joseph W., and Shelton, William C. *Revolution in United States Government Statistics, 1926-1976.* Washington, D.C.: U.S. Department of Commerce, Office of Federal Statistical Policy and Standards, 1978.

Farioletti, Marius. "Some Results from the First Year's Audit Control Program of the Bureau of Internal Revenue." *National Tax Journal* (March 1952).

———. "Some Income Adjustments Results from the 1949 Audit Control Program." *Studies in Income and Wealth* (1958):239-271.

"The Fast Growth of the Underground Economy." *Business Week,* 13 March 1978, pp. 73-74, 77.

Feige, Edgar L. "How Big Is the Irregular Economy?" *Challenge* (November-December 1979):5-13.

Ferman, Louis A. "Remarks Delivered Before the National Commission on Unemployment and Employment Statistics on June 13, 1978." Unpublished paper, Institute of Labor and Industrial Relations, University of Michigan-Wayne State University.

Ferman, Louis A.; Berndt, Louise; and Selo, Elaine. *Analysis of the Irregular Economy: Cash Flow in the Informal Sector.* Prepared by the Institute of Labor and Industrial Relations, University of Michigan-Wayne State University. Submitted to the Bureau of Employment and Training, Michigan Department of Labor. Ann Arbor: Institute of Labor and Industrial Relations, 1978.

Garcia, Gillian. "The Currency Ratio and the Subterranean Economy." *Financial Analysts Journal* (November-December 1978):64-66.

Garcia, Gillian, and Pak, Simon. "The Ratio of Currency to Demand Deposits in the United States." Research Program in Finance, Working Paper No. 69. Institute of Business and Economic Research, University of California at Berkeley, May 1978.

General Accounting Office. *Who's Not Filing Income Tax Returns? IRS Needs Better Ways to Find Them and Collect Their Taxes.* GGD-79-69. Washington, D.C.: U.S. Government Printing Office, 1979.

Goldfeld, Stephen M. "The Case of the Missing Money." *Brookings Papers on Economic Activity* 111(1976):683-739.

Goldsmith, Selma F. "Appraisal of Basic Data Available for Construction Income Size Distributions." In *Studies in Income and Wealth,* vol. 13, p. 302. New York, National Bureau of Economic Research, 1951.

_____ . "The Relation of Census Income Distribution Statistics to Other Income Data." *Studies in Income and Wealth* 23(1958).

Goode, Richard. *The Individual Income Tax,* rev. ed. Washington, D.C.: Brookings Institution, 1976.

Gutmann, Peter M. "The Subterranean Economy." *Financial Analysts Journal* (November–December 1977):26-27, 34.

_____ . "Statistical Illusions, Mistaken Policies." *Challenge* (November–December 1979):14-17.

_____ . "Professor Gutmann Replies." *Financial Analysts Journal* (November–December 1978):67-69.

Henrichs, John C. "The Relationships Between Personal Income and Taxable Income." *Survey of Current Business* 55(February 1975).

Iazo, H. "Scrip and Barter: Their Use and Their Service." Washington, D.C.: U.S. Department of the Treasury, 1933.

Kahn, C. Harry. *Personal Deductions in the Federal Income Tax.* Princeton, N.J.: Princeton University Press, for National Bureau of Economic Research, 1960.

_____ . *Business and Professional Income under the Personal Income Tax.* Princeton, N.J.: Princeton University Press, for National Bureau of Economic Research, 1964.

_____ . *Employee Compensation under the Income Tax.* New York: National Bureau of Economic Research, 1968. Distributed by Columbia University Press.

Kaufman, George G. "The Demand for Currency." In *Staff Economic Studies.* Washington, D.C.: Board of Governors of the Federal Reserve System, 1965.

Klein, Frederick C. "Americans Hold Increasing Amounts of Cash Despite Inflation and Other Drawbacks." *Wall Street Journal,* 5 July 1979, p. 28.

Laurent, Robert Dennis. "Currency Transfer by Denomination." Ph.D. diss. University of Chicago, December 1970.

_____ . "Currency and the Subterranean Economy." *Economic Perspectives,* Federal Reserve Bank of Chicago. (March–April 1979).

_____ . "Currency in Circulation and the Real Value of Notes." *Journal of Money, Credit and Banking* (May 1974):213-226.

Lenhart, Harry A., Jr. "How Tax Cheaters Get Away With Billions." *U.S. News and World Report,* 27 March 1978, pp. 102-105.

Long, Susan B. *The Internal Revenue Service: Measuring Tax Offenses and Enforcement Response.* Report to Law Enforcement Assistance Administration under Grant 78-NI-AX-0132 (White-Collar Crime Data Sources Project). BSSR 0583-01, 1979.

Mason, Robert, and Calvin, Lyle D. "A Study of Admitted Income Tax Evasion." *Law and Society Review* 13(Fall 1978):73–89.

McDonald, Stephen L. "Some Factors Affecting the Increased Relative Use of Currency Since 1939." *Journal of Finance* (September 1956):313–327.

McPheters, Lee R. "The Demand For Large Denomination Currency: An Empirical Analysis." Paper, Arizona State University, n.d.

Molefsky, Barry. "The Underground Economy: An Overview." Library of Congress, Congressional Research Service, 2 August 1979.

Paulus, John, and Axilrod, Stephen H. "Recent Regulatory Changes and Financial Innovations Affecting the Growth of the Monetary Aggregates." Federal Reserve Board, November 1976.

Pechman, Joseph A. *Federal Tax Policy,* 3rd ed. Washington, D.C.: Brookings Institution, 1977a.

Pechman, Joseph A., ed. *Comprehensive Income Taxation.* Washington, D.C.: Brookings Institution, 1977b.

Pechman, Joseph A., and Okner, Benjamin A. "Individual Income Tax Erosion by Income Classes." In *The Economics of Federal Subsidy Programs,* a compendium of papers submitted to the Joint Economic Committee, part 1: *General Study Papers,* 92nd Congress, 2nd Session (1972), pp. 13–40.

———. *Who Bears the Tax Burden.* Washington, D.C.: Brookings Institution, 1974.

Porter, Richard D. "Some Notes on Estimating the Underground Economy." Board of Governors of the Federal Reserve System, 10 August 1979.

Porter, Richard D., and Mauskopf, Eileen. "Some Notes on the Apparent Shift in the Demand for Demand Deposits Function." Board of Governors of the Federal Reserve System, May 1978.

Porter, Richard D., and Thurman, Stephan S. "The Currency Ratio and the Subterranean Economy: Additional Comments." Board of Governors of the Federal Reserve System, 26 January 1979.

Ross, Irwin. "Why the Underground Economy is Booming." *Fortune,* 9 October 1978, 92–98.

Roth, Jeffrey A., and Ekstrand, Laurie E. "Targeting Tax Law Enforcement: Some Preliminary Qualitative Results." Paper presented at the American Criminology Society Annual Meeting, Philadelphia, Pennsylvania, 16 November 1979. Prepared by Westat, Inc., supported by the Internal Revenue Service (Contract TIR-78-50).

Silk, Leonard. "The Hidden Economy." *The New York Times* 27 April 1979.

Stocker, Frederick D., and Ellickson, John C. "How Fully Do Farmers Report Their Income?" *National Tax Journal* (June 1959).

"The Underground Economy." *Newsweek,* 10 April 1978, pp. 35-36.

U.S. Department of Commerce. *Survey of Current Business* (June 1978).

U.S. Department of Commerce. Bureau of Economic Analysis. *The National Income and Product Accounts of the United States, 1929-74: Statistical Tables.* Supplement to *Survey of Current Business.* Washington, D.C.: U.S. Government Printing Office, 1977.

U.S. Department of the Treasury. Internal Revenue Service. *Annual Report of the Commissioner.* 1945-1978.

———. *Statistics of Income.* 1947-1976, 1977 (prel.).

———. *Estimates of Income Unreported on Individual Income Tax Returns.* Pub. 1104 (9-79).

Vito, Natrella. "Historical and Future Developments of Statistics of Income." Proceedings of the Business and Economic Statistics Section, American Statistical Association, pp. 154-159.

Weil, Ulrick. "A Note on the Derivation of Income Estimates of Persons Making Less Than $500 per Annum, 1944-1948." *Journal of the American Statistical Association* 45(1949):440.

# 7

# Crime and Economy in the Communist Countries

*Maria Łoś*

## The Criminal Economy

It would be misleading to discuss economic crimes without paying attention to the contradictions, deviations, and criminogenic nature of the economy itself. The main problem with the communist economy is that, contrary to the main assumption of Marxist theory, it is completely subordinated to an abstract political doctrine that is not generated by, and is in fact completely divorced from, the material base. As a result, the communist economy can make sense only on paper; thus it is not surprising that its constantly emphasized economic success is supported by "paper" evidence and ideological slogans that are in clear contradiction to the unsound and disorganized reality.

The one-party state monopoly over the means of production, as well as over all political and social processes, implies the full ideological unity of official political and economic interests and, therefore, the sheer impossibility of any legislation interfering with or curbing the centralized, plan-oriented organization of industry. Even more significant, it excludes the existence of any trade unions that would represent the interest of the employees rather than the employers (that is, the state). Further, the monopoly of the one-party state over the mass media excludes the possibility of any countercontrol or pressure by a nonparty majority.

The state's economic monopoly and its power to fix prices paralyzes the mechanisms of self-regulation in the communist nationalized economy. The exclusion of competition, a practice that is usually seen as criminal in the western countries, becomes the guiding principle under communism. The economy is geared towards the fulfilment of the plan and disregards the pressures of demand and of unsatisfied social needs. The macroeconomic decisions, especially the plan, cannot be criticized or adapted to the changing needs of society; their premises are secret, their directives legally binding.

Whatever is produced in agreement with the plan is treated automatically as adequate and socially useful, because the plan cannot be wrong. In fact, everything that is produced is officially contributing toward the fulfillment of the plan since all reports are prepared with the obligatory nature of the plan in mind. Therefore, any evaluation of the plan and all future planning are based on distorted information contained in reports modeled on legal expectations rather than real production. *The plan is, thus, fully arbitrary, and its soundness*

121

*can never be submitted to a systematic, practical test or any form of social control.*

Another factor limiting effectiveness of production in the communist countries is state ownership of the means of production. Not only do workers have no share or say under this form of ownership, but even the enterprise directors who are responsible for production are totally subordinated to state command.

A Polish economist, Stefan Kurowski (1980), clearly explained some important aspects of the economic failure of communism in a paper presented during a conference in Warsaw and later published outside the orbit of communist censorship:

> In the area of ownership, the enterprise stage has been skipped, and . . . state ownership, has been established. Thus, a new disproportion has emerged: state ownership of the means of production is not in harmony with the enterprise level of the production process, and this yields a new contradition. [p. 18; this author's trans. from Polish]

According to Kurowski, this contradiction consists in the simultaneous existence of the central plan, which embodies the principle of state ownership of the means of production, and of the enterprises, which organize the process of production in reality. The conflict between the producing units and the planners has been emphasized by many authors. For example, Katsenelinboigen (1977) observes that

> planning in the U.S.S.R. is, to a large degree, constructed on the principle of "power play" . . . there is a struggle between the administrators and the persons administered in the assignment of a plan.

Kurowski argued similarily with respect to the manner in which the central plan focuses its efforts largely on a struggle with the enterprises, seeking to subordinate them and thereby to curb their independence and destroy those barriers that make their separate existence possible. This also includes attempts to weaken their cooperative efforts to obtain data dealing with the state production process. In turn, the enterprises combat the central plan through the construction of an economic underworld that is directed by standards and motives operating in a manner contradictory to the designs of the central plan. This underground economy bypasses the orders and restrictions of the central plan and operates on the basis of apparently hidden reserves and unofficial networks. Larger enterprises evolve through the merger of smaller plants as, increasingly, decisions are placed in the higher levels of administration and corporations, in an effort to facilitate management from the top echelons of the central plan, or accomplish state ownership. (Kurowski 1980, pp. 18–19)

Clearly, this strategy requires an ideological somersault since it assumes that introduction by force of "more-progressive" forms of production relationships will provoke appropriate changes in the sphere of the means of production. This is a typical case of "putting the cart before the horse"; the only result can be, as Kurowski (1980) suggests, that "the horse will fall down and the cart will fall apart" (p. 20). Meanwhile, the central planner is involved in a battle on two fronts: conflict against consumers in the general population, and continuing conflict with the enterprises. And he is generally anxious about the ever present possibility of his two enemies joining forces to realize their common ends in the marketplace.

Such a union, although officially prohibited, emerges in the form of a black market; a second economy; and many other illegal, semilegal, or merely informal arrangements—all of them vital to the survival of both the economy and the individual members of the society.

In the second part of this chapter, I shall deal with these "survival techniques" as well as with more obviously criminal abuses of the economy, which are, however, stimulated and facilitated by its evident shortcomings.

## Economic Crimes

### Corruption

Disorganized and based on fictitious premises, the economy provokes—and in some cases even necessitates—various forms of corruption. Bribery is often the only effective way to keep production going. Directors are faced with the rigid requirements of the plan, on the one hand, and the insufficiently coordinated division of tasks among various enterprises on the other.

Chalidze (1977) observes that in the Soviet Union,

> the production goals of the Plan for an enterprise often cannot be fulfilled on schedule without violating the detailed prescriptions of the Plan for payroll, etc., or committing some other illegal act such as bribery to procure needed supplies. [ p. 172]

Similarly, the directors of the Polish enterprises interviewed by Kurczewski and Frieske (1977) stressed the importance of the following factors in maintaining the operative horizontal cooperation: use of personal contacts and relationships, reciprocity of services and exchange of goods, settling matters over a social drink, gifts, and so forth. Obviously, the directors interviewed could not speak of very widespread but deviously criminal practices such as bribery, forgery of documents, fabrication of false reports, fraud, and so forth. Bribery is most useful in the effort to obtain from one's collaborators unplanned supplies of needed materials, to expedite a delayed delivery, to cover up various deviations from the plan, to secure the tolerance of the controllers, and so on.

This common predicament stimulates a horizontal solidarity among the managers as well as among lower staff responsible for similar tasks in the cooperating units or enterprises, which counteracts the coercive fiction of the plan and the punitiveness of the vertical control. The authors of the aforementioned research report shed additional light on the significance of those informal and, strictly speaking, illegal developments in their description of how directors gave accounts of the manner in which top-level supervisory agencies would often enforce rules perceived by these agencies as irrational. This would create increased conflict in the professional role of the directors, for it is much worse to be obstructed by a rule that supervisors do not believe in than by one they find defensible. Given the opinions of the directors, it seems correct to conclude that the first-level supervisory agencies are inclined to exercise control, levy sanctions, and formulate rules as a means of avoiding sanctions in the form of severe criticism from the Central Planning Agencies or, possibly, of criminal prosecution (Kurczewski and Frieske 1977, p. 494).

Under such circumstances, illegal efforts to deceive or neutralize control agencies are seen by insiders as justified and necessary for the survival of an enterprise and the fulfillment of productive tasks. They create a solidarity of joint effort to do business despite all the rigid bureaucratic obstacles; yet "this climate of relations among managers may also undercut respect for the law by the employees and may legitimate criminal conduct in their eyes" (Kurczewski and Frieske 1977, p. 503). The workers, who are aware of this everyday lawbreaking by the management, are less likely to detect those situations when the system of illegalities becomes subordinated to individual rather than collective interests. In any case, the widespread methods of "stalling" the official administrative procedures, although vital in preventing the complete collapse of the centralized economy, lead nevertheless to a wasteful escalation of private resourcefulness, which inflicts large financial losses on the economy as a whole. Such a situation is clearly conducive to the widespread phenomenon of organized crime, which mushrooms in the general atmosphere of disdain for legality. This question will be dealt with later in this chapter.

Yet the corruption permeating the production processes represents only one aspect of the economy-related corruption prevalent in the communist countries:

> Internal corruption grows out of the very nature of the communist economies—a chronic shortage of consumer goods, their poor quality, the interminable delays in obtaining service and repairs, a centralized planning system that decides what people should wear or consume, whether they like the product or not. [Jacoby, Nehemkis, and Eells 1977, p. 38]

The failure of the centralized state economy and administration leads to the thorough corruption of the bureaucracy at all levels (see, for example, Staats

1972; Simis 1979). These developments are complicated even more by the preponderance of political criteria in the system of promotions and privileges, as well as the distribution of some restricted goods (for example, apartments, telephones, fur caps, and so on); welfare services (nurseries, reduced-price holidays, better hospitals); and other opportunities (entrance to university, passports to travel abroad, and so on). Therefore "what the elite gets legally through their special stores and system of privileges, ordinary people are forced to seek illegally in the country's counter-economy" (Jacoby, Nehemkis, and Eells 1977, p. p. 39).

Some ways around these political and bureaucratic barriers may be opened if one is able to find suitable connections to reach informally the responsible clerk or official, or if one finds the appropriate way to hand him a bribe or arrange a mutually acceptable exchange of services (favors). Very often a go-between is used, who can discuss more freely with both parties their conditions and mutual expectations. If one of the parties cannot meet the conditions set by the other party, the chain is broadened, often turning into a long network of mutual favors.

It is interesting, however, that such complex networks of corruption serve clearly as a stabilizing factor, for any change would disturb dangerously the existing, tested, and familiar arrangements and could bring to light common involvement in violation of the law. One may even claim that this gives to the system some sort of peculiar legitimacy.

> If behind the given legal system (which is rejected by the population at large as unjust, undemocratic, etc.) there operates a complicated infrastructure of mutually interdependent interests, then this legal system may become accepted, not on the basis of its own merits, but because it creates a convenient cover-system for the flourishing phenomenon of "dirty togetherness." Then each institution, factory and organization serves . . . as a formal network which gives a stable frame of reference for an enormous amount of mutual semi-private services, reciprocal arrangements. [Podgórecki 1979, p. 203]

The occurrence of such arrangements may not always be triggered by a spontaneous and grass-roots self-defense of the people who want to survive. Some of their forms may be manipulated and stimulated by the official power centers to counterbalance "private" cliques and to control profits flowing from corruption and tampering.

## Theft of Nationalized Property

A problem that greatly concerns the authorities in communist countries is the common lack of respect for nationalized property. This manifests itself above all

at workplaces, where theft is not only widespread but also is seen as fully legitimate under the circumstances, which themselves are generally perceived as
illegitimate and unjust. State property is perceived as nobody's, and its appro-
priation does not bear any criminal stigma. Chalidze (1977) describes bitterly
the early origins of this attitude:

> To obtain funds, both the Social Revolutionaries and the Bolsheviks
> were active in organizing armed robberies, which were euphemistically
> known as "expropriations." ... During the Revolution, the Bolsheviks
> declared that in the future all property of any magnitude would be held
> in common, and they incited the proletariat to pillage. [p. 21]

> With all its propaganda, the new regime did not succeed in persuading
> people to protect state property as their own; they continued to regard
> it as someone else's and treated it accordingly. This seems to be true
> today of the entire population; everyone steals a bit here and there.
> [p. 28]

In addition to the common feelings of hostility against "them"—those for
whom one works—there are also some other factors at work. The wasteful organization of work and the mindless subordination to the alien plan discourages
genuine involvement in productive tasks and stimulates an individualistic orientation that facilitates pilferage and cheating of the employer. Inadequate wages
make moonlighting a necessity; but there are no legal ways to acquire the parts,
materials, or tools to carry out one's side work (as the "means of production,"
they cannot be owned or purchased privately). Therefore, "A typical feature of
Soviet life is that people often steal socialist property not for personal use but as
a means of carrying on their lawful occupations" (Chalidze 1977, p. 195).

The penalties for theft of nationalized property were very harsh under
Stalin, but after his death a much more liberal policy was introduced into the
Soviet Union and the Eastern European countries. In most of these countries,
the Workers' Courts were established to deal with the problem by educational
rather than penal means. They have not proved effective, but there are no new
ideas for coping with the problem. In some countries, such as Poland, the
Workers' Courts have been so unpopular that most of them have gradually
ceased to exist. This has been caused to some extent by the high proportion of
white-collar backgrounds of the judges, in contrast to the defendants, almost all
of whom were blue-collar workers (see Podgórecki 1969; Łoś 1978, pp. 811-
814).

According to the existing statistics, the greatest losses (both in stolen goods
and in defrauded money) are usually sustained by the state and cooperative
commerce as well as by collectivized agriculture. Other extremely vulnerable
areas are the construction and food industries, both of which deal with goods
and materials that are often unavailable on the open market and thus are attractive to black-market operators.

*The Wasteful Use of Economic Resources*

Even though petty theft is routine and nearly ubiquitous, certainly much greater losses are caused by the wasteful organization of the economy: political rather than economic management of the processes of production; general disorganization and lack of coordination between various segments of industry; an oversized bureaucracy and inflexible planning. Surely these intrinsic features of the economy cannot be criminalized by the state. Only concrete cases of waste, usually on the level of the enterprise, can be penalized under existing law, although this rarely happens in reality. It is often difficult to separate willful waste or negligence on the part of individual employees from that caused by unrealistic, contradictory, or outdated plans. There are countless ways of wasting material resources and human labor. For example, the lack of any insight into consumer demand, coupled with the low quality of many consumer goods, leads to the growth of stocks of unsellable products. Lack of coordination between the production of parts and the planned amount of the final product causes enormous losses in scrapped parts and half-completed products. Great losses are also brought about by delays in delivery of necessary materials and parts, which cause frequent stoppages in the production processes. (The conventional penalties do not have any deterrent effect, since the fines paid by the unreliable supplier to the receiving enterprise are usually compensated by the penalties paid to him by his other cooperators because most of the enterprises involved in the chain of production are unable to meet the schedule. See Pawełko (1971, p. 202.) Moreover, enterprises have a tendency to order more materials than they actually need because they know that their orders are often cut. Additionally, they need some reserves in order to avoid at least some of the stoppages caused by the canceled, delayed, or thoroughly unusable deliveries. In some cases, this will mean simply using up accumulated stocks to continue production; in others, trading off some hard-to-get articles for the urgently needed materials or parts that are not kept in stock by the given enterprise. However, both the lack of reservers and the exaggerated stockpiling may lead to great losses, and both these practices are very common in the communist planned economy.

The examples of wasteful investment decisions are also numerous. Industrial plants, half-built and abandoned because of someone's change of heart; new, costly factories or machines, immobilized by the prohibitive costs of transporting raw materials from distant parts of the country, of importing of some necessary elements from abroad, or of training workers to use and service the modern equipment that is not synchronized with the traditional nature of production. Since the economy depends fully on political decisions made by party officials who are experts on ideology rather than economics, the tremendous scale of waste and carelessness can be anticipated.

Immense losses are also caused by incompetent or dishonest export agents

(Naumowicz 1970, p. 9). Jobs in foreign trade often tend to be distributed according to political rather than rational (that is, professional) criteria. Such jobs are considered not only politically sensitive, but also very attractive. Therefore, they are often given to incompetent but politically worthy people as a reward for their merits or as a consolation when they have been deprived of other, more-desirable offices. Naturally, information about this kind of economic wastefulness is suppressed and is spread largely through informal channels. This tendency to conceal the facts is even more pronounced in cases of gigantic waste of resources and of people's efforts caused by ideological mismanagement of an economy founded on fictitious premises and rules by secret decisions and policies.

*Organized Crime within the Nationalized Economy*

Significant economic losses are effected by organized cliques of those who do not steal just for themselves or for occasional dealing, but who organize their theft on a much larger and more-profitable scale. Large, Mafia-like organizations are probably relatively rare because of the fear of punishment, which may be extremely harsh (even including the death penalty, which was in fact not uncommon in the 1960s); fear of informers; limited opportunities for spending large amounts of money; and so forth. But the pattern in both large and small cliques is similar and is determined mainly by the specific features of the communist economy and the fact of suppression of private initiative.

The common characteristics of this economy—lack of incentives, waste and ineffectiveness in the organization of production—open up opportunities for the introduction of illegal incentives and increased productivity, the fruits of which are illegally appropriated. For example, Majchrzak (1965) describes in detail activities of criminal groups in the leather-tanning industry in Poland. One of the typical patterns consists of introducing to a tannery large amounts of illegally bought raw skins together with the legal ones and, at the end of the processing, withdrawing them for black-market sale. The members of the "gang" are selected according to their positions in the factory, and all they have to do is to avoid mixing up the two lots of skins and to do some double recording.

The cooperation of selected truck drivers, convoyers, guards, and so forth is also crucial for carrying out these tasks. If the goods are to be distributed through state stores (instead of on the black market), some of the stores' employees also must be included in the scheme. To achieve a satisfactory level of protection and security, it is usually necessary to buy the collaboration of internal and external control inspectors, as well as that of the director of the enterprise. The workers work harder, often with no extra pay, but may get some satisfaction from working in an unusually well-organized enterprise, with staff who care about the results and do everything to facilitate production processes, to avoid any unnecessary stoppages, and to achieve high-quality products. Such a technique for the creation of a parallel illegal enterprise within a legal one has been used in many other branches of production, for example, in the meat and food-processing industry. Modified versions of such a procedure can be introduced successfully in most state enterprises. According to Chalidze (1977), "unregistered production within a state enterprise" is a common type of offense in the Soviet Union; and "those who are brought to book for such activities are generally also charged with stealing socialist property and abusing their official position" (pp. 169–170).

It has been widely documented that securing the cooperation of the people who occupy strategic positions is, as a rule, very easy, whether it is done through the use of bribes (in the case of controllers and others); special payments for extra jobs (for example, to drivers); or shares in the profits (for directors, bookkeepers, foremen, and so forth). In the event of trouble, of course, various forms of blackmail or even physical terror may be employed.

The operators of such criminal cliques usually have splendid political reputations, skillfully use current ideological slogans, and have convenient connections with influential people. They may deal easily with eventual critics, either on political grounds or by charging them with defamation. (Majchrzak 1965; Daszkiewicz 1971).

It is worth emphasizing that the existence of a double structure and double recording of the ongoing productive processes is possible only because of the typical occurrence in communist enterprises of complicated patterns of spurious activities, which easily accommodate further fictitious expansion. In the organization of a communist economy, the only officially relevant and clearly formalized dimension of management is a hierarchical one; the only relevant types of activities are planning and reporting back on the fulfilment of the plan. These activities occupy much of the energies of any enterprise, although they are irrelevant from the point of view of the effectiveness of its real production. As indicated earlier, in order to carry on productive tasks and effective cooperation with other enterprises, very different types of relationships must develop— namely, a horizontal network of contacts, agreements, and exchanges. These are bound to be largely informal and to employ skillful means of evading the impractical and inconvenient implications of the centralized, hierarchical command.

Besides the illegal production that is fully simultaneous with the legal one, there exist many forms of private subsidiary shops within the factories, collective farms, service enterprises, and so on (see, for example, Grossman 1979). Their organizers share the profits with the "parent" enterprises in exchange for formal cover and protection. They often use stolen materials and, as a rule, "borrow" machines and other equipment from their legal hosts.

Large illegal gains are also obtained because of the often too tolerant estimates of materials and labor needed for planned production and of the size of the inevitable losses and waste. There are many ways in which such favorable norms can be secured (bribes, false reports about past performance, and so forth). The surplus can easily be sold on the black market or used for private production. Organized crime flourishes in state trade and services (for example, home repairs, appliance repairs, catering, and so forth) as much as in industry; in such cases, private consumers are often the immediate victims.

Although cases of very harsh penalties for the participants in organized gangs are known, communist law enforcement is usually rather lenient toward them. Moreoever, there are many instances in which people with previous convictions for economic crimes hold responsible positions in the state economy. For example, in a survey of 150 persons convicted for organized crime in light industry in the years 1959-1964 in Poland, it was found that in 1968, 57 of them were holding executive positions or posts connected with considerable responsibility for state property (Pawełko 1971, p. 182). Furthermore, organized crime in the communist countries, as in the capitalist ones, involves and benefits many high officials who determine and execute relevant legal economic and social policies. It should be emphasized that the countereconomy in the communist countries is very different from organized or corporate crimes in the capitalist countries. The criminalization of any private initiative and the subordination of the economy to an impractical ideology and to the state monopoly over production processes account for the origins and the nature of organized crime under communism. Under such conditions, any crime-prevention policies, short of total transformation of the economic structure, are doomed to remain a sterile exercise.

*Black Market and Speculation*

Crimes against the communist distribution of goods are very common because of the notorious failure of the state market. According to Chalidze (1977), "'speculation' defined as 'the purchase and resale of goods or other articles for gain' is more severely punished in the Soviet Union than any other form of private enterprise" (p. 174). Nevertheless, "speculation" is a common phenomenon in the communist countries, where many essential goods are in short supply because of the deficiencies of state planning and distribution, as well as regulations banning various goods from the consumer market. Chalidze (1977) quotes a typical example of "functional" speculation: "When, as often happens, goods are available in Moscow but not elsewhere, speculators who buy them in Moscow and resell them in the provinces are countering geographical discrimination" (p. 176).

These practices are so common that people no longer notice the illegality of the transaction when they routinely buy meat, eggs, and vegetables; foreign cloth and records; carpets and toilet paper from the door-to-door or corner salesmen; from "under the counter" in the state stores; from their own clients, customers, or patients; from some unidentified middlemen; and so on. (For the political functionality of these and similar arrangements, see Dobbs [1977]). Practically everybody is in need of something that he or she cannot obtain legally, but almost everyone often has access to goods or services that are scarce in the market. This is why, apart from the typical money transactions, there emerge numerous networks of complicated exchanges of goods, services, or even information. The survival of both the citizens and economic organizations (illegal, private ones, as well as state-owned enterprises) depends strongly on these mutual services. For instance, individuals and enterprises routinely acquire excess goods in order to trade (or exchange) them later with other enterprises or persons for other goods that are temporarily unavailable.

A general assumption that one's needs cannot be satisfied by ordinary, legal means leads to ubiquitous corruption and the emergence of an intricate web of illegal or semilegal bonds among people. It also leads to the emergence of many semilegal and illegal markets covering a remarkably diversified assortment of goods, services, and other commodities. The complexity of these multifarious markets is well described in a very useful article by Katsenelinboigen (1977).

In addition to black-market operators, speculators, and various sorts of middlemen, the state-shop salespeople play an important role as providers of numerous opportunities for illegal transactions. The basic reason for the emergence of this market is the apparent short supply ("deficitness") of commodities. Commodities in short supply include both producer and consumer goods. The reasons for such shortages vary, including, among other things, nonfulfillment of plans, planning mistakes, shortages due to lack of flexible relations between suppliers and consumers, and so forth. (Katsenelinboigen 1977, p. 75)

The salespeople in shops and wholesale trade bases engage routinely in selling goods under the counter in exchange for a bribe or another service; in selling stolen or illegally produced goods; in selling for untaxed provision products supplied by the private sector of the economy; in selling rejected, reduced-price articles for standard prices; in selling scarce goods to speculators or private producers for profit; and so forth.

In some communist countries, the so-called private sector plays a very important role in stimulating and sustaining illegal markets. This sector, despite its legality, encounters constant difficulties in securing adequate supplies of needed materials. In the following section, I shall comment on this issue.

## Crimes Related to the Private Sector

The communist economy, based on the principle of state ownership of the means of production, has been gradually forced to accommodate some degree of private economic enterprise. It has been realized that the rigid system of long-term planning and hierarchically centralized management is unable to respond to changing consumer demand and to individualized expectations in the area of some personalized services. After 1956, both the Soviet Union and the Eastern European countries relaxed to some extent their ban on private craft and small enterprise, but it continues to be a crime to engage in prohibited types of trade or industry. Naturally, the extent to which private initiative has been actually legalized varies very much both from country to country and from one ideological "wave" to another.

The dependence of illegal producers on the black market for the supply of tools and raw materials as well as for sales of their products is quite understandable. More striking is the fact that the legally established private enterprises must rely on them as well. The ideologically determined regulations of the market made it practically impossible for a private person to buy machines, materials, or other items necessary for carrying on production.

> Most people would doubtless prefer to buy their necessary supplies honestly, but the State makes this impossible. For instance, one cannot buy leather to make shoes, upholster chairs, or bind books. So when a man is charged with making shoes illegally, he is usually also charged with stealing leather from the State—an excellent example of how, by prohibiting a harmless activity, the State incites people to commit more serious offenses. [Chalidze 1977, p. 166]

A private producer may obtain authorization to purchase limited amounts of the required articles; but if he wants to make a profit and to be able to pay taxes, he must produce and sell more than is permitted and, often, more than he is prepared to reveal to the revenue office. Therefore, if his business is to make any sense economically, he is forced to pay black-market prices (or bribes) for the materials essential to his production. Moreover, the officially allotted supplies may be of such low quality that the profit-oriented producer may be better off paying black-market prices for more-suitable materials.

In some cases, tools, raw materials, construction materials, or chemical substances (for example, fertilizers) can be purchased legally only in "hard-currency" stores. Then, however, the producer must buy hard currency from black-market dealers (there is no legal exchange), or engage in even more risky criminal operations involving smuggling and contraband. There is no way in which legitimate private business in the communist countries could be freed of its criminal stigma and of the necessity to cooperate with the criminal underworld unless the basic principles of economic organization are rethought.

In his book on the prevention of economic crimes, published in Poland, Witold Pawełko emphasizes the high concentration of criminal activities in areas in which the state and private sectors interact. He uses official data of the state agencies of control to support his conclusion that the intersection of the two sectors in the agencies who determine the amount of allotted material result in abuses that lead to attempts to bribe officials in these agencies.

He describes three areas in which opportunities for such abuses exist. First, there are abuses related to the purchase of materials by state enterprises, institutions, or agencies from the private sector. Second, opportunities exist for such abuses where supplies for the state market are provided by private industry and trade. Both these types of economic crime, then, are basically due to the underdevelopment of some types of consumer goods and services in the nationalized economy. A third area that contributes to frequent abuse is the converse of the first two, that is, the purchase of materials—raw and other—from public or nationalized sources by private enterprises. Here the abuse grows out of the limited allotments that prevent the private enterprises from extending their activity beyond the maximum value of return established for them (Pawelko 1971, p. 74; this author's translation from Polish). However, even such a plain recognition of the failure of the state economy and disclosure of the mechanisms of the inevitable criminalization of the private sector cannot trigger any effective corrections of the status quo, since the required changes would violate the principles of the binding doctrine.

*State Crimes against Consumers*

In the communist countries, the state has a monopoly over prices, which, of course, is not in itself a crime according to communist laws. However, the communist economy, which is not directed by market laws and which proscribes competition, has not yet achieved any economically meaningful formula for determining prices.

The prices of consumer goods and food go up continuously, as in the West. Yet many complicated and often illegal tactics are used by the state to avoid open price increases and achieve the same effects in more hidden ways. A common trick consists in repacking and renaming products whenever prices of certain goods are to be raised. Another widespread practice consists in the introduction of new, supposedly better, more-expensive products, which give some range of choice to the consumers for a brief period before the older, cheaper articles are withdrawn. Another, often used tactic is the introduction of new stores with higher-quality goods sold at "market prices," which are much higher than the standard ones. This is a perfectly safe practice since no one has the right to question the economic meaning of the market prices in the nonmarket economy. The prices in these special stores are very high indeed, but for many scarce goods and food articles this may be the only—although not very egalitarian—chance to obtain them. There exist also many hard-currency stores in which otherwise unobtainable foreign and domestic goods are offered, ranging from food, cloth, and cosmetics to coal, agricultural machines, tools, chemicals, cars, apartments, and houses.

The quality of the articles on sale may also be manipulated. For instance, the price of butter may remain unchanged, but it may contain a higher proportion of margarine; sausages may be pumped with water, ground meat may contain ever more bread, and so forth.

These and many other similar practices are widely used in the communist countries. Naturally, some of them may occur also in the capitalist countries. Yet in the latter there are at least three factors that attempt (with varied success) to curb them: the courts, competition, and consumers' organizations. In the communist countries, first of all, one cannot expect any legal intervention in the policies and arrangements undertaken by the state; second, competition is illegal; and finally, any spontaneous organization against the state's policies is penalized; certainly, under the given circumstances, any consumers' movement would belong to this category.

Of course, some exemplary penalties may be administered against selected stores or producers in order to veil the real nature of the policy of deception practiced by the state. Yet even if a particular state enterprise is found guilty of producing substandard products (or, for that matter, of polluting the environment or maintaining unsafe or unhealthy working conditions), the penalties are purely symbolic. This is so not only because the average fine is not high enough —as is usually the case in the capitalist countries also—but, above all, because of the spurious nature of the punishment, which involves payment of the state's money from one state purse to another. No one is really bothered by the whole operation. In the worst case, workers' bonus payments would be stopped; but workers need not be perceived as a threat where strikes are banned.

## Summary

The two previous sections were devoted to the task of describing economic crimes under communism and exposing their roots in the organization of the economy itself.

For example, petty theft and fiddling in the nationalized economy of the communist countries is, to a significant extent, caused by the workers' realization that what is not stolen is going to be wasted anyway. The organization of production is very ineffective and wasteful because of the primary concern of the political authorities with the ideological criteria of the organization of the economy, which are contrary to the rational requirements of production processes. Another factor that contributes to the common occurrence of employee theft is connected with the total lack of legitimacy of the political and economic system and its laws. Moreover, ideological slogans about the workers' ownership of the means of production, entirely contradicted by reality, provoke feelings of bitterness and cynicism, as well as disrespect for state property.

In the light of empirical evidence, one may argue that under communism the enormity of economic tasks entrusted to the state must lead to the constant growth of state power and bureaucracy. Such a tendency is obviously contrary to Marx's thesis about inevitable progress toward the withering away of the state. In the democratic capitalist countries, the relative independence of the dominant economic interests from the political ones keeps in check the totalitarian tendencies of the state. Such tendencies remain unrestrained when economic interests are unified with political ones and subordinated to the single dominant ideology.

The only solution to the profit-seeking habits of many executives in communist countries is the creation of a parallel production that is profitable and that is not controlled by the state. Such private initiative counters and discredits the idologically based state economy because of its effectiveness, elasticity, and genuine human involvement—all features notably absent in state enterprises. Being illegal, the private countereconomy certainly brings significant financial losses to the state; but, above all, it reveals the weakness of the economic system, which does not recognize the fact that the reality in communist society is more forceful and real than the Marxist ideology that is supposed to guide it.

The dominant economic organization, with characteristic hierarchical relationships designed to transmit economic command, does not provide a sufficient base for carrying out production. The hierarchical relationships secure the routinized circulation of fictitious information (plans, reports), which is bound to lose touch with real production. Production-related relationships, exchanges, and cooperation are not incorporated into the ideological structure of the economy; therefore, they must develop spontaneously, in an unplanned (and therefore banned) manner. They must be outlawed since they evade the state plan—the fundamental legal document according to which economic processes are to be organized. Yet without these intricate illegal production relationships, the economy would exist only on paper. The inevitability of the development of an underground economic market is strengthened further by the contradiction between the social and economic necessity of the existence of a private economic sector and the ideological infeasibility of providing a legal and economic base for its functioning.

Economic crimes in communist and capitalist countries have some features in common, but they also differ significantly. These differences are caused by the different ideologies and economic realities of these countries. Capitalist ideology is discreet and hidden; it has acquired a high degree of consistency with the economic reality, which it has been able to mold effectively. Moreover, it has become more or less absorbed and legitimized by people's beliefs and life-styles. Economic crimes are shaped by the dominant values and are conditioned by market forces and economic cycles.

Communist ideology is coercive and doctrinaire; further, although it has influenced the formal structure of the economy, it has never been embodied in real economic practice. Moreover, it has not been accepted or even absorbed into social consciousness. Economic crimes are motivated, to a large extent, by a counterideology (a capitalist one?) that cannot be accommodated within the rigid structure of the communist economy. Both economic crimes and the country's economic development depend totally on the existence of black markets and social corruption, both generated by the official economic structure.

## Note

1. For a comparative analysis of economic crimes in the communist and capitalist countries, see Łoś (1980).

## References

Chalidze, V. *Criminal Russia. Essays on Crime in the Soviet Union.* New York: Random House, 1977.

Daszkiewicz, K. *Klimaty bezprawia. (Realms of Lawlessness).* Warsaw: Ksiażka i Wiedza, 1971.

Dobbs, M. "Will a Bit 'on the Side' Keep the Poles Quiet?" *The Sunday Times,* 25 September 1977, p. 8.

Grossman, G. "Notes on the Illegal Private Economy and Corruption." In U.S. Congress Joint Economic Committee, *Soviet Economy in a Time of Change,* vol. I. Washington, D.C.: U.S. Government Printing Office, October 1979.

Jacoby, N.H.; and Nehemkis, P.; and Ells, R. *Bribery and Extortion in World Business: A Study of Corporate Political Payments Abroad.* New York: Macmillan, 1977; London: Collier Macmillan.

Katsenelinboigen, A. "Coloured Markets in the Soviet Union." *Soviet Studies* 29(1977):62–85.

Kurczewski, J., and Frieske, K. "Some Problems in the Legal Regulation of the Activities of Economic Institutions." *Law and Society Review* 11(Winter 1977):489–505.

Kurowski, S. "Doktrynalne uwarunkowania obecnego kryzysu gospodarczego PRL" ("Doctrinal Determinants of the Present Economic Crisis of the Polish People's Republic"). Paper presented to the conference of the Polish Sociological Associations on Sociological and Economic Problems of the Planned Economy, Warsaw, 12 May 1979, Published in *Raport o Stanie narodu i PRL (Report on the State of the Nation and the Polish People's Republic).* Paris: Institut Litteraire, 1980.

Łoś, M. "Access to the Civil Justice System in Poland." In M. Cappelletti and G. Bryant, eds., *Access to Justice,* vol. 1: *A World Survey.* Milan: Dott. A. Giuffre Editore; Alphenaandenrijn: Sijthoff and Noordhoff, 1978.

Łoś, M. "Economic Crimes from a Comparative Perspective." In G. Newman, ed., *Crime and Deviance: A Comparative Perspective.* Beverly Hills, Calif.: Sage, 1980.

Majchrzak, I. *Pracownicze przestepstwo i jego sprawca (White-Collar Crime and White-Collar Criminal)*. Warsaw: Ksiażka i Wiedza, 1965.

Naumowicz, Z. "Niektóre zagadnienia dotyczace przestepczości gospodarczej" ("Selected Problems of Economic Crime"). In *Prawnicy, Socjologowie i Psychologowie o przestepczości i jej zwalczaniu*, trans. M. Łoś. Warsaw: Prokuratura Generalna, 1970.

Pawełko, W. *Zapobieganie przestepstwom gospodarczym (Economic Crime Prevention)*. Warsaw: PWN, 1971.

Podgórecki, A. "Attitudes to the Workers' Courts." In V. Aubert, ed., *Sociology of Law*. New York: Penguin Books, 1969.

Podgórecki, A. "Tertiary social control." In A. Podgórecki and M. Łoś, ed., *Multidimensional Sociology*. London: Routledge and Kegan Paul, 1979.

Simis, K. "The Machinery of Corruption in the Soviet Union." Survey, London, 23, no. 4(1979):35-55.

Staats, S.J. "Corruption in the Soviet System." *Problems of Communism* 2:(January-February 1972):40-47.

# 8

# The Level of Theft and the Size of the Public Sector: Some Empirical Evidence

## Michael K. Block

This paper has its origins in my preparation for a recent conference on white-collar and economic crime held at the State University of New York at Potsdam.[1] At that conference I served as a panelist at a session entitled "The Political Economy of White-Collar Crime: An Inevitable Consequence of Capitalism."

In my preliminary search of the available literature on the topic, I found a good deal of argument, but not very much evidence. Specifically, I discovered numerous assertions by social scientists who referred to themselves as radical or Marxist criminologists that criminal behavior was a direct consequence of the competition and inequality they claim characterize capitalist societies.[2] Lacking, however, in this literature was any empirical evidence on the relationship between the character of an economic system and the level of crime. Hence my preparation for the conference eventually took the form of a preliminary empirical investigation of the relationship between the level of a specific type of crime, theft, and several important characteristics of an economic system. The characteristics of the economy examined here are the degree of (1) direct collective control over resources in the economy and (2) equality in the distribution of income. This chapter is a brief report on that undertaking.

This investigation focuses on theft rather than white-collar crime for several methodological reasons. First, it was desirable to concentrate on an economic crime that was regularly recorded whether or not the offender was identified. This is simply not the case for most white-collar crimes. Second, and more significant, since an international comparison is most appropriate given the nature of the question being investigated, white-collar crime is the least-appropriate type of crime to consider. White-collar crime or, as some radical criminologists prefer to call it, corporate crime, is a particularly problematic type of crime to use in an empirical investigation involving international comparisons. Whereas economic crimes such as larceny involve some definitional problems across countries, white-collar crime is itself almost entirely definitional. After all, price fixing is only a crime if there are competing firms producing the same product. Moreover, since the radical analysis of crime applies to all types of crime in

I would like to thank Mark Nuti, Timothy Moore, and Jeanne Fleming for valuable research assistance. This paper was supported by Grant No. 79-NI-AX-0071 from the National Institute of Justice, U.S. Department of Justice. Opinions expressed are those of the author and do not necessarily represent the official opinion of the U.S. Department of Justice.

relation to the characteristics of the economy, our test of the hypothesis linking crime and capitalism loses little of its generality if we concentrate on the single, and numerically important, crime of larceny.

The crime data used to measure larceny in this analysis was obtained from the International Criminal Police Organization (INTERPOL).[3] According to this source, the crime of *larceny* includes "any act of intentionally and unlawfully removing property belonging to another person." Examples given for larceny include robbery, burglary, housebreaking, and theft. All means other than larceny of gaining unlawful possession of another person's property are classified as *fraud* in the INTERPOL data. There are, of course, a number of obvious problems with these definitions. Perhaps most bothersome is the possibility that what is unlawful possession in one country may not be unlawful in another. Nevertheless, the examples given for at least the larceny category appear to be actions that are quite universally considered crimes, such as robbery.

Table 8-1 reports the results of estimating the relationship between the size of the public sector and the larceny rate.[4] The variable GOVT represents government expenditure as a percentage of gross domestic product (GDP). The source for this data was the United Nations *Statistical Yearbook*.[5] As seen from the estimates in the first column of table 8-1, there appears to be a positive and statistically significant relationship between the size of the public sector in a country and the level of theft or larceny. Given that most socialist countries do not report their crime rates to INTERPOL, is this relationship between government expenditure and theft rates useful in illuminating the relationship between public ownership and control of the economy and crime rates?[6] The most-persuasive argument is the fact that the level of government expenditures is a logical proxy for the magnitude of direct public or collective control over the economy.[7] The larger the public sector as measured by government expenditures as a percentage of gross domestic product, the larger the percentage of total output that is subject to direct collective control.

An obvious determinant of the level of theft in any society is the vigor with which the law against theft is enforced. In column 2 of table 8-1 the level of law enforcement is in fact controlled for by using a measure of the clearance rate or solution rate, SOLVE.[8] The variable SOLVE represents the percentage of cases considered solved by the reporting authority.[9] Essentially, this means cases for which an offender has been either apprehended or identified. The results in table 8-1 reveal that the introduction of the law-enforcement or deterrence variable leaves the government-expenditure results unaltered. It is also interesting to note that the solution rate has the expected sign; that is, the higher the detection rate, the lower the theft rate. In other words, the evidence from this international data is consistent with the deterrence hypothesis.

Invariant as the results concerning the size of the public sector appear to be, one might argue that the government-expenditure variable in these regressions is simply a proxy for a higher level of economic development and hence a higher

**Table 8–1**

**Estimated Relationship between the Size of the Public Sector and the Larceny Rate, 1976**

| *Independent variables* | | | |
|---|---|---|---|
| GOVT[a] | 177.61[b] | 155.03 | 118.41 |
| | (3.99)[c] | (3.67) | (2.74) |
| SOLVE[d] | | −3,006.34 | −1,886.58 |
| | | (−2.62) | (−1.57) |
| PCAPINC[e] | | | 0.171 |
| | | | (2.20) |
| CONSTANT | −1,568.69 | −94.49 | −415.27 |
| *Number of observations* | 38[f] | 37[g] | 37 |
| $R^2$ | .31 | .42 | .50 |
| *F* statistic | 15.94 (1,36) | 12.52 (2,34) | 10.91 (3,33) |

Note: Larceny-rate data obtained from INTERPOL's *International Crime Statistics* (1975–1976).

[a]Government expenditures/gross domestic product obtained from United Nations, *Statistical Yearbook,* 1977.

[b]Estimated coefficient.

[c]Estimated coefficient divided by its estimated standard error.

[d]Larceny crimes solved/reported larcenies; see note 1.

[e]Per capita income; see note 2.

[f]Australia, Austria, Chile, Cyprus, Denmark, Fiji, Finland, France, Germany, Greece, Guyana, Hong Kong, Ivory Coast, Jamaica, Japan, Kuwait, Lesotho, Libya, Luxembourg, Madagascar, Malawi, Malaysia, Morocco, Netherlands, New Zealand, Nigeria, Norway, Peru, Philippines, South Korea, Singapore, Spain, Sri Lanka, Sweden, Syria, Tanzania, United Kingdom, West Indies.

[g]Same as previous note, except Greece.

level of recorded crime. The argument here is that the actual reporting and recording of crime is substantially higher for the developed than for less-developed countries, and the relative size of government may simply be a measure of economic development in this regression. In column 3 of the table we control for this possibility by introducing an explicit measure of economic development, per-capita income, into the regression. Again, although the size of the coefficient on government expenditure is somewhat reduced in magnitude, its sign and statistical significance remain unaltered. It does, however, appear to be true that higher-income countries have higher theft rates. The sign on the per-capita-income coefficient is positive and statistically significant.[10]

The relative size of the government is a logical indicator of direct collective control over the economy, but there are also other measures of this phenomenon.[11] In fact, what is perhaps the most-intuitive measure of "socialism," the percentage of the labor force employed in government enterprises, was available in consistent form for only a very small number of countries.[12] Unfortunately, not only is this sample small, containing only nine countries, but it also is composed almost entirely of countries in which the public sector is not the predominant or even the major producer of goods and services.[13] Hence, at best, this data provides a test of the relationship between theft rates and public-ownership patterns in fundamentally private-enterprise eocnomies. In any case, the relationship bewteen this variable, PUBENT, and the level of theft is given in table 8-2. Again, after controlling for the level of enforcement, SOLVE, there is a positive relationship between the magnitude of collective control over resources—this time measured by the percentage of the labor force employed in public enterprises—and the level of theft.[14]

There appears to be no empirical evidence that the greater the degree of direct collective control over an economy, the less crime prone a society. In fact, if anything, the converse appears to be the case. However, the so-called radical analysis of crime makes an additional and very specific assertion that we have not yet addressed, namely, that the degree of inequality in the distribution of income and crime are unambiguously and positively related (see, for example,

**Table 8-2**
**Estimated Relationship between the Extent of Public Ownership and the Larceny Rate**

| Independent variables | |
| --- | --- |
| PUBENT[a] | 306.36 |
| | (2.15) |
| SOLVE | −1,856.70 |
| | (3.06) |
| CONSTANT | 4,164.79 |
| Number of observations[b] | 9 |
| $R^2$ | .63 |
| F statistic | 5.05 |

[a]Percentage of labor force employed in government-owned enterprises (selected countries), *The Economist*, 30 December 1978.

[b]Austria, Denmark, France, Germany, Japan, Netherlands, Spain, Sweden, United Kingdom.

Gordon 1973; Quinney 1977). The greater the degree of inequality in the society, the higher the crime rate.

Table 8–3 introduces an explicit measure of income distribution (UNEQUAL) into the estimation. The variable used to measure the degree of inequality in the income distribution in this analysis in the Gini coefficient, which takes on values between zero and one, with the higher values indicating greater inequality in the income distribution.[15] Although there are some problems of timing—the Gini coefficients are generally for the 1960s, or in some cases even earlier; and the measure is available for only twenty-three çountries in our INTERPOL sample—the results of the estimation are quite revealing. The empirical results in table 8–3 are not consistent with the hypothesis that the greater the inequality in the distribution of income, the higher the crime rate. In fact, according to these estimates, theft rates are generally higher the more equal the distribution

**Table 8–3**
**Estimated Relationship between the Size of the Public Sector, the Distribution of Income, and the Larceny Rate**

| Independent variables | |
|---|---|
| GOVT | 167.14 (3.44) |
| SOLVE | −2,530.42 (−1.73) |
| PCAPINC | 0.17 (1.45) |
| UNEQUAL[a] | −50.43 (−1.98) |
| CONSTANT | 1,604.50 |
| Number of observations[b] | 23 |
| $R^2$ | .84 |
| F statistic | 23.29 |

[a]The variable UNEQUAL is based on the Gini-coefficient calculations found in J. Cromwell, "The Size Distribution of Income: An International Comparison," *Review of Income and Wealth* 23 (1977); and Felix Paukert, "Income Distribution at Different Levels of Development: A Survey of Evidence," *International Labour Review* 108(August–September 1973):97.

[b]Australia, Chile, Denmark, Fiji, Finland, France, Germany, Ivory Coast, Jamaica, Japan, Madagascar, Morocco, Netherlands, New Zealand, Nigeria, Norway, Peru, Philippines, South Korea, Sri Lanka, Sweden, Tanzania, United Kingdom.

of income in the society. Also of interest is the fact that the explicit introduction of a measure of the income distribution into the regression does not affect the sign or the significance of the coefficient on GOVT. There simply does not appear to be any empirical support for the proposition that greater direct collective control over the economy and/or greater equality in the distribution of income are associated with lower crime rates.

Perhaps the most-interesting finding in all of this is not that the available empirical evidence contradicts the hypothesis that increased direct collective control over the economic system implies lower crime rates, but that it appears that, at least for theft, the converse is true: A larger public sector appears to be systematically associated with higher theft rates. Why this should be the case is not transparent. Are we observing a causal relationship in the sense that large government is responsible for high theft rates?

Is it, as Milton Friedman suggests in the case of Britain, that "the growth of crude criminality . . . may well be a consequence of the drive for equality" (Friedman 1979, p. 145)? In other words, does the scale and pattern of government required for the redistribution of income actually result in an increased willingness to break the laws against theft? Assuming that the drive for equality is at least partially successful, the findings given previously on the relationship between the degree of equality in the income distribution and the level of theft are consistent with this hypothesis. Greater equality in income distribution is associated with higher levels of theft. However, if, as Friedman also asserts, the drive for equality decreases the respect for law and makes law enforcement a more-important controlling influence in society, then it might be argued that, although on balance crime rates increase as the relative size of government increases, law-enforcement efforts will increase to compensate for this erosion of respect for law. As one can see from the estimates in table 8-4, solution or clearance rates do not increase with the size of the public sector. To the extent, then, that an expanded public sector is required to redistribute income, the available empirical evidence is not entirely consistent with Friedman's hypothesis linking crime and the growth of government.[16]

Recent empirical work on the growth of government suggests that increases in equality of the distribution of income are not so much a consequence as a cause of the growth of government (see Pertzman 1980). Perhaps the same distributional forces that imply a larger role for public transfers via the government are also responsible for an increase in the tolerance of private involuntary transfers. That is, a more-equal distribution of income may lead to a demand for a lower solution rate. As is apparent from the results in table 8-5, the available evidence strongly suggests that this is not the case. In the first column of table 8-5 we note that our measure of degree of inequality in the income distribution (UNEQUAL) and the solution rate for larceny are negatively related. That is, we find in our international sample that the more equal the income distribution, the higher the solution rate.

**Table 8-4**
**Estimated Relationship between Solution Rates for Theft (SOLVE)**
**and the Size of the Public Sector, 1976**

| Independent variables | | |
|---|---|---|
| GOVT | −0.007<br>(−1.16) | 0.00004<br>(0.007) |
| PCAPINC | | −0.00003<br>(−2.72) |
| CONSTANT | 0.47 | 0.44 |
| Number of observations[a] | 37 | 37 |
| $R^2$ | .04 | .21 |
| F statistic | 1.36 (2,34) | 4.51 (2,34) |

[a]Australia, Austria, Chile, Cyprus, Denmark, Fiji, Finland, France, Germany, Guyana, Hong Kong, Ivory Coast, Jamaica, Japan, Kuwait, Lesotho, Libya, Luxembourg, Madagascar, Malawi, Malaysia, Morocco, Netherlands, New Zealand, Nigeria, Norway, Peru, Philippines, South Korea, Singapore, Spain, Sri Lanka, Sweden, Syria, Tanzania, United Kingdom, West Indies.

Although increases in the equality of the income distribution appear to make government redistribution more attractive, this same phenomenon makes private redistribution or theft less appealing. If the mechanism generating the demand for government is, as some have suggested, the broadening of the benefit base (that is, the growth of the middle class), then the fact that this change in the income distribution is accompanied by a decrease in the desired level of theft or, equivalently, an increase in the demand for law enforcement should not be surprising.[17] On this point it is interesting to note not only the results with respect to the variable UNEQUAL (Gini coefficient), but also those with respect to alternative indicators of the degree of inequality in the distribution of income. In table 8-5 the income-distribution variable BOT20 gives the percentage of income received by the lowest 20 percent of income earners and TOP5 the income received by the highest 5 percent. The results of table 8-5 clearly indicate that increases in the relative well-being of low-income earners in a society are associated with a demand for increased protection from theft. Moreover, it appears from the empirical evidence that high-income earners are not particularly effective in using the government to protect their property against theft. On this point, note especially the results in the last column of table 8-3. Law-enforcement efforts directed at solving larcenies decline as the share of income going to the highest earners increases—hardly a picture of the capitalist class with the state well under its control.

**Table 8-5**
**Estimated Relationship between Solution Rates for Theft and the Distribution of Income**

| Independent variables | | | |
|---|---|---|---|
| UNEQUAL | -0.009 (-2.56) | | |
| BOT20[a] | | 0.004 (2.39) | |
| TOP5[b] | | | -0.0006 (-1.83) |
| PCAPINC | -0.00005 (-5.39) | -0.00004 (-3.75) | -0.00005 (-4.71) |
| CONSTANT | 0.92 | 0.31 | |
| Number of observations | 23[c] | 22[d] | 22[e] |
| $R^2$ | .59 | .59 | .54 |
| F statistic | 14.54 (2,20) | 13.29 (2,19) | 11.14 (2,19) |

[a]Percentage of all income accounted for by the lowest 20 percent of income earners; Jerry Cromwell, "The Size Distribution of Income: An International Comparison," *Review of Income and Wealth* 23(September 1977):291, table 3.

[b]Percentage of all income accounted for by the highest 5 percent of all income earners; Cromwell, "The Size Distribution of Income."

[c]Australia, Chile, Denmark, Fiji, Finland, France, Germany, Ivory Coast, Jamaica, Japan, Madagascar, Morocco, Netherlands, New Zealand, Nigeria, Norway, Peru, Philippines, South Korea, Sri Lanka, Sweden, Tanzania, United Kingdom.

[d]Same as previous note, except New Zealand.

[e]Same as note d.

The results in table 8-5 should prove problematic for a radical or Marxist interpretation of crime. If crime is caused by the inequality in income distribution, then one might expect those whose interests the radical analysts assert the state represents to redouble their efforts to protect themselves as the distribution becomes more unequal. There is simply no evidence that this is the case. In fact, if anything the evidence in table 8-5 indicates that the desired level of law enforcement declines as the distribution becomes more unequal.[18]

In all the regressions reported in table 8-5, per-capita income is a statistically significant determinant of the solution rate for theft. In part, it appears that the wealthier the members of a society, the less law enforcement they demand.[19]

This might be the result of an increase in the relative cost of such enforcement as income increases. For example, since law enforcement appears to be labor intensive, its relative cost may rise and the demand for such enforcement will tend to encourage theft. Since the supply of theft also appears, from the results in table 8-1, to increase as per-capita income increases, the net effect of income growth under these conditions is unambiguously to increase the level of theft.[20]

Returning to our major concern, overall, no evidence was found to support the contention that greater direct collective control over resources or a greater degree of equality in the income distribution leads to lower property-crime rates. In fact, a reasonable amount of evidence was found to the contrary: Inequality and a large measure of direct collective control over the economy appear to be consistently associated with high levels of property crime. Moreover, far from being victims of laws against theft, it appears that the so-called workers are beneficiaries of such laws. Our evidence clearly shows that the demand for law enforcement actually increases as the degree of equality in the income distribution increases. We find the latter somewhat incongruous with the radical concept of a controlling elite. Finally, increases in per-capita income appear to be associated with increases in the equilibrium level of theft.

## Notes

1. "White Collar and Economic Crime: Trends and Problems in Research and Policy," Potsdam College of Arts and Science, Potsdam, New York, 7-9 February 1980.

2. See Chambliss (1975), Friedrichs (1980), Gordon (1973), Michalowski (1979), Quinney (1977), and Williams (1980).

3. International Criminal Police Organization (INTERPOL), *International Crime Statistics*, 1975-1976.

4. The results that appear in table 8-1 are for equations of the following form: Larceny Rate = Intercept + $\hat{\beta}_1$ GOVT, Larceny Rate = Intercept + $\hat{\beta}_2$ GOVT + $\hat{\beta}_3$ SOLVE, and Larceny Rate = Intercept + $\hat{\beta}_4$ GOVT + $\hat{\beta}_5$ SOLVE + $\hat{\beta}_6$ PCAPINC. The coefficients in the table are estimates of the $\hat{\beta}$s.

5. See United Nations, *Statistical Yearbook*, 1977 Public Finance, pp. 776-868, and the Economist, *The World in Figures*, 1978.

6. For example, in 1976 none of the Comecon countries reported their crime rates to INTERPOL.

7. The data used are for central-government expenditures and hence they also provide a measure of the degree of concentration in public control. However, it should be noted that government-expenditure data are not a very good proxy for the degree of collective control exercised through the regulatory process.

8. We ignore both the level of punishment and questions of simultaneity in this formulation, the former because of data constraints and the latter simply because this is an exploratory analysis.

9. For a discussion of the actual measure used, see INTERPOL (1976), p. xi, 1b "Detection Rates."

10. The statistical significance of this coefficient, although not its magnitude, is altered somewhat in the regression reported in table 8–3. Note, however, that not only is an additional variable added to the data set, but that the sample also is reduced quite substantially in this regression.

11. One measure of the size of the capitalist sector that has been used in other research in the share of the labor force working for wages and salaries. See Cromwell (1977). Applying this measure of the size of the capitalist sector in the context of the current problem would provide an interesting extension of this research.

12. The countries included in the sample are Austria, Denmark, France, Germany, Japan, the Netherlands, Spain, Sweden, and the United Kingdom.

13. The average value for PUBENT in the sample is 6.35 percent, with a range from 13.7 to 2.8 percent.

14. Whereas the percentage of the labor force employed by government entrepreneurs is an intuitive measure of socialism, it is not the measure suggested in the so-called radical analysis of crime (see note 10).

15. For a discussion of the Gini coefficient or concentration ratio, see Paukert (1973), appnedix 1, "Measures of Inequality of Income Distribution by Size."

16. It should be noted, however, that as reported in table 8–5, the more equal the distribution of income, the higher the solution rate. Although we provide an alternative explanation of the phenomenon, it is consistent with Friedman's assertion that the drive for equality will, because of its effect on attitudes, require greater reliance on law enforcement to control theft.

17. Peltzman (1980) makes the strongest empirical case for the relationship between increase in the size of the middle class and the growth of government. In summarizing his empirical work, he states: "our results imply that it is in fact the *levelling* of income differences across a large part of the population—the growth of the 'middle class'—which has been a major source of the growth of government in the developed world over the last 50 years."

18. It should be apparent at this point that, with the exception of the relationship between the level of law enforcement and the relative size of the public sector, all the results are consistent with Friedman's hypothesis concerning the relationship between attempts at redistribution of income through the public sector and the level of crime.

19. There is, of course, a potentially very important confounding factor at work here. Specifically, the proportion of crimes actually reported to the authorities may be a function of income per capita. If this is the case, the solution rate may, in part, be positively related to income per capita simply because of a reporting phenomenon.

20. The supply effect is inferred from the sign on the per-capita-income variable in table 8-1. Of course, this might simply reflect the fact that other— and, in this case, unmeasured—aspects of law enforcement such as punishment levels also fall as per capita income grows.

## References

American Academy of Political and Social Science. *Annals,* September 1973.

Chambliss, W. "Toward a Political Economy of Crime." *Theory and Society* 2 (Summer 1975):150-170.

Cromwell, Jerry. "The Size Distribution of Income: An International Comparison." *Review of Income and Wealth* 23(September 1977):291.

The Economist. *The World in Figures.* London, 1978.

Friedman, Milton. *Free to Choose,* chap. 5. New York: Harcourt Brace Jovanovich, 1980.

Friedrichs, D. "Radical Criminology in the United States: An Interpretive Understanding." In J. Inciardi, ed., *Radical Criminology: The Coming Crises.* Beverly Hills, Calif.: Sage Publications, 1980, pp. 35-60.

Gordon, D. "Capitalism, Class, and Crime in America." *Crime and Delinquency* (April 1973):163-185.

International Criminal Police Organization (INTERPOL). *International Crime Statistics,* 1975-1976.

Michalowski, R. "Crime and a Theory of the State: The Adolescence of Radical Analyses." *Criminology* 16(February 1979):561-580.

Paukert, Felix. "Income Distribution at Different Levels of Development: A Survey of Evidence." *International Labour Review* 108(August-September 1973):97.

Peltzman, Sam. "The Growth of Government." Center for the Study of the Economy and the State, University of Chicago, Working Paper No. 001-2, January 1980.

Quinney, R. *Class, State and Crime,* New York: David McKay, 1977.

United Nations, *Statistical Yearbook,* 1977.

Williams, F. "Conflict Theory and Differential Processing: An Analysis of the Research Literature." In J. Inciardi, ed., *Radical Criminology: The Coming Crises,* Beverly Hills, Calif.: Sage Publications, 1980, pp. 213-232.

# 9

## Critical Comments on Michael K. Block's "The Level of Theft and the Size of the Public Sector: Some Empirical Evidence"

*Laureen Snider*

In chapter 8, Michael K. Block has given us some interesting—and, to many, unexpected—findings. It appears there is a statistically significant relationship between the level of larceny (theft) and the amount of public ownership in a fair number of societies. Moreover, Block has tried to show that the more equal the distribution of income, the higher the larceny rate. He concludes that these two findings cast doubt on the "radical" thesis that crime is related to the inequality and competition generated by capitalism. I will focus my comments on two major areas: first, on the relationships themselves and the conclusions Block has drawn from these, and, second, on the validity of his theoretical and philosophical assumptions.

In this first section, I will examine the relationships between variables that Block has found *as if* they were a true representation of reality. We know from many sources, however, that INTERPOL data suffer from the same types of problems that afflict national records on crime—methodological deficiencies in recording and gathering the "facts"; technological problems; systematic inaccuracies engendered by dependence on a wide range of police forces as the primary source of data (due to the use of these facts to increase budgets and pay, as well as to biases of all types); differing legal definitions of similar behaviors; and so forth. Moreover, we now have a wide body of literature that points out that empiricism itself is not a value-free "objective" method of gaining knowledge about the human condition, but that it is biased toward a definition of reality that reflects a technocratic, individualistic, and rationalist world view.

However, to discuss this chapter at all necessitates a "suspension of disbelief" and a tacit acceptance of the notion that, despite all their problems, such statistics can tell us *something* about the real world. It must be remembered, then, that this is only an assumption.

With this caveat, let us look at the major relationships that Block has found and at the conclusions he has drawn. The relationship between public control of the economy (as revealed by the size of the public sector) and larceny is interesting. To know what it really means, however, we would have to have much more information than Block has here provided. Are we measuring and comparing older, more-established capitalist economies against younger ones still in the early stages of capitalism? The latter usually have less public ownership (although there are exceptions). Hence, the lower theft rates in such young societies may be rendered meaningless by much higher overall crime rates. That is, countries in this stage of development may not have matured and stabilized relations between the still-emerging classes; murder and kidnapping, more than theft, may then be the "crimes of choice" for redistributing resources. If this is so, public ownership may indeed be related to higher theft rates, but to lower "serious" crime rates.

Or this relationship could be accounted for by an underlying variable that I will call *traditionalism*. One could hypothesize that it is not the growth of government that "causes" higher larceny rates, but, rather, the destruction of a traditional way of life that such growth signifies. When the informal means of social control that are characteristic of traditional tribes or villages are destroyed by the anonymity, impersonality, and burgeoning urban growth that accompany what we call development or modernization (which is usually synonymous with the growth of the public sector), theft may well increase simply because people are no longer bound by the primary controls that marked their former way of life.

These explanations are, I would argue, just as plausible as those suggested by Block. He has completely ignored the well-known fact that the major western European countries, including Scandinavia and the United Kingdom, all of which have a much greater degree of public ownership than does the United States, also have much lower crime rates in every area *except* theft. Thus his interpretation must be examined skeptically.

The second major relationship discussed by Block is that between inequality and larceny. There is a serious defect here in the use of figures on income distribution to measure inequality. Real property ownership has been found to be a far more accurate index of inequality, whereas income data make ownership of resources and the distribution of life chances look far more equitable than they really are. Thus one might get very different results, in either direction, if one looked at stock ownership, for example.

Quite apart from this problem, the data presented here do not support the conclusions Block has reached. He says: "Law-enforcement efforts directed at solving larcenies decline as the share of income going to the highest earners increases—hardly a picture of the capitalist class with the state well under its control." In the first place, the members of the capitalist class in all capitalist societies employs all kinds of legal and quasi-legal devices—from electrical fences to armored cars to machine-gun-toting bodyguards—to protect the surplus they have amassed. That the monies expended on law enforcement against larceny are lower in states with more-unequal distribution of income may mean nothing more than that more state efforts are directed toward crimes of violence. (The rich can well protect their own property.) It may mean that the gross national product is not large enough to support enough police forces to concentrate on petty crimes such as larceny—a factor related to the aforementioned problem of lumping together capitalist societies that have different cultures and are in different stages of development. Or, if this relationship is valid (remembering that income statistics are suspect), it may reflect the increased needs of the national governments (the state) to promote legitimacy as the lower classes gain more power (which, again, is a necessary concomitant of obtaining a more-equitable distribution of income); that is, the state in such societies must act as if the protection of the relatively small amounts of equity amassed by the middle and working classes is a state priority—hence the increased expenditures on law enforcement vis-à-vis larcenies.

This dubious relationship poses one final problem. To assert, as Block does, that "increases in the relative well-being of low-income earners in a society are associated with a demand for increased protection from theft" does not allow one to conclude that the low-income earners actually *receive* more protection from theft. In fact, we have a considerable amount of evidence suggesting that law-enforcement priorities focus predominantly on the needs of the rich (Manning 1977; Bordua 1967; Chambliss 1974; Reiman 1979). A theft, an assault, or even a murder in which a poor person is victimized is given a lower priority, and results in the allocation of fewer police resources, than a similar offense involving an upper-class victim, all other things being equal.

In the foregoing, I have suggested that there are problems with the relationships found and the interpretations suggested in Block's chapter. Even if the relationships are valid, I have suggested, this may be due to intervening variables. Alternate explanations may well be more compatible with conflict/Marxist theory than with the consensus/functionalist approach assumed, if not articulated, by Block. In the following section I wish to remark on the deeper theoretical and philosophical problems with this study (and, by implication, with the other studies of this type taht abound in the literature).

In the first place, there is a basic misinterpretation of Marxist criminology here. This is hardly Block's fault—as he says, he is an economist who ventured into this area as a result of an invitation to attend the Potsdam conference. He has had time to acquaint himself only with the more-simplistic, predominantly American analyses. The vast literature developed over the past fifteen years in the United Kingdom and Europe, by Marxist scholars who are not necessarily criminologists, has therefore eluded him. Thus he asserts that "radical or Marxist criminologists [believed] that criminal behavior was a direct consequence of the competition and inequality they claim characterize capitalist societies." This simplistic statement provides a misleading view of the very complex body of Marxist theory on crime: Marx himself wrote very little on crime, but later scholars have developed a theory that sees law in capitalist states as an instrument of both legitimation and coercion. That is, the notion of "justice for all," which is meted out to rich and poor alike and which protects everyone in the

society from those who are "dangerous" and "antisocial," is part of an ideological system that stabilizes, explains, and justifies the status quo.

However, law (and the criminal-justice system) also fill a coercive function,
especially when the state is (or is perceived to be) threatened. Law is used to
neutralize and isolate real or potential "disruptive elements." Exploitation and
surplus value, not inequality and competition per se, are seen as a cause both of
criminal behavior and of the form and content of criminal law. Nothing in this
formulation implies that socialist countries will have no activities that will be
labeled "crimed" and no violators who will be labeled "criminal." The level of
theft in a given capitalist society, then, is seen as a function of the history of
that particular state, its culture, the nature of relationships between the classes,
the skill of the state elite in legitimatizing the status quo to its citizens, and so
forth (O'Connor 1973; Miliband 1969; Hall et al. 1978).

It *is* considered likely that, in a country like the United States, inequality
will generate traditional property crime and violence. However, this is due to
such factors as the prevailing tradition of individualism; the "vigilante spirit";
the weakness of working-class traditions and neighborhoods; and the undifferen-
tiated, universal, and incessant evocation of consumption through the mass
media. In Marxist theory, inequality of resource distribution *alone* does not
inevitably lead to high levels of larceny, nor does public ownership necessarily
decrease this.

This brings us to a second point. Block assumes throughout that he is
saying something about socialist states by looking at capitalist economies with
varying degrees of state ownership and state intervention. He is assuming, then,
that societies can be placed on a continuum from right to left—that the differences between a capitalist democracy like Canada and a socialist country like
the People's Republic of China are quantitative, not qualitative. In Marxist
theory, this is not so. There is a deep chasm between societies in which the
means of production are publicly owned and controlled (although small businesses and farms may be allowed) and those in which they are privately owned
(despite the fact that certain resources may be publicly owned). This difference
in the nature and composition of the ruling class has major effects on the whole
superstructure—on ideology, culture, religion, law, and so forth. Thus by analyzing only mixed capitalist economies and welfare states, to the exclusion of
socialist societies, Block has said something about capitalist societies only. No
inferences can be drawn from this about the shape that crime would take in
socialist societies, or whether or not a revolution in the societies he analyzed
would decrease or increase larceny rates. Even if the relationships he describes
are valid, they enable him to conclude, at most, that increased public ownership
of resources *in a capitalist society* does not lead to lower larceny rates. Whether
or not it this would be so in a socialist state is something that, contrary to his
conclusions, he cannot address.

## References

Bordua, David, *The Police: Six Sociological Essays.* New York: Wiley, 1967.

Chambliss, William. "The Political Economy of Crime." *Theory and Society 2, no. 2 (1974):149-1970.*

Hall, Stuart; Critcher, C.; Clarke, J.; and Roberts, B. *Policing the Crisis: Mugging, the State, and Law and Order.* London: Macmillan, 1978.

Manning, Peter K. *Police Work: The Social Organization of Policing.* Cambridge, Mass.: MIT Press, 1977.

Miliband, Ralph. *The State in Capitalist Society.* London: Quartet Books, 1969.

O'Connor, James. *The Fiscal Crisis of the State,* New York: St. Martin's, 1973.

Reiman, Jeffrey. *The Rich Get Richer and the Poor Get Prison.* Toronto: John Wiley and Sons, 1979.

# 10 The Production of Corporate Crime in Corporate Capitalism

*Harold C. Barnett*

## Introduction

The question of the inevitability of white-collar crime under capitalism has been posed. In this chapter I address the more-limited question: Why will corporate crime be reproduced under U.S. corporate capitalism? Although *capitalism* can refer to any system of private ownership of the means of production, *U.S. corporate capitalism* defines that variant in which large corporate entities control resources ultimately owned by private individuals, and make profit-oriented investment, production, and employment decisions that have a dominant impact on the character of national economic life. In the pursuit of corporate objectives, laws are violated and criminal damages are imposed on U.S. society. The magnitude of monetary and physical harm is large in relation to that associated with other types of white-collar crime.

The purpose of this analysis, then, is to consider how the political-economic structure of U.S. corporate capitalism has reproduced corporate crime up to now. Against this background I suggest changes in law and enforcement that could reduce the extent of such crime in the future. Finally, I ask whether the achievement of these necessary changes presupposes basic alterations in U.S. capitalism.

## A Schematic View of Corporate Crime

We may begin by considering the political-economic forces that generate criminal behavior on the part of large U.S. corporations. Such corporations pursue goals of profitability, growth, and expanded market share, subject to constraints imposed by markets and the state. Markets generate supply and demand constraints. The former are defined by technology, the nature of the production process, and the cost of factor inputs. The latter are a byproduct market structure, market share, and growth. The state or legal constraint is defined by laws and mechanisms of enforcement: It is the set of sanctions that relates to violation

An expanded version of this chapter appears in *Crime and Delinquency*, vol. 27, no. 1, January 1981. This chapter appears by permission of the editor of *Crime and Delinquency*.

of the rules regulating corporate behavior. The legal constraint arises historically to supplement or reinforce the market constraint.

Corporate crime will occur when management chooses to pursue corporate goals through circumvention of market constraints in a manner prohibited by the state. Illegal circumvention of market constraints can be translated into changes in cost relative to revenue, that is, into changes in profits. One can thus expect that a corporation will be more likely to engage in crime when the expected costs of its illegal action are acceptably low relative to the perceived gains. In this choice context, the type of offenses committed by the corporation will depend on the relevant market constraints and the severity of the related legal constraint; that is, a corporation will tend to violate those constraints that yield the greatest expected net change in profits.

As an example, we note that product quality and environmental constraints are more significant in relation to profits for manufacturing concerns than for firms in distributive or service industries. At the same time, labor and trade constraints are relatively more significant for firms in the latter industries. The data in table 10-1, adapted from *Illegal Corporate Behavior* by Clinard et al. (1979) indicate that the relative frequency of violations by sector follows this pattern of relative significance.[1]

We can also observe a correspondence between the type of offense committed and the distribution of the imposed crime costs among victims. Victims may be functionally categorized as labor, consumers, investors, taxpayers, or other corporations. To illustrate the relation of constraint to victimization, we can note that antitrust violations reflect a desire to diminish the negative impact of the demand constraint on the pursuit of corporate objectives. Such violations result in a redistribution of profits among corporations as well as in a redistribution of income from consumers to producers. A desire to diminish the supply constraint can result in such manufacturing violations as the production of hazardous goods. Corporate production costs are reduced (for example, the cost

**Table 10-1**
**Violations, by Sector**

| Sector | Percentage of Sector Violations, by Type | | | | |
|---|---|---|---|---|---|
| | Environment | Manufacturing | Labor | Trade | Financial |
| Manufacturing | 30.5 | 32.5 | 15.4 | 9.4 | 3.4 |
| Distribution[a] | 0.8 | 32.3 | 36.4 | 14.4 | 7.3 |
| Service | 0.0 | 7.7 | 53.8 | 23.1 | 7.7 |

Source: Marshall B. Clinard et al., *Illegal Corporate Behavior* (Washington, D.C.: National Institute of Law Enforcement and Criminal Justice, 1979), table 2, p. 281.

[a]Weighted average of wholesale and retail.

of testing and quality control, design change, or parts substitution) at the expense of some consumers of the product. In a similar fashion, environmental pollution shifts a cost of production from producers to consumers, other producers, or the public in general. Illegal antiunion activity can reduce corporate labor costs by diminishing the collective bargaining power of labor. Illegal discrimination may also allow an employer to reduce labor costs by, for example, paying a female employee a lower salary than that paid a comparable male employee. Violations of production-related health and safety standards also shift costs from producers to labor. The corporation's gain through these labor violations corresponds to a loss in present or future income for some members of the labor force.

In addition to illegal redistributions, corporate crime can have detrimental effects on the efficiency and stability of economic and political institutions. The Securities and Exchange Commission (SEC) has expressed concern that unreported foreign bribery could depreciate the value of corporate financial data to investors, resulting in a loss of efficiency in financial markets (see Clinard et al. 1979, pp. 199-230). Illegal campaign contributions and domestic political bribery diminish the extent to which the political process responds to the desires of a voting public and the extent to which government minimizes the cost of public goods to taxpayers.

The right to define and impose the legal constraint is within the domain of state power. Institutionally, the state may be defined as the government. In political-economic terms, it is a reflection of the current and historical distribution of power in society. To combine these two perspectives of the state, we note that the legal functions and powers of the government, the manner in which the government is organized to execute its authority, and the budget constraints related to its various functions emerge historically as the outcome of political competition among vested interests. The state is thus a reflection of a dialectical process in which a historical distribution of power shapes the options available to those who currently promote public and private interests.[2]

The state is thus the focus of pressure by victims and offenders to alter the aggregate and distributional impact of corporate crime. New conflicts over law and enforcement have developed as a result of changes in technology, industrial structure, the multinational nature of production, the political representation and labor-force participation of women and minorities, and regional specialization as related to production versus consumption of goods and raw materials. The question of the distribution of the costs of crime has resulted in confrontation between corporations and industries as well as between corporations, labor, consumer groups, and environmental interests. However, these various conflicts among economic interests have not resulted in the creation of a legal constraint that significantly restricts the ability of large corporations to profit from crime. An explanation of why this has not occurred is in turn an explanation of how U.S. capitalism has reproduced corporate crime up to now.

The historical development of the legal constraint can be understood in terms of the relationship of corporate crime to the state's primary functions of promoting profitable capital accumulation and maintaining social harmony. As noted previously, corporate crime is an illegal circumvention of constraints on corporate profits, growth, and market-share expansion. The achievement of these objectives, regardless of the legality of the means, may be associated with the dominant role of the large corporation in generating new capital formation, expanding job opportunities, and sustaining economic growth. It may also be associated with combating inflation (particularly in supply-side macro models), diminishing balance-of-payments deficits, and achieving energy independence. Although these outcomes may be deemed desirable in themselves, their achievement through illegal means can diminish the legitimacy of the state as a democratic embodiment of a system of legal procedure, as a guarantor of distributive and legal justice, and as a stabilizing institution.

The legal constraint, then, must achieve two often contradictory goals. On the one hand, it must be severe enough to maintain the legitimacy of the state. On the other, it must not be so severe as to diminish substantially the contribution of large corporations to growth in output and employment. This contradiction has a correspondence in the distribution of powers and resources within the government. Government departments and agencies have mandates to promote one or both of these functions. We observe conflict of function both within and between agencies. Congress, the executive branch, and individual departments and agencies are all subject to pressure from those who wish to ally their interests with the promotion of specific state goals. Beyond this political sphere is a system of economic production that embodies real and perceived limits on government action.

Thus, whereas corporations attempt to maximize profits subject to market and state constraints, the state must pursue objectives subject to the options and tradeoffs that are created through the historical development of productive relationships and the need to satisfy diverse economic interests.

## The Reproduction of Corporate Crime

The use of legal constraint vis-à-vis the production of hazardous products by the motor vehicle industry offers some insights into how this conflict among primary goals is resolved. The study by Clinard et al. shows that the motor-vehicle industry (primarily auto and tire producers) accounted for nearly 50 percent of the total violations involving the manufacture of hazardous products in 1975–1976. These violations represent 12 percent of the total violations by 477 large manufacturing corporations during that period (Clinard et al. 1979, p. 107; table 9, pp 105–106). Most of these violations resulted in voluntary recalls by the manufacturer.

Voluntary recalls, like cease-and-desist orders, require no admission of guilt and thus create no increased exposure to the cost of civil damage suits. From the corporation's point of view, the cost of a voluntary recall is presumably below the cost of a presale testing and quality-control process that would significantly reduce the probability of defective vehicles being sold. Given the sale of hazardous vehicles, the corporate costs of voluntary recall are less than those imposed if the National Highway Traffic and Safety Administration (NHTSA) were to force recall, establish corporate guilt, and thus socialize some costs of winning subsequent civil damage awards.[3] It can be argued that NHTSA is willing to accept voluntary recall as a suitable sanction given its need to economize on scarce budgetary resources.[4] It is also able to report to Congress and the public that the agency is responding to a serious and frequent corporate violation.

It may not take much to satisfy the public in this regard. If the consumer's choice among vehicles were significantly determined by safety considerations, then vehicle safety would be central to corporate competition for market shares. A severe legal constraint would be of less importance, and the public's demand for the use of the legal sanction would at the same time be less easily satisfied.

The enforcement behavior of the NHTSA can be understood given its relevant legal framework and enforcement resources. Law and funding may in turn be explained by the significance of the motor-vehicle industry to the national economy. The industry accounts for about 6 percent of total output by value and 5.4 percent of private-sector production employment. A highly effective legal constraint would raise costs of production and result in some combination of diminished profits and increased product price. Whereas the former outcome could create financial problems, the latter could create problems for price stability. Further, a concern with fuel efficiency defines another national-policy-related demand on industry resources. A more-severe legal constraint would force the industry to allocate scarce capital resources toward the production of safer vehicles and away from more-fuel-efficient vehicles.

The magnitude and nature of the costs of an effective legal constraint are uncertain. This uncertainty may be enhanced by the fact that estimates of the actual cost of enforcement must rely on data provided by the industry. Faced with this uncertain situation, Congress would be less willing to impose a stronger sanction lest the protection of consumers be purchased at the expense of unemployment or of diminished investment, price stability, or conservation. Although consumer groups have lobbied for stronger enforcement, one can take the Chrysler bailout as a demonstration of the ability of the industry to create an identity between its interests and the national interest. The periodic pushing back of dates for compliance with auto emission standards also indicates the industry's ability to forestall enforcement in the nation's economic interest.

A consideration of some characteristics of antitrust enforcement yields additional insight into the manner in which the structure of U.S. corporate capitalism establishes a link between a weak legal constraint and the promotion of state goals. A corporation can become vulnerable to antitrust prosecution when it attempts to circumvent the market-demand constraint by means of price fixing or anticompetitive mergers. Over 25 percent of the serious offenses by parent manufacturing corporations in the Clinard et al. (1979) study involved such violations (Posner 1974, table 7, p. 100). We can note that although these violations were the most likely to result in criminal fines, and although the maximum fine has recently been increased, the expected cost of the sanction remains low in relation to actual and potential gains.

The relative weakness of antitrust enforcement has been explained in terms of a conflict between limiting corporate market power while at the same time promoting economic growth.[5] Large oligopolistic firms are associated with technological advances, major capital formation, and labor-force employment. Size per se is seen as contributing to financial stability. Congress and the courts have been hesitant to deprive large oligopolistic firms of market power lest national economic performance be impaired in the process. Consequently, the law has emphasized the overt conduct of firms rather than the structural conditions that allow groups of oligopolists to act as a collective monopolist. Although the Department of Justice has powers to prosecute oligopolistic firms as shared monopolies, it has not been able to develop what it would consider to be a viable case. More commonly, the Justice Department's Antitrust Division and the Federal Trade Commission have prosecuted a disproportionate number of relatively small conduct-oriented cases in which the agency has a greater chance of success. As in the previous example, this enforcement-agency behavior can be explained by the need to win cases while economizing on limited enforcement resources, by the nature of the laws that are to be enforced, and by the absence of strong support by Congress and the courts.

It is not obvious who benefits from existing antitrust enforcement. Many cases involve conflicts between large corporations over profit and market share. It has not been established that the interests of consumers are significantly promoted in the process.

The need for state legitimation vis-à-vis business is partly satisfied through adjudication of corporate-sector disputes. These actions may also convey an impression of anticapital enforcement to the consuming public. Given an emphasis on conduct rather than structure, the corporations subject to active legal constraint are not necessarily those that receive the greatest sustained benefits through the illegal exercise of market power.

A similar conflict between material output and enforcement benefits can be observed in relation to environmental violations. Environmental enforcement falls far short of the classic condition of forcing large corporations to internalize the external costs of production. Penalties are low in relation to corporate cost savings. Despite relatively weak enforcement, environmental regulation is given credit for plant closures (for example, U.S. Steel); potential bankruptcy (for example, Chrysler); and corporate preference for mergers rather than new capital formation. In the extreme, former President Carter's Energy Mobilization Board proposal suggests the necessity of an override of those federal environmental standards that are deemed unacceptable constraints on energy development and energy independence.

Like manufacturing and environmental violations, antiunion labor-law violations are motivated by a desire to diminish a major cost of production and to maintain maximum managerial autonomy with respect to production decisions. The historic emergence of strong unions in major industries such as the automotive and steel industries was accompanied by a regularization of labor-management relationships and an enhanced legal protection of labor's collective rights. The strengthening of legal constraints in this area has reflected unionized labor's increased political-economic power and, in turn, has permitted a subsequent growth in that power. We must note, however, that the strongest unions are generally in those industries that exhibit relatively high capital-labor ratios and that employ skilled labor. High wages reflect high productivity and the presence of industrial market power. Within these industries, the presence of unions diminishes industrial strife; allows for a more-disciplined labor force; and, given corporate ability to pass wage costs on as price increases, does not necessarily pose a substantial threat to corporate profitability.

Although labor-law violations still occur in such highly unionized industries, they represent a smaller percentage of total industry violations than do the violations in other industries (such as textiles) or sectors (such as the distributive or service sectors) in which lower capital intensity, low labor productivity, the use of unskilled labor, and/or the absence of market power generate a less-avoidable conflict between union power and corporate profits (see table 10–1; Clinard et al. 1979, table 9, pp. 105–106). In these latter situations, the legal constraint is not severe enough to allow labor a collective claim over industry profits. At the same time, the legitimacy of the state as a protector of the rights of labor as well as those of capital is enhanced by the position of unions in those industries in which a labor-management accord has developed.

To generalize from the foregoing examples, we note that the concentration of productive assets within the corporate sector helps explain the contribution of large corporations to national economic performance as well as the criminal damages these corporations impose. To the extent that reduction in the latter implies a significant diminution of the former, we must conclude that a structural limit exists on the severity of the legal constraint. The nature of the conflict between limiting corporate crime and promoting corporate production is thus integrally related to the structure of production within U.S. corporate capitalism. This conflict is intensified when competing national demands on corporate resources are given priority over a reduction in the social costs of corporate crime (for example, vehicle safety versus fuel efficiency, environmental quality versus energy independence). In sum, it appears that those legal constraints that can be deemed the most anticapital vis-à-vis the impact of compliance on corporate profitability tend to be the least severe.

These observations are not inconsistent with the view that antitrust sanctions define the most-severe constraints on corporate criminality.[6] Adjudication of conflicts among corporations is in the long-run interest of the corporate sector. In contrast to other areas of enforcement, antitrust generally involves corporations as both victims and offenders. It contributes to a regularization of relations among corporations and imparts stability to a mode of production that is generally conducive to a pursuit of corporate goals.

These observations are also not inconsistent with the expectation that highly skilled unionized labor in capital-intensive industries is accorded greater legal protection than is other unionized and nonunionized labor. Although the unit labor costs facing large corporations have increased, the overall impact on corporate profitability has been minimized as a result of union willingness not to challenge other central aspects of managerial autonomy, corporate ability to substitute capital for labor, and the fact that corporate market power allows increased wage costs to be passed on to the consumer. From a market perspective, this last result is not necessarily adverse in that consumers are paying the price of the goods they receive—in this case, the price of goods produced with a diminished degree of labor exploitation. From a political perspective, however, this is divisive in that the redistribution related to the legal constraint involves a perceived conflict between labor and consumers, rather than a conflict between labor and consumers, on the one hand, and corporate interests on the other. The presence of such perceived conflicts does not contribute to a collective demand for a general increase in the severity of legal constraints vis-à-vis corporate crime. The expectation that corporate flexibility allows a maintenance of profits in the face of effective legal constraint does not alter the fact that the exercise of collective power by victims can reduce the criminal damage to which they are exposed.

This said, we must also note the direct relationship of large corporations to the process of state policy formulation. The expected economic impact of a more-severe legal constraint is associated with a considerable degree of risk. Both expected outcome and attendant risk are affected by the availability of information. In the case of corporate crime, much of the data on the basis of which decisions are made can come only from the offending corporation. The large corporation is thus in a position to increase uncertainty by withholding data, or to overestimate the economic impact of legal constraint through the provision of selective data. Large corporations are also the repositories of concentrated financial resources that can be made available, legally or illegally, to politicians who support corporate interests. The provision of selective or misleading information makes it easier for a politician to convince the public that a decision is in the public interest, as opposed to a corporate interest.

This combination of real economic impact, information, and financial resources has given large corporations an economic and political power that is greater in general than that of the victims of corporate crime. This historical imbalance of power has been institutionalized in law, in the funding and priorities of regulatory and enforcement agencies, in the privatization of socially relevant data, and in the process of political finance. It is manifest in an ineffective legal constraint and in the consequent reproduction of corporate crime.

## Confronting the Structural Problems

It has been argued that corporate crime has been historically reproduced under U.S. corporate capitalism. Does this imply an inevitable future link between the U.S. economic structure and corporate crime? We can approach this question from two interrelated perspectives. First, we can consider changes in the legal constraint that would negate reproduction, and ask whether the mode of production so defined would still be U.S. corporate capitalism. Second, we can consider the real opportunity costs of a significant reduction in corporate crime, and ask whether they are more likely to be absorbed without unacceptable side effects under a transformed political economy. To state these questions in a more-positive fashion: Can we postulate a mode of production that reproduces a system of constraints that would substantially reduce the profitability of corporate crime?

The legal constraint would become more severe in the presence of laws that impose progressive criminal fines and that fully establish corporate liability for damages consciously imposed in the course of production and labor-force decisions. The probability that such costs are imposed on corporations would be increased given a change in the funding, priorities, and organization of the federal enforcement agencies. Increased funding would allow greater prosecution of large offenders without necessitating a reduction in deterrence of the smaller offenders, who are now more likely to face successful prosecution. However, in the absence of a clear congressional mandate to pursue the larger, resource-rich offenders, one should not expect enforcement agencies to risk a reduction in their prosecutorial success rates. A reallocation of funds and legal powers among agencies could reduce some of the existing internal conflicts among agency priorities that tend to mitigate against strong enforcement. For example, consumer protection is often a secondary responsibility of federal agencies whose primary responsibility is defined in terms of promoting industry interests. An autonomous Consumer Protection Agency might yield a more-severe legal constraint without any sizable increase in the total funds currently allocated to consumer protection. Finally, an increased public enforcement effort could socialize some private costs of obtaining civil compensation. The probability of successful civil damage suits would be increased. These changes could significantly raise the expected costs of corporate crime, thus reducing the net benefits and the frequency of offenses.

Although such increases in expected costs could constrain the growth in manufacturing, environmental, and labor violations, they may not solve the problems associated with the illegal exercise of market power by firms in oligopolistic industries. First, we may find that successful prosecution of shared-monopoly cases will bring about corporate dismemberments that significantly reduce productive efficiency and financial stability. Second, we may find that forced divestitures do not significantly alter the degree of effective competition. If, given such findings, we must conclude that giant corporations are economically desirable, then limitations on their exercise of market power would require greater public representation on boards of directors and greater public oversight of managerial decision making.

Increased enforcement and increased public involvement in corporate decision making both presuppose a greater public or government access to corporate data. Reliable data are necessary to determine the existence of an offense, and to determine the corporate and social costs of compliance with legal requirements.

Taken together, these changes would define an altered distribution of decision-making power vis-à-vis productive capital. The public would have increased power to define the constraints corporations face, to determine compliance, and to oppose conscious circumvention effectively. In reducing the autonomy of corporate power, we would be transforming U.S. corporate capitalism into some more socially responsive mode of production.

The magnitude of the economic problems posed by a more-severe legal constraint depend in part on the magnitude of the various costs of corporate compliance. Compliance with product-safety regulations, environmental standards, and labor regulations will increase costs of production; compliance with trade regulations may reduce revenues. Given the elasticity of demand in the relevant markets, these costs of compliance will yield increases in product prices and reductions in net corporate income.

In the case of product safety and environmental standards, compliance would contribute to inflation in the short run regardless of the fact that higher prices result from corporate internalization of external costs of production. The impact on employment is uncertain. On the one hand, increased environmental safeguards and more-extensive product testing may be labor-intensive and/or employment-generating activities. On the other hand, increased cost and, hence, price for necessities may reduce demand elsewhere in the economy. A different problem is posed by prosecution of antiunion legislation that results in increased labor costs that cannot be passed forward because of foreign competition. In this case, we might consider national runaway-shop legislation to reduce the likelihood that increased enforcement is rapidly translated into the exportation of jobs. Alternatively, we could accept a further decline in the contribution of such industries to national employment and attempt to retain displaced labor for employment in industries in which profitable production is less dependent on the payment of inadequate wages.

A problem of adequate finance arises if compliance increases corporate expenditures relative to corporate net income. Corporations would be forced to rely more heavily on external sources of funding. This would be a positive effect if investors prefer to finance corporations that comply with legal requirements rather than to finance violators. Given higher expected costs of punishments, such behavior by investors would be self-interested, not altruistic. Corporate violations would now be more likely translated into increased liens on profits rather than into enhanced rates of return to corporate capital. Corporate behavior would be more subject to market constraint.

Investor choice aside, we would need to consider the problem of generating sufficient savings to match the increased corporate-investment expenditures required by some types of compliance. It is argued that corporate profits are already inadequate to finance necessary increases in capital formation (see, for example, Malkiel 1979). The problem is enhanced by a declining rate of household savings and a desire to increase investments that promote energy independence. If financial markets are inadequate to absorb increased capital requirements, then alternative means of finance would be necessary. Two possibilities might be noted. First, expanded union pension funds or other worker investment funds could supply needed capital. Expansion could come from an increase in wage costs as a percentage of gross national product or from a desire by workers to acquire a greater effective leverage over corporate behavior. Second, the state could use its existing powers to generate investment flows. Acting as a financial intermediary, it could bid resources away from less socially desirable investment expenditures. However, the use of these powers will not necessarily increase the total availability of financial resources. Since meeting financial needs through expansionary monetary policy has its own limitations in an inflationary period, the state might ultimately need to rely on its power to tax in order to redirect income from consumption to investment.

To summarize the foregoing, a more-severe legal constraint could induce greater compliance on the part of large corporations while simultaneously yielding an intensification of existing problems that have not been amenable to solution under U.S. corporate capitalism. Would these problems be more amenable to solution under a transformed U.S. political economy?

The transformation associated with a more-severe legal constraint will affect our perceptions and estimates of the cost of compliance. We will have redefined profitable production in terms of a corporation's ability to generate sufficient revenues relative to both private and currently social costs of production. Since we already absorb the social costs of noncompliance in the form of pollution, health and safety hazards, and wage exploitation, the fact that these costs are now made part of a market calculus does not mean that their total value has been increased. What is significant is that the distribution of the costs of compliance will be more equal than is the current distribution of the monetary and physical damage resulting from corporate crime.

Social access to corporate data will enhance our ability to determine the costs we will need to absorb while simultaneously reducing some of the uncertainty surrounding the magnitude of these costs. Current discussion of costs of compliance has been more political than scientific.[7] Corporations have publicized gross overestimates of the costs of regulation given current level of compliance. At the same time, private ownership of data allows for only rough estimates of the revenue and cost situations in relevant markets. The oil industry's monopoly over data on reserves, production, and distribution is a case in point. Although costs of compliance are in all likelihood below industry estimates, they are presumably great enough to make accurate estimation essential for rational, socially responsive policy formulation.

Transformation will not necessarily raise the costs of compliance, but it will make their magnitude more subject to accurate estimation and their distribution more equitable. This may in turn diminish some of the current problems associated with the absorption of these costs in a rational and equitable manner.

In speculating on such systematic changes, we must be conscious of the fact that in transforming the U.S. political economy, we are also altering access to the resources that have allowed the generation of illegal corporate incomes. Professor Radzinowicz has noted that each mode of production has its own type of crime (Radzinowicz 1971). It has also been noted that public officials are quite capable of abusing their access to state property (that is, to state-owned natural resources as well as to such legal resources as law enforcement, licenses, and public contracts). If we are thus to reduce production-related crime rather than merely to redistribute its gains, we must move away from either corporate or state capitalism and toward a more participatory economic democracy.

## Notes

1. M. Clinard et al. (1979) provides an analysis of a wide array of criminal acts by over 500 large U.S. corporations. It is a valuable work for its scope, methodology and data. This paper draws heavily on information contained in that study.

2. This analysis of the functions and dialectical development of the state draws on O'Connor (1973), Chambliss (1978), Korpi (1978) and Bates (1976).

3. "The reason for the non-admission of guilt is to protect the corporation from a civil suit in which the admission of guilt would make it unnecessary for there to be any trial of factual issues" (Clinard et al. 1979, p. 144). Although voluntary recalls can be expensive, their cost may be low in relation to civil damage claims that result when product defects are alleged to have caused death and injury. For example, Firestone estimates that its recall of the series-500 steel-belted radial tire will result in an after-tax cost of $114.5 million. This figure can be compared with the company's average net income (1975–1977) of

$113.3 million. Although the cost of recall is large in relation to a single year's earnings, it is small in relation to the billions of dollars in damages asked in various civil suits. The company notes that "an adverse adjudication of defective design in one law suit could have an adverse affect on other suits" (Firestone Corporation, *Annual Report,* 1978, 1979).

4. This is a generalization of the perspective offered by Posner (1974).

5. The following discussion draws on Barnett (1979).

6. "Generally, violations that directly affected the economy tended to receive the most severe sanctions (criminal fines and retroactive orders)" (Clinard et al. 1979, p. 128; table 10, appendix J, p. 291. Included in this category are unfair trade practices and most financial violations, except those related to consumer purchases.

7. Estimates of the costs of compliance with federal regulation vary considerably. At the upper end, Professor Widenbaum has offered a figure of $102.7 billion in 1979. In contrast, the GAO estimates a cost of $33.8 to $38.8 billion in 1975. The Business Roundtable estimates a cost to forty-eight large corporations of $2.6 billion in 1977. These estimates differ in terms of the inclusion of the benefits of regulation, which agency activities are defined as regulation, and the distinction between market versus state-induced compliance. See Green and Waitzman (1979) and Green and Waitzman, "A Challengeto Murray Weidenbaum," *The New York Times,* 29 October 1979.

## References

Barnett, Harold C. "Wealth, Crime and Capital Accumulation." *Contemporary Crises* 3(1979):171–186.

Bates, Timothy. *Economic Man as Politician: Neoclassical and Marxist Theories of Government Behavior.* Morristown, N.J.: General Learning Press, 1976.

Block, Michael K.; Nold, F.C.; and Sidak, J.G. "The Deterrent Effect of Antitrust Enforcement: A Theoretical and Empirical Analysis." Mimeographed, Center for Econometric Studies of the Justice System, Hoover Institution, Stanford University, 1978.

Chambliss, William J. *On the Take.* Bloomington: Indiana University Press, 1978.

Clinard, Marshall B., Peter C. Yeager, Jeanne Brissette, David Petrashek and Elizabeth Harries. *Illegal Corporate Behavior.* Washington, D.C.: National Institute of Law Enforcement and Criminal Justice, 1979.

Green, Mark, and Waitzman, Normal. *Business War on the Law.* Washington, D.C.: Corporate Accountability Research Group, 1979.

Korpi, Walter. *The Working Class in Welfare Capitalism.* London: Routledge and Kegan Paul, 1978.

Malkiel, Burton G. (1979), "The Capital Formation Problem in the United States," *The Journal of Finance,* XXXIV (2), 291–306.

O'Connor, James. *The Fiscal Crisis of the State.* New York: St. Martin's Press, 1973.

Posner, Richard A. "The Behavior of Administrative Agencies." In G.S. Becker and W.M. Landes, eds., *Essays in the Economics of Crime and Punishment.* New York: National Bureau of Economic Research and Columbia University Press, 1974.

Radzinowicz, Leon. "Economic Pressures." In L. Padzinowicz and M. Wolfgang, eds., *The Criminal in Society.* New York: Basic Books, 1971.

# Part III
# Social Control: Sanctions
# and Deterrent Effects

## Introduction

Analyses of efforts to control and sanction white-collar and economic offenses are, of course, of great practical as well as theoretical interest. Papers in this section discuss both the patterns and mechanisms of controls and the disparities that occur, particularly in comparison with traditional crimes.

The serious personal injury and violent death that can be the concomitants of faulty or inadequate control are the concern of chapter 11, by Carson, which focuses upon the high injury and death rates on offshore rigs in the scramble for oil in the North Sea. His case study of the "classically symbiotic relationship" between industry and state agencies provides data to support the application of Kramer's theory of organizations and Barnett's political-economy analysis (from part II) to the disparities and difficulties inherent in the social control of white-collar crime. Carson analyzes the interplay of capital sources and needs, oil use and development policy, and the licensing and regulation of oil production. He concludes that, despite the technological-frontier imagery used to justify high injury and death rates, the "same mundane factors" that exist in other workplaces are at play in offshore oil production, and that these could be controlled—if regulatory agency and business relationships were to be changed.

Chapter 12 by Parker, on social control and the legal profession, begins with an analysis of professional misconduct of attorneys that follows a Durkheimian perspective. Parker investigates the relationship between structural characteristics of state bar associations—types of social solidarity and degrees of centralization of power—and the rate and severity of sanctions and of readmissions to the bar. One of the most-interesting questions raised by this study is the utility of applying Durkheim's theory of the evolution of penal sanctions, conceived to explain societal development, to smaller organizational forms. Centrality of power and its effects on sanctioning are in many ways the issues raised by the other chapters in this section.

Laureen Snider, in chapter 13, uses Canadian data to contrast punishments given out for traditional as compared with corporate theft, and to develop a theoretical perspective on why, in Canada at least, punishments are in fact heavier for traditional than for "upperworld" crimes. Stressing the history of Canadian society and law, Snider urges that an explanation of disparities in sentencing be viewed in light of the different purposes and origin of laws on corporate crime and laws on traditional crime. The apparent leniency toward

171

upperworld offenders is not to be explained simply as a reflection of general public concerns.

Hagan, Nagel, and Albonetti further pursue the question of sentence disparity in chapter 14, using the U.S. federal courts as their focus. Using interviews, case studies, and quantitative data, they investigate the effects on sentencing of white-collar offenses of the social organization of the subsystems in the criminal-justice system and the nature of the legal statutes involved. Differences exist among federal jurisdictions, between state and federal courts, and between traditional white-collar offenses in factors such as victimization, which need to be taken into account in explaining the tendency for higher-income, white-collar offenders to receive lighter sentences.

# 11 Legal Control of Safety on British Offshore Oil Installations

## W.G. Carson

### Introduction: Images of Danger

In the summer of 1979, a widely traveled Englishman returned to Britain after a long absence and wrote a series of newspaper articles on the changed face and manners of the nation. Perhaps surprisingly, he chose as his starting point, not the continuing saga of Britain's economic decline, its highly publicized record of industrial unrest, or the allegedly imminent collapse of the politics of the center, but North Sea oil. Such a point of departure, he suggested, was a logical one because "the oil fields gushing beneath the North Sea have taken the place of the empire as the saviour of the British way of life." Under the title of "Empire and After—or Plain Tales from the Rigs," he pursued this theme in highly colorful terms:

> Any one who has ever ventured out into the North Sea off the Scottish coast knows it is just as wild a setting as India or Africa ever was in the empire days. Surely now, ten years after oil was first discovered there, it should have found its Kipling or Conrad to describe the incredible daring of bringing oil up from the sea-bed through the constant high swells and the sudden violent storms of this most untamed and unpredictable of environments. There certainly have been enough adventures to satisfy any chronicler—and enough violent deaths.[1]

I have not selected this quotation as the starting point for this chapter because of any pretensions or, indeed, even any wish to fill the literary gap referred to by the author. Rather, it has been selected because it provides a particularly good example of the extremely powerful imagery that the oil-related developments currently taking place on the British continental shelf can evoke.[2] Danger and daring, of course, are already well established as part of the folklore surrounding North Sea oil, often supported by the additional image of the cowboy worker who recklessly embraces any hazard in the pursuit of high wages, which are subsequently dissipated in riotous living back onshore. Similarly, the invocation of past imperial exploits is possibly just a satirical form of the much more common imagery depicting offshore operations as an adventure taking place at other kinds of frontiers.

A fuller version of this chapter appears in *Contemporary Crisis* 4, no. 3 (July 1980). This chapter appears by permission of the editor of *Contemporary Crisis.*

Preeminent among such images is the dual one of an industry facing all the risks associated with operating at the outer limits of existing technology and in physical conditions that are, at the very least, consistently more difficult than anywhere else in the world (Hamilton 1978, p. 69). As Guy Arnold remarks, "North Sea oil has created its own language: the leading jargon phrase is 'on the frontiers of technology' and everyone loves the image this creates" (1978, p. 9). Similarly, even the industry's own project engineers are said to have been left breathless by the pace of technological developments, which have been spurred along, not just for the sake of change in itself, but by "the peculiar circumstances than engineers have found themselves dealing with in the North Sea."[3] Nor is there any dearth of reports linking the challenge of the offshore enterprise in these respects to its implications for safety:

> The North Sea has presented man with one of his biggest challenges this century . . . a wealth of energy lying 12,000 ft. below turbulent 600 ft. deep seas. An area which can produce winds of up to 160 m.p.h. and waves of 100 ft.—as tall as an eight or nine story building. It is here that the offshore industry has constructed the necessary platform giants to extract oil and gas and send it ashore. . . . In such a hostile area, safety and the environment provide the starting point for all decision-making. . . .[4]

Whatever the priority allocated to safety in the planning and execution of offshore operations, the frontier image is one that readily reconciles readers to the inevitability of accidents. At inhospitable frontiers, people are killed. Thus, a further image that is often projected in discussions of offshore safety is that of necessary sacrifice for the common good. Although we may dismiss as mere (if possibly inappropriate) humor the view of one Treasury man who explained to an early collaborator on this project that "with the economy in the state that it was, the people who were dying there were dying for the greater good,"[5] the suggestion of necessary sacrifice is often quite explicit and quite serious. Thus, for example, in 1977 Anthony Wedgewood Benn, the secretary of state for energy, wrote about the reduction of offshore risks and, having outlined the vital contribution that oil and gas could make to Britain's future, turned his attention to "the penalties," which "as with all things . . . are to be paid." Somewhat melodramatically, he went on, "too many have already paid the ultimate penalty with their lives, which is tragically the price so often extracted of pioneers."[6] More recently, *The Guardian* deployed the metaphor of cost-benefit analysis to provide a stark caption for a discussion of "The human price of Britain's oil billions."[7] This and several of the other images already mentioned were cogently combined in one editorial in the *Aberdeen Press and Journal:*

> North Sea oil and gas will be worth a staggering £7,200 million this year—and we owe an enormous debt to all who have helped to bring

this about. The costs have been high and grievously so in regard to the loss of life which has been incurred. Only yesterday we had another grim reminder of the human toll involved in this vast and crucial operation, in often severe testing conditions which demand taking technology to its outer limits.[8]

Not all the images associated with offshore employment can be dismissed as false. More specifically, there is little doubt that, at least until very recently, the North Sea has been a very dangerous place indeed to work. Although the "human toll" of around 100 killed and 400 seriously injured may not seem particularly appalling in absolute terms, the incidence rates lying behind these stark statistics compare very unfavorably with other reputedly dangerous occupations.[9] Thus, for example, between 1974 and 1976 the overall risk of being killed on or around an oil installation in the British sector (excluding accidents on vessels, for which no employment figures are available) was around six times that for the quarrying industry, nine times that for the mining industry, and eleven times as great as the risk of death in the course of construction work.[10] When diving, probably the most-hazardous civilian occupation in contemporary Britain, is left out of the account, the gap narrows (to four times, six times, and eight times, respectively) but by no means disappears; when the figures relating to diving, itself, are calculated over the same period, the resulting incidence rate for fatalities is in the region of 8 per 1,000—twenty-six times the death rate in quarrying, thirty-eight times that in mining, and fifty times that in the construction industry. Although the record for diving, as for the industry as a whole, has shown very substantial improvement in 1977 and 1978,[11] there is no doubt that the North Sea thoroughly deserved its dangerous reputation during the most-crucial phase of its development in the mid-1970s.[12]

If this is the case, it becomes germane to ask why offshore employment has been so hazardous. This is a question to which some of the other images already mentioned have considerable relevance, since they suggest, at least by implication, that the casualty rate has been an inevitable consequence of working at technological frontiers and in consistently adverse climatic conditions. No less important, they imply that there is relatively little that law could have done, or can do, to minimize a human cost exacted by the unique exigencies of the offshore situation rather than by anything else. The other price of Britain's oil, they suggest, is not negotiable.

In the course of this research it has been possible to examine fatal-accident files compiled by the Scottish legal authorities in connection with nearly two-thirds of all oil-related fatalities that occurred in the British sector of the North Sea between 1971 and 1978.[13] Additionally, quarterly summaries of fatal- and serious-accident reports produced by the British Department of Energy have been scrutinized for the period from 1974 onward.[14] What emerges from these two sources is that although there is no denying the industry's technological sophistication or the harshness of the setting in which it has to conduct operations, neither of these factors—so salient in the imagery woven around the North Sea oil industry—can be held primarily accountable for the rate of death and injury that has taken place. On the contrary, the evidence overwhelmingly supports the view that offshore accidents largely emanate from the same set of relatively mundane factors that cause the majority of accidents in any industrial context. Thus, we should be wary of the superficially attractive explanation of high accident rates in terms of technological frontiers of adverse operating conditions. More important, we should remember that the causative factors underpinning the majority of offshore accidents are potentially amenable to regulation through law. Unsafe working practices, poor design and maintenance, inadequate communications and supervision, shortcuts taken under pressure, and lack of elementary safety precautions play an all-too-familiar role in the genesis of accidents in the North Sea; but these are also the kinds of issue on which properly constructed and systematically enforced law can purportedly intervene to create a safer working environment.

## The Regulatory Relationship

To understand the checkered history of how British law has dealt with the issue of safety in the North Sea, it is necessary to go back to the specific nexus of structural relationships that dominated offshore developments in their earliest stages during the 1960s. Throughout that decade, as writers such as Longstreth have argued, finance capital (banking and the City) maintained a position of institutionalized dominance within the British state, a dominance that was exercised through the Bank of England and its connections with the Treasury, and that found its expression in recurrent policy preoccupations with the value of the pound and with the balance of payments.[15] Thus, at a time when Britain's changed position in the world was belatedly dawning—not least as a result of the Suez debacle, which had finally brought home the limits of traditional British influence over the world's major oil-producing area—British economic policy continued to be constrained by "a dominant political-economic fraction which has outlived its 'world historical role' by some decades" (Crouch 1979, p. 184).

This nexus between finance capital and strategically located agencies within the state apparatus was to prove crucial in shaping British policy with respect to North Sea oil. As Adrian Hamilton has pointed out, the interdepartmental committee (Ministry of Power, Treasury, and Cabinet Office) that preceded the first North Sea licensing round in 1964 opted firmly for as rapid exploration and exploitation as possible in order to meet the "overriding need" for a balance of payments. Indeed, so pressing was the Treasury's preoccupation with this aspect of the matter that it even positively favored foreign investment in the early years "because of the immediate benefits to the capital account" (Hamilton 1978, p. 17). Although its voice may not have ultimately prevailed in this particular respect, there is no doubt that throughout the recurring fiscal crises of the 1960s, the potential effect of rapidly extracted North Sea oil on the balance of payments remained the dominant policy consideration. With the Yom Kippur War and the dramatically escalating cost of oil imports following the successive price rises imposed by the Organization of Petroleum Exporting Countries (OPEC) in the 1970s, this preoccupation was to remain central to government thinking until at least mid-1977 (Arnold 1978, p. 136).

Argument will long continue as to whether, ultimately, rapid exploration and exploitation was the optimal policy for Britain to follow in the North Sea; as to whether a slower approach might not have secured a bigger slice of the action for British industry; and, not least, as to whether the British exchequer has derived as much benefit as it might from offshore developments. Within the context of the present chapter, however, the germane point is that not only was speed adopted as a policy, but also that it required the cooperation of the major oil companies and the international capital market (including London) for purposes of raising the massive finance involved. Between 1965 and 1978, for example, total investment in the North Sea is estimated to have been in the region of £8.8 billion; a further £4.8 billion is estimated to have been spent in the period up to the end of 1980, a figure that will probably represent somewhere between 20 and 25 percent of total U.K. industrial investment in the same period (*Brown Book* 1979, p. 19). In the face of such expenditure, the potential strain on Britain's financial system was—and remains—great indeed:

> If the U.K. had had to go it alone—in the way that British companies built the railway systems of the mid-nineteenth century in this country, which is after all a comparable venture—then the strain on the financial system might have been much greater.

> But the key to the financing of the North Sea has been the involvement from the beginning of the established international oil companies, who have been large enough to treat North Sea exploration and development as part of their world-wide activities. . . . Further, so dominant has been London as a centre of the international capital market, that U.K. banks or international banks with branches operating aggressively through the international capital markets in London, have over the years developed a variety of techniques that have enabled them to put together financial packages to cope with the special demands of large scale oil development. . . .[16]

The fact that rapid exploitation of the North Sea's potential required this kind of assistance spawned a classically symbiotic relationship between the multinational oil industry and the strategic institutional apparatus of the British state. Initially, by all accounts, the nature of this relationship was comparatively straightforward, with the "giveaway" nature of the early licensing rounds (in which Britain has subsequently been described as behaving like a "gullible

Sheikdom" (Sampson 1976, p. 193) being justified on the grounds that only easy terms could ensure what government most wanted: "rapid and thorough exploration and exploitation" (Arnold 1978, p. 50). Similar arguments have been put forward in defense of the extent of participation allowed to U.S. companies comprising five of the famous "Seven Sisters," which alone could muster the finance, technology, and expertise required. Nor should it be forgotten that, once committed to development, there is a singular harmony of interest between oil companies and an official policy that places a high premium on speed: North Sea investment pays off quickly and handsomely as soon as production commences, but it is very front loaded and therefore highly sensitive to any possibility of delay.[17]

As time wore on, and particularly in the wake of the revelations of the Public Accounts Committee in 1973,[18] the relationship between host state and industry became increasingly fraught with tension, while still retaining its essentially symbiotic character. Thus, the newly elected Labour government of 1974 moved rapidly toward state participation through the creation of the British National Oil Corporation, toward a stricter tax regime, and even toward the assumption of powers to control depletion rates. In doing so, however, the secretary of state for energy gave a series of assurances "intended to dispel uncertainty about depletion policy and to encourage a rapid build-up of self-sufficiency by 1980" (*Brown Book* 1978, p. 53). As a result, and despite the belatedly tougher stand being adopted, undertakings were given to the effect that no delays would be imposed on the development of fields accounting for between one-half and two-thirds of estimated reserves and that no cutback in production from such discoveries would be imposed before 1982 at the earliest.[19] Similarly, the potential obstacle that the powers to control production and to revoke licenses could place in the way of the latter's use as security for loans was removed by devising "a form of assurance . . . which avoids fettering the Secretary of State's discretion but provides banks with the necessary assurance of the continuity of their security" (*Brown Book* 1978, p. 27). Not least, the uneasy symbiosis found repeated political expression during the post-1974 period in threats that any tightening of the regime, or any renewed uncertainty, would be countered by a decline in the rate of exploration.[20] Like finance capital itself, the multinational corporation has the ultimate sanction of invoking the nineteenth-century maxim that "its workings must be free as air; for at sight of human ties, it will spread the light wings of capital and fly away from bondage" (Ure 1835, p. 453). Although the profitability of the North Sea might render such a strategy improbable—one observer is reported to have said that "if you ringed the North Sea with gunships and then ordered the oil companies to go, they would refuse" (Arnold 1978, p. 11)—it nonetheless has been a constantly implicit bargaining counter in dealings with a government that, as late as 1978, was still seeing the "great benefit of North Sea oil" in its impact on the balance of payments (*Brown Book* 1978, p. 28).

At the heart of the regulatory relationship with respect to offshore developments, then, there lies not only a set of policies emanating from the institutionalized domination of strategic parts of the British state by finance capital, but also a related pattern of give and take between the state and the major oil companies. Just as the policy of rapid development required the assistance of the latter, so they, too, required the services of the state in creating the preconditions under which large amounts of capital could be safely raised and deployed. Although some traditional concerns, such as the maintenance of social peace and a stable political regime, may not have seemed so problematic in the British context—although they probably added to the attractiveness of the North Sea in the light of events elsewhere—others, like predictability in the terms of operation, could not so easily be taken for granted.[21] Most crucial of all, perhaps, development of the North Sea hinged on the establishment of a legal framework within which companies could operate, a framework that would fill the legal vacuum constituted by a maritime location outside territorial limits, and one that would create some kind of viable system of proprietary rights over any oil that might be found. It was within the context of attempts to meet this vital requirement that the issue of legislative provision for the safety of operations in the North Sea first raised its head.

## Law and Enforcement

It is the central thesis of this chapter that discussion of how the law relating to offshore safety has developed, of how the administration of its enforcement is structured, and of how it is implemented in practice cannot be divorced from the broader regulatory relationship that has already been examined. In touching briefly on each of these issues, I shall attempt to clarify this connection through the presentation of evidence that, although necessarily inconclusive, is highly suggestive in terms of a working hypothesis for explaining the current situation with respect to the legal regulation of working conditions in the North Sea. In so doing, I hope to move beyond mere description or criticism of what is widely acknowledged to be an unsatisfactory state of affairs in this connection.

### The Development of Legal Controls

As already suggested, the issue of safety in the North Sea first arose in the context of attempts to supply the legal framework needed for offshore developments to get under way. By the early 1960s, surveys had indicated the existence of promising geological structures in the area; the stage had been reached at which further progress could be made only by undertaking the expensive task of offshore drilling. Although the international basis for the creation of the necessary system of law already existed in the Continental Shelf Convention of 1958 (see Daintith and Willoughby 1977, p. 167 ff), which was still awaiting British ratification (ultimately to be the twenty-second of the twenty-two ratifications required for it to take effect), there was no British legislation to cover the now imminent exploratory activities on its continental shelf (Arnold 1978, p. 44). Thus, under pressure from the industry to rectify these omissions, a bill was brought before Parliament in 1964.[22] As the then minister of power explained to the Commons, "at this point the companies have very reasonably turned to the Government and asked that their operations and investments shall have the protection of a proper system of law."[23] The bill's "main purpose," despite many "incidental provisions," was the "highly desirable and urgent" one of enabling "the natural resources of the Continental Shelf to be exploited for the benefit of all concerned."[24]

The act that resulted was primarily concerned with these objectives and, apart from taking the vital step of vesting rights with regard to the seabed and its resources in the crown,[25] made provision for the necessary system of licensing by extension of the "landward regime" already contained in the Petroleum (Production) Act of 1934.[26] Increasingly, the use of this strategy did not necessarily entail the granting of licenses or concessions to private operators, since the latter enactment is merely permissive in this respect and permits government to exploit its own resources. As Daintith has pointed out, however, there is no evidence to suggest that any other mode of legal organization was ever contemplated at this time. In terms of this chapter's central argument, his explanation is significant:

> Good economic reasons can be found for this basic decision: rapid exploitation of the resources was desired, mainly for balance of payments reasons, and the requisite expertise and capability did not exist in the United Kingdom public sector (nor indeed, if the first aim were to be vigorously pursued, in the private sector either). Hence it seemed natural, particularly to the Conservative Government in power in those years, to continue, through the concession system, to make the maximum call on the resources of the world-wide private oil industry. [Daintith and Willoughby 1977, pp. 12 ff.]

Although the Continental Shelf Act provided the requisite work for exploration to get under way, it also contained provisions relevant to the issue of safety. Thus, as part of what appears to have been a fairly panic-stricken effort to preempt "all the incidental matters" that might arise, "provision for law and order" was made by an extremely convoluted Section,[27] which applied the civil and criminal law of the United Kingdom to acts and omissions taking place on or around installations.[28] Moreover, as a result of worries voiced by Labour backbenchers about the adequacy of the protection being afforded to offshore workers in the course of this "first-class scramble,"[29] it was stipulated that model clauses pertaining to safety, health, and welfare should be incorporated into any licenses granted.[30] In the event, the standard clause that was used in this respect was one that required the licensee to "comply with any instructions from time to time given by the Minister in writing for securing the safety, health and welfare of persons employed in or about the licensed areas" (Kitchen, p. 47).

These provisions created an extraordinary situation with respect to the law governing offshore safety. Although the extension of the civil and criminal law to the continental shelf would subsequently, when exploration moved northward, be temporarily construed as giving the Scottish legal authorities powers to investigate North Sea fatalities (to be discussed later in this chapter), it did not have the effect of extending the application of the Factories Acts, the main body of onshore safety legislation, to the offshore situation.[31] The fond hopes of some members of the House of Lords notwithstanding,[32] offshore installations did not fall within the definition of a "factory" given in the relevant legislation (Kitchen 1977, p. 60). In consequence, the principal legal protection with respect to occupational safety lay in the instructions issued under model clauses that made up part of the license itself. Although there has been some debate as to whether these model clauses and attendant instructions were of a contractual or regulatory character (see Daintith and Willoughby 1977, p. 26); Kitchen 1977, p. 48), there is no doubt about the nature of the sanctions that they made available in the event of noncompliance. The minister could either effect entry and carry out necessary rectifications at the licensee's expense, a somewhat improbable scenario, or he could fall back on the contractual nature of the licensing arrangement and revoke the license (Kitchen 1977, p. 48).

The regulatory implications of exercising control over safety by these methods became tragically apparent within some eighteen months of the act's passage when, on 27 December 1965, the "jack-up" rig Sea Gem collapsed and sank, with the loss of thirteen lives. Although the Tribunal of Inquiry into the causes of this accident and the operation of relevant safety procedures did not report for nearly another two years, when it did, the point quickly became clear.[33] "It is perhaps as well to make it clear this early," said the report's introduction, "that the only sanction for ensuring the proper operation of the safety procedures is the revocation of the license."[34] Accordingly, the three-man inquiry went on to include in its list of recommendations a crucial proposal for a *statutory* code "supported by credible sanctions."[35]

It was this proposal that led directly, albeit after a further delay of nearly four years, to the creation of a more-familiar system whereby safety matters are subjected to statutory regulation. In 1971, a new Conservative government took over a bill that its Labour predecessor had been preparing, and the Mineral Workings (Offshore Installations) Act was passed,[36] the legislative process once again betraying a nice concern for the views and interests of the industry. Thus, for example, the undersecretary of state for trade and industry, head of a new department into which the Ministry of Power had been absorbed, made it clear that although the "typically British tradition" of keeping "ahead with our safety regulations" must be maintained, this should not be done in such a way as to "cramp initiative and enterprise" or to curtail the exciting prospects of new developments in what he called "oceaneering."[37] Similarly, his response to suggestions that the promulgation of detailed regulations under the act's enabling auspices should be obligatory rather than discretionary was that the latter more easily allowed time for the consultation that the act insisted must take place with interested parties: "we must ensure that we carry the industry with us in believing that the regulations are fair, reasonable, effective and practicable."[38] Even the issue of nomenclature or, more specifically, whether the title of "master" was inappropriate for persons in charge of installations because of its authoritarian merchant-navy connotations, was something to be referred to the industry.[39]

"Taking the industry with us" in the matter of making regulations has subsequently proved to be a protracted affair. Although some regulations, such as those relating to registration, maintenance of log books, and the appointment of "installation managers," emerged fairly rapidly in the wake of the 1971 act,[40] others have been rather longer in the making. Those pertaining to the inspection of installations and the reporting of casualties did not become operative until the end of 1973,[41] whereas regulations covering "operational safety, health and welfare" did not come into force until November 1976, more than five years after the act was passed.[42] What appear to have been particularly protracted negotiations delayed the appearance of detailed rules for firefighting equipment until 1978.[43]

Although the Mineral Workings (Offshore Installations) Act of 1971 and the regulations made thereunder constitute the main body of statutory controls specific to the safety of offshore oil operations, they do not exhaust the catalogue of British law purporting to have some application in this connection. Thus, the Merchant Shipping Acts apply to certain aspects of such operations,[44] whereas the Petroleum and Submarine Pipe-lines Act of 1975 makes provision for regulating the safety, health, and welfare of those engaged on pipeline works.[45]

Most important of all for what follows, it was announced in mid-1976 that the government intended to extend the overarching body of onshore safety legislation, the Health and Safety at Work Act of 1974, to the offshore situation.[46] With its attempt to get away from the piecemeal approach to specific industries by the imposition of general duties on all employers and by the creation of a unified enforcement apparatus to cover all health and safety at work (the Health and Safety Commission and Executive), this act's application to the North Sea might have seemed to augur a sharp change of direction with respect to the regulation of offshore safety. As we shall see, however, attempts to implement the relevant decision were to prove very difficult, not least because they cut across the special regulatory relationship that had already been established. At the time of writing (see author's postscript at end of chapter), it seems probable that the highly unsatisfactory state of affairs that resulted will be resolved, not by further efforts to bring North Sea operations more firmly under the general umbrella of the Health and Safety Executive, but by the (at least partial) rescindment of the decision itself.[47] Such an outcome would be entirely comprehensible within the context of the central argument advanced in this chapter, namely, that the development and application of safety provisions with respect to the British sector of the North Sea have been shaped and constrained by the symbiotic nature of the relationship between the industry (including its financers) and crucially located apparatuses within the British state.

## Administration and Enforcement

Just as the forces that generated and sustained rapid exploration and exploitation of the North Sea had a profound influence on the development of laws relating to the safety of such operations, so, too, they have permeated the structure and practice of how those laws are enforced. At one level, this is apparent in the way that responsibility has been distributed between the different official agencies with an interest in the area of offshore safety; at another, it is evident in some of the problems encountered by the Scottish legal authorities within whose jurisdiction something approaching two-thirds of the British sector is located. Not least, the same consideration and constraints that have influenced British North Sea policy at the highest level over the past fifteen years can be seen to have penetrated down to the level of routine enforcement practice.

At the time when the Mineral Workings (Offshore Installations) Act was passed in 1971, the Ministry of Power had recently been absorbed into the new Department of Trade and Industry under an ex-oilman, John Davies. However, responsibility for most of the matters encompassed by the act soon passed to another body when, during the oil crisis of 1973–1974, a newly developed Department of Energy was created. Since then, it has been this department and, more specifically, its Petroleum Engineering Division, that has been in the forefront of the development and enforcement of regulations under the act. Staffed by inspectors selected for their experience in oil or related industries, this division maintains a close relationship with the industry, a relationship that was perhaps epitomized, at an extreme, when the director of operations and safety resigned from the department in 1978 to become technical secretary to the United Kingdom Offshore Operators Association—the body that represents the major operators of licenses and that is prone to regard itself as speaking for the total offshore oil industry.[48] More generally, at many points in this research instances were encountered in which personnel from the Petroleum Engineering Division seemed to be acting more as the industry's advocates than as its overseers. In one particularly pointed case, when members of a commercially organized seminar were told that the offshore safety record was not a good one, it was not the oilmen present but the Department of Energy's representative who rose to refute this allegation against an industry "that has come further in seven years than any other comparable one has in three years that time."

A more-important point about the role played by the Department of Energy, however, is that at least until recently it has meant that control over both the formulation and the implementation of laws relating to offshore safety have been vested in the same body, which has held responsibility for licensing, for the encouragement of exploration, and for maintaining the impetus toward self-sufficiency in oil. Hence, what many observers would see as the sine qua non of a good safety policy—that the authority responsible for safety not be synonymous with that responsible for production—was set aside in the case of the North Sea.[49] In fairness, of course, it is not difficulty to see why, initially, this should have happened. As we have already seen, installations could scarcely have been classified as factories in order to bring them under the control of the Factory Inspectorate, nor could they have been designated as ships and brought within the purview of the Merchant Shipping Acts. What is surprising, however, is the fact that despite the passage of the Health and Safety at Work Act in 1974 and the subsequent incorporation of virtually every other British inspectorate into the Health and Safety Executive (HSE), responsibility for North Sea safety was not completely transferred to that body.

Several reasons have been advanced for the failure to take this obvious step. In particular, it has been claimed that the Health and Safety Executive and the Factory Inspectorate (which is now subsumed) lacked the necessary expertise, whereas the Department of Energy did not. Against this, however, it must be said that the evidence alluded to briefly in the first part of this chapter strongly suggests that the vast majority of offshore accidents, including many of the most technologically complex ones, arise out of circumstances with which Health and Safety Executive personnel are perfectly familiar. Moreover, although a case may perhaps be made that this familiarity does not extend to production hazards such as the risk of blowouts, or to technical aspects of an installation's structural integrity, this still does not provide a priori support for the retention of responsibility for these matters within the Department of Energy. In the first instance, the requisite expertise on the hazards associated with tapping the reservoir could have readily been made available by the transfer of relevant personnel, if not the entire Petroleum Engineering Division, to the Health and Safety Executive; with respect to structural safety, a similar redeployment of staff would have dealt with the problem. This aspect of safety is in any case "farmed out" by the Department of Energy to "independent" certifying authorities such as Lloyds, and there is no reason that this procedure could not have continued under Health and Safety Executive auspices.

An alternative explanation, and one that is very much in keeping with the theme of this chapter, is that rationalization along the foregoing lines might have compromised the delicate symbiotic relationship encapsulated in the

Department of Energy's dealings with the oil industry. Although it would be historically inaccurate to portray the Factory Inspectorate, by far the largest component of the HSE machine, as always having acted autonomously of the productive requirements and interests of the industries it controlled, or indeed of the "requirements" of the economy in general, the inspectorate does none-theless maintain a stance of relative independence from those concerns.[50] Indeed, in ideological terms, its historical significance probably lies primarily in its ability to maintain this position, which is signified by a small but steady stream of prosecutions each year.[51] In contrast, the relationship between the Department of Energy—often officially referred to as the "sponsoring agency"—and the oil industry has been not only much closer but also one in which the objective of rapid exploitation has been substantially and overtly shared.

To have transferred responsibility for offshore safety to a relatively independent body such as the HSE could have jeopardized this relationship in several ways. At one level, as a senior Petroleum Engineering official explained, the Health and Safety Executive has a tendency "to fuss about small details which barely touch on the major hazards offshore," and this could obviously have become a considerable irritant to the industry, although we may add that such a tendency would certainly have had more than a slight bearing on many of the accidents examined in the course of this research. On an equally crucial plane, such a transfer of responsibility could have slowed down the rate of exploration and exploitation as a consequence of a relatively more independent stance being adopted toward the issue of production. The point was put nicely by another Department of Energy official when he pointed out that "they [the HSE] could not balance the exigencies of safety against the requirements of production in the way that we can."

The "special relationship" between the industry and its sponsoring department seems to have shaped events crucially when the decision was finally taken to extend the Health and Safety at Work Act of 1974 to the continental shelf. Although the prime minister's announcement of this decision in July 1976 was predicated on the need for "a more rational redistribution of responsibility,"[52] the administrative arrangements that were laid down presaged the resilience that the basic regulatory relationship would exhibit in the face of any attempt to bring offshore safety within the unified framework of British safety legislation as applied onshore. Thus, although responsibility for structural and production safety was left with the Department of Energy, occupational safety on installations (and on pipe-laying barges),[53] was passed over the Health and Safety Commission, whose executive arm is the Health and Safety Executive. But the Petroleum Engineering Division of the Department of Energy was still to retain the task of actually inspecting installations in connection with occupational safety, by virtue of an "agency agreement" to be worked out with HSE. Thus, the latter body came to hold responsibility for policy in this area, though having only a tenuous grasp of the means of seeing that it was carried out in practice.

Moreover, it is by no means certain that even this complex and limited intrusion into the regulation of offshore safety will long continue. A committee of inquiry, set up within the Department of Energy, was due to report early in 1980 and seemed poised to endorse, at least by implication, the unanimous view of the industry—that policy and enforcement should be reunited under one roof, that of the Department of Energy.[54]

In the space of this chapter it is not possible to detail all the other respects in which this basic nexus underpinning the regulation of offshore safety has permeated the structure of law enforcement in this area. Thus, for example, we cannot go into the complexities of how the anomalies bequeathed by the "panic-stricken" nature of the Continental Shelf Act created a situation in which the jurisdiction of the Scottish courts with regard to the holding of Fatal Accident Inquiries could be successfully challenged, with the result that all such inquiries had to be abandoned for almost two years.[55] Nor, unfortunately, can we trace out the checkered relationship between the Scottish authorities and the Department of Energy, a relationship that reached its nadir in 1975 when the latter's reluctance to release its "confidential" reports on fatal accidents led to complaints that the investigation of cases was being impeded. It suffices to say that in these instances, as in that of the part to be played by the Health and Safety Executive, there seems to have been more to the story than simple legislative confusion or interdepartmental misunderstanding.

When the focus shifts to the actual practices of enforcement under the auspices of the Department of Energy, the picture that emerges is one of conflict emanating from the performance of different roles. At the most-immediate level, such conflict is probably rendered inevitable by the fact that, within existing resources, the Petroleum Engineering Division has had to fulfill its own immediate responsibility for structural and production safety on the one hand, and its agency responsibilities for occupational safety on the other. As is common in cases of such conflict, of course, officials sometimes deny the existence of any distinction between these two categories of safety, asserting that occupational risks can simply be subsumed under the heading of structural and production hazards. At other times, however, they concede that their approach has indeed been dominated by the risk of major catastrophes such as blowout or structural collapse, and defend their position on the grounds that these dangers are potentially much greater than those associated with the world of routine occupational safety. In so doing, they not only acknowledge the distinction but also leave the department open to the suspicion of having paid less attention than it might to its responsibility for occupational safety. Such suspicions would not be out of keeping with the offshore accident record, which shows that, although there has indeed been no major disaster since Sea Gem, there has been a high casualty rate stemming from the more-mundane types of circumstances with which occupational safety is primarily concerned. The point was put cogently by one member of another department with an interest in North Sea risks:

Quite often they get the big things right—the big things are politically more dangerous for an enforcing authority, and sure, you've got to get that right as well—but I sometimes think we get it right because the current political implications of not getting it right would be far worse. But, you know, you've got to get the little things right. That's where you make the biggest impact on accidents, and how the Department of Energy are on that kind of thing I have no idea at all. . . .

The other major source of potential conflict within the enforcement practice of the Department of Energy stems from the fact that, as already discussed, the department holds front-line responsibility not only for offshore safety but also for licensing and the maintenance of progress toward self-sufficiency. Thus, there is the very real possibility of inspectors being caught between what could be the contradictory demands of their own regulatory function and wider considerations emanating from the nature of the relationship between the industry and the department as the state's main agency for dealing with North Sea oil. As one recent critic puts it, "the men for the P.E.D., through no particular fault of their own, seem bound to be torn between interest in engineering problems associated with the production and process capability of an offshore oil installation and the need to ensure satisfactory occupational safety for the workforce."[56]

Not surprisingly, relevant officials at the Department of Energy vehemently deny any suggestion that production might ever be allowed to take priority over safety in their approach to regulation of offshore activities. Others, however, are less certain that the matter is always quite so straightforward. According to one union official, for example, there is "no shadow of doubt" that there are divided loyalties and conflicts as a result of the department's functions in relation to the "economic and production side"; and another described the enforcement process as always taking place in the knowledge "that over their shoulder there is a government which is determined to get the oil out of the North Sea as quickly as possible." Nor were they alone in voicing such misgivings. Health and Safety Executive personnel expressed similar doubts on this same score:

> . . . the danger is always there, I think, that, you know, the production side of it might, well, you know. . . . There's good reasons way they've got to produce this oil, you know—the good of the country and all this stuff. And that's pressure on the inspectors as it is on anybody else, no matter who it is, and these are conflicting pressures. . . .

In view of the Department of Energy's failure to permit access to anything more than fragmentary documentation relating to its enforcement activities, it has not been possible for this research to substantiate or refute such suggestions in any systematic fashion. From even the limited amount of data available, however, a serious doubt arises as to whether the department's own categorical denials are justified. Such a charge is a grave one; since, therefore, it cannot be

left entirely unsupported, the following brief case history of one major North
Sea production platform will be left to speak for itself.

In late 1974, this particular installation was inspected while it was still,
in effect, little more than a maritime construction site; and it was noted that
the intention was to house 122 persons in temporary "portacabins," six to ten
to a cabin, during the construction phase. However, no Certificate of Fitness
under the Construction and Survey Regulations (1974) was required at this
point because the absence of any "oil related function" on an installation in
this stage development has been interpreted by the department as exempting
it from this requirement,[57] and because, in any case, the deadline fixed for
certification by the regulations was August 1975.[58] Such a certificate, with its
prescription of appropriate accommodation standards, escape routes, and protection from hazards such as fire, would therefore become necessary only when
drilling commenced, a stage that was reached in June 1975, some eight or nine
weeks before the deadline was due to expire. During an inspection carried out
at this point, it was noted that 120 men were still housed in a three-tier stack
of portacabins; and the inspector suggested that "it would be very difficult to
evacuate this installation quickly and safely should an emergency arise." As one
of his superiors baldly noted on the file's minute sheet, "they are *drilling* with
330 people on board."

Some three weeks before the certification requirement was due to take
effect, the platform was visited again; it was noted that the first well was about
to be perforated, with 214 persons still on board, and that, indeed, *production*
was now expected to begin before the end of the month. The inspector recorded
his personal view that to embark on this phase of the operation while construction (not to mention drilling) was still in progress would be "hazardous" and of
debatable good sense "from other than an economic point of view." But the
platform received its Certificate of Fitness some ten days after the prescribed
date, as a result of the department having instructed the certifying authorities
"to virtually ignore" temporary accommodation carried over from the construction phase into the drilling and subsequently into the production phase on this
and other northern North Sea platforms. Approximately one month later, a
further visit confirmed that production had commenced, although completion
was "still months ahead" and although at least 55 construction workers were
still on board. In voicing his own misgivings on this occasion, the inspector
demonstrated how some of the wider forces discussed in this chapter do indeed
penetrate down to the day-to-day level of enforcement:

> The economic plight of the country and the political significance of
> producing oil yesterday are understood and appreciated, but in my
> opinion from a purely safety aspect "start-up" has been 3 months too
> soon. I state this so that no-one is in any doubt that corners are being
> cut and calculated risks are being taken to obtain objectives. I myself
> consider that the risks are valid, but I would be failing in my duty if

my peers are not aware of the situation. The position is that construction work is going ahead simultaneously with well drilling, oil/gas
separation and pumping activities.[59]

If such a flexible approach to the imposition of statutory regulations is in
any way characteristic of the Department of Energy's general approach to law
enforcement in the North Sea—and it is for that department to demonstrate that
it is not—then it comes as no surprise to discover that the Petroleum Engineering
Division's attitude to the application of legal sanctions is, to say the least, un-
enthusiastic. To some extent, of course, the department is not alone in this;
other agencies purporting to regulate business activities and "white-collar crime"
have never been renowned for the alacrity with which they resort to the courts
in instances of violation. At the same time, however, it seems likely that the
Department of Energy would fall well toward the "nonpenal" end of any continuum that might be constructed in this respect, a position that is evidenced in
its tendency to "deprecate the attitude sometimes displayed of looking for
breaches of regulations rather than ways to prevent similar accidents." Although
never specified, such deprecation is almost certainly an oblique reference to
what is perceived as the unduly legalistic approach of the Health and Safety
Executive, whose own activities with respect to the use of prosecution could
scarcely be described as overly rigid (see Carson 1970).

As far as the Department of Energy is concerned, resort to the penal sanctions available under the relevant legislation is deemed largely irrelevant to the
regulation of North Sea operations, save in the most exceptional circumstances.
To date, there have been six prosecutions arising out of offshore violations, two
of which involved fatalities included among the files thus far made available by
the Scottish legal authorities. In one instance, a major oil company was fined
£200 following an accident in which a pipefitter standing on one of a number of
inadequately secured sections of deck grating fell 80 feet to his death in the sea
below. A similar fine was imposed on a diving company after the death of two
divers who had been sent into the turbulent seas around anchor bolsters at night,
with an adequately secured "buddy line," with no standby diver, and in the
absence of any written rules for the conduct of diving operations.[60] The motivation for taking this case tells its own story with respect to the place that prosecution had hitherto held in the enforcement of the Offshore Installations (Diving)
Regulations of 1974:

. . . the motivation of the Department in submitting the case is that
they wish to be seen to have the ability to institute a prosecution if
they think fit. Since the establishment of the Diving Inspectorate, the
Department has proceeded by exhortation, to obtain compliance with
first of all logical safety measures and later compliance with the Diving
Regulations. The Inspectors now feel that since there have been no prosecutions, the companies may adopt the attitude that there will be no
prosecutions.[61]

Such motivation is entirely in accordance with a general approach that sees prosecution as nothing more than an occasional sharp corrective, or something to be countenanced for other and extraneous reasons.[62] Indeed, it would be no exaggeration to describe the enforcement of safety laws in the British sector of the North Sea as being organized in such a way that legal proceedings are rendered highly improbable. Thus, the inspectors lack training in the investigative procedures that are necessary for purposes of court action, and indeed, there is even some doubt as to their power to take statements from witnesses.[63] Similarly, as far as Scots law is concerned, the department has been very slow to adjust its activities to the procedural requirements of that jurisdiction. Visits by a single inspector, for example, raise real, though not insurmountable, problems with respect to corroboration, with the consequence that one inspector could assert roundly, if incorrectly, that in most instances prosecution would not be possible even if it were desirable. Even in the case of fatalities, where the Scottish police also investigate on behalf of the Procurator Fiscal, officials have sometimes been totally confused as to whose task it is to identify any grounds for prosecution. "This we have left to the police because the police force investigates," explained one senior member of the department; "but the police don't go out looking for offences," said a Procurator Fiscal; "when the inspector goes out, he is looking for offences." Similar confusion characterized one extraordinary period in which the department claimed to be awaiting the results of "inquests" (fatal-accident inquiries) from Scotland before deciding whether a prosecution should be proposed; since in Scotland the normal procedure is to prosecute first, the Scottish authorities were therefore awaiting recommendations from London on this score before holding fatal-accident inquiries!

If prosecution is unlikely, what other strategies does the department adopt in order to secure compliance? Here, a great deal is made of the inspectors' power to close down an installation, a sanction that both they and the industry claim to be entirely adequate. Superficially convincing as this claim may be, however, it leaves certain important questions unanswered. Would this power, for example, be sufficient to overcome the political and economic pressures to maintain continuity of production? Given the department's wider concerns, is it likely that such a sanction would be used or threatened with any regularity? "Very rarely" was the estimate of one official who went on to explain that when a "direct confrontation" between production and safety had arisen in connection with a number of the older gas platforms, the issue had been resolved by granting temporary exemptions and partial certificates. Others merely offered isolated anecdotal accounts from their own experience of the dramatic impact that a threat to close down an installation could have. Sometimes, as when one inspector described how he had threatened to take such action on discovering that an installation lacked a single life-saving capsule with a startable engine, such stories revealed just how high the other price of British oil could have been.

Most of all, however, the claims made for the efficacy of this sanction tend to divert attention from what, in the light of the North Sea's record so far, is very arguably an equally important issue—what action is taken in connection with all those other mundane deficiencies that could result in injury but that are not deemed to warrant contemplation of such draconian measures? It is here, I suggest, that the really big gap in offshore enforcement practice is to be found. Written instructions deposited with the installation manager by inspectors who, in any case, are untrained in the routine of general (as opposed to specialist) inspection scarcely seem likely to be any more efficacious than the system formerly employed by the Factory Inspectorate, whose main enforcement action used to comprise letters simply notifying occupiers of "matters requiring attention" (Carson 1970). As a result, it is difficult to avoid the suspicion that there are and will continue to be significant lucunae in the extent of the legal protection afforded to workers employed in the British sector of the North Sea.

**Conclusion**

In this chapter I have suggested, first of all, that the tendency to attribute the very real dangers of offshore employment to the technological and other exigencies of North Sea operations is misleading in that it tends to minimize the potential role of law in creating a safer working environment. I then examined the broad structural context within which North Sea developments have taken place, and traced out the concatenation of forces that produced an essentially sumbiotic relationship between the industry and the state agencies most concerned with offshore oil. This relationship was depicted as one within which the objective of rapid exploration and exploitation was substantially shared and a classic process of give and take grew up betwen multinational corporations and the host state.

It was this basic relationship that shaped the development, administrative structure, and enforcement of laws relating to the safety of offshore developments. Initially an afterthought in the wake of the need to provide a legal framework for North Sea operations, regulations relating to safety emerged slowly through a process of negotiation in which the need to carry the industry's support was crucial. The administrative structure for the enforcement of such regulations consistently placed effective power in the hands of the same agency that was instrumental in facilitating rapid development toward self-sufficiency in oil supplies. Attempts to displace some of this power onto the relatively independent body responsible for nearly all onshore safety regulation were confounded by complex administrative arrangements that generated both tension and an impetus toward rationalization that would restore the regulatory status quo. Similar interagency problems that arose in connection with other departments and authorities concerned with legal aspects of safety in the North Sea could not be discussed here. Finally, it was suggested that the practice of enforcement under the auspices of the British Department of Energy has exhibited several features that are in keeping with the nature of the basic regulatory relationship described earlier. Heavily permeated by the department's wider concern with the rate of offshore progress, it has tended to elevate the priority of production requirements, and to exhibit a reluctance to prosecute that is extreme even for a regulatory body of this kind. Not least, it has tended to revolve around procedures that, although possibly successful in helping to avert major catastrophe, have left large areas of routine safety comparatively underregulated. It was precisely these areas that the first section of this chapter suggested were the main locus of the North Sea's high casualty rate.

### Author's Postscript

Since this chapter was written, two events have occurred which are of considerable relevance to its content. On the evening of 27 March 1980, the *Alexander Kielland,* an accommodation platform located in the Norwegian sector of the North Sea, capsized with the loss of 123 lives. Although the cause of this tragedy will not be known until the Norwegian authorities have completed their investigation, it may prove to have been a notable, if lamentable, exception to the argument advanced vis-à-vis technology in the first part of the chapter. Such an outcome would not necessarily run counter to the chapter's central thesis, however. Commenting on the possibility that metal fatigue not only may have been responsible in this instance but also may be present in other North Sea structures, one eminent metallurgist has suggested that the oil industry is using technology that is unproven, with design running ahead of research and development. The reverse order, he points out, would be more sensible, "but in the case of oil . . . we are in a great hurry because of the energy crisis. . . ."[64] Such comments are consistent with those of engineers responsible for testing platform designs, who have been quoted as claiming that "until 1977, no realistic tests were conducted into metal fatigue or into the potential buckling of hollow steel components of the structures, such as the legs."[65]

The other event that has occurred since the chapter was written is the publication of the report alluded to earlier (the Burgoyne Committee, *Cmnd. 7841*). Apart from offering little reassurance that a disaster on the scale of the *Alexander Kielland* could not take place in the British sector—the British National Oil Corporation, for example, submitted evidence suggesting that construction defects have been encountered on many occasions and may well still exist in some offshore structures—the report came out strongly in favor of responsibility for offshore safety being vested in a single agency, the Department of Energy (p. 18). This recommendation is in keeping with both the argument and the prediction contained in the chapter, which, I hope, was persuasive in its opposition to such a step being taken. A further and regrettable effect of the *Alexander Kielland* disaster may well turn out to be that the British government will decide to demonstrate the urgency of its concern about safety in the North Sea by implementing this recommendation without due regard to its wider implications.

## Notes

1. *The Guardian*, 20 August 1979, p. 11. Reprinted with permission.

2. Throughout this chapter I shall refer almost exclusively to oil. It should not be forgotten, however, that North Sea developments initially centered on the possibility of substantial gas deposits, and that such deposits indeed were found in the southern sector.

3. "Offshore Europe 79", *The Scotsman*, 3 September 1979.

4. *The Press and Journal*, Aberdeen, 10 August 1979, p. 10. Reprinted with permission.

5. This story is recounted by Dr. J. Kitchen, who collaborated with the author during a preliminary investigation to assess the feasibility of conducting research in this area.

6. *The Guardian*, 21 June 1977.

7. Ibid., 10 August 1979.

8. *The Press and Journal*, Aberdeen, 10 August 1979, p. 18. Reprinted with permission.

9. These figures are taken from the Department of Energy's report entitled *Development of the Oil and Gas Resources in the United Kingdom* (London: HMSO, 1979). Hereafter these annual publications will be referred to as the *Brown Book,* the title that they are commonly given in the field.

10. Calculated from figures given in *Brown Books* 1975–1979, and from *Health and Safety Statistics,* Health and Safety Executive (London: HMSO, 1975, 1976). Because of the relatively small numbers employed offshore, such comparisons should be treated with some caution.

11. Indeed, although four men were killed on vessels in 1978, there were no fatalities on or around installations. This improvement is usually attributed to the fact that the industry is now moving into the production phase, which does not involve the same hazards, although the risk of a major catastrophe is probably increased. However, figures for 1979 will almost certainly show a marked deterioration.

12. The offshore industry also compares badly, although not quite so sharply, when fatal and serious accidents are combined.

13. Under Scots law, Procurators Fiscal investigate fatal accidents (using the police) and make recommendations as to whether a Fatal Accident Inquiry should be held in the Sheriff Court.

14. These documents give the bare details of each accident, along with a brief comment, usually on the cause of the accident.

15. See C. Crouch, "The City, Industry and the State" in Crouch (1979). The position adopted here obviously raises important questions about how the "state" should be theorized, but I do not propose in this chapter to enter into the heated debate on this subject. It is suggested, however, that whatever stance is adopted on this score, the nexus referred to here would have to be acknowledged as exerting a vital influence in the specific instance of North Sea oil.

16. *The Oilman,* 18 November 1978, p. 18. Reprinted with permission.

17. Hamilton (1978, p. 71) points out that "capital costs in the North Sea are as much as ten times the on-shore figure, or anything between £3,000 and £8,000 per daily barrel of production capacity compared to a few hundred dollars onshore in the Middle East. . . ." The Department of Energy also recognizes this as an important factor to be considered in the context of depletion policy (*Brown Book* 1978, p. 54).

18. *First Report from the Committee of Public Accounts,* Session 1972/ 1973.

19. Statement by the secretary of state for energy, 6 December 1974; *Brown Book* (1975, p. 36).

20. See, for example, *The Oilman,* 21 October 1978.

21. For a good discussion of the symbiotic relationship between nation-states and multinational corporations, see Martinelli (1975).

22. *Continental Shelf Act,* 1964 (c. 29).

23. *Parliamentary Debates,* vol. 668, 1963–1964, p. 218.

24. Ibid., p. 224.

25. Sec. 1. Whether these rights are proprietary or jurisdictional is not entirely clear, although Daintith favors the former interpretation (Daintith and Willoughby 1977, p. 21).

26. *24 & 25 Geo. V* (c. 36).

27. *Parliamentary Debates,* vol. 668, 1963–1964, p. 235.

28. Sec. 3.

29. *Parliamentary Debates,* vol. 668, 1963–1964, p. 235.

30. Sec. 1(4).

31. *1961 Factories Act,* 9 & 10 Eliz. II (c. 34).

32. *Parliamentary Debates,* vol. 668, 1963–1964, p. 239.

33. *Cmnd. 3409,* October 1967.

34. Ibid., p. 2.

35. Ibid., p. 24.

36. *1971* (c. 61).

37. *Parliamentary Debates,* vol. 816, 1970–1971, p. 649.

38. *Parliamentary Debates,* Reports from Standing Committee G, vol. IV, 1970–1971, p. 6.

39. Ibid, pp. 31–33.

40. *S.I. 1972, 702; S.I. 1972, 703; S.I. 1972, 1542.*

41. *S.I. 1973, 1842.*

42. *S.I. 1976, 1019.*

43. *S.I. 1978, 611.*

44. Particularly, of course, to the activities of ancillary vessels.

45. *1975* (c. 74).

46. Implemented by *S.I. 1977, 1232.*

47. An independent committee of inquiry set up by the Department of Energy under the chairmanship of Dr. J. Burgoyne was due to report early in 1980.

48. Notably, however, most offshore workers are employed not by the companies making up this association, but by contractors, a fact that creates great difficulty for attempts to regulate safety conditions offshore.

49. This point is made, for example, by Peter Watson, whose forthcoming dissertation on conditions of employment offshore will almost certainly turn out to be the definitive work on this subject, although its treatment of specifically health and safety matters will necessarily be brief.

50. For a discussion of the significance of this body in historical terms, see Carson, 1980.

51. Between 1974 and 1976, for example, prosecutions were running at around 1,400 per annum. *Health and Safety Commission Report, 1974-1976* (London: HMSO, 1977).

52. *Parliamentary Debates*, 30 July 1976.

53. This responsibility does not, however, include crew members engaged in normal manning of ships.

54. Although there is certainly a case for reunification, the pratical implication of the argument advanced in this chapter is that it would be much more appropriate to achieve this by transferring complete responsibility for safety to the Health and Safety Executive.

55. Following the death of a welder in 1974, Brown & Root (U.K.) Ltd. challenged the right to hold public inquiries into offshore fatalities. They contended that although Section 3 of the Continental Shelf Act extended the criminal and civil law of Britain to the North Sea, inquiries held under the Fatal Accidents Inquiry (Scotland) Act of 1895 were not, strictly speaking, civil or criminal proceedings. As a result, all such inquiries were suspended until a new act, the Fatal Accidents and Sudden Deaths Inquiry (Scotland) Act of 1976, could be passed.

56. *Offshore Engineer*, November 1979.

57. Interestingly, it was pointed out during discussion of the Mineral Workings (Offshore) Installations Bill that the construction phase created the very circumstances in which it was crucial to have strict observance of construction and survey regulations. Significantly too, the undersecretary of state indicated that the proposed power to grant exemptions would be used not to

provide loopholes, but only to allow for "the remote possibility" of someone in the future undertaking "some activity where this legislation would be totally unsuitable". *Parliamentary Debates,* Reports of Standing Committee, vol. IV, 1970–1971, pp. 13–17.

58. *S.I. 1974, 289,* Sec. 3.

59. Eighteen months later, the company was still seeking further permission to retain "construction quality" accommodation, but was told that as of May 1977 the regulations would be enforced.

60. The diving supervisor in this case was also fined £25.

61. *S.I. 1974, 1229.*

62. Thus, for example, the following point was made in connection with another case, although no prosecution ensued:

> In a previous case . . . regarding the failure to report a fatality . . . in April 1974, we accepted your advise not to prosecute. This fatality has now, for other reasons, become a cause celebre in some Union circles and, in hindsight, it was a mistake not to prosecute.

63. Section 3 of the Offshore Installations (Inspectors and Casualties) Regulations 1973 seems to omit this vital requirement.

64. *The Oilman,* 5 April 1980.

65. *The Observer,* 30 March 1980.

### References

Arnold, Guy. *Britain's Oil.* London: Hamish Hamilton, 1978.

Carson, W.G. "White Collar Crime and the Enforcement of Factory Legislation." *British Journal of Criminology* 10(1970).

――――. "White Collar Crime and the Institutionalization of Ambiguity." In G. Geis and E. Stotland, eds., *White-Collar Crime.* Beverly Hills, Calif.: Sage Publications, 1980.

Crouch, C., ed. *State and Economy in Contemporary Capitalism.* London: Croom Helm, 1979.

Daintith, T., and Willoughby, G. *A Manual of United Kingdom Oil and Gas Law.* London: Oyez Publishing, 1977.

Department of Energy. *Development of the Oil and Gas Resources in the United Kingdom.* London: HMSO, various years. Cited as *Brown Book.*

Hamilton, Adrian. *North Sea Impact: Offshore Oil and the British Economy.* London: International Institute for Economic Research, 1978.

Kitchen, J. *Labour, Law, and Offshore Oil.* London: Croom, Helm, 1977.

Sampson, Anthony. *The Seven Sisters.* London: Coronet Books, 1976.

Ure, A. *Philosophy of Manufactures.* London, C. Knight, 1835.

# 12 Social Control and the Legal Profession

*Jerry Parker*

*After three years of studying lawyer discipline throughout the country, this committee must report the existence of a scandalous situation that requires the immediate attention of the profession. With few expections the prevailing attitude of lawyers toward disciplinary enforcement ranges from apathy to outright hostility. Disciplinary action is practically nonexistent in many jurisdictions; practices and procedures are antiquated; many disciplinary agencies have little power to take effective steps against malefactors.*

(American Bar Association Special Committee
on Evaluation of Disciplinary Enforcement,
1970, p. 1)

## Introduction

The foregoing quotation begins, and perhaps best summarizes, the most-systematic study of the legal profession's attempts to deal with misconduct by its own members. The study, now commonly referred to as the Clark report, brought to the attention of the legal profession a perennial problem, which Watergate would make apparent to the general public some three years later—that membership in the legal profession is no guarantee of professionally competent, ethically sound, or even legally acceptable behavior by a lawyer.

The problems surrounding the competence, ethicality, and legality of professional behavior are, of course, not limited to the legal profession. As both recent exposes (Mitford 1963) and more-systematic studies (Quinney 1963; Freidson 1960) have demonstrated, they are common to many professions. Historically, the professions have been allowed to police themselves under an arrangement that Rueschemeyer (1973) describes as a "bargain model":

> Professions strike a bargain with society in which trust, autonomy from lay control, protection from lay competition, substantial

Revised version of a paper presented at the State University at Potsdam Conference on White-Collar and Economic Crime, 7-9 February 1980. The author wishes to thank John Clark, Pat Lauderdale, James Inverarity, Joel Samaha, Peter Wickman, Tim Dailey, and Barry Feld for suggestions and comments on earlier revisions of this chapter. Additional thanks are due to the staff of the American Bar Foundation, the Standing Committee on Professional Discipline, and the Center for Professional Discipline of the American Bar Association for their aid in collecting the data. This research was supported in part by a Faculty Development Grant from Florida Atlantic University.

remuneration, and high status are exchanged for individual and collective self-control designed to protect the interests of both clients and the public. [p. 13]

Recently, however, both the adequacy of the conception of professions that underlies this model and the capability of professions to uphold their end of the bargain has been challenged.[1]

This is especially so in the case of the legal profession. With regard to the adequacy of the model, Rueschemeyer (1973) notes, "For attorneys and advocates the mesh of role obligations is complicated by a number of factors that derive from the distinctive characteristics of the law and the legal profession" (p. 20). That is, the lawyer must successfully balance the potentially conflicting role expectations placed on him by courts, clients, colleagues, and a general sense of public duty toward the institution of the law itself. These competing role expectations—when combined with the pecuniary nature of the lawyer-client relationship, the specialized nature of legal knowledge, the perception that this knowledge may allow the lawyer to break the law with some greater degree of impunity, and substantial problems of trust regarding the confidentiality of information—make the exercise of professional social control within the legal profession especially problematic.[2] Additionally, the problematic nature of professional self-control in the legal profession is further complicated by the internal stratification of the profession. As several studies have indicated, the lawyer's place in the stratification system of the bar may affect his perception of the need for disciplinary action (O'Gorman 1963; Smigel 1964); his experience of role conflict (O'Gorman 1963; Carlin 1966); his knowledge of unprofessional conduct (Wood 1959); and his ability to exercise power with respect to bringing or avoiding disciplinary action (Carlin 1966; Handler 1967; Auerbach 1976; Heinz et al. 1976; Laumann and Heinz 1977; Riesman 1957; ABA 1970).

With respect to the legal profession's ability to fulfill its portion of the bargain, the evidence suggests rather extensive failure. Steele and Nimmer (1976, p. 982) note that in four jurisdictions having large bar populations (California, Illinois, Michigan, and New York City) 10,558 complaints were made against lawyers during the period 1974-1975. Based on previous studies, it is likely that the majority of these cases involved neglect of client's cases, fee disputes, and conversion or misappropriation of client funds (see Carlin 1962, p. 151; Steele and Nimmer 1976, pp. 970-976). Although these are relatively minor breaches of the Code of Professional Responsibility, it is nonetheless surprising that 95 percent of these cases were administratively dismissed without investigation. Of course, this could indicate great efficiency on the part of administrative officers in screening out unfounded cases. However, of the 5 percent of cases investigated, only 33 percent received any sanction more severe than an informal reprimand. Thus, only 1.6 percent of complaints resulted in any form of sanction being imposed, a processing rate not likely to inspire extensive public confidence in the seriousness of the bar's efforts to police itself. Nor is the Clark report's list of abuses and problems likely to inspire public confidence. As that report notes:

> The Committee has found that in some instances disbarred attorneys are able to continue to practice in another locale; that lawyers convicted of federal income tax violations are not disciplined; that lawyers convicted of serious crimes are not disciplined until after appeals from their convictions have been concluded, often a matter of three or four years, so that lawyers convicted of serious crimes, such as bribery of a governmental employee, are able to continue to practice before the very agency whose representative they have corrupted; that even after disbarment lawyers are reinstated as a matter of course; that lawyers fail to report violations of the Code of Professional Responsibility committed by their brethren, much less conduct that violates the criminal law; that lawyers will not appear or cooperate in proceedings against other lawyers but instead will exert their influence to stymie the proceedings; that in communities with a limited attorney population disciplinary agencies will not proceed against prominent lawyers or law firms and that, even when they do, no disciplinary action is taken, because the members of the disciplinary agency simply will not make findings against those with whom they are professionally and socially well acquainted; and that, finally, state disciplinary agencies are undermanned and underfinanced, many having no staff whatever for the investigations or prosecution of complaints." [ABA 1970, pp. 1-2]

Thus the nature of the legal profession itself and the nature of past disciplinary enforcement suggests certain problems in the exercise of professional social control.

## Previous Studies of Misconduct in the Legal Profession

These problems are not entirely new, nor have they escaped the attention of the legal profession and sociologists concerned with occupational behavior. The legal profession has devoted considerable attention to the origins and incidence of professional misconduct, and numerous programs have attempted to resolve the problem of lawyer misconduct.[3] However, the majority of these studies and programs are reminiscent of the simplistic and archaic views of the social pathologists in that they have seen professional misconduct as caused either by inadequate socialization to professional standards or by personal inadequacy in meeting those standards (see Freidson 1964; Carlin 1966; Steele and Nimmer 1976).

Recent sociological studies that have sought to investigate the effects of social structure of professional misconduct are somewhat less individualistic in focus. Of particular note are the works of Wood (1959); O'Gorman (1963); Smigel (1964); Reichstein (1965); Simon (1966); Carlin (1962, 1966); Handler (1967); and Rueschemeyer (1973). These studies all suggest that a lawyer's place within the social structure of the legal profession has some effect on his attitudes toward professional misconduct and, by inference, on his own behavior regarding ethical questions. Wood (1959) reports that: (1) criminal lawyers without a college degree are more likely to be aware of instances of professional misconduct; (2) degree of specialization in criminal law and income show no consistent relationship with attitudes toward matters of ethics; and (3) criminal lawyers, although more aware of instances of professional misconduct, are less involved with bar activities designed to deal with such instances. O'Gorman (1963) notes that the degree to which an attorney specializes in matrimonial cases affects his or her view of ethical questions arising from matrimonial practice. In particular, ethical questions were more problematic for those practitioners for whom matrimonial practice was a peripheral or minor specialization. Smigel (1964) demonstrates the importance of informal organizational pressures as determinants of opinions and attitudes toward professional ethics, suggesting that firm lawyers are subject to a quite different set of pressures regarding both ethical conformity and the violation of ethical standards. Reichstein (1965) reports that opinions toward personal-injury solicitation (ambulance chasing) became less favorable as: (1) size of firm increased, (2) amount of corporate practice increased, (3) clientele status increased, and (4) participation in bar activities increased. Reichstein's work is also worthwhile in that he is perhaps the first to view ethical enforcement from a conflict perspective, to seek to investigate the role of the state in the management of such conflict, and to investigate actual cases in which sanctions were imposed. Since his work is neither longitudinal nor comparative across jurisdictions, his conclusions regarding the foregoing areas of investigation must be viewed more as suggestive than as definitive. Simon (1966) reports that the existence or lack of program in professional ethics produces no significant differences in law-school graduates' opinions regarding ethical questions. Carlin (1962, 1966) finds that professional status is the most-important determinant of attitudes toward professional ethics. He concludes that the individual practitioner, by virtue of his lower status and the type of practice into which he is relegated, "generally finds it difficult if not, in some instances, impossible to conform to the ethical standards of practice" (Carlin 1962, p. 209). Furthermore, location in the stratification system of the bar is the most-important determinant of situational inducements to violate (see Carlin 1966, pp. 170-176). Handler (1967), in his replication of Carlin's 1966 work reaches a similar conclusion regarding ethical conduct among the nonmetropolitan bar in "Prairie City." Rueschemeyer (1973), in his comparative study of the German and U.S. bars, reiterates the importance of status within the legal profession as a determinant of professional ethics, at least for the U.S. lawyer. He notes (Rueschemeyer 1973) that "In contrast to its American counterpart, the German Anwaltschaft does not even in its lower strata in large cities appear to have comparable 'pockets' of structured deviance, defined by field of practice, status of practitioners, and types of clientele and/or public agencies involved" (p. 192). His work is of particular interest because he attributes this difference between the German and American bars to the greater homogeneity and lesser stratification of the German bar (see Rueschemeyer 1973, p. 192).

Although these studies are more informative than the individualistically focused studies conducted by the legal profession, they nontheless share certain theoretical and methodological problems. With the exception of Reichstein (1965), none appear to be informed by recent developments in the field of deviance; and the unit of analysis remains the individual attorney. This focus on the individual attorney ignores the contributions of the classical functionalist, labeling, and conflict perspectives. That is, the aforementioned studies see professional misconduct as behavior that is a priori defined by a professional code of ethics rather than as an outcome of a negotiation process between an attorney and some organization charged with the investigation and adjudication of alleged cases of professional misconduct. Further, such a focus—again with the exception of Reichstein (1965)—ignores conflict between segments of the legal profession over definitions of professional misconduct. Also, these studies ignore the importance of structural characteristics of the bar itself, both as a factor in the etiology of professional misconduct and as a factor that, from Durkheim's classical functionalist perspective, could be expected to influence organizational processing of professional misconduct. Finally, previous researchers have shown little interest in comparative research. Although some of the studies (Wood 1959; Reichstein 1965; Carlin 1962, 1966; Handler 1967) are comparative across strata within one organizational jurisdiction, only the Rueschemeyer (1973) work deals with differing jurisdictions. However, even this work does not deal with organizational differences in processing, but rather focuses on how differing professional organizations impinge on the individual attorney. Thus, a remaining need in the study of professional misconduct among lawyers is for a comparative study of the structural determinants of the sanctioning behavior of state bar associations. We feel such a study is desirable because it would both supplant the individualistic focus of previous studies and allow the introduction of concepts from modern deviance theory. Specifically, since modern deviance theory has moved toward a classical sociology of law, it would allow the study of the sanctioning behavior of the legal profession from a sociology-of-law perspective. It is toward such a study that this chapter is directed.

## Research Design

Although the sociology of law has a number of intellectual forebears, the Durkeimian thesis that the nature of punishment found in a society is dependent on the society's structural characteristics (specifically its level of solidarity and the degree to which power is centralized within the society) is perhaps one of its more-central themes. In this chapter we conceptualize the legal profession of each state as a social system and seek to investigate the effects of its structural characteristics on the punishment of professional misconduct. Specifically, we propose that three salient characteristics of disciplinary behavior (the rate at which attorneys are sanctioned, the severity of sanctions imposed, and the rate of readmission following sanctioning) are primarily effected by the level of social solidarity that characterizes a state bar and the degree to which power is centralized within a state bar.[4] The hypothesized relationships between level of solidarity, centrality of power, and the three salient characteristics of sanctioning behavior follow.

**Hypothesis 1**: The greater level of solidarity that characterizes a state bar, the lower the rate of sanction.

**Hypothesis 2**: The greater the level of solidarity that characterizes a state bar, the less the severity of sanctions.

**Hypothesis 3**: The greater the level of solidarity that characterizes a state bar, the lower the rate of readmissions.

**Hypothesis 4**: The greater the centrality of power within a state bar, the higher the rate of sanctions.

**Hypothesis 5**: The greater the centrality of power within a state bar, the greater the severity of sanctions.

**Hypothesis 6**: The greater the centrality of power within a state bar, the lower the rate of readmissions.

**Hypothesis 7**: The greater the level of solidarity that characterizes a state bar, the less the centrality of power within that state bar.[5]

Although there is some variation among state bars as to what sanctions are public and the publicity given to those sanctions, all state bars make public in some sense four types of sanctions: (1) disbarment, (2) resignation in lieu of disbarment, (3) suspension or probation, and (4) formal letters of reprimand or censure. Thus we shall be concerned only with these sanctions; realizing that they represent only the more-severe end of the disciplinary continuum (see appendix 12A for a list of specific types of disbarments, resignations, suspensions, probations, and letters of reprimand and censure).

We are concerned with three salient characteristics of sanctioning behavior:

*Rate of sanction:* The total number of disbarments, resignations, in lieu of disbarment, suspensions and probations, and formal letters of reprimand occurring in a particular state during the four-year period 1967-

1970 per 1,000 attorneys in the average lawyer population for the period 1967-1970.

*Rate of severity:* The ratio of severe sanctions (disbarments and resignations in lieu of disbarment) to total sanctions.[6]

*Rate of readmission:* The ratio of readmissions to the total number of disbarments, resignations in lieu of disbarment, and suspensions and probations occurring in a particular state during the four-year period 1967-1970.[7]

Data used in the operationalization of all dependent variables are taken from the American Bar Association Center for Professional Discipline National Disciplinary Data Bank (ABA 1978) and are available for fifty-one jurisdictions (the fifty state bars plus the District of Columbia bar).[8] In order to maximize the availability of data on independent variables, we have chosen the period 1967-1970 for the analysis. Although this somewhat dates the research, the choice of this time period allows maximum usage of available data on independent variables since it allows us to use both the 1967 and 1970 Lawyer Statistical Reports (American Bar Foundation 1967, 1971) and the 1967 Census of Business Select Report on Law Firms (U.S. Bureau of the Census 1970). Additionally, the choice of this time period allows us to investigate our hypotheses without having to control for the disruptive effects of the Clark report; see Steele and Nimmer (1976) for a discussion of the effects of this report on sanctioning.

Having operationalized the dependent variables, we now turn our attention to the operationalization of the independent variables—level of solidarity and centrality of power. As Durkheim (1964) notes:

> Social solidarity is a completely moral phenomenon which, taken by itself, does not lend itself to exact observation nor indeed to measurement. To proceed . . . we must substitute for this internal fact which escapes us an external index which symbolizes it and study the former in light of the latter." [p. 64; see Inverarity 1976, pp. 72-73, and Cohen 1969, pp. 129-130 for further discussion of indicators of solidarity.]

Similarly, although centrality of power is not a "completely moral phenomenon," the variety of meanings that Durkheim attaches to "absoluteness of power" and the number of discrepant operationalizations of centralization of power used by later researchers (see Price 1972) suggest the need for multiple external indicators of this variable as well. Thus, we treat level of solidarity and centrality of power as induced variables (see Heise 1972; Hauser and Goldberger 1971) and seek to form two sets of indicators that will serve as their representations.

Durkheim (1964, pp. 190-193) suggests that organic solidarity is characterized by a high concentration of population in relation to resources, which
thereby produces an increased division of labor and an increase in overall diversity within the social system. Hence, we operationalize level of solidarity in terms
of (1) concentration of potential clients (as the primary resource of interest to
the legal profession) relative to the size of the state bar; (2) the degree of specialization within the state bar; and (3) the diversity displayed by the state bar.
The first of these operationalizations is achieved by the average ratio of state
population to lawyer population, as reported in the 1967 and 1970 Lawyer
Statistical Report (American Bar Foundation 1967, 1971). Thus, a high average
population/lawyer ratio would indicate an abundance of resources and little
need for division of labor; a low average population/lawyer ratio would indicate
a relative scarcity of resources and would encourage the division of labor. As a
measure of specialization we use the percentage of associates reporting specialized practice in the 1967 Census of Business,[9] and the average percentage of
lawyers in nonrural practice (that is, practicing in cities of population over
50,000, since specialization is primarily an urban phenomenon), as reported in
the 1967 and 1970 Lawyer Statistical Reports.

As a measure of diversity we include an average diversity measure relative
to location of practice (that is, in cities of less than 50,000 population, cities
of 50,001 to 200,000 population, cities of 200,001 to 500,000 population, and
cities of over 500,001 population).[10] The diversity measure used is that developed by Lieberson (1969) for measuring diversity within a population.

As noted earlier, centrality or centralization of power has been quite
variously operationalized. Unfortunately, the most frequently used measures
of centralization rely on subjective reports (see Price 1972, p. 43) and, since we
are dependent on official records of state bars, are impractical for the present
research. However, since a variety of data is available from official records, we
may still formulate measures of centrality of power. As an initial measure we
choose the distinction between integrated bars and nonintegrated bars (that
is, bars in which membership is mandatory versus bars in which membership
is voluntary). We reason that integration per se influences the ability of state
bars to exercise power over member attorneys because integrated bars may
effectively stop an attorney from practicing law by denying membership in
the state bar.

The measure of centrality of power previously discussed is essentially
an organizational-level measure and may only tangentially reflect the concentration of power within the hands of specific groups of actors. Therefore, we
suggest two additional operationalizations of centrality of power, which focus
on the entrenchment of bar elites. In each case we reason that the greater the
degree to which certain members of the bar elite are entrenched as members
of that bar elite, the greater the degree to which they may exercise positional
power, whether this is due to greater reputational, experiential, positional,

or charismatic authority. Thus, we suggest that greater entrenchment, however measured, is associated with greater centrality of power. Our first measure of positional entrenchment deals with the extent to which certain individual members of the bar elite are able to retain positional power over a given period of time. Thus, we calculate the average holdover ratio for bar officers and members of the board of governors for the period 1967-1972. That is, the average proportion of each year's cohort of bar elites who are retained in the succeeding year's cohort. Additionally, since power may not be concentrated in the hands of all bar-elite members but rather in a smaller subset of positional elites, we also suggest a measure of centrality of power that taps the entrenchment of this smaller subset. For this measure we use the ratio of bar elites that have retained membership for a five-year period to the average size of the bar elite itself. Thus, the model with which we shall be concerned throughout the rest of the analysis contains seven indicator variables. The first four of these tap dimensions of level of solidarity—respectively, resource concentration, specialization, locational diversity, and urbanization. The remaining three indicator variables tap dimensions of centrality of power—respectively, bar integration, positional entrenchment, and long-term elite entrenchment. The model also contains three dependent variables, which tap, respectively, the rate of sanctioning, the severity of sanctioning, and the rate of reintegration.

Having specified a number of measures of our induced variables, we are now in a position to present the final model and discuss the limitations of the data used to investigate the model. The expanded model is presented in figure 12-1.

It should be noted that our investigation of this model is to some extent limited by the nature of the data available. Although we have complete data (that is, for fifty-one jurisdictions) on sanctioning behavior, we do not have complete data for all the indicator variables. In particular, data on specialization are available for only thirty jurisdictions (see appendix 12B for jurisdictions included). Even for those jurisdictions that are included in the census report, data are based only on firms with four or more employees (associates, secretaries, receptionists, and so forth) since these were the only firms sampled. Additionally, there is of course the problem of response rate within the sample, which is unfortunately unreported. Likewise, data on bar elites are available for only thrity-one jurisdictions (see appendix 12B for jurisdictions included). Unfortunately, the jurisdictions present are not common among subsets of original data. Thus, we have complete data for only twenty-two jurisdictions. Although this severely limits the sample from which we may generalize, we note that these twenty-two jurisdictions are diverse (bar populations ranging from 2,681 to 44,646); representative of both integrated ($N = 10$) and non-integrated ($N = 12$) bars; and extensive (the twenty-two jurisdictions represent 77 percent of the total lawyer population in 1967).

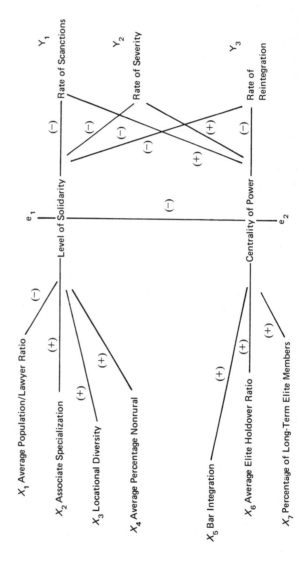

**Figure 12-1.** Level-of-Solidarity and Centrality-of-Power as Determinants of Sanctioning Behavior

## Results: Hypothesis Testing

We may make a preliminary evaluation of our hypotheses by inspection of the magnitude and direction of correlations in the zero-order correlation matrix presented in table 12-1. For our first hypothesis—that level of solidarity is inversely related to rate of sanctioning—to be supported, we should obtain a significant positive correlation between the average population/lawyer ratio and rate of sanctions, and significant negative correlations between associate specialization, locational diversity, average percentage nonrural, and rate of sanctions. Although the direction of all obtained correlations is as predicted, the correlation between average population/lawyer ratio and rate of sanctions is so small as to be meaningless, and of the remaining obtained correlations only one is statistically significant at the .05 level. Thus there is weak support for our first hypothesis.

For our second hypothesis—that level of solidarity is inversely related to sanction severity—to be supported, we should again obtain a significant positive correlation between average population/lawyer ratio and rate of severity, and significant negative correlations between the remainder of level-of-solidarity indicator variables and rate of severity. Although the correlation between average population/lawyer ratio and rate of severity is positive and significant at the .05 level, the direction of the remaining obtained correlations is counter to what we would expect, and one is significant at the .05 level. Thus we have contradictory indications regarding our second hypothesis.

For our third hypothesis—that level of solidarity is inversely related to rate of readmissions—to be supported, we should obtain the same pattern of correlations between the level-of-solidarity indicator variables and rate of readmission as was described previously. Although the correlation between the average population/lawyer ratio and rate of readmission is positive and the correlations between locational diversity, average percentage, nonrural, and rate of readmission are negative, none of these obtained correlations are statistically significant; the obtained correlation between associate specialization and rate of readmission is positive, although statistically insignificant. Thus there is only the most-minimal support for our third hypothesis.

For our fourth hypothesis—that centrality of power is positively related to rate of sanctioning—to be supported, we should obtain significant positive correlations between the centrality-of-power indicator variables and rate of sanctions. In fact, the obtained correlations are all positive but are so small as to provide no support for our fourth hypothesis.

For our fifth hypothesis—that centrality of power is positively related to sanction severity—to be supported, we should obtain significant positive correlations between the centrality-of-power indicator variables and rate of severity. Here, however, the obtained correlations are all negative, and one is significant beyond the .05 level. Thus the obtained correlations tend to disconfirm the fifth hypothesis.

**Table 12-1**
**Zero-Order Correlations for Final Model**

| | Rate of Sanctions | Rate of Severity | Rate of Readmissions | Average Population Lawyer Ratio | Associate Specialization | Locational Diversity | Percentage Nonrural | Bar Integration | Average Elite Holdover Ratio | Percentage of Long-Term Elite Members |
|---|---|---|---|---|---|---|---|---|---|---|
| Rate of sanctions | 1.0 | | | | | | | | | |
| Rate of severity | −.06 | 1.0 | | | | | | | | |
| Rate of readmission | .10 | −.27* | 1.0 | | | | | | | |
| Average population/Lawyer ratio | .02 | .25* | .14 | 1.0 | | | | | | |
| Associate specialization | −.24 | .04 | .09 | −.57* | 1.0 | | | | | |
| Locational diversity | −.17 | .25* | −.14 | .07 | −.37* | 1.0 | | | | |
| Average percentage nonrural | −.27* | .13 | −.17 | −.42* | .43* | .42 | 1.0 | | | |
| Bar integration | .07 | −.08 | .28* | .20 | −.13 | .11 | −.16 | 1.0 | | |
| Average elite holdover ratio | .04 | −.46* | .26 | −.07 | .19 | .21 | −.05 | .22 | 1.0 | |
| Percentage of long-term elite members | .04 | −.25 | .37* | .00 | −.04 | .34* | .10 | −.11 | .63* | 1.0 |
| Mean | 4.101 | .447 | .303 | .785 | .566 | .483 | .572 | .549 | .642 | .257 |
| Standard Deviation (S.D.) | 3.111 | .267 | .287 | .201 | .100 | .197 | .242 | .503 | .170 | .203 |

*Significant beyond the .05 level.

For our sixth hypothesis—that centrality of power is inversely related to rate of readmission—to be supported, we should obtain significant negative correlations between the centrality-of-power indicator variables and rate of readmission. Here again however, the direction of the obtained correlations is counter to that predicated, and two of the obtained correlations are statistically significant beyond the .05 level. Thus the obtained correlations tend to disconfirm our sixth hypothesis as well.

Our seventh hypothesis—that level of solidarity is inversely related to centrality of power—cannot be evaluated at this time because we are dealing with sets of indicator variables rather than single indicators of each concept.

It should be remembered that our interest in the indicator variables is not so much in their use as single indicators of level of solidarity and centrality of power, but rather in their use to form induced variables. The pertinent question then becomes how best to form induced variables that serve as summary representations of level of solidarity and centrality of power. Index construction would, of course, be one alternative. However, because of the lack of any theoretical guidance as to the weights to be assigned to each single indicator, this appears a somewhat arbitrary exercise. Likewise, a factor-analytic solution would be a possibility. However, we do not conceive the indicator variables to be caused by some set of external and unmeasurable factors, but rather to be the reflection of the causes of level of solidarity and centrality of power. Hence, the logic of factor analysis is not strictly applicable to the problem at hand. Thus, we have chosen to use canonical correlation analysis to form measures of the induced variables. Although space does not permit a full exposition of canonical correlation analysis, we may briefly indicate some of the results. The canonical correlation analysis using all indicator variables produced only one significant canonical variate, and the pattern of loadings on that canonical variate was not consistent within sets of indicator variables.[11] Two separate canonical correlation analyses, one using only the level-of-solidarity indicator variables and one using only the centrality-of-power indicator variables, failed to produce a significant canonical variate.

However, as was the case in the initial canonical correlation analysis, it is the first canonical variate (linear compound) that extracts the majority of the redundant variance. Therefore, we chose to use the canonical-variate scores generated from this canonical variate, for each analysis (level of solidarity only and centrality of power only), as summary measures of level of solidarity and centrality of power, respectively. And we may examine the direction and magnitude of the correlations between these canonical variate scores and the dependent variables as a test of our first six hypotheses.[12] Additionally, we may examine the direction and magnitude of the correlation between these canonical-variate scores as a test of our seventh hypothesis. These correlations are presented in table 12-2.

With respect to hypothesis testing, the obtained correlations suggest the following results:

Table 12-2
**Correlations between Canonical-Variate Scores and Dependent Variables**

|  | Rate of Sanctions | Rate of Severity | Rate of Readmissions | Centrality-of-Power Canonical-Variate Score |
|---|---|---|---|---|
| Level-of-solidarity canonical-variate score | .1669 | −.3922* | −.0375 | −.0869 |
| Centrality-of-power canonical-variate score | −.0256 | −.2544* | −.4499* | |

*Significant at the .05 level.

1.  Hypothesis 1, that level of solidarity is inversely related to rate of sanctioning, is not supported. Although the correlation between the canonical-variate score for level of solidarity and rate of sanctions is not significant, its direction suggests that level of solidarity is positively related to rate of sanctioning.
2.  Hypothesis 2, that level of solidarity is inversely related to severity of sanctioning, is supported.
3.  Hypothesis 3, that level of solidarity is inversely related to rate of reintegration, is not supported. The magnitude of the correlation between the canonical-variate score for level of solidarity and rate of readmissions is so minimal as to suggest no relationship.
4.  Hypothesis 4, that centrality of power is positively related to rate of sanctioning, is not supported. Again, the magnitude of the correlation between the canonical-variate score for centrality of power and rate of sanctions is so small as to suggest no relationship.
5.  Hypothesis 5, that centrality of power is positively related to severity of sanctioning, is not supported. The direction and magnitude of the correlation between the canonical-variate score for centrality of power and rate of severity suggests a counterhypothesis—that centrality of power is inversely related to severity of sanctioning.
6.  Hypothesis 6, that centrality of power is inversely related to rate of readmission, is not supported. The direction and magnitude of the correlation between the canonical-variate score for centrality of power and rate of readmissions suggests a counterhypothesis—that centrality of power is positively related to rate of readmission.
7.  Hypothesis 7, that level of solidarity and centrality of power are inversely related, is not supported. Although the direction of the correlation between the canonical-variate score for level of solidarity and the canonical-variate

score for centrality of power is negative, the magnitude of the correlation offers only the very weakest support for this hypothesis.

We note that the results from this method of analysis are, for the most part, consistent with the results from our earlier evaluation of the hypothesis. In particular, the negation of hypotheses 5 and 6 is noteworthy. Likewise, the support of hypothesis 2 is of interest. Whereas the earlier method of analysis offered contradictory evidence as to the validity of this hypothesis, this later method of analysis offers quite clear support for the hypothesis. Finally, the lack of support for hypothesis 7 is consistent with the failure of the initial canonical correlation analysis to produce two significant canonical variates.

## Prediction of the Dependent Variables

We now turn our attention to determining the combination of indicator variables that best predicts each of the dependent variables separately. This may be accomplished by a straightforward stepwise regression analysis. The results of that analysis are presented in table 12-3.

Results of the regression analysis indicate that the best predictive standardized regression equations are:

Rate of sanctions = 0.1808 (average percentage nonrural)
−0.7109 (associate specialization)
−0.5523 (locational diversity)
+0.2681 (average elite holdover ratio)
+0.0555 (bar integration)
+0.0120 (percentage of long-term elite members)

Rate of severity = −1.0778 (average elite holdover ratio)
+1.2444 (locational diversity)
+1.3357 (associate specialization)
−0.8326 (average percentage nonrural)
+0.5112 (average population/lawyer ratio)
+0.1477 (percentage of long-term elite members)
−0.0218 (bar integration)

Rate of readmissions = 0.6928 (percentage of long-term elite members)
+0.3999 (bar integration)
−0.1183 (locational diversity)
−0.3160 (average elite holdover ratio)
+0.3845 (associate specialization)
+0.1639 (average population/lawyer ratio)
−0.2332 (average percentage nonrural)

**Table 12-3**
**Standardized Beta Coefficients for Indicator Variables in Multiple Regression Analysis**

|  | Rate of Sanctions | Rate of Severity | Rate of Readmissions |
|---|---|---|---|
| Average population/lawyer ratio | −.2568 | .5112* | .1639 |
| Associate specialization | −.7109 | 1.3557* | .3845 |
| Locational diversity | −.5523 | 1.2444* | −.1183 |
| Average percentage nonrural | .1808 | −.8326* | −.2332 |
| Bar integration | .0555 | −.0218 | .3999 |
| Average elite holdover ratio | .2681 | −1.0778* | −.3160 |
| Percent of long-term elite members | .0120 | .1477 | .6928* |
| $R^2$ | .2224 | .8446** | .3921 |

*Significant at the .05 level using partial $F$ test.
**Significant at the .05 level using total $F$ test.

Several conclusions are indicated by these results.

1.  The stepwise regression equation obtained for rate of sanctions does not predict a statistically significant proportion of the variance in this variable. Thus, the rate of sanctioning is dependent on factors other than level of solidarity and centrality of power.

2.  None of the indicator variables themselves account for a statistically significant proportion of the variance in rate of sanctions when the effects of other indicator variables are controlled.

3.  The stepwise regression equation obtained for rate of severity does predict a statistically significant proportion of the variance in this variable. Thus, sanction severity is dependent on dimensions tapped by this set of indicator variables.

4.  Five of the indicator variables (in decreasing order of importance: associate specialization, locational diversity, average elite holdover ratio, average percentage nonrural, and average population/lawyer ratio) account for statistically significant proportions of the variance in the rate of sanctions when the effects of other indicator variables are controlled.

5.  The stepwise regression equation obtained for rate of readmissions does not predict a statistically significant proportion of the variance in this variable.

6.  One of the indicator variables (percentage of long-term elite members) does account for a statistically significant proportion of the variance in rate of readmissions when the effects of other indicator variables are controlled. Thus, rate of reintegration appears to be dependent only on this particular aspect of centrality of power and not dependent on level of solidarity.

The most-economical (in the sense that addition of further independent variables does not significantly increase the proportion of variance explained) predictive equations are thus:

Rate of sanctions     = −0.2681 (average percentage nonrural)

$$R^2 = 0.0719$$

Rate of severity      = −0.9783 (average elite holdover ratio) +1.2292 (locational diversity) +1.3025 (associate specialization) −0.7823 (average percentage nonrural) +0.5066 (average population/lawyer ratio)

$$R^2 = 0.8312$$

Rate of readmissions = 0.3701 (percentage of long-term elite members)

$$R^2 = 0.1370$$

We note that these results are consistent with results obtained from a multiple regression analysis using the canonical-variate scores for level of solidarity only and centrality of power only as independent variables. The results of this multiple regression analysis are presented in table 12-4.

## Conclusion

The results from both the hypothesis testing and predictive phases of our analysis are, for the most part, consistent, and suggest the following:

1.  Neither level of solidarity nor centrality of power is either significantly

**Table 12-4**
**Standardized Beta Coefficients for Canonical-Variate Scores as Independent Variables in Multiple Regression Analysis**

|  | Rate of Sanctions | Rate of Severity | Rate of Readmissions |
| --- | --- | --- | --- |
| Level-of-solidarity canonical-variate score | .1659 | .4175* | .0016 |
| Centrality-of-power canonical-variate score | −.0111 | −.2907* | .4500* |
| $R^2$ | .0280 | .2377** | .2024** |

*Significant at .05 level using partial $F$ test.
**Significant at .05 level using overall $F$ test.

associated with or a suitable predictor for the rate at which sanctions are applied.

2.  Both level of solidarity and centrality of power are both associated with and suitable predictors for the severity of sanctions applied. The canonical correlation analysis and the multiple regression analysis using canonical-variate scores suggest that both level of solidarity and centrality of power are negatively associated with severity of sanctions applied.

3.  Only centrality of power is associated with the rate of reintegration/readmission. And although the canonical-variate score for centrality of power is a suitable predictor of rate of reintegration, only the extent of long-term elite entrenchment is a suitable predictor when single independent variables are considered. The results of the canonical correlation analysis and the multiple regression analysis both suggest that centrality of power is positively associated with rate of reintegration.

These results suggest that any application of Durkheim's theory of penal evolution to the sanctioning behavior of state bar associations must remain quite conditional and will require additional theoretical specification. In particular, additional theoretical work is necessary with respect to the following questions: (1) What factors or combination of factors influence the rate at which sanctions are applied? (2) Why is increased centrality of power associated with both greater leniency in sanctioning and greater willingness to readmit persons to whom sanctions have been applied?

With respect to the first of these questions, the finding that much of the considerable variation in rate of sanctioning is unexplained by structural characteristics, such as level of solidarity and centrality of power, is noteworthy. This finding suggests that rate of sanctioning might be more dependent on: (1) other structural factors, (2) organizational factors, or (3) personal factors. One additional structural characteristic that might be profitably investigated is the effect of threats to the solidarity of the bar. That is, do state bar associations respond to external threats to solidarity in a manner analagous to that described by Erikson (1966)? What would be required here, of course, is a comparative longitudinal study of the disbarment rate of various state bars that controlled for organizational differences in processing and sought to determine the effects of a priori defined boundary crises. Auerbach's (1976) social history of the bar seems to suggest that the formation of the "alphabet agencies" under Roosevelt's first administration, the McCarthy era, and the implementation of the Office of Economic Opportunity legal-services programs in the 1960s were in fact such boundary crises. Steele and Nimmer's (1976) study of the effects of the Clark report suggests that the issuance of that report was likewise a boundary crisis of significant dimensions. Given certain similarities between state-bar ethics committees and traditional courts, we might also wonder whether organizational variables affect the rate at which sanctions are applied.

Thus perhaps future studies of sanctions applied by professional associations might consider the organization and resources of these committees in addition to structural characteristics of bar elites generally. This chapter, in demonstrating variation in centrality of power of bar elites, suggests that investigation of the degree to which power is centralized within disciplinary committees might also be of interest in future research. What we have in mind here could range from a positional analysis such as that developed by Domhoff (1967) to a more-complex network analysis of bar decision making along the lines suggested by Laumann and Pappi (1976). Finally, Simon's (1966) work notwithstanding, future studies of the rate at which sanctions are applied might wish to consider variation in personal responsiveness to ethical codes induced either by characteristics of practice situation (as Carlin's work would suggest) or by variation in educational inputs relative to ethics (for example, whether states in which a larger proportion of attorneys attend part-time or evening law schools apply sanctions more frequently). Which of these levels of analysis future researchers choose will, or course, be dependent on both their own perspectives and the availability of required data. At present we can only suggest that further research on the rate at which professional associations apply sanctions remains a pressing need in the study of professional social control.

With regard to the second question, the association between high centrality of power, on the one hand, and, on the other, both leniency with respect to sanction severity and willingness to readmit persons sanctioned, suggests that the effects of centrality of power are different in corporate social systems such as bar associations from the effects that Durkheim suggests for larger social systems. That is, centrality of power produces less-severe sanctions and, because of this, a greater readiness to readmit the persons to whom such sanctions are applied. We suggest that the explanation of this finding lies in the difference in "absoluteness" of power in corporate and larger social systems. Thus, although the power of elites in larger social systems may approach absolute levels, the power of elites in corporate social systems can approach absoluteness (become centralized) only with respect to intraorganizational operation. Elites in corporate social systems will be restained in the exercise of intraorganizational power by the conditions of the power relationships between their organization and the larger social systems. Hence, elites whose power is relatively centralized may exercise that power to apply less-severe sanctions and thereby preclude bringing intraorganizational deviance to the attention of the larger social system. Unfortunately, the data examined in the present study do not allow us to test this hypothesis of the relationship between centrality of power and leniency. However, we may suggest that future studies of professional social control not only give attention to intraorganizational concentrations of power but also consider comparative and temporal variation in power relationships between professional associations and their environments.

Fortunately, the research efforts that these theoretical considerations would imply are, particularly with respect to the legal profession, amenable to examination using existing or easily obtainable data. In particular, the data necessary to deal with organizational variables and the centralization of power in state bar associations, per se, and in disciplinary committees specifically, can generally be obtained from state bar-association journals. Indeed, the availability of committee rosters for state bar associations over significant periods of time and the availability of biographical information on attorneys from the Martindale-Hubbell directories suggest interesting possibilities for research on the social characteristics of bar and disciplinary elites and analysis of changes in elite structure over time. Likewise, the availability of officially published records of the American Bar Association (ABA) and the state bar associations and, in particular, recent compilations of ethics opinions suggest opportunities for longitudinal studies of the relationship of these associations and their environment. The establishment of the National Disciplinary Data Bank at the ABA Center for Professional Discipline provides a comprehensive and centralized source of data on recent sanctioning behavior. Although the data on sanctioning behavior in earlier years are quite variable in quality, the accumulation of reliable time-series data for at least a sizable subsample of jurisdiction is certainly possible. Finally, the increasingly public nature of individual-case data, either from clerks of superior courts or from published records, suggests possibilities of extensive analysis of personal factors involved in professional misconduct.

Thus, the prospects for both theoretically interesting and methodologically sophisticated research on professional misconduct by attorneys as an instance of white-collar crime appear quite good. It remains only to suggest that such research will necessarily involve the use of multiple levels of analysis and that it may, in doing so, generally enrich our knowledge of white-collar crime and organizational responses to such crime.

## Notes

1. Several works suggest that the bargain model exaggerates the service orientation of the professions, downplays the importance of governmental and legal control, underemphasizes the extent to which patterns of social control are historically derived from the class position of members of a profession, stresses homogeneity and the learning of a common core of universal values, and ignores the stratified and factional nature of professions (see Rueschemeyer 1973, p. 14; Ladinsky 1963, p. 50; Bucher and Strauss 1961, p. 334).

2. See, for example, the works of Carlin (1966), Handler (1967), and Lortie (1959) on the stratification and factional nature of professions. For discussions of the difficulties of competing loyalties, see Curtis (1951), Frank (1949), and Blumberg (1967). See Carlin (1970), Brill (1973), and Krislov (1959) for discussions of lawyers as agents of social change. A good additional

discussion of role conflict peculiar to the legal profession is given in Parsons (1952, 1956).

3. Studies of professional misconduct by the legal profession include Phillips and McCoy (1952), Drinker (1955), Schroeder (1967), and Blaustein and Porter (1954). Phillips and McCoy (1952) discuss the integrated bar movement as a solution. For better professional education as a solution, see Blaustein and Porter (1954), Simon (1966), Eron and Redmount (1957), and Marden and Sacks (1962).

4. In proposing that level of solidarity and centrality of power are the primary determinants of sanctioning behavior, we assume that variation in sanctioning behavior caused by differing levels of ethicality and competence among individual lawyers is randomly distributed across state bars and is negligible. Relative to competence, this assumption appears somewhat viable given both the homogeneity of law-school programs (see Swords and Walwer 1974) and bar admissions-examination pass rates. Relative to ethicality, the assumption is probably less viable. As Carlin (1962, 1966) has demonstrated, ethicality is negatively related to position within the stratification system of the bar. Thus we might expect that in states in which a greater proportion of lawyers are in the lower levels of the stratification hierarchy, a greater proportion would engage in unethical behavior and that hence santioning behavior would at least be more frequent. However, there is no assurance that unethical behavior by a lawyer will be sanctioned by a state bar. Additionally, given the variety of individual etiologies of unethical behavior, the assumption of random and negligible variation in ethicality is at least as viable as the assumption of systematic variation. Finally, given extreme variations in rule application even when individual behavior has remained constant (see Steele and Nimmer 1976; Auerbach 1976; Freedman 1975), we suggest that a study of rule application separate from a study of individual unethical behavior remains worthwhile (see figure 12-1).

5. The formulation of hypotheses about rate of sanctions and rate of readmissions is something of a stretch of Durkheim's logic. He is clearly most concerned with the severity of punishment. However, the works of Lukes (1973), Inverarity (1978), Wimberly (1973), Spitzer (1975), Schwartz (1974), Silver (1978), and Schwartz and Miller (1964) and the entire tradition of legal evolution studies suggest the need for such expansions. They do not, however, all suggest these particular hypotheses.

6. We note that disbarment and resignation in lieu of disbarment are both theoretically and practically distinct from other sanctions. Theoretically, both imply more-permanent placement of individuals outside the moral boundaries of the collective. Practically, although persons who are disbarred or who resign in lieu of disbarment may be readmitted, such readmissions are more problematic (in the sense that they may require proof of rehabilitation or retaking of bar examinations) and are not automatic (as is the case with certain types of suspensions).

7. We have not included letters of reprimand in the denominator of this ratio since this sanction does not imply the need for readmission. Additionally, we have not distinguished, in the numerator, between readmissions for violations within the four-year period and readmissions that may occur during the four-year period, but pertain to violations occurring before the four-year period. Although this may bias the figure slightly, we know of no means of determining the time period over which to consider violations that may lead to the need for readmission. For consistency, therefore, we have utilized the same arbitrary four-year time period.

8. As Steele and Nimmer (1976) indicate, "the unavailability of data is an old problem in this area" (p. 920). After finding that few states have systematic reports on disciplinary enforcement and that the data that are compiled are seldom available in easily reached sources. I contacted the American Bar Association and American Bar Foundation regarding summary data sources. Fortunately, one outgrowth of the Clark report was the establishment of the National Disciplinary Data Bank as a reasearch arm of the Center for Professional Discipline. The data bank has compiled summary statistics on disciplinary actions from the various state bars since 1971. Data from approximately 1975 to the present are judged to be very reliable and roughly comparable among the states. Historical data from 1955 to 1975 are judged to be less reliable but still represent the best source of data. Very little data on disciplinary enforcement prior to 1955 exist, although the response forms from the 1948 Survey of the Legal Profession are available in the Cromwell Library of the American Bar Foundation. Since there is extreme variation in the quality of response to that survey, the number of states on which sufficient longitudinal data exist is relatively limited. I estimate that there are sufficiently reliable data for approximately thirteen states from 1928 to present. I am currently attempting to analyze what data exist and to add to the data base by researching state bar-association journals. The series of variously titled Lawyer Statistical Reports provide excellent demographic data on the legal profession from 1949 to 1970. Unfortunately, that series has been discontinued. I am simultaneously trying to compile demographic data from samples taken from the Martindale-Hubbell directories for the years 1973, 1976 and 1979.

9. *Specialized practice* is operationally defined as greater than 25 percent of effort or time devoted to one field of law. We have used associated specialization because it implies specialization by partners and by firms. Measures of partner and firm specialization are available from the census of business and were used in a preliminary analysis. The results are essentially the same regardless of which measure of specialization (firm, partner, or associate) one uses.

10. A lesser value on this measure indicates greater homogeneity, and a greater value indicates greater heterogeneity. Since we are using four categories and not assuming sampling with replacement, the actual maximum value attainable is 0.75. The categories of city size used in the 1967 and 1970 Lawyer

Statistical Reports are not consistent. In 1967 the categories are as indicated but in 1970 the categories are: (1) less than 50,000, (2) 50,001 to 250,000, (3) 250,000 to 500,000, and (4) 500,001 and over. Therefore, we have figured each diversity measure separately and then averaged them. The actual formula for the diversity measure is

$$A_w = 1 - \left[ (p_1)^2 + (p_2)^2 + (p_3)^2 + (p_4)^2 \right]$$

where $p_1$, $p_2$, $p_3$, and $p_4$ are the proportion of the state's lawyer population in each city-size category.

11. The result of the initial and the separate (that is, level of solidarity only and centrality of power only) canonical correlation analyses are in tables 12-5 to 12-10 and figure 12-2.

Figure 12-2 is conceptualized as follows:

$X_I$, $X_{II}$ and $X_{III}$ are induced variables described by the first, second, and third canonical variates (linear compounds), respectively, and are solely dependent on the set of indicator variables.

$X_{Ie}$, $X_{IIe}$, and $X_{IIIe}$ are induced variables described by the first second and third canonical variates (linear compounds), respectively, and three specific error terms. The dependent variables are conceived as solely dependent on these canonical variates and their respective error terms.

$\bar{R}^2_{c/p}$ and $\bar{R}^2_{c/p}$ are mean squared multiple correlations between the dependent or indicator variables and the set of indicator or dependent variables as described by the three canonical variates. Thus, the mean squared multiple correlation for SANRATFY ($\bar{R}^2_{c/p}$ = 1.4388) is the average multiple correlation between SANRATFY and the three linear compounds described by $X_{Ie}$, $X_{IIe}$, and $X_{IIIe}$. See Stewart and Love (1968) for a further discussion and computational formulas.

Lines indicate correlations between canonical-variate scores and variables that are significant at or beyond the .05 level. See table 12-10 for the values of these correlations.

12. This is analogous to developing an orthogonal-factor solution for each set of indicator variables. See Van de Geer (1971, pp. 156-162) for a further discussion of this approach.

**Table 12-5**
**Results of Canonical Correlation Analysis**

| | Canonical Variate | R | R² | Variance Extracted by Level-of-Solidarity Indicators | Variance Extracted by Centrality-of-Power Indicators | Total Variance Extracted | Redundancy Level of Solidarity | Redundancy Centrality of Power | Total Redundancy | Proportion of Redundancy |
|---|---|---|---|---|---|---|---|---|---|---|
| Indicator Variables | 1 | .9937 | .9874 | .0756 | .0160 | .0916 | .0746 | .0158 | .0904 | .5022 |
| | 2 | .6438 | .4145 | .0796 | .0877 | .1673 | .0330 | .0363 | .0693 | .3850 |
| | 3 | .2780 | .0773 | .1862 | .0769 | .2631 | .0144 | .0059 | .0203 | .1128 |
| | | | | .3414 | .1806 | .5220 | .1220 | .0580 | .1800 | |

| | Canonical Variate | R | R² | Variance Extracted Rate of Sanctions | Variance Extracted Rate of Severity | Variance Extracted Rate of Readmissions | Total Variance Extracted | Redundancy Rate of Sanctions | Redundancy Rate of Severity | Redundancy Rate of Readmissions | Total Redundancy | Proportion of Redundancy |
|---|---|---|---|---|---|---|---|---|---|---|---|---|
| Dependent Variables | 1 | .9937 | .9874 | .0399 | .2458 | .0031 | .2888 | .0394 | .2427 | .0031 | .2852 | .6433 |
| | 2 | .6438 | .4145 | .0073 | .0212 | .2926 | .3210 | .0030 | .0088 | .1213 | .1331 | .3002 |
| | 3 | .2780 | .0773 | .2498 | .0504 | .0228 | .3230 | .0193 | .0039 | .0018 | .0250 | .0564 |
| | | | | .2970 | .3174 | .3185 | .9328 | .0617 | .2554 | .1262 | .4433 | |

**Table 12-6**
**Loadings and Correlations for Canonical Correlation Analysis**

|  | First Canonical Variate (CV1) | | Second Canonical Variate (CV2) | | Third Canonical Variate (CV3) | |
|---|---|---|---|---|---|---|
|  | Loading | Correlation | Loading | Correlation | Loading | Correlation |
| Average population/lawyer ratio | .6162 | .3931* | .2135 | .2316 | -.1617 | .2230 |
| Associate specialization | 1.6302 | .3433* | .4755 | .3168* | -.5168 | -.7477* |
| Locational diversity | 1.3416 | .4380* | -.2630 | -.3149* | -.0351 | -.4281* |
| Average percentage nonrural | -.9222 | -.2553* | -.3940 | -.5512* | -.5359 | -.7152* |
| Bar integration | .0673 | .0773 | .6480 | .5072* | .0647 | .0132 |
| Average elite holdover ratio | -1.2080 | -.3135* | -.5145 | .2775 | -.5769 | -.6115* |
| Percentage of long-term elite members | .3218 | -.0872 | 1.1102 | .5290* | .0965 | -.4054* |
| Rate of sanctions | -.3037 | -.3460* | .2607 | .1478 | .9264 | .8657* |
| Rate of severity | .9614 | .8587* | .0758 | -.2520* | .3974 | .3888* |
| Rate of readmissions | .2618 | .0969 | 1.0111 | .9369* | -.0620 | -.2614* |

*Significant at the .05 level.

**Table 12-7**

**Results of Canonical Correlation Analysis with Only Level-of-Solidarity Indicators**

|  | Canonical Variate | R | $R^2$ | Variance Extracted | Redundancy | Proportion of Redundancy |
|---|---|---|---|---|---|---|
| Indicator variables | 1 | .6353 | .4036 | .1687 | .0681 | .5871 |
|  | 2 | .3222 | .1038 | .3577 | .0371 | .3198 |
|  | 3 | .1722 | .0297 | .3629 | .0108 | .0931 |
|  |  |  |  | .8893 | .1160 |  |

|  | Canonical Variate | R | $R^2$ | Variance Extracted | Redundancy | Proportion of Redundancy |
|---|---|---|---|---|---|---|
| Dependent variables | 1 | .6353 | .4036 | .2877 | .1161 | .7414 |
|  | 2 | .3222 | .1038 | .2829 | .0294 | .1877 |
|  | 3 | .1722 | .0297 | .3740 | .0111 | .0709 |
|  |  |  |  | .9446 | .1566 |  |

**Table 12-8**
**Loadings and Correlations for Canonical Correlation Analysis with Only Level-of-Solidarity Indicators**

|  | First Canonical Variate (CV1 - LOS) | | Second Canonical Variate (CV2 - LOS) | | Third Canonical Variate (CV3 - LOS) | |
| --- | --- | --- | --- | --- | --- | --- |
|  | Loading | Correlation | Loading | Correlation | Loading | Correlation |
| Average population/lawyer ratio | -.9663 | -.5591* | -.3825 | -.4992* | .2859 | .5090* |
| Associate specialization | -1.2531 | -.2995 | -.2995 | .1276 | -.8328 | -.9432* |
| Locational diversity | -.8435 | -.5139* | .1341 | .5035* | .1414 | .5155* |
| Average percentage nonrural | .2449 | .0930 | .8387 | .9550* | .2901 | .1925 |
| Rate of sanctions | .4568 | .5514* | -.6671 | -.5632* | .6039 | .5392* |
| Rate of severity | -.8375 | -.6862* | -.1780 | .0897 | .5957 | .6477* |
| Rate of readmissions | -.4579 | -.2971* | -.8562 | -.7235* | -.3897 | -.6418* |

*Significant at the 0.5 level.

**Table 12-9**
**Results of Canonical Correlation Analysis with Only Centrality-of-Power Indicators**

| | Canonical Variate | R | $R^2$ | Variance Extracted | Redundancy | Proportion of Redundancy |
|---|---|---|---|---|---|---|
| Indicator variables | 1 | .5114 | .2615 | .5355 | .1400 | .7388 |
| | 2 | .4309 | .1857 | .2646 | .0491 | .2591 |
| | 3 | .0331 | .0011 | .3681 | .0004 | .0021 |
| | | | | 1.1682 | .1895 | |

| | Canonical Variate | R | $R^2$ | Variance Extracted | Redundancy | Proportion of Redundancy |
|---|---|---|---|---|---|---|
| Dependent variables | 1 | .5114 | .2615 | .3791 | .0991 | .7023 |
| | 2 | .4309 | .1857 | .2246 | .0417 | .2955 |
| | 3 | .0331 | .0011 | .3232 | .0003 | .0021 |
| | | | | .9269 | .1411 | |

Table 12-10
Loadings and Correlations for Canonical Correlation Analysis with Only Centrality-of-Power Indicators

| | First Canonical Variate (CV1 - CP) | | Second Canonical Variate (CV2 - CP) | | Third Canonical Variate (CV3 - CP) | |
|---|---|---|---|---|---|---|
| | Loading | Correlation | Loading | Correlation | Loading | Correlation |
| Bar integration | .5413 | .7571* | .6231 | .6379* | -.7063 | -.8405* |
| Average elite holdover ratio | .1955 | .7342* | -1.3564 | -.6193* | -.2407 | .0070 |
| Percentage of long-term elite members | .7286 | .7031* | .9312 | -.0591 | .6841 | .6307* |
| Rate of sanctions | .1950 | .1232 | .1620 | .0457 | -.9768 | -.9595* |
| Rate of severity | -.3868 | -.6238* | .9686 | .7320* | -.0148 | -.0085 |
| Rate of readmissions | .8150 | .8561* | .6411 | .3687* | .1393 | .2213 |

*Significant at the .05 level.

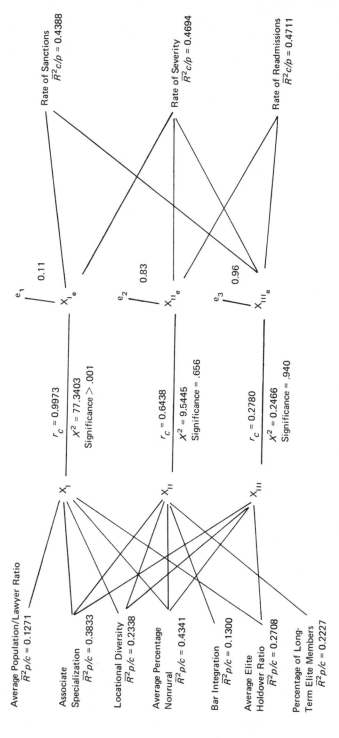

**Figure 12-2.** Schematic Diagram of Canonical Correlation Model

## References

American Bar Association (ABA). *Problems and Recommendations in Disciplinary Enforcement: Report of the American Bar Association Special Committee on Evaluation of Disciplinary Enforcement.* Chicago: American Bar Association, 1970.

_____. *Statistical Report Re Public Discipline of Lawyers by State Disciplinary Agencies, 1974-1977.* Chicago: Standing Committee on Professional Discipline and Center for Professional Discipline of the American Bar Association, 1978.

American Bar Foundation. *The 1967 Lawyer Statistical Report.* Chicago: American Bar Foundation, 1967.

_____. *The 1970 Lawyer Statistical Report.* Chicago: American Bar Foundation, 1971.

Auerbach, Jerome S. *Unequal Justice: Lawyers and Social Change in Modern America.* New York: Oxford University Press, 1976.

Blaustein, Albert P., and Porter, Charles O. *The American Lawyer: A Summary of the Survey of the Legal Profession.* Chicago: University of Chicago Press, 1954.

Blumberg, Abraham S. "The Practice of Law as a Confidence Game: Organizational Cooptation of a Profession." *Law and Society Review* 1 (1967): 15-39.

Brill, Harry. "The Uses and Abuses of Legal Assistance." *The Public Interest* 31 (1973):38-55.

Bucher, Rue, and Strauss, Anselm. "Professions in Process." *American Journal of Sociology* 66 (1961):325-334.

Carlin, Jerome E. *Lawyers on Their Own: A Study of Individual Practitioners in Chicago.* New Brunswick, N.J.: Rutgers University Press, 1962.

_____. *Lawyer's Ethics: A Survey of the New York City Bar.* New York: Russell Sage Foundation, 1966.

_____. "Store Front Lawyers in San Francisco." *Transaction* 7 (1970):64-74.

Cohen, Yehudi A. "Ends and Means in Political Control: State Organization and the Punishment of Adultery, Incest and Violation of Celibacy." *American Anthropologist* 71 (1969):658-687.

Curtis, Charles P. "The Ethics of Advocacy." *Stanford Law Review* 4 (1951): 3-23.

Domhoff, G. William. *Who Rules America?* Englewood Cliffs, N.J.: Prentice-Hall, 1967.

Drinker, Henry S. "Legal Ethics." *Annals of the American Academy of Political and Social Science* 297 (1955):37-45.

Durkheim, Emile. *Professional Ethics and Civic Morals*, trans. Cornelia Brookfield. London: Routledge and Kegan Paul, 1957.

_____. *The Division of Labor in Society,* trans. George Simpson. Glencoe, Ill.: Free Press, 1964.

_____. "Two Laws of Penal Evolution," trans. T. Anthony Jones and Andrew T. Scull. *Economy and Society* 2 (1973):285-308.

Erikson, Kai T. *Wayward Puritans: A Study in the Sociology of Deviance.* New York: Wiley, 1966.

Eron, L.D., and Redmount, R.S. "Effect of Legal Education on Attitudes." *Journal of Legal Education* 9 (1957):431-443.

Frank, Jerome. *Courts on Trial: Myth and Reality in American Justice.* Princeton, N.J.: Princeton University Press, 1949.

Freedman, Monroe H. *Lawyers' Ethics in an Adversary System.* Indianapolis: Bobbs-Merrill, 1975.

Freidson, Eliot. "Client Control and Medical Practice." *American Journal of Sociology* 65 (1960):374-382.

_____. "The Organization of Professional Behavior." Paper presented at the Annual Meeting of the American Sociological Association, Montreal, 1964.

Handler, Joel F. *The Lawyer and His Community: The Practicing Bar in a Middle Size City.* Madison: University of Wisconsin Press, 1967.

Hauser, Robert M., and Goldberger, Arthur S. "The Treatment of Unobservable Variables in Path Analysis." In Herbert L. Costner, ed., *Sociological Methodology,* pp. 81-117. San Francisco: Joseey-Bass, 1971.

Heinz, John P.; Laumann, Edward O.; Cappell, Charles L.; Halliday, Terence C.; and Schaalman, Michael H. "Diversity, Representation, and Leadership in an Urban Bar: A First Report on a Survey of the Chicago Bar." *American Bar Foundation Research Journal* 3 (1976):717-785.

Heise, David R. "Employing Nominal Variables, Induced Variables, and Block Variables in Path Analysis." *Sociological Methods and Research* 1 (1972): 147-173.

Inverarity, James M. "Population and Lynching in Louisiana, 1869-1896: A Test of Erikson's Theory of the Relationship Between Boundary Crises and Repressive Justice." *American Sociological Review* 4 (1976):262-280.

_____. "Law, Political Power and Social Structure: A Critique of the Conflict Theory in the Sociology of Law." Mimeographed, University of Minnesota, 1978.

Krislov, Samuel. "Constituency versus Constitutionalism: The Desegregation Issue and Tensions and Aspirations of Southern Attorneys General." *Midwest Journal of Political Science* 3 (1959):75-92.

Ladinsky, Jack. "Careers of Lawyers, Law Practice and Legal Institution." *American Sociological Review* 28 (1963):47-54.

Laumann, Edward O., and Heinz, John P. "Specialization and Prestige in the Legal Profession: The Structure of Deference." *American Bar Foundation Research Journal* 1 (1977):155-216.

Laumann, Edward O. and Pappi, Franz U. *Networks of Collective Action: Perspective on Community Influence Systems.* New York: Academic Press, 1976.

Lieberson, Stanley A. "Measuring Population Diversity." *American Sociological Review* 34 (1969):850-862.

Lortie, Dan C. "Laymen to Lawmen: Law School Careers and Professional Socialization." *Harvard Educational Review* 29 (1959):352-369.

Lukes, Steven. *Emile Durkheim, His Life and Work: A Historical and Critical Study.* New York: Harper and Row, 1973.

Marden, O.S., and Sacks, H.R. *Education for Professional Responsibility in the Law School,* Chicago: National Council of Legal Clinics, American Bar Association, 1962.

Mitford, Jessica. *The American Way of Death.* Greenwich, Conn.: Fawcett, 1963.

O'Gorman, Hubert J. *Lawyers and Matrimonial Cases: A Study of Informal Pressures in Private Professional Practice.* New York: Free Press, 1963.

Parsons, Talcott. "A Sociologist Looks at the Legal Profession." Paper presented at the fiftieth anniversary celebration of the University of Chicago Law School. Chicago: University of Chicago Press, 1952.

_____. "The Law and Social Control." In William M. Evan, ed., *Law and Sociology,* pp. 56-72. New York: Free Press, 1962.

Phillips, Orie L., and McCoy, Philbrick. *Conduct of Judges and Lawyers: A Study of Professional Ethics Discipline and Disbarment.* Los Angeles: Parker, 1962.

Price, James L. *Handbook of Organizational Measurement.* Lexington, Mass.: D.C. Heath and Company, 1972.

Quinney, Richard. "Occupational Structure and Criminal Behavior: Prescription Violation by Retail Pharmacists." *Social Problems* 11 (1963):179-185.

Reichstein, Kenneth J. "Ambulance Chasing: A Case Study of Deviation and Control within the Legal Profession." *Social Problems* 13 (1965):3-17.

Riesman, David. "Law and Sociology: Recruitment, Training and Colleagueship." *Stanford Law Review* 9 (1957):669-670.

Rueschemeyer, Dietrich. *Lawyers and Their Society: A Comparative Study of the Legal Profession in Germany and in the United States.* Cambridge, Mass.: Harvard University Press, 1973.

Schroeder. Oliver, Jr. *Lawyer Discipline: The Ohio Story.* Cleveland: Ohio Legal Center Institute, 1967.

Schwartz, Richard D. "Legal Evolution and the Durkheim Hypothesis: A Reply to Professor Baxi." *Law and Society Review* 8 (1974):653-668.

Schwartz, Richard D., and Miller, James C. "Legal Evolution and Societal Complexity." *American Journal of Sociology* 70 (1964):159-169.

Silver, Burton B. "Social Structure and Legal Evolution: A Longitudinal Analysis of the California Gold Rush Camps." Paper presented at the annual meeting of the American Sociological Association, San Francisco, 1978.

Simon, Rita James. "An Evaluation of the Effectiveness of Some Curriculum Innovations in Law Schools." *Journal of Applied Behavioral Science* 2 (1966):219-237.

Smigel, Erwin O. *The Wall Street Lawyer: Professional Organization Man?* New York: Free Press, 1964.

Spitzer, Steven. "Punishment and Social Organization: A Study of Durkheim's Theory of Penal Evolution." *Law and Society Review* 9 (1975):613-637.

Steele, Eric H., and Nimmer, Raymond T. "Lawyers, Clients, and Professional Regulations." *American Bar Foundation Research Journal* 3 (1976):917-1019.

Stewart, Douglas, and Love, William. "A general Canonical Correlation Index." *Psychological Bulletin* 70 (1968):160-163.

Swords, Peter de L., Walwer, Frank K. *The Costs and Resources of Legal Education.* New York: Council on Legal Education for Professional Responsibility, 1974.

U.S. Bureau of the Census. *Census of Business, 1967. Selected Service, Law Firms:* BC67-SS5. Washington, D.C.: U.S. Government Printing Office, 1970.

Van de Geer, John P. *Introduction to Multivariate Analysis for the Social Sciences.* San Francisco: Freeman, 1971.

Wimberley, Howard. "Legal Evolution: One Further Step." *American Journal of Sociology* 79 (1973):78-83.

Wood, Arthur Lewis. "Professional Ethics among Criminal Lawyers." *Social Problems* 7 (1959):70-83.

# Appendix 12A
# National Disciplinary
# Data Bank Codes Used
# in Formulating
# Categories of Sanctions

Because of terminological differences in the ways in which state bar organizations report to the National Disciplinary Data Bank, some uniform scheme of coding had to be developed. The details of that scheme, which follows the National Disciplinary Data Bank coding system as closely as possible, are as follows.

## Disbarment

Removed from office
Name struck from roll
Disbarred on consent
Indefinite disbarment
Permanently enjoined from practice
Removed from office of attorney
Resigned—disbarred
License revoked
Certificate revoked
License annulled
Disbarment
Disbarment—temporary

## Resignation

Name struck from role on consent
Surrendered license
Resignation accepted with prejudice
Disbarment on consent/resignation

## Suspension

Suspension, nonpayment of fees
Suspension, indefinite
Suspension, until license to practice restored by state

Suspension, on consent
Suspension, on condition of probation
Suspension, until further order of court
Suspension, temporary, pending final order
Suspension, pro hoc vice (for this fault)
Suspension, on specific conditions
Suspension, for definite period
Suspension, with automatic reinstatement
Suspension, reinstatement on application only
Suspension, disciplinary disability

## Letter of Reprimand

Restricted practice/other
Order of restriction
Public reproval
Admonishment
Probation
Public reprimand/other public censure
Court censure
Censured
Fines
Fines

## Reinstated after Disbarment

Reinstated after disbarment
Reinstated after disbarment on consent

## Reinstated after Suspension

Suspension vacated
Reinstated after disciplinary suspension
Reinstated after other
Conditional reinstatement
Reinstated after conditional reinstatement

Three additional categories were assigned to either "reinstated after disbarment" or "reinstated after suspension," depending on the specifics of the action. These were:

Judgement vacated
Reinstatement
Discipline removed by order of court

# Appendix 12B
# Integrated-Bar States
# and States for which
# Data on Centrality of
# Power Are Available

| State | Year of Bar Integration | Centrality-of-Power Data |
|---|---|---|
| Alabama | 1923 | Yes |
| Alaska | 1956 | Yes |
| Arizona | 1933 | No |
| Arkansas | 1938 | Yes |
| California | 1927 | Yes |
| Colorado | N.I. | Yes |
| Connecticut | N.I. | Yes |
| Delaware | N.I. | No |
| District of Columbia | 1974[a] | Yes |
| Florida | 1949 | Yes |
| Georgia | 1964 | Yes |
| Hawaii | N.I. | Yes |
| Idaho | 1923 | No |
| Illinois | N.I. | Yes |
| Indiana | N.I. | No |
| Iowa | N.I. | No |
| Kansas | N.I. | Yes |
| Kentucky | 1934 | Yes |
| Louisiana | 1940 | Yes |
| Maine | N.I. | No |
| Maryland | N.I. | Yes |
| Massachusetts | N.I. | Yes |
| Michigan | 1935 | Yes |
| Minnesota | N.I. | Yes |
| Mississippi | 1930 | Yes |
| Missouri | 1944 | Yes |
| Montana | N.I. | No |
| Nebraska | 1937 | Yes |
| Nevada | 1929 | Yes |
| New Hampshire | 1970[a] | No |
| New Jersey | N.I. | Yes |
| New Mexico | 1925 | No |
| New York | N.I. | Yes |

| | | |
|---|---|---|
| North Carolina | 1933 | No |
| North Dakota | 1921 | Yes |
| Ohio | N.I. | No |
| Oklahoma | 1939 | Yes |
| Oregon | 1935 | No |
| Pennsylvania | N.I. | Yes |
| Rhode Island | N.I. | Yes |
| South Carolina | 1970[a] | No |
| South Dakota | 1931 | No |
| Tennessee | N.I. | Yes |
| Texas | 1939 | Yes |
| Utah | 1931 | No |
| Vermont | N.I. | No |
| Virginia | 1938 | No |
| Washington | 1933 | No |
| West Virginia | 1945 | No |
| Wisconsin | 1956 | Yes |
| Wyoming | 1939 | No |

N.I. = Not integrated

[a]Not coded as integrated for this study because of date of integration.

# 13 Traditional and Corporate Theft: A Comparison of Sanctions

*Laureen Snider*

## Introduction

This study aims to discover, first, whether the punishments given to those who commit traditional nonviolent economic offenses are more severe than those given to offenders against "upperworld" nonviolent economic laws. Second, and perhaps more importantly, it addresses in theoretical terms the question of why this condition exists, and outlines problems with traditional methods in conceptualizing traditional and upperworld offenses.

By *nonviolent economic offenses,* I mean simply those that involve loss of property without the actual or threatened use of force. The term *economic* refers to the type of loss suffered by the victim(s), in contrast to crimes against the person (such as violent offenses) or against the state. "Upperworld" offenses are those that Geis (1974) has defined as

> a label designed to call attention to the violation of a variety of criminal statutes by persons who at the moment are generally not considered . . . to be the "usual" kind of underworld and/or psychologically aberrant offenders [p. 120]

and

> it points at a group of people engaged in a variety of acts contrary to the law; . . . It is employed to call attention to a wide range of law-breaking that usually escapes public attention, indignation and to persuade that offenses such as advertising fraud, anti-trust violation, and water pollution ought to be attended to seriously. . . . [p. 120]

In Canada, they are often not found in the traditional repository of offenses, the Criminal Code, but in individual acts (such as the Combines Investigation Act or the Food and Drug Act), under both federal and provincial jurisdiction, with special inspectors or boards provided for enforcement purposes. Moreover, only people who occupy certain positions in the social structure can commit these offenses. One cannot conspire to fix prices or pollute streams unless one is in a senior executive position in an industrial enterprise. Thus the population most at risk of breaking these laws is upper or upper-middle class.

The "traditional" property offenses, such as theft or breaking and entering, have the opposite characteristics. They are almost always in the Criminal Code; they can be enforced by municipal, provincial, and federal police forces; and they can (theoretically) be committed by anyone in the society. In practice, however, the lower and working classes are at much greater risk because the majority of such offenses are utilitarian, committed for gain; since these offenses are much less lucrative and much riskier than the acquisitive acts available to those employed in bureaucracies or professions, few people with these latter alternatives are tempted. It has been well documented that it is lower-class male youths who are primarily arrested, charged, and convicted for these offenses (Chambliss 1969; Turk 1969; Green 1970; Arnold 1971; Weiner and Willie 1971; Thornberry 1973; Tepperman 1977.) Middle- and upper-class people have a wide range of both legal and illegal options available to them when they need money, most of which involve less visibility, less chance of being caught, less stigma, and/or lighter sanctions than do the traditional offenses. These range from falsifying expense accounts to charging government aid plans for extra patients or clients, or for extra services. Moreover, they are less likely to *need* to break the traditional laws governing private property, since they can borrow money from a bank rather than from a loan shark, or can raise money on other possessions (such as houses or heirlooms) in a crisis. The laws are written in a way that defines as legal, or quasi-legal, the ways in which middle- and upper-class people typically get money. They can sell their professional services or their manufactured products at whatever price the market will bear. In Canada, they can use materials in a building or put additives in a food that have not been proved safe, as long as they have not been "conclusively" demonstrated to be unsafe. They can make any amount of profit from land speculation or from ownership of an apartment building (except in the periodic rent-control phases that governments go through near election time). On the other hand, the legal system defines as illegal most acts available to members of the lower class, who have no resources behind them and nothing but their bodies and their labor power to sell in a buyer's market (Lefcourt 1971; Taylor, Walton, and Young 1973; Zinn 1971; Cloke 1971; Quinney 1974; Chambliss 1975; Reich 1973).[1]

Thus we have two kinds of nonviolent offenses: those in which the suspects are primarily middle and upper class (upperworld crimes) and those in which they are primarily lower class (property offenses).

No explicit comparisons of these two types of crimes appear to have been made although many writers have talked about the leniency accorded to upperworld offenders and the reasons for this (Sutherland 1940, 1949; Blumberg 1974; Edelhertz 1970; Geis 1974; Goff 1975; Green 1972; Reich 1973; Stanbury 1975). Are upperworld offenders really getting off more lightly than individuals who steal in different settings and use different techniques? Perhaps *all* offenders charged with nonviolent property offenses are lightly sanctioned, because these crimes do not involve any direct harm to other human beings. This chapter aims to analyze this issue and provide some tentative answers.

## The Study

The study described in this chapter consists of two parts: first, an analysis of the law as it is written, and, second, an analysis of the law as it is practiced—as it is enforced. Both parts were necessary because the law on the books determines the limits to which the system can go. It defines the parameters within which legal officials can act. No judge, whatever his or her personal feelings, can sentence a corporate official to life imprisonment for price fixing if the maximum prescribed penalty in law is two years. Since the rationale of the study depends on the equation of traditional and upperworld property offenses, there is one further point that must be considered here. Traditional offenses are commonly recognized and officially designated as criminal acts and are sanctioned in the Criminal Code of Canada. The criminality of upperworld offenses is still a matter of debate. I would argue, first, that the continuing noncriminal legal status of the latter activities reflects not their lack of harmfulness but, rather, the superior resources of upperworld criminals and corporations. They have been successful in defining their own acquisitive acts as noncriminal and even harmless, despite the reams of data that have documented the heavy dollar losses and the even heavier loss of life and limb they cause (Reiman 1979; Schur 1969; Edelhertz 1970; Geis 1968; Jaspan and Black 1960). Although the political authorities may not be legally able to criminalize these acts, that does not mean that we, as analysts, cannot. As both Sutherland (1949) and Geis (1974) have argued, acts can be considered criminal provided that: (1) the state has implicitly or explicitly recognized them as socially injurious by assigning penalties; and (2) a person (or persons) is directly or indirectly victimized, deprived, or made to suffer in some sense. Such victimization may involve financial loss, but it may also refer to the violation of state-recognized rights (to clean air or water, for example). *Excluded* from this definition are acts that are perhaps morally wrong but that have not (yet) been officially labeled. Examples are acts that deprive children of "adequate" nutrition, recreation, and mobility opportunities; or that deprive adults of their "right" to a "decent" standard of living, medical care, and so forth.

The traditional nonviolent economic offenses chosen for analysis were:

1. *Theft:* Under and over $200 value; typically occurs as shoplifting from retail stores. This is an indictable offense.[2]
2. *Possession of stolen goods:* An indictable offense, typically involving those believed to "fence" or resell stolen property.
3. *Breaking and entering:* An indictable offense, often referred to as *burglary*. The law specifies life imprisonment as a maximum penalty when the target is a residential home or apartment (a "dwelling house," in legal language).
4. *Taking a motor vehicle without consent:* A summary offense, involving the "borrowing" of automobiles. (The vast majority are recovered unharmed within forty-eight hours.)

These four offenses are the most-common property offenses in Canada. They account for approximately 70 percent of the charges laid annually under the Criminal Code (Canada 1980).

The comparable corporate offenses chosen for analysis were:

1.  *Food and Drug Act:* This act attempts to ensure that only pure food and approved drugs are offered for sale to the public. Prosecution for most sections is either indictable or summary, at the discretion of the crown prosecutor. Heavier sanctions are prescribed for the former than for the latter.
2.  *Packaging and Labelling Act:* This act provides regulations and penalties for defrauding the public by not providing sufficient, accurate, and valid information about the product being offered for sale. Violations can be prosecuted either summarily or by indictment, at the discretion of the crown.
3.  *Hazardous Products Act:* This act is meant to ensure that no products that are dangerous are offered for sale in Canada. Key sections provide for either summary or indictable prosecution, at the discretion of the crown.
4.  *Weights and Measures Act:* This act provides regulations and sanctions to ensure that consumers are not defrauded by incorrect sales and measuring devices. Again, prosecution is summary or indictable, at the crown's discretion.
5.  *Combines Investigation Act:* Roughly analogous to the Sherman Act in the United States, this long, complex piece of legislation forbids all kinds of corporate misbehavior, from combining to fix prices or restrict supplies of goods to misleading advertising. For five sections (combines, illegal monopolies, refusal to supply, misleading advertising, and resale-price maintenance), prosecution must be by indictment; for one section (that forbidding misleading price representation, double ticketing, and various other "shady" selling techniques), it is either summary or indictable, at the crown's discretion. Other penalties available to the crown include the Order of Prohibition, forced dissolution of illegal mergers or monopolies, removal of tariffs protecting the guilty industry, and removal of patents or trademarks.

Now let us look at the maximum sanctions prescribed for each. For reading convenience, they have been averaged and set out in table 13-1 (see Snider 1977 for original tabulation).

It is obvious from table 13-1 that the maximum prison times specified are much greater for traditional than for upperworld offenses, be they indictable or summary. Since the two major pieces of legislation were passed in the same era (the Combines Investigation Act in 1889, the Criminal Code in 1886), this discrepancy does not seem to be the result of legislators in recent times turning away from the punitive orientation of bygone eras (indeed, for combines offenses,

**Table 13-1**
**Average Maximum Sanctions Prescribed for Traditional and Upperworld Nonviolent Economic Crimes**

|  |  | Indictable | | Summary | |
|---|---|---|---|---|---|
|  |  | Average Maximum Prison | Average Maximum Fine | Average Maximum Prison | Average Maximum Fine |
| Traditional economic offenses[a] |  | 11.5 years | Limitless | 2 years (only one case) | $1,000 |
| Upperworld offenses[b] | Excluding new Combines Act | 2.3 years | $5,750 | 7.7 months | $1,428 |
|  | Including new Combines Act | 3.3 years | $217,571 | 9 months | $9,200 |

[a]Source: *Martin's Annual Criminal Code* (Toronto: Cartwright Law Books, 1978).

[b]The source for each act here is the law itself, as published by the relevant department.

the trend in the written law has been toward heavier sanctions rather than the reverse) (Snider 1978). It seems, instead, that there has been a marked feeling that certain kinds of people—namely, corporate executives—do not "deserve" prison sentences. However, it does look as though this has been compensated for (if, indeed, a monetary payment can even be equated with the loss of freedom and security of a prison sentence) by heavier maximum fines. Even though the fines for indictable traditional offenses are theoretically limitless, in practice the fines assessed are usually under $200. Even if we exclude the very high average fine of $217,571 on the grounds that it is atypical (the average was badly skewed by the new $1,000,000 maximum for illegal combines), the fines still appear much higher for upperworld offenses. (It is true, however, that a fine of $100 to the average 18-year-old defendant may represent a higher percentage of monthly income than does a fine of $9,200 to a corporation. The corporation often can pass the cost on to consumers or customers or claim it as a tax-deductible business expense, whereas the individual cannot. Moreover, the defendant in the upperworld offense has usually realized a much greater economic gain from his act than has the traditional offender.)

It is also apparent from these data that the courts have more choices in dealing with upperworld offenses. Most are *either* summary or indictable, at the discretion of the prosecuting attorney and/or the attorney-general. There are alternate sentencing sanctions for those found guilty, such as the provisions to remove customs duties, trademarks, or patent protection. In two cases (the Hazardous Products Act and the Combines Investigation Act), boards of review are sandwiched between the offender and the legal process. These are supposed to amass and review evidence, but they also serve as a buffer between the upper-class offender and the law. And there is that ubiquitous sanction for combines offenses, the Order of Prohibition. This is an ingenious device, which, when decreed by the judge after a guilty verdict, removes much of the stigma of criminality and provides no punishment to the corporation for having committed an offense. It says, in effect, "Don't do it again." Theoretically, one can be fined or even imprisoned for disobeying an Order of Prohibition (Section 31-2 of the Combines Investigation Act); but this had never yet been done. This provision of a second chance has no parallel in the written legislation governing traditional offenses.[3]

To sum up, the written law sanctions upperworld crimes less punitively than traditional crimes, though the prescribed fines are somewhat heavier. The pre-scribed maximum terms of imprisonment are much lighter; and the Crown has many more choices before resorting to the stigmatizing and punitive criminal justice system.

### Laws as Enforced

*Traditional Offenses*

Now let us look at the actual sanctions that have been meted out under tradi-tional and upperworld laws. The written laws tell us very little about the reality of the legal system, because the officials of the criminal-justice system, from the cop on the beat to the judge him- or herself, have so much discretion. In fact, despite what the laws we have just examined say, it would be entirely possible and legal for traditional offenders to be put in prison much less often than upperworld offenders. For this reason, data were gathered on the sanctions imposed for both traditional and upperworld offenses, from 1949 to 1972. For newer legislation, data date from the inception of the law up to the most-recent published statistics. This is illustrated in tables 13-2 through 13-5.

Several interesting tendencies are highlighted by this data. Looking first at the sentences given for breaking and entering, we find that judges seem to view this as a crime similar to theft or possession, but as slightly more serious.[4] There has developed, over the years, a greater tendency for judges to allow the person charged with theft the option of a fine, or to give the suspect a suspended sen-tence without probation, whereas the person charged with breaking and entering is still more likely to be placed on probation or given a short prison term. But considering the substantial differences in sanctions prescribed by the Criminal

**Table 13-2**
**Average Sentences for Breaking and Entering, 1949-1972**

| Year | Suspended Sentence, No Probation | Suspended Sentence with Probation | Fine | Jail | Penitentiary, 2-14 years | Reformatory | |
|---|---|---|---|---|---|---|---|
| 1949-1952 | 12.5 (1,741) | 9.5 (1,302) | 3.2 (444) | 41.1 (5,678) | 16.7 (2,326) | 16.2 (2,242) | (13,733) |
| 1953-1956 | 10.4 (1,639) | 12.5 (1,945) | 3.3 (523) | 40.6 (6,335) | 18.6 (2,914) | 13.0 (2,030) | (15,386) |
| 1957-1960 | 10.6 (2,463) | 18.2 (4,212) | 2.9 (659) | 38.7 (8,956) | 16.3 (3,766) | 13.1 (3,027) | 99.8 (23,083) |
| 1961-1964 | 9.9 (2,829) | 23.3 (6,727) | 2.3 (666) | 40.2 (11,568) | 14.5 (4,167) | 9.6 (2,775) | 99.8 (28,732) |
| 1965-1969[a] | 9.8 (3,201) | 31.1 (10,170) | 2.4 (809) | 34.3 (11,312) | 11.6 (3,790) | 10.4 (3,422) | 99.6 (32,605) |

| Year | Suspended Sentence, No Probation | Suspended Sentence with Probation | Fine | Under 1 year | 1 to Under 2 | 2 to Under 5 | 5 and Over | |
|---|---|---|---|---|---|---|---|---|
| 1970-1972 | 6.1 (1,125) | 41.2 (7,585) | 1.7 (321) | 32.5 (6,156) | 9.2 (1,753) | 7.2 (1,340) | .5 (95) | 98.4[b] (18,375) |

Source: *Canada Statistics of Criminal and Other Offences, 1957-1972*

[a]Since method of reporting sentences was changed in 1970, 1969 was included with previous four years.

[b]501 cases were unaccounted for in the 1971 statistics given.

**Table 13-3**
**Average Sentences for Theft, 1949-1956**

| Year | Suspended Sentence, No Probation | Suspended Sentence with Probation | Fine | Jail | Penitentiary, 2-14 Years | Reformatory | |
|---|---|---|---|---|---|---|---|
| 1949-1952 | 14.5 (5,774) | 11.8 (4,771) | 18.2 (7,231) | 44.9 (18,042) | 3.5 (1,449) | 6.3 (2,527) | (39,794) |
| 1953-1956 | 13.8 (4,928) | 15.4 (5,467) | 19.0 (6,790) | 40.4 (14,417) | 4.4 (1,575) | 5.2 (1,893) | (35,070) |
| 1957-1960 | 16.2 (8,267) | 19.5 (10,028) | 22.5 (11,527) | 33.3 (17,000) | 3.0 (1,547) | 5.2 (2,662) | (51,031) |
| 1961-1964 | 14.0 (8,884) | 22.3 (14,178) | 25.6 (16,280) | 31.4 (19,941) | 2.6 (1,650) | 3.9 (2,507) | (63,440) |
| 1965-1969[a] | 14.4 (12,092) | 20.2 (16,987) | 35.7 (29,932) | 24.7 (20,707) | 1.7 (1,450) | 3.1 (2,624) | (83,790) |

| Year | Suspended Sentence, No Probation | Suspended Sentence with Probation | Fine | Under 1 year | 1 to Under 2 | 2 to Under 5 | 5 and Over | |
|---|---|---|---|---|---|---|---|---|
| 1970-1972 | 9.2 (5,255) | 22.3 (12,646) | 48.0 (27,217) | 18.0 (10,214) | 1.6 (915) | .8 (460) | .1 (19) | (56,699) |

Source: *Canada Statistics of Criminal and other Offences*, 1957-1972.

[a] Since method of reporting sentences was changed in 1970, 1969 was included with the previous four years.

**Table 13-4**
**Average Sentences for Possession of Stolen Goods, 1949–1972**

| Year | Suspended Sentence, No Probation | Suspended Sentence with Probation | Fine | Jail | Penitentiary, 2–14 Years | Reformatory | |
|---|---|---|---|---|---|---|---|
| 1949–1952 | 12.3 (432) | 10.6 (372) | 14.9 (527) | 47.4 (1,667) | 5.8 (206) | 7.6 (272) | (3,476) |
| 1953–1956 | 13.7 (506) | 12.3 (459) | 17.0 (629) | 43.3 (1,605) | 5.6 (211) | 5.2 (199) | (3,604) |
| 1957–1960 | 13.0 (739) | 17.6 (1,001) | 16.4 (918) | 40.5 (2,296) | 5.9 (337) | 6.6 (380) | (5,671) |
| 1961–1964 | 12.4 (1,042) | 19.5 (1,638) | 14.9 (1,262) | 40.8 (3,447) | 7.0 (597) | 5.4 (464) | (8,450) |
| 1965–1969[a] | 11.8 (1,466) | 22.6 (2,835) | 17.8 (2,239) | 37.3 (4,681) | 4.9 (623) | 5.6 (712) | (12,556) |

| | Suspended Sentence, No Probation | Suspended Sentence with Probation | Fine | Under 1 Year | 1 to Under 2 | 2 to Under 5 | 5 and Over | |
|---|---|---|---|---|---|---|---|---|
| 1970–1972 | 7.4 (1,742) | 34.8 (3,466) | 19.3 (1,950) | 30.5 (3,030) | 5.1 (504) | 2.6 (262) | .1 (13) | (9,969) |

Source: *Canada Statistics of Criminal and Other Offences,* 1957–1972.
[a]Since method of reporting sentences was changed in 1970, 1969 was included with the previous four years.

**Table 13-5**
**Average Sentences for "Taking Motor Vehicle without Consent", 1957-1972**

|  | Suspended or Other Disposition | Probation | Option of Fine | Committed without Option | Other |
|---|---|---|---|---|---|
| 1949-1952 | 14.7 (773) | 11.4 (601) | 53.7 (2,827) | 11.4 (601) | (5,258) |
| 1953-1956 | 13.0 (726) | 13.4 (746) | 53.3 (2,966) | 20.1 (1,119) | (5,557) |

|  | Suspended Sentence, No Probation | Suspended Sentence with Probation | Fine | Institutional Sentence | Other | |
|---|---|---|---|---|---|---|
| 1957-1960[a] | 10.6 (519) | 22.6 (1,107) | 44.8 (2,183) | 21.6 (1,051) | .4 (20) | (4,880) |
| 1961-1964 | 10.9 (694) | 24.4 (1,599) | 42.9 (2,790) | 21.7 (1,401) | .1 (5) | (6,489) |
| 1965-1968 | 8.5 (600) | 29.9 (2,085) | 41.5 (2,897) | 19.7 (1,375) | .4 (18) | (6,975) |
| 1969-1972 | 8.2 (487) | 31.8 (1,884) | 38.2 (2,266) | 19.9 (1,179) | 1.9 (120) | (5,936) |

Source: *Canada Statistics of Criminal and Other Offences*, 1949-1972.

[a]Figures for 1957 and 1958 were identical in all categories. If this is a mistake, it had not been corrected at this time of writing (1981).

Code among the offenses, the differences in sentencing severity are less than might be expected.

The tables also show several other interesting trends. Over time, the use of probation as an integral part of a sentence has doubled. This may reflect an increasing awareness on the part of judges of the deleterious effects of incarceration with the result that judges are sending only "serious" offenders to prisons. In fact, institutional sentences have become markedly less common from 1949 to 1972 for both theft and breaking and entering. They have fallen from an average of 54.7 percent of all those convicted of theft between 1949 and 1952, to 20.5 percent between 1970 and 1972, and from 74 percent to 49.4 percent during the same periods for those convicted of breaking and entering; and from 60.8 to 38.3 percent for those convicted of possession. But it must be remembered that many of those who were ordered to pay fines actually went to jail for inability to pay, and many others served time before their court appearance because they were unable to raise bail for their release. (The Bail Reform Act, allowing release of selected defendants without bail payments, was not in effect until 1972; and even now 94.2 percent of all defendants are kept in custody until their first court appearance (Hann 1973, p. 196).

Although the sanctions prescribed for theft and for possession of stolen goods are the same, in practice judges are harder on those charged with possession. This may be because many of those charged with theft are first offenders or females; because judges think that those charged with possession are professionals making a living as fences; or because higher dollar losses are involved. Moreover, we know from U.S. studies that those charged with theft are a minority of those who steal and are usually either professionals or members of discredited groups, such as blacks, the poor, and teenagers (Cameron 1970; Robin 1967). One would suspect from the statistics that, in Canada, many more nonprofessional, "respectable" people are hauled into court.

In contrast to the indictable offenses first analyzed, for which the numbers of persons charged increased every year, the numbers charged with taking a motor vehicle without consent have remained remarkably constant throughout the postwar period (see table 13-5). Considering the increased population of Canada and the increased number of cars per family, the rate has actually decreased. This may reflect a greater inclination on the part of police and prosecutors to lay the more-serious charge of theft of an automobile; the greater availability of credit to poor youths, which enables more to buy their own cars; or the increased security measures taken by automobile owners and manufacturers—there are any number of possibilities but no definitive answers.

The sentences given have also changed little compared with those for the indictable offenses, except that there has been a considerable increase in the use of probation as a sanction. This rose from 11.4 percent of all cases in 1949-1952 to 22.6 percent in 1957-1960 to 31.8 percent in 1969-1972. But rather than indicating a greater leniency in sentencing, it seems from the data—hard as they are to interpret with any confidence—that those who might formerly have received a straight suspended sentence are now more apt to get probation in addition to the suspension. The percentage of offenders being sent to prison has remained constant over the years at approximately 20 percent. As noted before, however, it must be remembered that some unknown (but higher) number of people actually served time in jail because of an inability either to raise bail or to pay a fine, or both.

A comparison of table 13-5 with table 13-3 shows dramatically how little the written law can mean in determining the sanctions handed out. Over the years, despite the fact that taking a motor vehicle is a summary offense, and theft of some types calls for up to ten years' imprisonment, the sanctions handed down for each have become more and more similar until, in the 1969-1972 period, the number of people receiving institutional terms for each crime is nearly identical. Sanctions differ mainly in that those charged with taking a motor vehicle without consent are more likely to receive a suspended sentence with probation, whereas those charged with theft are more likely to get fined.

*Upperworld Offenses*

Tables 13-6 to 13-11 show the sanctions handed out for upperworld offenses, as reported by the agencies responsible for enforcement. Only two sections of the Combines Investigation Act (misleading price representation, Section 36, and misleading advertising, Section 37) are included for analysis here, because the remaining sections governing restraint of trade, resale-price maintenance, and mergers and monopolies are too complex to be strictly compared with sentences for traditional offenses. Moreover, these sections have been analyzed in detail elsewhere (Goff and Reasons 1978; Snider 1978).

The unit of analysis employed in these tables is the case, rather than the charge. There are often five or six charges laid in a particular case; and the defendant or defendants may, typically, be fined $100 on each of two charges, be acquitted on one, and have the other three withdrawn by the government. This would appear in the tables as one case with one $200 fine. Per charge, the fines are even lower—the mode or most-common fine per charge is $100 under Section 36 and $200 under Section 37. Even per case, the fines are very low. However, there may be a tendency toward assessment of more-severe sanctions for false-advertising offenses. The maximum fine of $25,000 (before the amendments took effect on 1 January 1976) was assessed only once, in 1973; but there were three fines of $5,000 and one of $8,000 in 1974. There was no parallel trend for cases under Section 36, misleading price representation—the average fines were lower than in the late 1960s, taking into account the decreased value of the dollar.

Another change that is noteworthy is the declining use of alternate criminal sanctions in sentencing in recent years, and the greatly increased use of the

**Table 13-6**
**Enforcement Record and Sanctions for Misleading Price Representation (Section 36)**

| Year | Number of Cases Tried | Number of Cases Convicted | Average Fine | Suspended Sentence | Acquittal | Number of Cases Withdrawn or Dismissed |
|------|------|------|------|------|------|------|
| 1962 | 6 | 5 | $520 | 1 (Fine option) | 1 | 0 |
| 1963 | 6 | 3 | $591.66 | 1 (Fine option) | 1 | 2 |
| 1964 | 2 | 1 | $200 | | 0 | 1 |
| 1965 | 5 | 5 | $190 | 2 (Fine option) | 0 | 0 |
| 1966 | 6 | 6 | $283.66 | 0 | 0 | 0 |
| 1967 | 5 | 5 | $180 | 1 (No fine) | 0 | 0 |
| 1968 | 16 | 14 | $218 | 0 | 2 | 0 |
| 1969 | 31 | 13 | $318 | 1 (Fine option and 1–15 days or fine option) | 5 | 3 |
| 1970 | 29 | 29 | $245 | 0 | 0 | 0 |
| 1971 | 34 | 28 | $232 | 0 | 3 | 3 |
| 1972 | 28 | 23 | $211 | 0 | 2 | 3 |
| 1973 | 21 | 20 | $258 | 0 | 1 | 0 |
| 1974 | 26 | 20 | $327 | 1 (10-day term with fine option) | 4 | 2 |

Source: Canada, 1973, plus 1974 and 1975: Annual Reports of the director of investigation and research, Combines Investigation Act.

**Table 13-7**
**Enforcement Record and Sanctions for False Advertising (Section 37)**

| Year | Number of Cases Tried | Number of Case Convictions | Average Fine | Suspended Sentence | Acquittal | Number of Cases Withdrawn or Dismissed |
|------|------|------|------|------|------|------|
| 1970 | 11 | 7 | $ 330 | 0 | 4 | 0 |
| 1971 | 55 | 45 | $ 461 | 0 | 5 | 5 |
| 1972 | 60 | 47 | $ 620 | 1 (Fine option) | 5 | 8 |
| 1973 | 54 | 47 | $1,789 | 0 | 4 | 3 |
| 1974 | 78 | 63 | $ 959 | 4 (1 day in jail) (120 days in jail) (Keep peace 1 year) (2 years suspended, plus restitution) | 4 | 11 |

Source: Canada, 1973; plus 1974 and 1975 Annual Reports of director of investigation and research, Combines Investigation Act.

**Table 13-8**
**Sanctions for Food and Drugs Act**

|  | Firms or Individuals Convicted | Number of Charges | Total Fines | Average Fine per Case | Average Fine per Charge |
|---|---|---|---|---|---|
| *1974* | | | | | |
| January–June | 23 | 37 | $ 4,380 | $190.43 | $118.37 |
| July–December | 34 | 56 | 14,275 | 419.85 | 254.91 |
| *1975* | | | | | |
| January–June | 40 | 55 | 13,675 | 341.87 | 248.63 |
| July–December | 51 | 61 | 12,300 | 241.17 | 232.07 |
| *1976* | | | | | |
| January–June | 44 | 53 | 10,300 | 234.09 | 194.33 |

**Table 13-9**
**Sanctions for Weights and Measures Act**

|  | Firms or Individuals Convicted | Number of Charges | Total Fines | Average Fine per Case | Average Fine per Charge |
|---|---|---|---|---|---|
| *1974* | | | | | |
| January–June | 19 | 65 | $ 4,219 | $222.05 | $ 64.90 |
| July–December | 17 | 50 | 2,875 | 169.11 | 57.50 |
| *1975* | | | | | |
| January–June | 16 | 37 | 14,625 | 914.06 | 395.27 |
| July–December | 27 | 60 | 9,070 | 335.92 | 151.16 |
| *1976* | | | | | |
| January–June | 46 | 183 | 64,505 | 1,402.28 | 352.48 |

**Table 13-10**
**Sanctions for Hazardous Products Act**

|  | Firms or Individuals Convicted | Number of Charges | Total Fines | Average Fine per Case | Average Fine per Charge |
|---|---|---|---|---|---|
| *1974* | | | | | |
| January–June | 2 | 2 | $400 | $200 | $200 |
| July–December | 0 | 0 | 0 | 0 | 0 |
| *1975* | | | | | |
| January–June | 0 | 0 | 0 | 0 | 0 |
| July–December | 1 | 1 | 50 | 50 | 50 |
| *1976* | | | | | |
| January–June | 1 | 1 | 250 | 250 | 250 |

**Table 13-11**
**Sanctions for Packaging and Labeling Act**

| | Firms or Individuals Convicted | Number of Charges | Total Fines | Average Fine per Case | Average Fine per Charge |
|---|---|---|---|---|---|
| a | – | – | – | – | – |
| a | – | – | – | – | – |
| *1975* | | | | | |
| January–June | 0 | 0 | 0 | 0 | 0 |
| July–December | 0 | 0 | 0 | 0 | 0 |
| *1976* | | | | | |
| January–June | 3 | 7 | $7,000 | $2,333.33 | $1,000 |

Source: Consumer and Corporate Affairs, news releases, 15 October 1974–20 September 1976.

aNot proclaimed in effect until January 1, 1975.

Order of Prohibition. Even though nobody actually served any time in jail until 12 December 1974, when a Dartmouth man was sentenced to two years in a federal penitentiary, the alternate penal sanctions serve the important function of reminding both the defendant and the court that these are criminal offenses. However, those who typically received optional penal sanctions were small entrepreneurs in nonestablished or "disreputable" businesses, such as fortune telling or weight-reducing salons. When any major (dominant) company was involved, the charge was likely to be against the corporation alone, not against individuals *and* the corporation; and the sanction was typically a fine and/or an Order of Prohibition. In only one case was restitution ever ordered; and, again, the defendant was not a powerful corporation but an individual in Montreal. He was given a two-year suspended sentence and was placed on probation with the condition that he refund $9.95 to each of approximately 400 people who had purchased his useless electronic television antennas. This is equivalent to a $4,000 fine and a public lesson. In the same year, under the same section of the act, the T. Eaton Company, a major retail chain, was assessed a $200 fine, General Mills Canada Ltd. was fined $750 and Robert Simpson Company was assessed $5,000. No executives were charged in any of these three cases, and no restitution was required.

Finally, we will look at the sanctions handed down under the other four acts administered by the Department of Consumer and Corporate Affairs that fit our definition of nonviolent economic crimes.

The data are less than complete. Three of the acts are fairly recent legislation (the Food and Drugs Act is the exception), but it was not until 1974 that the department began systematically releasing enforcement data. Prior to this, statistics were reported only in "Statistics of Criminal and Other Offences" and in Annual Reports of the department responsible for enforcement (food and drugs used to be under the aegis of the Department of Health and Welfare). Neither source gave comprehensive, consistent, reliable data: The former lumped many statutes together under the heading "other Federal Statutes" and, in any event, reported neither the size of the fine nor the details of the sentence, if any; the latter provided only general information on the numbers charged. Thus we have data only from 1974 to the first half of 1976.

The greatest activity (in terms of number of charges laid) has been under the Food and Drugs Act. The size of fines varies widely from judge to judge and from area to area. There appears to be a slight increase in the number of convictions registered (from 57 in 1974 to 91 in 1975) and in the total fines assessed (from $18,655 in 1974 to $25,975 in 1975), but the average fine per case or per charge has not systematically increased. A factor not revealed in the table is that virtually all the charges were laid against small retail merchants (for example, Monk Fish Market, Montreal; Pulsateri Supermarket, Toronto; Epicerie Michaud Enrg., Rimouski), generally for short volume, adulteration, or substitution of meat or fish products. Prior to 1976 only one major retail chain was convicted (a Dominion store in St. John's, Newfoundland), although in the first six months of 1976, four Loblaws stores, Dominion Dairies, and two A&P stores (all dominant companies) were charged. Perhaps some policy changes are being made; but on the basis of the data we now have, it is safe to say that most of the enforcement activity under the Food and Drugs Act has been directed against small businesses.

The Weights and Measures Act shows a similar enforcement pattern, although convictions increased dramatically in the 1975–1976 period. Fines per charge appear to have been increasing steadily, if erratically, although the drastic increase in the first half of 1976 is due to one $46,000 fine against a motor-vehicle dealer in Calgary for odometer tampering. In fact, the act has been enforced chiefly against two businesses: car dealers for odometer tampering, and retail merchants (again in small stores) for short-weight scales.

There have been far fewer charges laid under the Hazardous Products Act. But of the four charges laid in two-and-one-half years, three have been against major retailers. However, despite the sanctions allowed by the act and the size of the firms involved (Steinbergs and the T. Eaton Company), the fines are very small, amounting to far less than the court costs.

The Packaging and Labelling Act will be an interesting one to watch in the future. With an eye, perhaps, to precedents, the first three cases laid were against the three major food retail chains in Toronto (Dominion Stores Ltd., Loblaw's Ltd., and Steinberg's Ltd.), and resulted in substantial fines. In view of the overall record of enforcement of the Department of Consumer and Corporate Affairs (they are responsible for all the upperworld crimes analyzed here), it will be surprising if this pattern continues.

Let us look at the data another way. We are comparing two types of theft: that committed by lower- and working-class people *from* the business enterprise or from other individuals, (traditional offenses), and that committed *by* the business enterprise from consumers (upperworld offenses). We will look at the most-recent data, from 1970–1972. Judging by the written law, both types are serious offenses. Both are relatively simple and easy to prove in court—in fact, misleading advertising is a "strict liability" offense. This means that to convict a person or firm of this offense, the crown must prove only that the advertising was misleading to the "average man," not that the company or corporate executive responsible for its approval knew that it was or intended that it should be. Moreover, advertisements suspected of being false, like traditional thefts, are highly visible and relatively straightforward; the crown does not have to hire economists and lawyers and spend two years sorting out the evidence (as is often the situation for combines cases). Traditional theft, similarly, is a visible, uncomplicated act that is relatively easy to prove in court. False advertising has recently experienced a surge of enforcement activity, with the budgets of the enforcers going up substantially. Thus, the two are roughly parallel in ease of prosecution.

We can see from Table 13–12 that traditional theft is treated much more harshly than corporate theft. The number of people charged and the sanctions dealt out are all much, much higher for theft. We know that the average traditional theft causes far less loss, in monetary terms, than does the average corporate theft (Schur 1969; Cameron 1970; Robin 1967; Law Reform Commission 1974). We know also that corporate theft has far greater repercussions on, and does much more damage to, the social order itself and the tacit "consent" on

Table 13–12
**Theft Compared with Misleading Advertising, 1970–1972**

|  | Theft | Misleading Advertising |
|---|---|---|
| Number of cases prosecuted | 56,699[a] | 126 |
| Number fined | 27,217 | 99 |
| Average fine per case | Unknown | $470.33 |
| Number given suspended sentence (with or without probation) | 17,901 | 1 |
| Number sentenced to prison | 11,608 | 0 |

[a]Excluding Quebec and Alberta.

which this order is thought to be based (Schur 1969; Edelhertz 1970; Geis 1974). How, then, can we explain such anomalies?

## Discussion

It has been shown quite clearly that the sanctions for the traditional crimes analyzed are very much heavier than for the upperworld crimes; moreover, enforcement efforts are much more energetic, and many more offenders are charged. That this should be true is not surprising, in view of the literature. The more-important issue is why this is so.

There are two possible explanations. The paradigm that dominated the fields of criminology and sociology prior to 1967 or so—the functionalist or consensus school of thought—would explain these results in terms of public opinion.[5] People worry about "real" crimes, such as theft, but not about mere "regulatory" offenses. I would argue that the alleged public acceptance of serious upperworld crimes is virtually nonexistent. Researchers have mistaken cynicism and impotence for acceptance. The few studies done indicate that people would support heavier, not lighter, penalties for violators (Newman 1968; Rossi et al. 1974; McDonald 1976). Moreover, even if this were true, the crucial question would be how this amazing state of affairs was achieved in view of the damage done by such offenses.

The key theoretical question of corporate crime is "why does it exist?" Why do certain capitalist states enact strong legislation,[6] ostensibly against the interests of the capitalist class in that state?[7] What factors, historical and sociocultural, affect the passage and enforcement of these laws? And what effects do the laws ultimately have on the state and on the offenders? It will be argued next that regularly enforced criminal laws essentially serve two major and very different functions: (1) social control and (2) legitimation.

### Social Control

Traditional criminal laws primarily help the state to control a potentially dangerous class of people—the underclass. Since they have little property, little prestige or status, and little security in their employment (when they can get employment), they have the least to lose and the most to gain by breaking the law. This is not to say that they *are* in any sense a revolutionary class; evidence has discredited that notion quite convincingly. However, they are viewed as the class most capable of disrupting the old order, if not of building the new. These criminal laws are also enforced against middle- and upper-class people, especially on the rare occasions when they commit visible or dramatic traditional crimes.

*Legitimation*

Laws are also passed in response to citizen dissent and pressure, to stave off further social conflict, to pacify disaffected groups, to restore or ensure the legitimacy of the judicial system. As Miliband (1969), Hall et al. (1978), Poulantzsas (1975), and others have pointed out, the consent of the citizens is crucial to both the long-term survival and the short-term success of the advanced capitalist state. (People must want the goods that are produced, and they must "freely" contribute their labor in the belief that they are getting a fair deal.) But as monopoly capitalism develops, power becomes increasingly concentrated in fewer and fewer hands. This process is dangerous because middle- and working-class people may come to see that this development blocks upward mobility and negates equality of opportunity, and because monopolies and oligopolies present increased potential for abuse of the captive consumer market. The state, in order to ensure the long-term survival of capitalism, *must* intervene to prevent dangerous citizen disenchantment. Thus, an interventionist state is a sine qua non of capitalism, which must improve (or appear to be improving) the life chances of the average citizen through programs of reform. Laws against corporate crime, then, are among a series of statutes designed to make it appear that the state is acting against the interests of the capitalist class to retain the integrity of the liberal democratic system.

I would argue that these are the dynamics that underlie the discrepancies in the writing and enforcement of laws that we have seen in the earlier analysis. Laws on traditional offenses, because they have a general social control (or "deterrence") function, are enforced in such a way that the offense committed has less to do with the sentence handed down than does the perception of the judge and other officials of the need to control this particular offender. Hence, we see the emphasis on his or her attitude, demeanor, and background (Hogarth 1970). This also explains why laws that have very different maximum penalties prescribed in the legislation turn out to be enforced in a very similar fashion. The essentially similar sanctions given for breaking and entering a dwelling house (maximum life imprisonment in law), and receiving stolen goods (maximum ten years in law), are a case in point.

The laws on corporate crime, however, are there for a very different reason. Since the state is tied to the capitalist class in a whole range of structural and instrumental ways, and in fact must set policy that will facilitate the extraction of surplus (the function referred to as accumulation by O'Connor 1973), lawmakers do not have any vested interest in controlling those they are forced to regulate. These people are no threat to the status quo, even though individual members do sometimes get too greedy. The capitalist class must sometimes be protected from its own internal disagreements and excesses, and from its often shortsighted views on social policy. Moreover, the history of the individual nation-state is relevant for understanding the role of different types of laws within it. In Canada, this means that the state elite cannot afford to jeopardize in any real sense its close ties to the corporate class. The ties that bind are too personal, too direct, too close (Porter 1965; Clement 1975). More importantly, they do not even need to *appear* to be independent of this class, because the working class generally lacks political consciousness and an effective political voice in Canada. The middle class is split but is no more "radical," even in defending the rights of its members as consumers, than is the working class. The Canadian state, then, has not been pushed to extend or enforce corporate-crime laws in the interests of legitimating itself to, and defending itself in front of, an aroused coalition of working- and middle-class interests. The weakness of both the written and the enforced law on corporate crime is the result.

This history of the Canadian state also helps explain the laws surrounding traditional economic crime. Lacking a strong working-class movement, accepting the ideology promoted by the ruling class with respect to the dangerousness of the average criminal, believing in the concept that "only bad people commit (traditional) crimes," the bulk of the Canadian population has passively (and sometimes actively) supported the punitive criminal-justice system and the Criminal Code. They have not identified with their "brethren" in courts and prisons. Thus, on the organizational level of analysis, the police and court officials have been able to give vent to their own predilections with very little interference. And these predilections have been shaped on the macro level by ideological and political forces emanating from the ruling-class/state nexus (as well as by the micro- and organizational-level factors with which we are all so familiar in the literature).

In conclusion, I am arguing that it is a mistake to try to interpret all law-breaking activities as if they were fundamentally similar by virtue of the fact that they are all illegal. The history and uses to which each type of law is (or can be) put are key variables that determine how the laws will be written and enforced. The forces that shaped and are still shaping the culture of the controllers (the police, inspectors, lawyers, judges, and so forth) are also important (although I have not dealt with them in detail here for lack of space). In particular, I have argued for a bifurcation of the analysis, with laws that appear to restrain the ruling class being analyzed independently of laws that appear to restrain the rest of the population.[8] Because they arose in different ways and serve very different purposes, one must use a different explanatory framework for laws governing traditional and corporate offenses. In this final section, I have suggested in a preliminary way some of the variables that are central to such an analysis.

## Notes

1. I am not arguing here that upper-class offenders who do commit traditional lower-class crimes, and are arrested for them, will necessarily be treated

leniently because of the inconsistencies of their position. Indeed, as the cases of Patty Hearst or, arguably, Harold Ballard, illustrate, sanctions may be imposed that are within the average range for the offense. This seems to happen because such cases, being rare, are highly publicized, and because the state, in the interests of legitimacy, *must* be seen to dispense evenhanded justice.

2. *Indictable offenses* are those considered more serious, with severe maximum penalties. *Summary offenses* carry lighter fines and never more than two years' maximum in prison. Some offenses, such as theft, forgery, and murder, are indictable only; others, such as taking a car without permission or failing to signal a turn properly, are summary only; and still others can be either summary or indictable, at the discretion of the prosecutor's office. This decision is supposed to depend on the seriousness of the offense, taking into consideration the characteristics of the offender and any mitigating circumstances.

3. The alternative of probation provided for many traditional offenses does not serve an analogous function, I would argue, because this is *not* written into the law as a possible alternative. Moreover, probation provides for close personal supervision, which is usually obvious to the community and therefore creates further loss of status and of autonomy for the offender.

4. This is to be expected, not only because the maximum sanctions in the Criminal Code are much heavier, but, more significantly, because this offense is officially classified as a crime of violence. I have not followed this usage because it differs from simple theft only by the location of the property stolen—it is inside a private building to which access is already restricted by law, rather than inside a building open to the public such as a retail store, or in an unprotected location such as a park or street. Thus the theft necessitates getting in and out of the protected territory, which calls for usually greater premeditation, potentially greater gain, and a possible risk of greater property damage in effecting an entrance and exit. A more-serious offense against private property (in terms of monetary loss, premeditation, and so forth) it may be; but a violent offense, it is not. For if a weapon or a toy resembling a weapon is carried by the offender, regardless of whether it is used or shown or intended for use, if any threat of personal violence is uttered, whether or not the threat is acted on, the offender is charged with robbery, an indictable offense carrying a maximum of life in prison. As Waller and Okihiro (1978) have shown, breaking and entering is typically a type of petty theft from temporarily vacant homes and businesses.

5. In fact, consensus theorists would be most unlikely to do this kind of study, since by and large they did not expect much lawbreaking to occur in the middle and upper classes, which were not generally seen as anomic or as suffering from a means–goal disjunction. Moreover, because they assumed, for the most part, a "scientific" stance that ruled out ideology, their concerns and interests were shaped by the concerns of the dominant class of the day (Habermas 1971) who were best able to coopt public opinion and to identify as social problems those behaviors that threatened them. Third, the "background assumptions" (Gouldner 1970) of this study and the questions it asks are inimical to the world view of most consensus theorists.

6. The term *state* or *capitalist state* refers to six major institutions: the government, the administration, the military and police, the judicial branch, sub-central (state or provincial) governments, and parlimentary or congressional assemblies. The *state elite* refer to those people who occupy positions at or near the top of these institutions—presidents, premiers, governors, ministers and deputy ministers, judges of the highest civil courts, and senior military men (Miliband 1969, pp. 46–51).

7. The term *capitalist class,* or *ruling class,* refers to that class which owns and/or controls the means of production. I prefer the term *capitalist* to *ruling class* because the latter term implies a totality of monolithic control. I would argue that the nature and degree of this control in each capitalist state is the very issue we are empirically and theoretically exploring.

8. Such laws go far beyond the narrow sample discussed here. They include environmental protection; laws governing the stock market; and laws regulating the production, sale, transportation, and processing of goods on the one hand; and most (if not all) traditional property offenses, plus laws governing morality and "public order," on the other.

## References

Arnold, William "Race and Ethnicity Relative to other Factors in Juvenile Court Disposition." *American Journal of Sociology* 77(September 1971):211–227.

Bliss, Michael. *A Living Profit: Studies in the Social History of Canadian Business, 1883–1911.* Toronto: McClelland-Stewart, 1974.

Blumberg, A.S., ed. *Current Perspectives on Criminal Behavior.* New York: Knopf, 1974.

Cameron, Mary Owen. "The 5-Finger Discount." In Smigel and Ross, *Crimes Against Bureaucracy,* pp. 97–118.

Canada. *Statistics of Criminal and Other Offenses.* Ottawa: Information Canada, Statistics Canada (Judicial Division), 1949–1972.

——. *Crime and Traffic Enforcement Statistics.* Ottawa: Statistics Canada, 1980.

Chambliss, William, ed. *Crime and the Legal Processes,* New York: McGraw-Hill, 1969.

——, ed. *Criminal Law in Action,* Santa Barbara, Calif.: Hamilton, 1975.

Clement, Wallace. *The Canadian Corporate Elite: An Analysis of Economic Power.* Toronto, McClelland and Stewart, 1975.

Clinard, M., and Quinney, R. *Criminal Behaviour Systems: A Typology.* New York: Holt, Rinehart and Winston, 1973.

Cloke, K., "The Economic Basis of Law and State." in Lefcourt, *Law Against the People,* pp. 65–80.

Edelhertz, H. *The Nature, Impact and Prosecution of White Collar Crime.* Washington, D.C.: U.S. Government Printing Office, 1970.

Geis, Gilbert. "The Heavy Equipment Anti-trust Case of 1961." In Geis, ed., *White Collar Criminal.* New York: Atherton, 1968.

——. "Upperworld Crime." in Blumberg, *Current Perspectives,* pp. 114–138.

Goff, Colin H. "Corporate Crime in Canada." Master's thesis, Department of Sociology, University of Calgary, November 1975.

Goff, C., and Reasons, C. *Corporate Crime in Canada.* Toronto: Prentice-Hall, 1978.

Gouldner, Alvin. *The Coming Crisis of Western Sociology.* New York: Basic Books, 1970.

Green, Edward. "Race, Social Status and Criminal Arrest." *American Sociological Review* 35(June 1970):476–490.

Green, Mark J. *The Closed Enterprise System.* New York: Grossman, 1972.

Habermas, Jurgen. *Knowledge and Human Interests,* trans. J.J. Shapiro. London: Heinemann, 1971.

Hall, Stewart; Critcher, C.; Clarke, J.; and Roberts. B. *Policing the Crisis: Mugging, the State and Law and Order.* London: MacMillan, 1978.

Hann, Robert. *Decision Making in the Canadian Criminal Court System: A Systems Analysis.* Toronto: Centre of Criminology, Research Report, University of Toronto, 1973.

Hogarth, J. *Sentencing as a Human Process.* Toronto: University of Toronto Press, 1970.

Jaspan, R., and Black, D. *The Thief in the White Collar.* New York: Lippincott, 1960.

Law Reform Commission of Canada. *Principles of Sentencing and Dispositions,* Working Paper No. 3. Ottawa: Information Canada, 1974.

Lefcourt, R., ed. *Law Against the People.* New York: Random House, 1971.

Lefebvre, H. *The Sociology of Marx,* trans. Guterman. New York: Vintage, 1968.

Lemert, E.M. *Human Deviance, Social Problems and Social Control.* Englewood Cliffs, N.J.: Prentice-Hall, 1967.

Marchak, M. Patricia. *Ideological Perspectives on Canada.* Toronto: McGraw-Hill Ryerson, 1975.

McDonald, Lynn. *The Sociology of Law and Order.* London: Faber, 1976.

Miliband, Ralph. *The State in Capitalist Society.* London: Quartet Books, 1969.

Mitton, G.I. *A Survey of Indictable Offences in Canada.* Halifax: Dalhousie University Law School, 1960.

National Council of Welfare. *Press and the Poor: A Report on How Canada's Newspapers Cover Poverty.* Ottawa: Information Canada, 1973.

Newman, Don J. "Public Attitudes Towards a Form of White Collar Crime." In Geis, *White Collar Criminal,* pp. 287–293.

O'Connor, James. *The Fiscal Crisis of the State.* New York: St. Martin's Press, 1973.

Porter, John. *The Vertical Mosaic.* Toronto: University of Toronto Press, 1965.

258                                    White-Collar and Economic Crime

Poulantzsas, Nico. *Classes in Contemporary Capitalism.* London: Verso, 1975.
Quinney, Richard. *Critique of Legal Order.* Boston: Little, Brown, 1974.
Reich, Charles. "Law and the Corporate State." In W.J. Chambliss, ed., *Sociological Readings in the Conflict Perspective,* pp. 445–455. Reading, Mass.: Addison-Wesley, 1973.
Reiman, Jeffrey. *The Rich Get Richer and the Poor Get Prison.* Toronto: Wiley, 1979.
Robin, Gerald. "The Corporate and Judicial Disposition of Employee Thieves." *Wisconsin Law Review,* Summer 1967, pp. 685–702.
Rossi, P.; White, E.; Rose, C.E.; and Berk, R.E. "The Seriousness of Crimes: Normative Structure and Individual Differences." *American Sociological Review* 39(April 1974):224–237.
Schur, E. *Our Criminal Society.* Englewood Cliffs, N.J.: Prentice-Hall, 1969.
Smigel, E.O., and Ross, H.L. *Crimes Against Bureaucracy.* New York: Van Nostrand, 1970.
Snider, D. Laureen. "Does the Legal Order Reflect the Power Structure: A Test of Conflict Theory." Ph.D. diss., University of Toronto, October 1977.
——. "Corporate Crime in Canada: A Preliminary Report." *Canadian Journal of Criminology* 20, no. 2 (April 1978).
Stanbury, W.T. "Canadian Attitudes Toward Competition Policy: The Dominance of Business Interests." Unpublished paper, written for Canadian Research Council, February 1975.
Sutherland, E.H. "White Collar Criminality." *American Sociological Review* 5(February 1940):1–12.
——. *White Collar Crime.* New York: Dryden, 1949.
Taylor, I.; Walton, P.; and Young, J. *The New Criminology: Towards a Social Theory of Deviance.* London: Routledge and Kegan Paul, 1973.
Tepperman, Lorne. *Crime Control.* Toronto: McGraw-Hill Ryerson, 1977.
Thornberry, T.P. "Race, Socio-economic Status and Sentencing in the Juvenile Justice System." *Journal of Criminal Law and Criminology* 64(March 1973): 90–98.
Tigar, M. "Socialist Law and Legal Institutions." In Lefcourt, *Law Against the People,* pp. 40–64.
Turk, Austin T. *Criminality and Legal Order.* Chicago: Rand McNally, 1969.
Vaz, E., and Lodhi, A. *Crime and Delinquency in Canada.* Toronto: Prentice-Hall, 1979.
Waller, Irvin, and Okihiro, Norman. *Burglary: The Victim and the Public.* Toronto: University of Toronto Press, 1978.
Weiner, N.L., and Willie, C.V. "Decision by Juvenile Officers." *American Journal of Sociology* 77(September 1971):199–210.
West, Gordon. "Serious Thieves: Lower Class Adolescent Males in a Short-Term Deviant Occupation." In Vaz and Lodhi, *Crime and Delinquency in Canada.* 1979.
Zinn, Howard. "The Conspiracy of Law." In R.P. Wolfe, ed., *The Rule of Law.* New York: Simon and Schuster, 1971.

# 14

## The Social Organization of White-Collar Sanctions: A Study of Prosecution and Punishment in the Federal Courts

*John Hagan, Ilene Nagel,* and *Celesta Albonetti*

This chapter is concerned with the legal sanctioning of white-collar offenders. It builds on an earlier analysis of sentencing decisions in ten federal district courts (see Hagan, Nagel, and Albonetti 1980). The earlier study revealed that college-educated persons convicted of white-collar crimes received the most-lenient sanctions in a federal district court that was unique in the relatively large volume of white-collar crime prosecuted. The findings of the former analysis are suggestive of an inverse relationship between social class and legal sanctions that has been the subject of an enduring debate among sociologists (see Hagan 1974; Nettler 1979, pp. 40–46). However, the further implication of the analysis is that the likelihood of a class-sanction relationship increases with the number of white-collar offenders prosectued, and that therefore the presence of such a relationship may be contingent on the *type* of jurisdiction studied. Thus issues surrounding the sanctioning of white-collar offenders may be issues of social organization as much as of social stratification.

In the current chapter we explore further the legal sanctioning of white-collar crime. Whereas our earlier analysis focused on education as one aspect of social standing, in this chapter we focus on the offender's income. One purpose of this chapter, then, is to demonstrate that our findings for education can be replicated with income. Also, we elaborate theoretically our explanation of why the findings we are attempting to replicate should be expected to hold both here and for other data. We then go on to outline a program of research directed toward the resolution of several issues posed by the findings of this and previous studies.

### Previous Studies

There is considerable doubt in the research literature about the presence or absence of a relationship between social class and legal sanctions, particularly

This research was made possible by a grant from the Crime and Delinquency Section of the National Institute of Mental Health.

those sanctions imposed by the courts in the form of criminal sentences. Thus, although a number of studies of sentencing find little (see Bernstein et al. 1977) or no (see Chiricos and Waldo 1975) class-sanction relationship, there are also studies that find this relationship to be substantial (see Swigert and Farrell 1977; Lizotte 1978). One general source of concern about these studies is that they are based on samples that consist almost entirely of low-status defendants, making this research mainly a matter of "within-class" rather than "between-class" comparisons (see Greenberg 1977; Hopkins 1977; Reasons 1977). In simple terms, there is little of what most observers would regard as white-collar crime—income-tax evasion, price fixing, violation of pollution laws—in these data sets (Hopkins 1977, p. 177).

There are several reasons that few white-collar cases are found in these data. First, most white-collar crimes can safely be assumed to be "beyond incrimination" (Kennedy 1970), in the sense that such activities are usually undetected or, if detected, dealt with under civil law. However, there is also a second and increasingly important point to be made. That is, when white-collar crimes are dealt with under criminal law in the United States, they are most frequently dealt with in the federal courts. To date, almost all research on criminal sentencing has focused on state courts. The quantitative data analyzed in this paper consist of cases prosecuted and sentenced over a period of several years in ten federal district courts, including one of the first U.S. attorney's offices in this country reputed to have made the prosecution of white-collar crime a high priority; qualitative data as well were gathered through observations and interviews in these courts, and through a consideration of several well-documented white-collar cases prosecuted and sentenced in the U.S. attorney's office just mentioned.[1] The latter qualitative data are used first to establish a theoretical foundation for the analysis that follows. Our use of the quantitative data is restricted by an agreement not to identify individual districts in our data; this agreement is therefore observed in our discussion of the qualitative data as well.

## The Social Organization of Crime and Punishment

It is a premise of this chapter that to understand the sanctioning of white-collar and other kinds of crime, we must develop an understanding of the system in which it occurs.[2] We begin, following Reiss (1971, 1974), by conceptualizing the criminal-justice system generally as a loosely articulated operating network of input-output relationships among a series of subsystems; a set of relationships that we will refer to as a "loosely coupled system" (see Hagan, Hewitt, and Alwin 1979; Hagan, Nagel, and Albonetti 1980; Meyer and Rowan 1977). Thus, whereas most research to date on criminal-justice decision making has been almost exclusively concerned with decisions made with reference to individual offenders, the perspective we are proposing suggests that these individual case

decisions be understood within the larger context of input and output relationships that exist between the various organizational components of the criminal-
justice system. For many, perhaps most, types of crimes and circumstances, the
organizational components of the criminal-justice system will have an interest
in maintaining operational autonomy through these input-output relationships.
One consequence of this situation may be a high degree of apparent randomness
in the decisions made about individual cases, leading to complaints by policymakers that discretion is being exercised in an unbounded fashion, and to the
frustration of social scientists who seek to explain the presumed disparities that
result. The character of the system operations we are attempting to conceptualize is well captured by the observation of Gibbs (1978) that ". . . the system
actually appears to be an ungoverned mishmash" (p. 105), and by the suggestion
of Eisenstein and Jacob (1977) that even "the judge does not rule or govern, at
most, he manages, and often he is managed by others" (p. 37).

The occurrence of loose coupling in the criminal-justice system is an obvious impediment to those who would attempt to change it; there is a resistance to the
coordination that policies of change require. In place of such coordination, Reiss
(1971, p. 120) notes that in most criminal-justice systems, "the major means of
control among the subsystems is *internal* to each," with the significant consequence that "each subsystem creates its own system of justice." Indeed, one
of the fascinating features of loosely coupled systems is their ability to circumvent changes in policy (see Meyer and Rowan 1977), often seeking instead to
maintain subunit autonomy.

For the purposes of this chapter, the important questions that emerge from
the foregoing portrayal of criminal-justice operations have to do with how and
when conditions of loose coupling are *circumvented*. We will argue that it is
only when loose coupling is circumvented that extensive prosecution of white-
collar crime will occur. We are left, then, with the questions of *how* and *when* we
should expect a *tightening* of organizational couplings to occur in criminal-
justice systems.

Taking the second question first, one obvious condition for a tightening to
occur will involve a mutuality of interests among policymakers at various levels
of a criminal-justice system in achieving a particular, well-specified goal. One
such goal in the U.S. Department of Justice, and in some exceptional U.S.
attorney's offices, has been the increased prosecution of white-collar crime.
Whereas the first condition we have identified can be thought of as coming from
*above*, in a hierarchical sense, the second condition can be considered to come
from *below*.

Thus a second condition in which a tightening of organizational couplings
may occur is that in which an effort is made to pursue a type of crime that
involves no immediately obvious source of information about the criminal events
in question. Again, much white-collar crime is an example. White-collar crime
usually involves a diffuseness and subtlety of victimization that removes victims

themselves as sources of information about the criminal events of concern. We will return to this point shortly. Here it is enough to suggest that for criminal-justice agencies to pursue white-collar crime effectively, it is necessary to co-ordinate their activities toward the collection of information, evidence, and testimony in ways not necessary for the prosecution of many other kinds of crime. The question remains: *How* can this be done?

The answer to this question focuses on the role of the prosecutor in Anglo-American system of law. Reiss (1974) indicates why and how:

> By legal authority and by practice, prosecutors have the greatest discre-tion in the formally organized criminal justice network. . . . The way that prosecutors exercise discretion over input and output varies con-siderably among jurisdictions. This variation is due partly to the organ-ized forms of discretion available to a prosecutor in a given jurisdiction and partly to historical praactice within that office. The discretionary decisions of prosecutors whether or not to file information can exercise substantial control over input into the system, while the quantity and quality of output are determined mainly by their decisions to nol pros or to plea bargain. [p. 690]

Drawing from Reiss (1971) and Black (1973) and from our own interviews, we suggest that this prosecutorial power can be exercised in two principal ways.

One possibility is to organize prosecutorial resources in a *reactive* fashion. Prosecutors following this approach essentially respond to police initiatives in the same way that the police do to citizen complaints. Indeed, in most state courts the influx of cases, the absence of ready avenues of diversion, and the scarcity of resources are such that it is not possible to do much more than react. Many federal prosecutors also are reactive. Their assumption is often that court resources can be most efficiently organized to satisfy existing demands of en-forcement agencies. This view is well articulated in one of our interviews with a U.S. attorney:

> For the most part, they (the enforcement agencies) are the experts. They know whether there is a crime and they know how to prove it. They will get the facts and bring us a package and there it is. I don't know the FBI in Chicago, but I would imagine . . . more [the U.S. attorney] sitting down with the FBI and saying, "Okay, I want to go after political corruption, let's go get it." . . . We are basically a reactive agency and before setting priorities we have to consider that. . . . We have to respond to the needs of all agencies and enforce the law.

An alternative view of the prosecutorial role is reflected in what we will call a *proactive* policy. Four features of federal jurisdictions encourage the possibility of a proactive approach:

1.  Federal statutes can be interpreted to include a wide range of white-collar as well as common crimes.

2. Federal prosecutors retain the discretion to decline cases or defer them to state courts, making it possible to reserve resources for cases assigned higher priority.
3. The ratio of personnel to cases is often more favorable in federal than in state courts.
4. Federal prosecutors often have at their disposal investigatory resources, particularly federal agencies like the FBI, the Securities and Exchange Commission, and the IRS, that state prosecutors do not.

As a result, U.S. attorney's offices in several large U.S. cities have reorganized their resources to initiate proactively and encourage the investigation and prosecution of high-priority cases. One way this is done is suggested in the following excerpt from an interview with an assistant U.S. attorney in what we regard as a proactive office.

> [T]he way I operate is I basically initiate grand jury investigations where I think it is appropriate. The _____ case, which was a major land sales fraud case, is a very good example of that. Basically my philosophy is that the resources here are limited. . . . You can never prosecute all the crimes that are being committed, and you can never prosecute all the white-collar crimes. Going into the decision-making process for me are the following: (1) I want it to be obviously a case with federal impact—that is, a federal problem that we are looking at, and not a local state problem; (2) that the impact is broad; and (3) for me particularly I prefer to make cases in areas where nothing has been done. In other words, to focus on an industry or problem where there has not been a criminal prosecution. . . . So, I will pick an area such as land fraud where there was a lot of good information about serious abuses but no criminal prosecutions and begin a grand jury investigation. And that resulted in the _____ case being brought and successfully prosecuted. And there are other areas. . . . I will just focus on areas where there really hasn't been federal criminal enforcement, areas which have a consumer impact, and develop cases in those areas.

This proactive attitude toward the use of grand juries is summarized in the observation of another U.S. attorney that "We don't sit back and wait for cases to walk in the door. We go out and make them."

However, the use of grand juries is not sufficient to build most white-collar cases in a proactive fashion. The problem is that information and evidence are necessary to begin building a case. As we have noted earlier, whereas in other types of crime such information frequently comes from victims and witnesses, white-collar cases usually are different: The complexity and diffuseness of the victimizations reduces the visibility of the crime and, therefore, the likelihood of obtaining evidence from unimplicated persons. Beyond this, even when such evidence might be obtained through record searches, accounting, checks and audits, and the analysis of documents, the amounts of material and the methods of investigation are so costly in both man-hours and resources, both to develop and to present in court, that such efforts rarely are undertaken. Discounting the likelihood of the latter approach, a U.S. attorney sums up the practical problem this way:

> You've got to do something. And in these sort of activities, the only people with the information that you are going to have to convict are the participants. It is not like a bank robbery where innocent people watch and see and identify. The only way you get these kinds of criminals is through information supplied by participants. You have to peel off the layers . . . and that is difficult. That is a burden that is tougher than the burden prosecutors in the past had to deal with.

The nature of the "burden" described here is the development of cooperative witnesses (as sources of information and evidence) through plea bargaining. The following series of questions and answers from an interview with a federal prosecutor is suggestive of the means by which this bargaining is accomplished.

*Q:* How do you urge cooperation from defendants?

*A:* We threaten to send them to jail. It's the most effective way we've ever done it. We make a good, solid case on them and hang it over their head like a hammer.

*Q:* And what are the mechanics of doing that, how exactly do you present it to the defendant?

*A:* We tell them "if you don't cooperate, we will convict you. And we will do it in a way that will make you look—we'll do it so well that you would get really good jail time, a solid big chunk of time."

*Q:* At what stage do you do this?

*A:* Well, we are willing to make deals with people in a whole host of ways running all the way from giving them a "pass" to they just don't get prosecuted at all in return for testifying.

*Q:* Do you usually indict them first?

*A:* We make deals at all stages. . . . We talk to them before indictment in the very big cases. Then we have all kinds of pleas like a guy has committed a felony. We'll let him plead to a misdemeanor and won't prosecute . . . a whole range of things all the way 'til he pleads to the principal count . . . to charging him with exactly what he did and saying nice things about him at sentencing.

The proactive prosecution of white-collar crime therefore comes down to the problem of how to get the leverage required to "turn witnesses," and the key to obtaining this leverage is to forge a connection between plea negotiations and concessions and coercion in the sanctioning process. In other words, prosecutors must overcome the tendency toward loose coupling between most parts of the criminal-justice system, establishing instead a direct connection between plea bargaining and sanctioning decisions in white-collar cases. In terms of sentencing, this can be accomplished in at least two ways: *by carefully managing the severity of the charges in these cases, so that judges can use statutory guidelines in arriving at lenient sentences,* and *by getting judges to reward negotiated pleas directly.* Our suggestion is that the overall implication of such a connection between negotiation and sentencing in white-collar cases will be a tendency toward lenient sanctions. In other words, in white-collar cases, coercion will be less frequent than concession as a means tightening the organizational connections that make the proactive prosecution of white-collar crime possible. We consider next some examples of how this process actually occurs in major white-collar cases.

## Two White-Collar Cases

In this section we will review events surrounding the prosecution and sentencing of two major white-collar cases.[3] The first case involves a national price-fixing conspiracy, the second the bribery of state legislators. To illustrate aspects of the theoretical perspective outlined previously, we draw in this section on documentation that resulted from extensive litigation surrounding these cases. Both cases illustrate how the diffuseness of victimization in white-collar offenses complicates their prosecution and encourages a tightening of links between the prosecutorial and judicial subsystems. The first case in particular illustrates how organizational concerns about the consumption of time and resources in the prosecution of white-collar cases encourages the judiciary to reward with lenient sentences the decisions of white-collar offenders not to go to trial; the second case illustrates more directly the role plea bargaining can play in generating the information and evidence required to prosecute white-collar cases successfully. In both types of cases the consequence is a tightening of the coupling between the prosecutorial and judicial subsytems that is reflected in the rewarding of guilty pleas with lenient sentences.

The first case involves a group of defendants in the paper folding-carton industry convicted of price fixing. The folding-carton industry is a large industry engaged in the production of containers for a wide range of foods and manufactured products. The basis of this industry's prosperity is the premise that cartons can be produced more cheaply by the carton manufacturers than they could be by the companies using them for packaging their products. Nonetheless, amost all of the relatively large carton corporations (such as Weyerhauser, St. Regis, and American Can) and many of their executives were charged with fixing prices in this case. The strategy involved in this price-fixing scheme was simple and efficient. The conspirators in the case accounted for over 70 percent of cardboard-box sales. Thus, when a purchaser indicated a desire for boxes, it was usually possible to identify an existing supplier, who would then set a price that the other conspirators would agree to exceed in their respective bids. The result was that existing patterns of production and profit were preserved. In a description of this case, Ermann and Lundman (1980) note that although these conspiracies existed across several decades and cost purchasers millions of dollars in inflated charges, none of the victimized corporations (including Falstaff Brewing, Pepsi Cola Bottling Company, and Sambo's Restaurants Inc.) ever indicated a public awareness that they were paying fixed prices. Rather, a personal communication is cited from the head government prosecutor in the case indicating that this was a proactive, government-initiated case.

There are several direct and indirect indications that the proactive character of this case resulted in lenient sanctions. For example, the chief judge in the district responsible for sentencing of offenders in this case indicates in a brief that "It is a case in which the most prolific wrongdoers are not available for sentencing because they have been immunized from prosecution in return for their testimony against the others." A further complicating factor acknowledged in the same brief is the potential toll in time and resources that pleas of innocence and lengthy trials would have brought in the case: "it is a case in which, had all of the defendants demanded one trial, with or without a jury, no judge could guarantee each defendant a fair, impartial, and an independent trial." Although noting that these factors should not unduly influence the sentences imposed, the chief judge in this case nonetheless candidly notes that these factors "nevertheless are inescapable considerations which place great impediments in the path of the fair and wise performance of a judge's most difficult task." The final dispositions in this case followed guilty pleas and resulted in a *maximum* sentence of ten days in jail and a fine of $35,000. Most of the sentences in this case were much milder.

It is interesting to note that a point of contention in the folding-carton case involved the proper statutory guideline to be followed in determining appropriate sentences. Prior to the sentencing of the offenders, Congress raised the status of the offense charged from a misdemeanor to a felony, increasing the potential maximum fine from $50,000 to $100,000 and raising the potential maximum imprisonment from one year to three years. Nonetheless, the chief judge ruled in this case that "the defendants must be tried for, found guilty of, and sentenced within the limitations of the statute as it existed at the time of their violation of the law." Thus it would seem that the low statutory severity of the offense was a partial justification for the mild sentences imposed. Beyond this, it is clear that not even the maximum possibilities of the misdemeanor provisions were applied. Thus all three of the factors we have emphasized in our theoretical discussion have come to play in this case: (1) the case was proactively generated, and the immunity given some potential defendants in building the case was a factor considered in sentencing the others; (2) the savings in court resources realized through the defendants' guilty pleas was also an acknowledged point of consideration; and (3) the low statutory maximums provided for this particular type of white-collar crime became a basis for justifying the lenient sentences imposed. None of this is to say that the sentences imposed in this case represented a miscarriage of justice—certainly not in the legal sense; the pattern exemplified is fully consistent with existing legal principles. Rather, our argument is that the problem is one of organizational considerations as much as of law.

The second case is rather different from the first. For one thing, it involves politicians as well as businessmen. The case begins with a trade association that represented the interests of the ready-mix cement industry. One specific interest of the industry and its association involved increasing by one cubic yard, per truck, the amount of ready-mix cement that industry trucks could transport on state roads. To this end, a representative of the industry met with an attorney who offered to draft the necessary legislation and, more importantly, to contact and form agreements with legislators who could help to get the legislation passed. Such contacts and agreements were made with legislators on both the Republican and the Democratic sides of the state house of representatives and senate. These agreements involved payments of up to $10,000 on each side of both legislative bodies. In sum, arrangements were made through the trade association and its attorney to bribe a number of state politicians for the passage of a weight-relief bill. This bill, which was ultimately passed by both houses, with the bare number of votes required, was vetoed by the governor. Arguments then ensued among the parties involved as to whether the promised bribes should be paid. Nonetheless, the bribes were paid and prosecutions followed.

The proactive character of this case is made clear by arguments offered during its appeal. Here it is freely acknowledged that, in order to obtain the evidence necessary to achieve convictions in the case, the U.S. attorney's office had to plea bargain with a state representative and partially immunize him against full prosecution. The nature of this agreement was that the representative would plead guilty to failing to report income from the bribe on an income-tax return (an offense punishable by a maximum of three years' imprisonment), and that he would not be charged along with his coschemers with a selection of offenses (punishable by up to five years imprisonment on one of these counts alone). Additionally, the prosecution agreed to recommend to the court that a sentence of probation be imposed in this case. In return, this individual was to assist in the collection of tape-recorded evidence and to provide testimony for the prosecution.

At sentencing, the cooperating politician did indeed receive a disposition of one year on probation. The other legislators in this case were charged with mail fraud, conspiracy, and violations of the Travel Act. All the legislators pled *not* guilty; and, although one was acquitted, the remainder were convicted and received three-year prison sentences and fines. The rest of the corporate executives were charged with the same offenses, entered guilty pleas, and received one to two years' probation and fines. At least one member of the latter group entered into negotiations with the prosecution about cooperating in the development of the case, in exchange for favorable treatment at sentencing. Again, then, this case illustrates the role of plea bargaining and of statutory considerations in the prosecution and sentencing of white-collar cases.

A final point of interest in this case involves the specific charges used to obtain convictions in a federal rather than a state court. Over the past decade federal statutes have been used with increasing flexibility or, as one participant-observer (Henderson 1977) has put it, "legal craftsmanship," to obtain federal jurisdiction in cases of white-collar crime and political corruption. In particular, the Mail Fraud Statute and the Travel Act have been used to obtain federal jurisdiction over cases that could have been prosecuted under other kinds of state laws, which probably would have more accurately portrayed the nature of the offense involved. This point was made in a rather provocative way in a dissenting opinion offered in the aforementioned case.

> I conclude by depicting a scenario which I have little doubt approximates the facts of this prosecution. Federal officials, getting wind of a deal between . . . state legislators and the . . . industry, assign agents to investigate. In due course, immunity is promised to some of the involved legislators and company officials in return for their cooperation and testimony. Recording devices are placed on some of the immunized persons to obtain inculpating admissions from those who are the targets of the prosecution. Once the investigation is completed, consideration is then given to what federal offense, if any, has been committed. The mail fraud statute? The federal travel act? The investigation files are searched to find some mailings or evidence of interstate travel. The United States attorney's office sifts through the mailings in the file and then constructs a legal theory in order that they may be used to form the basis for a charge of mail fraud. One fortuitous trip, totally incidental and unforeseen, by an unindicted coschemer forms the basis of the two Travel Act counts. A conspiracy count is, of course, added. In this fashion, the Mail Fraud Statute and the Travel Act are subverted to purposes for which they were never intended. No longer are the mailings and travel considered essential or an integral part of the scheme; they are seen and used to obtain federal jurisdiction.

It should be emphasized that the foregoing was a dissenting opinion. Nonetheless, the point is well made that statutory considerations can play a very important role in the manner in which white-collar cases are pursued.

We have now presented a theoretical approach to our data and material that illustrates by way of example the central features of this approach. We turn next to a quantitative treatment of the issues we have raised.

## An Analysis of Sentencing Decisions in
## Ten Federal District Courts

The quantitative data to be considered next consist of 6,562 cases sentenced in our ten district courts over a period beginning in 1974 and ending in 1977. These data were collected by the administrative office of the U.S. courts.

Our analysis is premised on an operational definition of white-collar crime that allows consideration of both the offender and the offense. A procedure described in Hagan et al. (1980) was first used to identify thirty-one offenses that, according to U.S. attorneys interviewed in our research, consensually were recognized as white-collar crimes; the remaining offenses in our data were designated as common crimes. This dichotomy was then cross-classified with the offender's income, dichotomized in two groups: less than $13,777 per year, and $13,777 or more per year, in 1974–1977 dollars. The latter cut point is consistent for this period with a division in Featherman and Hauser's (1978) data between the highest grouping of occupations in their research and those that fall below. The resulting cross-classification that is central to the remainder of our analysis includes the following four kinds of cases: the common crimes of lower-income persons; the common crimes of high-income persons; the white-collar crimes of lower-income persons; and the white-collar crimes of high-income persons. For obvious reasons, it is the last type of case that is of greatest interest to us.

In the previous work (Hagan et al. 1980) on which this chapter builds, we found that nine of our ten districts displayed a common distribution of cases into the four cells of the cross-classification described here. The tenth district, which we will call District C, was made unique by its disproportionate prosecution of white-collar persons involved in white-collar crimes. The distinctiveness of District C is reflected in table 14–1, where 12.1 percent of the offenders charged are of high income and have committed white-collar crimes. In the remaining districts, the comparable figure is 2.4 percent.

We have also included in table 14–1 mean sentence-severity scores for the various offender-offense groupings. The sentence-severity scale used is adapted

## Table 14–1
## Distribution of Cases and Mean Sentence-Severity Scores for Offender-Offense Combinations in District C and Other Districts

| Offender-Offense Combinations | District C | | Other Districts | |
|---|---|---|---|---|
| | Percentage of Total | $\bar{x}$ Sentence | Percentage of Total | $\bar{x}$ Sentence |
| High-income white-collar crime | 12.1 (84) | 3.55 | 2.4 (142) | 4.98 |
| High-income common crime | 7.8 (54) | 8.11 | 6.3 (371) | 6.18 |
| Low-income white-collar crime | 11.7 (81) | 4.10 | 9.1 (536) | 4.38 |
| Low-income common crime | 68.4 (475) | 7.60 | 82.1 (4819) | 7.31 |

Note: See text for description of sentence-severity scale

from Tiffany, Avichai, and Peters (1975) and presented in Hagan et al. (1980). These scores reveal that white-collar crimes overall result in lighter sentences than common crimes and that these disparities are greatest in District C. Beyond this, in District C white-collar persons prosecuted for white-collar crimes receive the most-lenient sentences, whereas in the remaining districts the lightest mean sentences are received by lower-income persons prosecuted for white-collar crimes. Most interesting for our purposes, however, is the finding that when comparisons are made between the same offender-offense groupings in District C and in the remaining districts, the second-largest disparity is in the mean sentences received by the high-income white-collar criminals ($\bar{X}$ = 3.55 and 4.98). An implication of these findings, consistent with the perspective developed previously, is that the proactive prosecution of white-collar crime in District C results in the more-lenient sentencing of white-collar crime, particularly for white-collar persons. However, before we draw inferences from these findings, we will consider the roll of a number of other potentially relevant variables.

A variety of other variables are considered in the tables that follow. These variables are included on the basis of the perspective outlined previously, prior research (Hagan 1974; Chiricos and Waldo 1975; Burke and Turk 1975; Bernstein et al. 1977; Nagel 1980; Swigert and Farrell 1977), concerns for multicollinearity, and suggestions arising from our interviews. These variables include prior adult felony convictions (the actual number); the statutory seriousness of the offense (measured from low to high in terms of the maximum sentence allowed by statute for the offense); the number of charges for which the defendant was convicted; the presence of multiple defendants; ethnicity (nonwhite = −1, white = 1); sex (male = −1, female = 1); age (from low to high); employment status (unemployed = −1, employed = 1); whether the defendant was undergoing treatment for physical and/or mental illness (no = −1, yes = 1); bail status (ordinally ranked from personal recognizance to remand on a scale from 1 to 10); plea (not guilty = −1, guilty = 1); and the extent of any charge reductions that may have occurred (on a scale from −3 to 3). Finally, we added to the foregoing those offenders with high incomes who were prosecuted for white-collar crimes. Inclusion of this variable in a multiple regression analysis will allow us to determine whether the disparity observed earlier in the sentences received by higher-income white-collar criminals, as compared with other types of criminals, persists when the other independent variables discussed previously are taken into account. The dependent variable in the following tables is the sentence-severity scale outlined previously.

Our analysis of the variables described earlier is based on conventional regression procedures. The results of the first part of this analysis are presented in table 14-2. Tests of significance are not reported in either this table or table 14-3 because we are dealing in this chapter with populations or subpopulations rather than with samples.

**Table 14–2**

**Regression of Sentence Severity on Independent Variables in District C**

| Independent Variables | b | B |
|---|---|---|
| Prior convictions | 0.44 | 0.13 |
| Statutory seriousness | 0.04 | 0.05 |
| Number of charges | 0.08 | 0.04 |
| Multiple defendants | 2.90 | 0.05 |
| Ethnicity | 0.34 | 0.06 |
| Sex | −0.55 | −0.06 |
| Employment | −0.71 | −0.13 |
| Physical illness | 0.35 | 0.05 |
| Mental illness | 0.54 | 0.03 |
| Age | 0.28 | 0.04 |
| Bail status | 0.67 | 0.28 |
| Plea | −1.04 | −0.13 |
| Charge reduction | 0.58 | 0.11 |
| High-income white-collar criminal | −1.08 | −0.17 |

$R^2 = .296$

Intercept = 4.46

Note: $N = 694$.

**Table 14–3**

**Regression of Sentence Severity on Independent Variables for White-Collar Offenders Convicted of White-Collar Crimes in District C**

| Independent Variables | b | B |
|---|---|---|
| Prior convictions | −.32 | −.16 |
| Statutory seriousness | .53 | .47 |
| Number of charges | .12 | .18 |
| Multiple defendants | −.30 | −.16 |
| Ethnicity | −.07 | −.03 |
| Sex | −.49 | −.12 |
| Employment | −.06 | −.02 |
| Physical illness | .11 | .04 |
| Mental illness | −.65 | −.16 |
| Age | −.17 | −.10 |
| Bail status | .03 | .04 |
| Plea | −.81 | −.13 |
| Charge reduction | .21 | .10 |

$R^2 = .36$

Intercept = 2.47

Note: $N = 84$.

Table 14-2 reports the results of regressing sentence severity on our independent variables in District C, the proactive district in the analysis presented earlier. Our primary interest in this regression is to determine whether, other variables held constant, the sentencing of higher-income persons for their white-collar crimes remains more lenient. The unstandardized ($b = -1.08$) and standardized ($B = -.17$) regression coefficients presented in table 14-2 reveal that in District C, the proactive district, higher-income white-collar criminals do receive more-lenient sentences than other ,,offenders. Thus table 14-2 provides provisional support for the perspective we have proposed: With a variety of other important variables held constant, our proactive district does grant lenient sentences to higher-income persons convicted of white-collar crimes. In the next part of our analysis, we are interested in examining the role that considerations of plea and charge play in the lenient sanctioning we have identified.

In table 14-3 we find that, consistent with the perspective we have adopted, within District C statutory seriousness (the seriousness of the initial charge) has the biggest effect on the severity of sentences received by higher-income white-collar offenders ($B = .47$). As well, we find that the offender's plea ($B = -.13$) has a notable impact on sentence severity. These are not the only notable findings in table 14-3. As expected, however, two important variables explaining the tendency in District C to sanction high-income white-collar criminals more leniently are their pleas and the initial charges placed against them.

## Conclusions and Suggestions for Further Research

The qualitative and quantitative data presented in this chapter have reinforced the findings of our previous analyses (Hagan et al. 1980). More specifically, we have demonstrated that use of income as a measure of social standing produces findings similar to those found in our earlier analyses based on educational attainment. Here, as in our earlier analyses, we have argued that most white-collar crime involving white-collar persons is characterized by a diffuseness of victimization and an absence of unimplicated witnesses. As a result, a proactive organization of legal resources usually is required to seek out and build these white-collar cases in what is regarded as a cost-efficient manner. Thus it is frequently only the participants in these criminal events who can provide information essential to build successful cases, and prosecutorial negotiation becomes a key part of the proactive prosecution of these cases. Furthermore, to make this negotiation work, a connection must be forged between the prosecutorial and judicial subsystems, such that the promises and concessions offered white-collar offenders actually are confirmed at sentencing. We have argued that this type of connection may be the exception more than the rule in a criminal-justice process we have otherwise called a loosely coupled system. In any case, both this and our previous analysis indicate that the tightening of connections we expected in white-collar cases involving the proactive prosecution of white-collar persons does indeed occur, as indicated by the role charge severity and guilty pleas play in the sentencing of these white-collar offenders in our proactive district, and in the lighter sentences these white-collar offenders receive in this jurisdiction.

Nonetheless, there are issues left unresolved by this research. For example, the exact nature of the interplay between organizational and stratification factors in producing the patterns we have observed is unclear. To the extent that the organizational factors we have emphasized are salient, it should be possible to replicate the kinds of findings we have produced in other areas of law enforcement that require proactive prosecution, for example, in the areas of drugs and prostitution. On the other hand, there may be an interplay of organizational and stratification factors that uniquely produces the kinds of findings reported here. Only further research will resolve this issue adequately.

Additionally, it is important to point out that this analysis has dealt only with sentencing as its dependent variable. However, if we are to understand sanctioning more generally, then it is important that we consider earlier stages of the criminal-justice process as well. The type of proactive prosecution discussed in this chapter probably results in distinctive patterns of outcome at early as well as later stages of the legal process; and further resolution of the issues we have raised in this chapter will therefore require a more-comprehensive coverage of the larger criminalization process.

Finally, this chapter has emphasized an understanding of individual case decisions within the larger context of relationships among component parts of the criminal-justice system. Obtaining this type of understanding will require that future research consider more directly the character of these subsystem relationships. This will require the development of new types of measures of the links that exist between subsystem parts and the forms of exchange that characterize these links. In this chapter we have confined our attention largely to plea negotiation and sentencing. Future research will need to expand the focus of attention.

## Notes

1. The districts and their principal cities are Eastern and Southern New York (Brooklyn and Manhattan), Northern Illinois (Chicago), Eastern Pennsylvania (Philadelphia), Maryland (Baltimore), Northern Texas (Dallas), Eastern Missouri (Kansas City), Northern Georgia (Atlanta), Central California (Los Angeles), and Eastern Michigan (Detroit). During site visits to each of these districts we observed 200 hours of court proceedings and conducted approximately 600 hours of interviews with the following court personnel: 9 chief judges and 43 presiding judges, 8 U.S. attorneys and 48 assistant U.S. attorneys,

14 probation officers, 15 administrators of Pretrial Services Agencies, 31 magistrates, and 10 chiefs of public defender's offices. The first two authors of this chapter conducted the interviews together, using a set of structured, open-ended interview schedules that are available on request.

2. This section of the paper restates and elaborates a theoretical perspective developed in Hagan and Bernstein (1979) and Hagan et al. (1980).

3. In deference to our agreement not to identify any of the districts in our study, no specific attributions of quotes will be offered in this section.

## References

Bernstein, Ilene Nagel; Kelly, William R.; and Doyle, Patricia A. "Societal Reaction to Deviants: The Case of Criminal Defendants." *American Sociological Review* 42(1977):743–755.

Black, Donald. "The Mobilization of Law." *Journal of Legal Studies* 2(1973): 125–149.

Burke, Peter, and Turk, Austin. "Factors Affecting Postarrest Dispositions: A Model for Analysis." *Social Problems* 22(1975):313–332.

Chiricos, Theodore G., and Waldo, Gordon P. "Socioeconomic Status and Criminal Sentencing: An Empirical Assessment of a Conflict Proposition." *American Sociological Review* 40(1975):753–772.

Eisenstein, James, and Jacob, Herbert. *Felony Justice.* Boston: Little, Brown, 1977.

Ermann, M.D. and Lundman, Richard. *Corporate Deviance.* New York: Holt, Rinehart and Winston, 1980.

Featherman, David, and Hauser, Robert. *Opportunity and Change.* New York: Academic Press, 1978.

Gibbs, Jack P. "Deterrence, Penal Policy, and the Sociology of Law." In Rita Simon, ed., *Research in Law and Sociology.* Greenwich, Conn.: JAI Press, 1978.

Greenberg, David F. "Socioeconomic Status and Criminal Sentences: Is There an Association?" *American Sociological Review* 42, no. 1(1977):174–176.

Hagan, John. "Extral-Legal Attributes and Criminal Sentencing: An Assessment of a Sociological Viewpoint." *Law and Society Review* 8(1974):357–383.

Hagan, John, and Bernstein, Ilene Nagel. "The Sentence Bargaining of Upperworld and Underworld Crime in Ten Federal District Courts." *Law and Society Review* 13(1979):467–478.

Hagan, John; Hewitt, John; and Alwin, Duane. "Ceremonial Justice: Crime and Punishment in a Loosely Coupled System." *Social Forces* 58(1979):506–527.

Hagan, John; Nagel, Ilene; and Albonetti, Celesta. "The Differential Sentencing of White Collar Offenders in Ten Federal District Courts." *American Sociological Review* 45(1980):802–820.

Henderson, Thomas. "The Expanding Role of Federal Prosecutors in Combating State and Local Political Corruption." *Cumberland Law Review* 8(1977): 385–401.

Hopkins, Andrew. "Is There a Class Bias in Criminal Sanctioning?" *American Sociological Review* 42(1977):176–177.

Kennedy, Mark C. "Beyond Incrimination." *Catalyst* 5(1970):1–27.

Kerlinger, Fred, and Pedhazur, Elazor. *Multiple Regression in Behavioral Research*. New York: Holt, Rinehart and Winston, 1973.

Lizotte, Alan J. "Extra-Legal Factors in Chicago's Criminal Courts: Testing the Conflict Model of Criminal Justice." *Social Problems* 25(1978):564–580.

Meyer, J.W., and Rowan, B. "Institutionalized Organizations: Formal Structures as Myth and Ceremony." *American Journal of Sociology* 83(1977):340–363.

Nettler, Gwynn. "Criminal Justice." *American Sociological Review*, annual. 5(1979):27–52.

Nagel, Ilene. "The Behavior of Formal Law: A Study of Bail Decisions." Paper presented at the Law and Society Association Meetings, Madison, Wisconsin, 1980.

Reasons, Charles E. "On Methodology, Theory and Ideology." *American Sociological Review* 42(1977):177–180.

Reiss, Albert J., Jr. *The Police and the Public*. New Haven: Yale University Press, 1971.

_____ . "Discretionary Justice." In Daniel Glaser, ed., *Handbook of Criminology*. Chicago: Rand McNally, 1974, pp. 679–699.

Swigert, Victoria Lynn, and Farrel, Ronald A. "Normal Homicides and the Law." *American Sociological Review* 42(1977):16–32.

Tiffany, Lawrence P.; Avichai, Yakov; and Peters, Geoffrey W. "A Statistical Analysis of Sentencing in Federal Courts: Defendants Convicted After Trial, 1967–1968." *Journal of Legal Studies* 4(1975):369–390.

# Index

# About the Contributors

**Celesta Albonetti** is a graduate student at the University of Wisconsin (Madison). She is currently working on an analysis of the impact of structural effects on the frequency and type of organizational contacts among treatment programs for adjudicated delinquents, and she is interested in further research in the application of organizational concepts to the analysis of the criminalization process.

**Harold C. Barnett,** associate professor of economics at the University of Rhode Island, received the Ph.D. in economics from the Massachusetts Institute of Technology. Dr. Barnett has written on the political economy of traditional property crime, rape and prostitution, tax fraud, and corporate crime. He is currently researching crime and punishment in Sweden.

**Michael K. Block** is Senior Research Fellow and director of the Center for Econometric Studies of the Justice System at the Hoover Institution, Stanford University, and principal at Block and Nold, Palo Alto, California. He has taught at Stanford University, the Naval Postgraduate School, and the University of Santa Clara. The areas of research he is currently pursuing include assessing the deterrent effects of antitrust activity and analyzing the long-term trends in the costs of crime control.

**W.G. (Kit) Carson** studied at Queen's College, Oxford, and Churchill College, Cambridge. He is senior lecturer in criminology at the University of Edinburgh; coeditor of *Crime and Delinquency in Britain;* author of various articles on white-collar crime and the sociology of law and author of *The Other Price of Britain's Oil* (forthcoming). He is currently on leave—funded by the Social Science Research Council—working on the first sociologically oriented history of policing in Scotland.

**John P. Clark** is professor of sociology and associate dean for social sciences, University of Minnesota. He has conducted research and taught in the areas of social deviance, criminology, social-control organizations, and the sociology of youth. His publications have appeared in many of the leading sociology journals. Current research focuses on how work group, occupations, and work organizations produce deviance in the workplace.

**Gilbert Geis** received the Ph.D. from the University of Wisconsin; taught at the University of Oklahoma; the State University of New York, Albany; and California State University, Los Angeles; and has been on the faculty of the University of California, Irvine (Program in Social Ecology) since 1971. Dr. Geis's recent research has resulted in publications in the areas of forcible rape, white-collar crime, victimless crime, and victimology. He is coauthor of *Man, Crime and Society; White-Collar Crime; White Collar Crime Theory and Research;* and *Forcible Rape.* He was president of the American Society of Criminology in 1975–1976.

**Colin Goff,** a doctoral candidate at the University of California, Irvine, in the social-ecology program–criminal-justice option, is currently involved in research on the sociology of law, with specific focus on laws and legal procedures that attempt to regulator corporate interests. He is coauthor (with C. Reasons) of *Corporate Crime in Canada: A Critical Analysis of Anti-Combines Legislation,* and has published an article on corporate crime as well as various articles in the *Criminal Law Quarterly.*

**John Hagan** is a professor in the Department of Sociology, University of Wisconsin (Madison). His monograph, *The Organizational Domination of Criminal Law: A Study of Victim Involvement in the Criminal Justice System,* is being published in 1981. He has published various studies relevant to the sentencing of offenders–including white-collar criminals–and is involved in a study of the sanctioning of stocks and securities violators in Toronto.

**Ronald Kramer** received the Ph.D. in sociology from The Ohio State University in 1978. He is currently assistant professor of sociology at Western Michigan University, where he teaches courses in criminology, deviance, and social issues. His research interests include corporate crime and the control of corporate behavior.

**Susan B. Long** is currently visiting research Fellow in the Department of Statistics, Princeton University, and a visiting Fellow of the National Institute of of Justice, U.S. Department of Justice (on leave from her assistant professorship in the Department of Quantitative Methods, Syracuse University). The work reported here is part of a larger research project she is conducting on federal tax administration.

**Maria Łos** received the Ph.D. in sociology from the University of Warsaw. She has had academic appointments at the University of Warsaw, the Polish Academy of Science, and the University of Sheffield; visiting appointments at universities in Florence, Oslo, and Montreal; in 1973–1974 was a Ford Foundation Fellow; and is currently at Carleton University. She has coauthored two books in Polish and one, *The Multidimensional Sociology,* in English, as well as various articles in English, Polish, and other languages.

**Ilene H. Nagel** is associate professor, School of Law, Indiana University. During the fall of 1980 she was a visiting Fellow at the Institute of Criminology,

Cambridge University and at the Netherlands Institute for Advanced Study in the Humanities and Social Sciences. She has recently published "Sentencing of White-Collar Offenders" (with C. Albonetti and J. Hagan) and various research essays on evaluation in criminal justice. She has a forthcoming book (with J. Hagan) on prosecutorial and judicial discretion, with emphasis on the differential import of numerous variables.

**Jerry Parker** received the Ph.D. in sociology from the University of Minnesota and is currently assistant professor of sociology and criminal justice at the University of Tulsa, where he teaches in the areas of deviance and the sociology of law. He is continuing his research on the ethics of the legal profession.

**Charles E. Reasons,** received the Ph.D. in sociology from Washington State University and is professor of sociology at the University of Calgary. He has published numerous articles and books concerned with social issues and crime; his recent works include, among others, *Corporate Crime in Canada* (with C. Goff), *Sociology of Law: A Conflict Approach, The Ideology of Social Problems* (with W.D. Perdue), and *Assault on the Worker: Workers' Health and Workers' Struggles in Canada.*

**Leon Shaskolsky Sheleff** holds a law degree from the University of Cape Town and the Ph.D. in sociology from the Ohio State University. He has a joint appointment as senior lecturer in the Department of Sociology and the Institute of Criminology and Criminal Law at Tel Aviv University. Dr. Sheleff has published various articles on law and criminology. His published books include: *Generations Apart: Adult Hostility to Youth and the Bystander: Behavior, Law, Ethics* (Lexington Books, 1978). His research interests include the sociological study of criminal law and the case of capital punishment (political implications).

**Dwight C. Smith, Jr.** received the B.A. from Yale University and the M.P.A. from Syracuse University, and is currently associate professor, School of Criminal Justice, Rutgers University. He has published various articles dealing with organized and economic crime over the past fifteen years and the well-known book, *The Mafia Mystique.*

**Laureen Snider** is an assistant professor in the Department of Sociology at Queen's University, Canada. She has published articles in the field of corporate crime and has recently completed an overview and analysis of the Canadian criminal-justice system. Her current research interests center on legal-aid legislation and delivery systems and on the concept of reform in the capitalist state.

# About the Editors

**Timothy Dailey** received the Ph.D. in sociology from the University of Massachusetts, Amherst, in 1975, and has taught at The Ohio State University and Clarkson College of Technology.

**Peter Wickman** received the Ed.D. from Michigan State University and did post-doctoral study in sociology at the New School of Social Research and Emory University. He is professor of sociology at the State University of New York at Potsdam. Professor Wickman's research interests have focused on problems of community corrections and on social-policy issues. He has published articles dealing with community corrections, youth attitudes, and penal systems in Scandinavia. His most recent books include *Readings in Criminology*, of which he was coauthor, and *Criminology: Perspectives on Crime and Criminality*. His current research interests focus on public opinion of white-collar offenders and citizen involvement in criminal justice.